THE INTELLIGENCE GAME

The Illusions and Delusions of International Espionage

James Rusbridger

I.B.Tauris & Co Ltd
Publishers
London · New York

Revised paperback edition
published in 1991 by
I.B.Tauris & Co Ltd
110 Gloucester Avenue
London NW1 8JA

First published in 1989 by The Bodley Head

A CIP record for this book is available from the British Library

Typeset by J&L Composition Ltd, Filey, North Yorkshire

CONTENTS

LIST OF ILLUSTRATIONS

ACKNOWLEDGEMENTS

A great many people, far more than I had expected, helped me with material for this book. Unfortunately, because of the present climate of legal threats and injunctions, a number of contributors asked that their assistance remain anonymous. No author likes to use information on this basis but because some of it threw new light on old stories I felt it important to do so since I personally knew the sources to be totally reliable. Hopefully the day will soon come when people can talk about intelligence matters without having to look over their shoulder.

In Britain, Dr Meryl Foster and T. R. Padfield of the Public Record Office tirelessly put up with my requests and so too did Phillip Reed at the Imperial War Museum. The late Ronald Lewin was a kind and generous tutor, while Michael Montgomery, Dr John Chapman, Richard Deacon, Chapman Pincher, Phillip Knightley, Ralph Erskine, Nigel West and Graham Smith all generously shared their information with me. Elaine Jones, Muriel Rogerson, Martyn Thomas and John Stevens were a constant source of support in providing a ready flow of essential reference material from the Cornwall library services.

I am also most grateful to Sir Stuart Milner Barry, Sir Dick White, Howard Baker, Cedric Brown, Jane Thynne, Colin Gibbon, Dr Toby Baker, Mrs Jean Howard, the late Professor G. C. McVittie, Colonel Maurice Buckmaster, Miss Jean Overton Fuller, M. R. D. Foot, Christopher Woods (SOE archivist, Foreign Office), Roy Davies and Robert Marshall (BBC Television) for their help.

In the United States, John Taylor, Richard von Doenhoff, Charlotte Seeley and Wilbert B. Mahoney, of the Military Reference Section, National Archives, Washington DC, with unfailing courtesy put themselves at my disposal to lead me through the maze of their voluminous files, while George

Henriksen and Commander Newman at the US Naval Security Group in Washington DC were a valuable source of hitherto classified information. I am also particularly grateful to the help I received from Dr Dean Allard and Bernard Cavalcante on my visits to the US Naval Historical Center at the Washington Navy Yard.

John Costello not only criticised my efforts and encouraged me to better things but also generously placed at my disposal his files and experience, and I am also grateful to Robert Haslach, Robert Lamphere, Arnold Kramish, Louis Kruh and Hayden Peake for their expert assistance.

In Australia, my gratitude goes to Tim Bryant and Moira Smythe of the Australian Archives who, despite all the pressures from the British government, helped me unearth many new documents, and to John Griffiths of the Department of Defence who supplied much new and useful historical information. Others who willingly gave up their time to see me included Sir Charles Spry, Captain T. E. Nave, Lt Col G. B. Courtney, Martin Clemens, Dr Wilson P. Evans, my cousin Peter Wright, Creighton Burns, editor of *The Age* in Melbourne, and Professor John Rickard. In New Zealand, it was Ellen Ellis at the National Archives whose persistent searches on my behalf finally uncovered a treasure trove of hitherto unknown material.

Finally my thanks to Melvin Lasky who originally gave me the courage to write, Penny Deane who showed me how to come to terms with word processing, Andrew Lownie for having made it all come true, the generous and critical encouragement from Chris Holifield and Derek Johns at The Bodley Head who helped me turn an idea into words, and the infinite patience and skill of Jan Boxshall who created a book from my tattered manuscript.

INTRODUCTION

It is frequently said about advertising that half the money spent is wasted but no one knows which half. Much the same can be said about intelligence services in peacetime. In wartime their value is easier to quantify. You can count the number of ships sunk, the number of aircraft you intercept and destroy, and the land battles you win as the result of advance knowledge of your enemy's intentions. Whether intelligence actually wins wars is doubtful. The intelligence fraternity will naturally claim that it does. Indeed there have been so many exotic claims about intelligence operations shortening World War II in favour of the Allies that one wonders why it took so long to defeat the Germans. In reality wars are won by the side that makes the fewest mistakes.

Equally, it is relatively easy to judge intelligence failures in war time. As as example, consider the case of the British War Cabinet minutes[1] of August 1940 which fell into Japanese hands. This came about only because someone foolishly sent them to Singapore as sea mail in a freighter[2] that was seized[3] by a German surface raider[4] whose captain[5] was astute enough to recognise their importance and rush them to Tokyo.[6] The papers showed in stark detail that Britain was unable to defend the Far East, including Singapore, against a Japanese attack. This was something so secret that not even the Australian[7] and New Zealand governments had been told. Thus the Japanese realised for the first time it would be safe to attack the American fleet at Pearl Harbor without interference from the British and to capture Malaya and Singapore with a relatively small military force.[8]

The ability of the Japanese to peer over Churchill's shoulder and read his innermost secrets a year before hostilities began helped bring about one of the worst intelligence disasters of World War II and led to the most humiliating defeat Britain's armed forces have ever suffered. And all because a mailbag was wrongly handled by some minor civil servant.

Even the best intelligence is sometimes ignored simply because it does not agree with the commander's own views and wishes. This is known as 'cognitive dissonance' – believing only what you want to believe. In September 1944 Field Marshal Montgomery was warned by his own intelligence officers that the Germans had *Panzer* forces around the area of Arnhem in Holland where he proposed making a dramatic airborne landing.[9] Montgomery chose to ignore this and allowed his airborne forces to be dropped without any anti-tank weaponry. Not surprisingly the result was a disaster.

In peacetime things are very different. Although we may not actually be fighting enemies on the battlefield that does not mean they do not exist. The problem is to identify them and assess their importance. The most obvious examples are spies from foreign countries (not necessarily unfriendly ones), who want to learn our economic and military secrets, and traitors in our midst who are motivated by reasons ranging from ideology to greed. As will be explained elsewhere this type of espionage in peacetime is of very limited value since most of the secrets that are so eagerly sought can be acquired quite openly and without difficulty. So, rather like drunken sailors propping each other up, the intelligence agencies of East and West need one another as an excuse to justify this aspect of their activities.

Another example is the growth in recent years of terrorism on the part of organisations like the IRA and other, foreign, groups that are prepared to resort to violence to further their aims; and no one would deny that these conditions dictate that the security services give close attention to them as part of their peacetime role. However, as this book will show, attitudes towards terrorism are hypocritical and are often manipulated to justify what is really political expediency, so that a terrorist outrage in one country can be considered legitimate behaviour by another. The difference between a freedom fighter and a terrorist is a very narrow and subjective one.[10]

Neither terrorism nor espionage is as widespread and important as the security services would have us believe, nor are they particularly good at preventing either. In the post-war years Britain's security service has seldom caught a spy or traitor on its own, while the IRA is no nearer defeat after twenty years of intensive security operations that have turned much of Britain into an armed fortress. On the basis of this very typical record, intelligence agencies cannot possibly justify their hugely expensive peacetime organisations and their extensive files that poke into people's private lives.

But just as turkeys do not vote for Christmas, the intelligence fraternity are not going to admit that there is less for them to do in peacetime. Quite the reverse. In order to justify their ever-increasing budgets they continually invent all manner of windmills to tilt at and seek to persuade their political paymasters that new and even more deadly enemies lurk around every corner. One way of achieving this is to claim that those who disagree with government policy are dangerous subversives who must be treated as enemies of the state – which automatically provides a limitless supply of suspects. Because politicians suffer from even worse paranoia than those who work in intelligence it is not hard to create this aura of suspicion, which security services the world over find a ready breeding ground for their bureaucratic empire building.

Since intelligence operates in a secret and unaccountable world, and we are assured that this is the only way it can work, it is impossible to judge whether the aims and activities of any given agency are justified or that the results demonstrate that it is giving value for money. For a start, no one knows how much is spent on intelligence around the world. The official budgets that are published are quite meaningless because so much by way of secret subvention is taken from other budgets or from contingency funds.

America spends at least $12 billion a year on its intelligence community, but if one allows for illegal activities such as the Iran/Contra business the true total is certainly much higher. Overall, a total of $24 billion[11] is available from two secret budgets for funding all America's intelligence operations. In Russia intelligence operations are so inextricably mixed with military defence spending that no accurate figures can ever be arrived at, but if one bears in mind that they try to copy the Americans in every sphere of operations, it seems logical that their annual bill is of the same size.

In Britain the official cost of the two main intelligence services MI5 and MI6, is put at around £100 million a year, but the real figure is nearer four times this. Then there is the cost of running the Government Communications Headquarters (GCHQ) at Cheltenham with its 12,000 employees, which adds a further £300 million; and to this must be added the cost of the various listening stations around the world that are run by the British army. Some British operations are shared with the Americans in order to lessen the cost as well as to obscure their illegality.

Whatever the final sum may be – and one suggests that the total worldwide cost of the intelligence fraternity is near $30 billion a year – all such agencies have two things in common. First, they are very inefficient. Second, they multiply like rabbits. The bureaucracy of the intelligence world is staggering and makes even the most inept government department seem quite efficient. For example, when the Central Intelligence Agency (CIA) was first created by President Harry Truman in 1946 under the name of Central Intelligence Group (CIG), the intention was to have a small organisation gathering intelligence from around the world for the benefit of the President and his advisers. In 1947 Allen Dulles, a leading American wartime intelligence officer and later director of the CIA, told Congress how he envisaged such an agency:

> I do not believe in a big agency. If this thing gets to be a great big octopus, it will not function well. Abroad, you will need a certain number of people but it ought to be scores rather than hundreds.[12]

Fine words indeed. But they had no effect at all. A year from the time of its founding the CIG began to expand, and after it became the CIA in 1947 the process continued rapidly. From an original budget of $5 million, its running costs jumped to $80 million in five years and $200 million a few years later.

The same thing happens everywhere else in the world, and no politician, East or West, has any real idea of what is being spent or what is going on in these vast organisations. As each year passes technology becomes more complex and politicians busier, so that accountability goes by default. This suits the intelligence fraternity perfectly. All they need to do is to find out what the particular politicians want to hear and then tailor the information[13] to please them. The most important form of intelligence for pleasing politicians is imaginary intelligence (Imaginint).

Ideally all intelligence agencies would like to be totally secret from the public that pays for them. But in today's inquisitive society that is plainly impossible no matter what draconian legislation governments may introduce. The problem before the intelligence services is how to present themselves to the public. To justify their cost they naturally want to be thought of as efficient and essential. To that end they leak disinformation consisting of tales of alleged achievements, either through tame, gullible journalists or through journals and magazines with which the agency has influence sometimes amounting to control.[14] Publicity of that kind is easy to recognise because it either makes incredible claims about the abilities of the Western nations (our satellites can read a Russian soldier's badges of rank from 600 miles out in space), or alarmist claims about the success of the Russian spy network. Such tales are based on vague claims form supposediy well informed sources or so-called experts who appear with monotonous regularity on television and in the press.

The danger for the intelligence services is that if people start believing they are efficient then they will be expected to achieve things like catching spies or stopping the IRA from letting off bombs. In place of those successes the services plant bogus tales in the media of having foiled non-existent plots. It was claimed, for example, that the intelligence services had foiled an attempted IRA attack on the wedding of Prince Andrew to Miss Sarah Ferguson on 23 July 1986. Or we are told that MI5 and MI6 foiled an attempt by the IRA to shoot down with surface-to-air missiles the aircraft[15] taking Mrs Thatcher to a conference in Canada.

Some years ago it was alleged that Russia had supplied chemical weapons to Vietnam which had been used in Cambodia and Laos. This was confirmed by American intelligence sources. Details of how a yellow rain had been found on the leaves of trees in the affected areas were carefully given to the press. Enormous publicity followed these reports, which just happened to come at the time when proposals were being made to upgrade and increase Western stocks of chemical weapons. An independent committee of respected scientists subsequently visited Cambodia and Laos where the attacks were alleged to have taken place, and they discovered that the yellow rain was in fact nothing more than bees' droppings.[16] There was no evidence that chemical weapons had ever been used. But the committee's report enjoyed little publicity, and today many people still believe the original story because it agrees with what they want to hear.

The other popular piece of intelligence mythology that has helped sustain the agencies operations for the past forty-five years is that World War III is just around the corner. Like all good fairy tales it appears in many different forms. But the central theme is the same: millions of highly trained Russian soldiers, backed up by thousands of the latest battle tanks all in perfect condition, and an equally perfect airforce with battle-honed pilots, are waiting for the signal that will send them surging through the Fulda Gap[17] and on to the Channel ports[18] within 48 hours.

In preparation for this Armageddon the Russians maintain the world's most efficient intelligence service, which, day and night, is beavering away in the West, stealing our secrets, planting spies in the innermost recesses of government, and setting up secret arms dumps with the help of local Communist sympathisers so that, when war begins, sabotage groups will emerge and wreak havoc throughout Britain and Europe, destroying essential services just when they are most needed.

A typical sort of horror story that appears from time to time in the right-wing sections of the Western press is that the drivers of East European lorries arriving in Western Europe and Britain are really all senior Russian and East European intelligence officers.[19] During their journeys they contrive to get lost and deviate from their proper itinerary in order to prepare maps of the best routes, so that the Russian tanks can sweep through the West's defences. Naturally no facts can be produced to substantiate the claim because all the evidence is secret.

It is a terrible scenario. But is it true? Just consider the situation in Britain. Over the past forty years a succession of tawdry traitors and spies have been uncovered in our midst. Some have been described as very important, right in the heart of our diplomatic and intelligence services. Others less so. On the occasions that they have brought to trial virtually all have confessed their guilt. But though our enemies know what secrets they have betrayed and what damage they have done to our nation's security, the British people are not allowed[20] to be told. Yet if one looks back over these same forty years it is very hard to see any evidence that we have slept less soundly in our beds at night as a result of these peoples' activities.

If Burgess and Maclean had not defected to Russia, what difference would it make today? Fuchs and other atom spies are credited with allowing the Russians to build the atom bomb and later the nuclear bomb earlier than would have been the case. Even if this were true, and there is good reason to believe that it is not, what difference did it really make? No nuclear weapon has been used since 1945, and no one seems particularly anxious to do so now – least of all the Russians. Equally, are the Russians any more fortunate? Over the years there has been a steady stream of Russian defectors reaching the West. On each occasion we are assured that they have brought with them information of great value.[21] But is Russia less secure because Gordievsky or Golitsin have poured out their secrets to MI6? All that happens is that we grandly expel a few alleged spies. Then we have the risk of finding out which of their replacements are also spies, so the whole rigmarole begins again.

A large part of intelligence work is connected with the gathering of the other side's technology. But technical information is quite perishable. What is secret and new today will be on show at a military exhibition in six months time. By then it will have been described, illustrated, and dissected, in a score or more technical journals. It is safe to assume that at any given moment scientists around the world are all working on much the same sort of projects, although not always with equal success. Technical assessments of other countries' military prowess is always exaggerated by intelligence experts. Often this is the result of endless quarrelling between different agencies as they try to impress politicians and get a larger budget for their agency or particular branch of the armed services. And sometimes it is simply an index of the inefficiency of the rival agencies.

Russia is credited with possessing immense industrial capability that out-produces America in every field, and especially in building warships. Yet, in reality, the US Navy is launching and commissioning more new warships than the Russians. In 1989 it was claimed that the Russian air force[22] had 300 of the latest MiG-29 *Fulcrum* fighters. In fact they had only 30. American experts have discovered a new Russian tank called the T-80 that does not exist, and an even better one called the FST-1 that no one has ever seen. By crediting Russia with arms it does not have, or expertise it has not achieved, all we have done is to frighten ourselves, which is precisely what the intelligence fraternity have wanted to happen these past forty-five[23] years. They know that a frightened nation and its political leaders will always spend money on what they believe is self-preservation.

Russia has not fought a land and air battle with an equal enemy since 1941–42. Since that time, apart from Afghanistan, Russian forces have not fired a shot in anger. In Afghanistan the 100,000-strong occupation force was defeated by a motley group of *mujahideen* fighters in the hills who killed, over an eight-year period of sporadic fighting, 15,000 Russian soldiers and wounded 50,000 more. The huge Russian mechanised army that arrived wrapped in its myth of superiority was no more successful than were the American military forces in Vietnam, and in the end had to make an equally ignominious withdrawal. What defeated the Russians in Afghanistan was the *Stinger* surface-to-air missile, a relatively cheap, unsophisticated, hand-held weapon that simply made it impossible for them to give air support to their ground forces.

As far as NATO is concerned, the hoary old Fulda Gap scenario has long been out of date. The area around Fulda is densely urbanised, and far from sweeping across open plains the Russians would find themselves bogged down in street battles. The notion of Russian superiority in armoured equipment is grossly misleading since much of it is old, poorly maintained, lacks spares, and seldom leaves barracks for extended exercises. The much-vaunted Russian air force spends most of its time on the ground, and even shooting down an unarmed 747 civilian airliner took two hours to achieve and threw the entire air defence system into chaos.

Russian servicemen are conscripted largely against their will, poorly educated and trained, lack motivation, and spend much of their time either stoned on drugs or drunk. Apart from not speaking one another's language, the majority come from backgrounds where a telephone and flush toilet are a rarity. Long before the Russian fighting machine crossed the West German border it would have run out of fuel, food, and spares, and lost its way through lack of maps, as happened during the Russian invasion of Czechoslovakia in 1968.

For years the West had been assured by its intelligence experts that Russia would survive any nuclear attack because it possessed a highly efficient civil defence organisation directly controlled by the army, which, unlike the civil defence organisations[24] of the West that are cosmetic agencies run on shoestring budgets, had huge resources at its disposal to cope with the worst nuclear catastrophe. Yet when the Armenian earthquake[25] of December 1988 occurred, the Russian civil defence organisation failed completely, and the Russian health minister, Dr Yevgeny Chazov, described it as totally bankrupt.[26] All the army could do was to stand around as bewildered as the unfortunate victims. Chaos prevailed at every level. Nothing worked. There was no organisation. Food and medical supplies were non-existent despite the fact that, unlike nuclear attacks, earthquakes have happened before in this region. It is hard to believe that this is the same organisation that for forty-five years we have been told will sweep across Europe in two days, defeat NATO, and take over the West.

The art of scaring people with mythological spy mania that can neither be proved or disproved is one of the oldest tricks of the intelligence trade in order to get extra money and make its organisations seem more important. The Western nations have always been so anxious to believe the worst about Russia that they never stop to query even the most bizarre claim.

Creating spy mania[27] is not new. It began at the turn of the century with stories of hordes of Prussian spies infiltrating Britain. At the start of World War II it was an imaginary Fifth Column of traitors that had been responsible for the collapse of Europe in the face of Hitler's attacks.

Even today the same sort of scaremongering finds a ready audience. Two years ago a highly reputable weekly defence magazine reported that the Russians had infiltrated[28] some of their sabotage troops, (known as *spetsnaz*), into the women protesters' peace camps at the US Cruise missile airbase at Greenham Common, near Reading. The story apparently originated from a Russian emigré in America, and although it caused a sensation at the time no one was able to produce any proof. It was a classic example of a story that simply fitted in with what some people wanted to believe. If we are willing to frighten ourselves in this manner, we do the enemy's work for him. Russian intelligence must be very pleased and highly amused at some of the achievements we so readily credit them with.

Russian intelligence and military experts had less to laugh about when a £50,000 light aircraft, piloted by 19-year-old West German, Mathias Rust, flew across the most heavily defended sector of Russia's air defence system and landed, ironically, on Border Guard Day, right in the heart of Red Square, unchallenged and undetected.[29] The incident caused much embarrassment within Russia where several senior officers in charge of air defence were sacked, and considerable amusement in the West – although there is every reason to assume that a light aircraft could penetrate Britain's airspace just as easily.[30]

All too often intelligence fails us just when we would expect it to work. On the morning of 2 April 1982, while the Prime Minister, Mrs Margaret Thatcher, and her cabinet slept soundly in their beds, a piece of sovereign British territory fell to an invader and for the first time in thirty-five years British troops were obliged to surrender. Contrary to all that we had been told since the end of the war, these invaders did not have snow on their boots nor did they speak Russian. They came from Argentina and their target was the Falkland Islands, which in a matter of hours they captured. Even more alarming was that shortly before the invasion there was a complete communications blackout with the Falklands, so that the government in London was obliged to learn of the surrender from the enemy's capital.

So here was a country that over many decades had spent billions of pounds on the latest intelligence technology that was specifically designed to warn us of any attack, so that Britain could use its independent nuclear deterrent within a matter of minutes. Yet all this technology failed. Was this just bad luck or was it Britain's Pearl Harbor?

After the war with Argentina, Britain turned to the time-honoured custom of holding an inquiry conducted by eminent people ignorant of intelligence matters. They politely questioned civil servants and the heads of the intelligence services and received equally polite, uninformative replies. The inquiry concluded that no one was to blame. It seemed that MI6 was so impoverished that all it could do was read the newspapers in Buenos Aires to find out what General Galtieri was planning. No mention was made of what GCHQ had managed to monitor, either alone or in conjunction with the American National Security Agency (NSA), or the Central Intelligence Agency (CIA). It seemed that our expensive intelligence agencies had suddenly been struck deaf and blind. The report was filed and forgotten. Now we could go back to watching Ivan the Terrible at the Fulda Gap.

But a startlingly different version of events has since been told by a retired Deputy Director of MI6.[31] He has stated that British intelligence recived a very full assessment of the Argentinian intentions, including the fact that the story that the Argentines were conducting a joint naval exercise with the Uruguayan navy was a deception plan designed to conceal their invasion preparations. All this information reached GCHQ, who had a very good picture of what was in the enemy's mind. But, like MI6, GCHQ is controlled by the Foreign Office, which at the time was busily engaged in trying to give away these troublesome islands whose tiny population had the annoying desire to remain British.

In Britain, convention dictates that government ministers do not have direct access to raw intelligence but get their information from summaries prepared by a series of committees, the most important of which is the Joint Intelligence Committee (JIC), in which the Foreign Office has the dominant role. By contrast, during World War II, Churchill would have none of this:

> I had not been content with this form of collective wisdom and
> preferred to see the originals myself ... thus forming my own opinion.
> I do not wish [Ultra] reports to be sifted and digested by the intelligence
> authorities ... Major [Desmond] Morton is to be shown everything and
> submit authentic documents to me in their original form.[32]

As a result Churchill usually knew more about the enemy's intentions than his Chiefs of Staff (who greatly resented his access to raw intelligence), which was why he was able to make such swift and prescient decisions.

In post-war years it is very unlikely that any British prime minister or foreign secretary has ever visited[33] GCHQ at a time of crisis, sat down next to the codebreakers to see what raw material was coming in, and seek the opinion of those actually dealing with it on a daily basis. In America things ought to be slightly different because President Bush was once head of the CIA, but here again the bureaucratic nature of an organisation of that size almost certainly precludes the director-general from having time to see raw material.

In the case of the Falklands in 1982, it was not difficult for the Foreign

Office to ensure that any information that might have upset their delicate hand-over negotiations was so diluted or obscured that it would not be taken seriously by ministers. The Foreign Office gambled for high stakes, for had the Argentines stayed their hand for six months either the islands would have been theirs by negotiation, or the British navy would have had insufficient aircraft carriers to support a task force.

Either Galtieri was very stupid not to read the Foreign Office signals correctly or he was pushed into a premature invasion. The one country that has emerged from the Falklands War highly satisfied is the United States, which now has an unsinkable aircraft carrier in the South Atlantic controlled by a friendly power from which it would be very easy to defend the Cape Horn sea route if ever the Panama Canal were closed or fell under the control of an unfriendly government.[34]

Eight years later the same scenario occurred again when, in August 1990, President Saddam Hussein of Iraq invaded Kuwait, and in a matter of hours had siezed the tiny state and its important oil wells. Throughout July – and indeed even earlier – both America and Britain had gathered a vast amount of intelligence (mainly from electronic sources), showing that Hussein was massing large numbers of troops and tanks on the Kuwait border. Although the American Joint Chiefs of Staff had a contingency plan, called Operations Plan 90–1002 (first drafted in the 1980s, and envisaging a war against Russia or Iran to protect the Gulf oil fields), no action was taken, both the British and American ambassadors in Baghdad were on holiday at the time, and the Foreign Office did not even warn a British Airways 747 airliner about to land in Kuwait that an invasion had taken place; its crew and passengers were taken hostage by Iraq.

Was this yet another Pearl Harbor? Far from it. The intelligence was accurate, but the political willpower to use it was lacking because, throughout the ten-year Iran-Iraq war, both America and Britain, although officially neutral, had covertly backed Iraq, believing that Hussein was a better victor than some mad Iranian *mullah*. Indeed, so strong was Britain's and America's commitment to Iraq, that they conveniently overlooked shipments of equipment and chemicals from West Germany with which Hussein made poison gas to massacre thousands of Kurdish women and children.

At the end of the Iran-Iraq war, Britain's Foreign Office encouraged British firms to visit Baghdad and rebuild its shattered industry, hoping to secure large numbers of profitable contracts. A blind eye was turned to the export of military equipment, such as radar systems,[35] and even bizarre projects like Hussein's 'super-gun'.[36] A slight hiatus occurred when a British journalist, Farzad Bazoft,[37] who had visited Iraq to investigate a story of a mysterious explosion, was arrested and later hanged as a spy. At the time the British government did everything possible to play down the importance of Bazoft's execution, leaking convenient stories to the media about a previous criminal conviction which encouraged some to suggest that he was, in reality, a spy. His innocent companion, a nurse called Daphne Parish, was sentenced to 15 years imprisonment but later released in curious circumstances.[38]

Immediately William Waldegrave, a Foreign Office minister, went on television to say that her release would lead to a new chapter in Anglo-Iraqi relations. Under the circumstances, it was hardly surprising that intelligence reports that Hussein was massing tanks and troops on the Kuwait border were deliberately downplayed as being merely bluff, so that Mrs Thatcher and President Bush were completely ignorant of events until the invasion was almost complete. It is interesting to compare this attitude to the traditional bias both Britain and America have always shown towards any intelligence reports about the Soviet Union, which always automatically assume the 'worst case' scenario.

The Iraq invasion also showed the limits of electronic intelligence, for, although it showed details of troop concentrations and movements, and eavesdropped on all forms of communications, it could not penetrate the mind of an unbalanced, autocratic dictator like Hussein who operates within a small tribal cabal. Here, only human intelligence (Humint), will provide the final piece to the intelligence jigsaw, and, although the Foreign Office have always prided themselves on knowing the Arab mind far better than the Americans, evidently their skill failed completely on this occasion.

A great deal of intelligence work is a matter of bluff, with each side pretending to know more, or less (as it suits them), about the other. In 1956, the British actor and writer, Peter Ustinov, produced a play in London called *Romanoff and Juliet*. This contains a scene in which the prime minister of a small, unaligned country (played by Ustinov), learns of some secret operation planned by the Russians. Ustinov tells the Americans, who smile knowingly and admit they know about the plan. He then tells the Russians that the Americans know about their plan. 'We know they know', reply the Russians. Back he goes to the Americans to warn them, who merely say, 'We know they know we know'. The ploy is continued until the point is reached when the Americans are told by a puzzled Ustinov that 'They know you know they know you know' at which point, having counted up the permutations, the Americans are horrified.

Of course some intelligence operations are a necessary part of any nation's defence against both external and internal enemies. That does not mean that the agencies should automatically be excused from accountability merely on the grounds of national security. Even the most modern and efficient army, navy, and air force, is constantly scrutinised to ensure it provides the country and the taxpayer good value for money. Sometimes a particular military role is abandoned altogether because it is considered neither cost-effective nor essential. Naturally generals and admirals complain that without larger budgets the security of the nation and its alliances will suffer. But commonsense prevails, and the armed services become leaner and more efficient. No one thinks this odd.

But to suggest that intelligence agencies should have to undergo the same evaluation is akin to producing a crucifix in Transylvania. Everything they do is vital and if enemies cannot be shown to exist today they will be invented tomorrow. Even the most investigative politician finds it difficult to penetrate this labyrinthine web of mythology, and those that try too hard are immediately deflected by the ever-present talisman of national security.

Politicians are particularly vulnerable to the lure of intelligence. While in opposition they may demand greater accountability, more openness, and more control over illegal operations, yet upon taking office they soon succumb to its mystique. Inevitably a nation gets the intelligence service it deserves, but unless these organisations can be made more accountable and operate with far less secrecy, there is the very real danger that they will lose the public's confidence to the point that they are totally emasculated, as has happened, for example, in Australia where the anti-intelligence lobby now holds power to disastrous effect.[39] The main difficulty is to let in a little daylight on people who spend their time in a secret, twisted twilight world of their own reflections and morality. The purpose of this book is to open the window of accountability still further, and show the pointlessness of so much of the work of intelligence services everywhere.

CHAPTER I

THE PLAYERS

Virtually every country in the world has some sort of intelligence agency. Most have at least two, one to look after security within the country (usually called counter-intelligence) and the other to engage in spying abroad. In addition there are often separate intelligence-gathering sections in each armed service. The general rule is that the efficiency of a country's intelligence operations is in inverse proportion to the number of agencies it operates. This is because each agency has to fight for its share of the overall intelligence budget and in the process exaggerates and distorts its reports so as to pander to the whims of those who hold the purse-strings. Large intelligence organisations are very hierarchically structured, affording plenty of opportunity for individual empire-building and internecine jealousies, all of which waste an enormous amount of time and effort, sow the seeds of discontent and distrust and frequently obscure and distort the important issues.

In recent years the lifestyle of the intelligence officer has acquired a glamorous image thanks to the literary world and the screen. Though most people recognise that this is only fiction there nevertheless remains a feeling that the work is rather exciting, possibly because it lacks any clearly defined morality. In truth it is not. Nor, despite its supposed importance in terms of national security, is it very well paid. The obvious attraction is job security, since the world of intelligence never suffers from lay-offs. One source of recruitment has always been the armed services, not only because their staff have already been security vetted, but also because they are used to carrying out dull repetitive chores and filling out the endless paperwork that forms the major part of any intelligence operation. University graduates are another obvious source and in Britain are headhunted, initially under another government department's name, to sound out their loyalty and motivation.[1]

Some countries are less coy about recruiting. In America and Australia, for example, advertisements appear quite regularly for intelligence staff. Those for the Australian Security Intelligence Organisation (ASIO), which is the equivalent of Britain's MI5, offer 'a unique opportunity to make an important contribution to Australia's security'. One recent advertisment carried a photograph of a rather seedy individual in a large hat and dirty raincoat which it stressed was precisely the type of applicant not required. Aside from employing field officers who go out on to the streets, intelligence agencies gobble up an incredible amount of technically skilled manpower, simply to run their huge banks of computers, and large numbers of foreign-speaking translators.

In Britain there are three main intelligence organisations[2]: Military Intelligence, Department Five (MI5), responsible for counter-intelligence within Britain; Military Intelligence, Department Six (MI6), often referred to as the Secret Intelligence Service, responsible for espionage abroad; and the Government Communications Headquarters (GCHQ), which is responsible for the security of the British government's own communications and intercepting those of other countries.

MI5 began life in 1909. It came about as the result of a committee set up under the chairmanship of that impeccable Liberal, Lord Haldane, to consider 'The Question of Foreign Espionage in the United Kingdom'. Although officially named as a branch of the military, MI5 was placed under the control of the Foreign Office.

MI5's initial task was to counter alleged German plans to secretly invade Britain by infiltrating thousands of spies. This proved a difficult task as the story was completely false. Its first real test came during World War I when 30 genuine German spies were arrested between 1914–18. After the war MI5 turned its attention to the growing menace of Bolshevism which the government feared would soon engulf the country. Its greatest achievements came during World War II when it caught every one of Hitler's spies sent to England.[3] This was not a particularly difficult task since they were all pathetically trained and equipped and stood out conspicuously as they wandered around the countryside asking stupid and suspicious questions in foreign accents.

Many of these spies subsequently agreed to work for MI5. The alternative was to be hanged, so there was a powerful incentive. Through the Double Cross Committee, usually known as the XX Committee,[4] these turned spies sent back to Germany a steady stream of fictitious information garnished with sufficient truth to give it credibility, which the Germans apparently accepted without question. Whether the Germans were quite as easily fooled as history would have us believe is open to some question. Since the war there has been a remarkable lack of comment on this issue from the German side. This may be because no one likes to admit they have been fooled or because many German records relating to their intelligence operations against Britain were amongst the captured archives not returned to Bonn in 1956. But it probably does not matter much anyway. As the war progressed Hitler tended to listen only to advice that agreed with his own views and no one was willing to disagree with him.

After the war there was a complete review of Britain's security services and in 1952 MI5 came under the control of the Home Office. It moved back to London from its wartime headquarters at Blenheim Palace in Oxfordshire and established its headquarters at Leconfield House in Curzon Street. In the late 1970s MI5 moved again to its present address, still in Curzon Street. It also has another office which houses K Section (counter-espionage), and the liaison section that works with MI6.

Back in 1952 the then Home Secretary, Sir David Maxwell Fyfe, laid down specific guidelines to the Director-General of MI5 as to how it should operate in the future. It is worth looking at these in detail:

1   In your appointment as Director-General of the Security Service you will be responsible personally to the Home Secretary. The Security Service is not, however, a part of the Home Office. On appropriate occasion you will have right of direct access to the Prime Minister.

2   The Security Service is part of the Defence Forces of the country. Its task is the Defence of the Realm as a whole, from external and internal dangers arising from attempts of espionage and sabotage, or from actions of persons and organisations whether directed from within or without the country, which may be judged to be subversive of the State.

3   You will take special care to see that the work of the Security Service is strictly limited to what is necessary for the task.

4   It is essential that the Security Service should be kept absolutely free from political bias or influence and nothing should be done that might lend colour to any suggestion that it is conerned with the interests of any particular section of the community, or with any other matter than the Defence of the Realm as a whole.

5   No inquiry is to be carried out on behalf of any government department unless you are satisfied that an important public interest bearing on the Defence of the Realm, as defined in Paragraph 2, is at stake.

6   You and your staff will maintain the well-established convention whereby ministers do not concern themselves with the detailed information which may be obtained by the Security Service in particular cases, but are furnished with such information only as may be necessary for the determination of any issue on which guidance is sought.

One can readily deduce from this directive that Maxwell Fyfe was a civil servant, a member of the legal profession and an optimist. As Sir Robert Armstrong, former Cabinet Secretary, pointed out in a recent court case,[5] economy of truth and interpretation plays an important part in how the behaviour of MI5 is determined. For this reason the directive deserves careful study in three specific areas. First, though MI5 is notionally under the control of the Home Secretary he will be told nothing about its day-to-day operations. Second, MI5 alone determines who and which organisations are judged to be subversive. And third, ministers will not be given any detailed information about MI5's work.

The fundamental flaw in Maxwell Fyfe's directive is that, though it is admirable in theory, there is no supervisory machinery to ensure that it is carried out. Those members of MI5 who have written or spoken publicly about their work say quite clearly that the directive is consistently and deliberately ignored. The absence of any system of accountability is not a mistake. Maxwell Fyfe's guidelines were never meant to be taken seriously but were merely a piece of bureaucratic window-dressing.

In post-war years MI5 has been remarkably unsuccessful at catching spies and traitors in our midst, going right back to Guy Burgess and Donald Maclean who in the summer of 1951 defected under the noses of MI5 despite supposedly being under surveillance. Following them was Kim Philby, who escaped to Moscow just ahead of MI5 in 1962, and Anthony Blunt, who finally confessed in 1964 to being a long-time and important Russian spy only after having been granted immunity from prosecution.

Since then a succession of tawdry traitors have been unmasked as the result of information passed to the intelligence services by a defector. Some of the more important include George Blake, who worked for MI6 (see Chapter 2); John Cairncross, who betrayed Ultra secrets from the Government Code & Cipher School (GCCS) at Bletchley Park during the war to the Russians; John Vassall, a sad homosexual who gave away naval secrets while working at the Admiralty; Frank Bossard, who gave the Russians details of British and American guided weapons systems (which must have amused them greatly as the Russians were far ahead of the West at the time); and William Marshall, who had worked as a cipher clerk at the British Embassy in Moscow.

Then there was the famous Portland spy ring comprising Peter and Helen Kroger and 'Gordon Lonsdale', whose real name was Konon Molody, all of whom were professional Russian spies living in England with false identities. The British end of the network consisted of Harry Houghton and Ethel Gee who passed on secrets of sonar and submarine development. More recently there was Geoffrey Prime, who worked in the very heart of GCHQ (see Chapter 4), and Michael Bettaney, an MI5 officer whose drunken and strange behaviour was in many ways reminiscent of Guy Burgess's yet similarly went undetected until reported by a defector (see Chapter 4).

The common factor in all these cases is that they were not discovered by MI5. Why is MI5 so useless at finding spies and traitors? Some argue that the reason is that MI5 has been penetrated by Russian intelligence so deeply that even its own Director General, Sir Roger Hollis, was a Russian mole and therefore every investigation has been frustrated. This lacks credibility for two reasons: first, there is no evidence to prove Hollis was a Russian mole, and second, no investigations were ever planned that would have tracked down any of these spies, despite the fact that they all displayed behaviour patterns that were highly suspicious, until a defector alerted MI5.

Vassall was recognised at once by the Russians in Moscow as a homosexual and blackmailed. He later lived in an expensive flat surrounded by antique furniture far beyond his official income. Prime was recognised as a paedophile by East German intelligence and blackmailed, yet passed six positive vetting checks. He gave up a well-paid senior post at GCHQ in order to become a taxi driver but no one thought it strange. Houghton's wife reported him to naval security for being in possession of large sums of cash. No one took any notice. Burgess was a drunken homosexual yet no one seemed concerned.

The reason for MI5's inefficiency is that it wastes far too much time and resources chasing after the wrong sort of people who it believes to be subversive, while real enemies of the state are able to go on spying undetected for decades. This is the result of allowing a counter-intelligence agency to become politicised. MI5 maintains a large registry of files on individuals and organisations it considers of 'interest'. Peter Wright recalls that when he joined MI5 in 1953 there were some two million files held on individuals.[6] During the 1960s and 1970s, when there was much student and industrial militancy in Britain, the numbers of personal dossiers rose dramatically. In recent years the entire MI5 registry has been transferred on to a computer at a Ministry of Defence office in Mount Row, Mayfair.

The original system used a £25 million ICL 2960 computer with 100 on-line EDS-200 disc stores capable of holding 30 million separate dossiers[7] but in 1984 (an apt year indeed) two ICL 2980 computers were ordered which provide enough capacity to store a 1,000-word report on every adult in Britain. As it is hard to believe that even MI5 thinks there are that many subversives, spies and traitors in the country, it must keep a lot of files on innocent people. Here is a straightforward example of how the Maxwell Fyfe directive is ignored. Special Branch, which works closely with MI5, has its own computer system[8] which keeps records on many millions of people none of whom have committed any offence (if they had they would be on the Police National Computer) split into 27 different groups such as 'interesting', 'controversial' and 'subversive'.

Cathy Massiter made it very clear in her television interview[9] that MI5 and Special Branch alone decide who merits a dossier and which group they belong to and can open a file on any person or group of people or organisation they please, put into it anything they like, be it only gossip or hearsay, and once opened the file remains there indefinitely. Furthermore, Miss Massiter explained that information gathered by MI5 was shared with other government departments for political purposes and gave examples of how trade-union leaders had their telephones tapped by MI5 during wage negotiations with government departments. Since no minister would authorise a warrant for such tapping it must have been done illegally. All this is in clear breach of the 1952 directive.

In addition MI5 has representatives permanently stationed at the central registry of the Department of Social Security (DSS) at Newcastle, which maintains records – which the DSS claim are confidential – on every adult in the country.[10] MI5 is able to extract any information it wants about individuals, which is often useful when it is smearing someone's character. This registry is in the process of being transferred, at a cost of £1.6 billion,[11] on to what will become the country's single largest computer system with terminals at every DSS office throughout Britain. The man chosen to run this is 51-year-old Dr John Spackman who previously held the rank of brigadier in the British Army running its computers.[12] It will be easy to interface the new DSS computer with those of MI5 and Special Branch.[13]

MI5 taps large numbers of telephones, sometimes with the authority of a signed warrant but more frequently without. Hotels where visiting politicians regularly stay[14] and conference headquarters like Lancaster House are permanently bugged.[15] MI5 and Special Branch also open mail illegally and break into so many properties that they have one section that does nothing else.[16]

Turning to the final point of the 1952 directive, it is noteworthy that ministers are to be given only the information MI5 decides they need. In other words, if a minister does not know the right question to ask MI5 about a particular operation or allegation then MI5 will not volunteer any information on its own.[17] This leaves MI5 in the enviable position of being accountable to no one nor having to explain anything it does or is alleged to have done.

If MI5 had obeyed the 1952 Maxwell Fyfe guidelines then there would have been little cause for complaint about its activities over the past 35 years. But MI5 deliberately ignored them as and when it suited because it believed no prime minister or Home Secretary would interfere[18] nor would any member of the service break ranks and tell the truth about what really went on inside MI5.

By 1988 the number of leaks about MI5's illegal activities, from people like Peter Wright and Cathy Massiter who had first-hand experience, had reached such proportions that they could no longer be ignored, even though the government made every attempt to denigrate the motives and character of such people. As a result in December 1988 the government was forced to introduce the Security Service Bill to replace the Maxwell Fyfe guidelines and clearly identify MI5's role, providing legal safeguards against improper behaviour. Amongst the proposals is one requiring MI5 to seek the Home Secretary's authority before premises are burgled. As is explained later in the book, despite the high-sounding words with which the Bill was presented to Parliament it is a complete sham. MI5 will remain as unaccountable as it always has been and since it blatantly ignored the 1952 directive for over three decades without once being publicly called to account there is no reason to believe that MI5 will be any more law-abiding now.[19]

MI6, the Secret Intelligence Service (SIS), began life in 1911 under the control of the Foreign Office, which had been spying on other countries for over 400 years. After World War I its activities were severely limited by lack of funds and its inability to recruit good personnel. It seemed to have the knack of attracting some of the most bizarre characters who spent a great deal of the inter-war years building up little empires for themselves with scant regard for any overall espionage policy.

As a result, by the time war was declared in 1939 MI6 had failed to establish any worthwhile network of agents in Europe and those it had were of very dubious quality, some even dishonest and fraudulent. MI6 never appreciated the amount of opposition that existed within Germany to Hitler and the Nazi party in its early days and as a result failed to exploit the very considerable amount of information that was offered to it by well-placed anti-Nazi groups. In 1939 MI6 received the famous Oslo Report[20], a package of technical information delivered to the British Legation in Oslo, containing a wealth of priceless data about secret weapon developments in Germany including rocket design at a then unheard of location called Peenemünde. Because MI6 possessed no one with any technical qualifications to analyse the Oslo Report it was rejected as worthless and ignored. It turned out to be accurate in every respect.

MI6 also had advance warning of the German plan to invade the Low Countries in May 1940 but decided the maps it had been shown were forgeries and again ignored the information. The main problem with MI6 at the time was that all the senior people were amateurs who had joined MI6 only because they had gone to the right school,[21] wore the right sort of tie and dined at the right clubs. They in turn recruited their friends in the belief that together they would make a jolly good team. This view lingered on for a long time and probably still exists to this day.

During World War II MI6 produced few worthwhile results, largely because it had no agents in place before Hitler occupied the whole of Europe. MI6 was greatly upset by Churchill's decision to create Special Operations Executive (SOE),[22] which it saw as infringing upon its sacred duties. But to no avail. Churchill wanted action of a dramatic kind and had little use for MI6. MI6 accepted his decision with ill-grace and throughout the rest of the war did all it could to hinder the work of SOE. On at least one occasion it infiltrated a double agent of its own into SOE who betrayed some 400 British and French agents to the Germans.[23]

MI6's wartime reputation also suffered from the fact that several of its senior members were Soviet agents so that, as with MI5, it required some drastic reorganisation after the war. MI6 remains to this day a secret organisation that does not officially exist despite the fact that in recent years there have been numerous books written about its activities. There is a childlike belief at the Foreign Office that if it does not admit to the existence of MI6, foreign governments will believe Britain does not spy on them. At the *Spycatcher* trial in Sydney in 1987 Sir Robert Armstrong, then the Cabinet Secretary, said he could not confirm the existence of MI6. Had Armstrong bothered to look in the government's own internal telephone directory (the Government Telecommunications Network), he would have found that MI6 is listed with four addresses.

Since the telephone directory is circulated to all government offices throughout the country one must assume that by now the Russians have managed to see a copy. Over 600 people work for MI6 in its main office. In 1988 the head of MI6, known as 'C', was Sir Christopher Curwen. Official letters to MI6 are addressed to a mythical person called Mr G. H. Merrick. MI6 cooperates with MI5 through a liaison office in London.

MI6 is still controlled by the Foreign Office but the Foreign Secretary neither admits to this publicly nor asks any questions about how MI6 goes about its daily business. MI6 is supposed to operate only outside Britain although it does occasionally get involved in projects within Britain such as the Crabb affair of 1956 (see Chapter 3), which was bungled from start to finish. Some years ago MI6 became involved against the IRA in Northern Ireland, much to the annoyance of MI5. The result of the two intelligence services, army intelligence, the Royal Ulster Constabulary's Special Branch, and various odd freelancers all having a go at the same time was, not surprisingly, a total disaster.

It is hard to judge how effective MI6 is today because on the only recent occasion it was needed, to warn us of the Argentinian invasion of the Falkland Islands in 1982, it either failed completely or the Foreign Office deliberately presented MI6's information to the government in a way that precluded it being taken seriously.[24] If the Foreign Office cannot agree with MI6 as to who are Britain's enemies, the effectiveness of MI6 is at risk of being submerged by political expediency, calling into question the whole point of having such an organisation in the first place.

From time to time fringe elements in MI6 dream up hare-brained schemes like the plot to assassinate President Nasser of Egypt,[25] or sending midget submarines into the Russian naval base at Leningrad.[26] Much of its time is now spent targeting potential defectors amongst other foreign diplomatic staff. In this respect MI6 has had a number of successes although it is difficult to know how useful defectors really are (see Chapter 2). MI6 makes considerable use of freelancers, such as businessmen, who can openly visit sensitive parts of the world without arousing suspicion, but the overall value of the information such people can produce is very limited.

To a large extent technology has eroded much of MI6's original style of work while modern communications make it difficult for political decisions to remain secret for very long even behind the Iron Curtain. While there will always be a place for human intelligence (Humint), past experience suggests that MI6 is unable to produce anything that remotely justifies its annual cost.

Britain's third intelligence service is the Government Communications Headquarters (GCHQ), located at Cheltenham in Gloucestershire and employing some 12,000 staff with a secret budget of around £500 million a year.[27] It is part of MI6 and thus controlled by the Foreign Office. Like MI6, for many years GCHQ did not officially exist despite the fact that it was listed in several yearbooks.

GCHQ began in 1919[28] as the Government Code and Cipher School (GCCS), picking up the few remaining members of the army and naval teams of codebreakers who had operated in Britain during World War I. A very small team was formed, working on a tiny annual budget in MI6's offices at 56 Broadway, in London.

The public function of GCCS was: 'To advise as to the security of codes and ciphers used by all government departments and to assist in their provision.'

The secret function of GCCS was: 'To study the methods of cipher communication used by foreign powers.'

As more money became available and the number of codebreakers could be increased GCCS managed to penetrate all the really important codes of Britain's friends and foes alike during the inter-war years.

Additionally, it read all cable traffic entering and leaving Britain. At first this was arranged on a private basis. At the time there were only three cable companies operating in Britain: Cable & Wireless, which was owned by the British government so presented no problem, and the two American cable companies, the Commercial Cable Postal Telegraph Company and Western Union, who did not acquiesce so easily. The tacit threat of having their operating licences removed was required before they agreed to cooperate with GCCS and let it see their messages each day.

In December 1920, during a US Senate Sub-Committee hearing in Washington, one of the cable companies publicly revealed the duress under which it had been placed by the British Government.[29] Acutely embarrassed by this unexpected disclosure, the British government hastily added a clause to the 1911 Official Secrets Act giving it the right to see copies of all cables if an emergency existed. In 1919 a single warrant was signed alleging such an emergency (the excuse being the threat of Bolshevism) and interceptions have continued on this basis, with the exception of wartime censorship from 1939–45, to this day without debate or approval by Parliament. As the years passed, telephone, telex, facsimile and computer data traffic all came under this original warrant, so that not a single communication enters or leaves Britain without being subject to interception by GCCS's successor, GCHQ.

GCCS made particularly good progress breaking the Japanese naval attaché cipher traffic, both in London and elsewhere in Europe, since many foreign cable companies routed their signals through repeater stations in places like Malta where GCCS could acquire all interesting traffic without having to go through the charade of obtaining a warrant. The naval attaché's telephone in London was also intercepted. Eventually GCCS in London and Singapore was in a position to read all Japanese naval signals, right up to the attack on Pearl Harbor, although Churchill carefully kept this information from the Americans.

Progress against German cipher traffic was less successful because Britain ignored developments in machine cryptography so that by 1939 GCCS was unable to read the German Enigma cryptograph. Many years after the war the story of how the Enigma code was eventually broken was told[30] and, as is often the case with officially approved histories, it was implied that the success was entirely that of GCCS. In truth Enigma was broken by Polish intelligence[31] with the help of the French and although Britain was invited to join in the work before the war, it declined to do so. Only when Polish intelligence made a gift of its work to GCCS in August 1939 was it able to break its first German messages.

How much effect this had on the final outcome of the war is hard to say. Claims that it shortened the war by several years cannot be proved one way or the other. Intelligence, even codebreaking, is at best only a fragmented adjunct to strategic planning. Nevertheless the breaking of the German Enigma codes, which became known as the Ultra secret, played a vital role in winning the war and was the only good thing to come out of MI6. With apparent benevolence Britain and America later sold off to many smaller countries reconditioned Enigmas at extremely cheap prices, urging them to adopt the system for their most secret traffic. As a result for many years their messages were read with ease.

At the end of World War II, GCHQ[32], as GCCS had become, moved from its wartime headquarters at Bletchley Park, north of London, to Cheltenham, where it swiftly sprawled over two large sites – Oakley and Benhall.[33] Its tasks remained much the same. Only the technology was different. The first would be to protect Britain's own secrets by developing the necessary cipher machines, codes and operating procedures. This is the work of the Communications Security Department (Comsec).

The second task was the interception of everyone else's messages around the world and, where possible, decoding them. This work is concealed under the cover-title of the Composite Signals Organisation (CSO).

The cost of all this was too large for a war-weary, bankrupt Britain. As a result in 1947 an agreement was signed with the Americans, known as the UK-USA Treaty, whereby the world would be split up into different areas of operation and GCHQ and its American counterpart the National Security Agency (NSA), would share out the intelligence work on the most economical basis. In some parts, where Britain still had old colonial links, GCHQ would run the eavesdropping stations. In others where American money had more influence the NSA would operate. All the information gathered would be shared freely between GCHQ in Cheltenham and the NSA at Fort Meade in Virginia.

The work of GCHQ's CSO is straightforward eavesdropping. Around the world GCHQ and the NSA have a series of powerful listening stations that scoop up every transmission that ventures into the ether. No matter how faint or how brief each transmission may be it can be snatched out of the air and analysed.

In 1986 the leader of the Labour Party, Neil Kinnock, telephoned Malcolm Turnbull, the lawyer representing Peter Wright during the *Spycatcher* trial in Australia which was causing the British government and the security services endless embarrassment.[34] As Turnbull's number was pressed-out in London the group of numbers, converted into digital pulses, sped on their way to Sydney via Mondial House, the British Telecom international switching centre in London, to the Post Office tower and west across Britain via the main microwave link down to the earth satellite station at Goonhilly in Cornwall.

As the first group of pulses were directed to the satellite high above the Indian Ocean, mixed up with all the other transmissions going out to the Far East, they were snatched out of the ether by the NSA's giant aerials at Morwenstow 60 miles up the coast to the east of Goonhilly, and compared with the watch lists of 'interesting' numbers on their computer memories. As

Turnbull's calls were of great interest to the government at the time any calls to him from Britain would be separated from the surrounding chaff and monitored. Within seconds of Kinnock completing the call a full recording of his conversation was on its way back to Fort Meade and, from there, back to GCHQ in Cheltenham. By allowing the NSA to tap the call in Britain GCHQ had not been involved and, since the presence of the NSA in Britain is not officially admitted, the government could claim the interception never happened.[35]

Millions of calls are intercepted like this every day in Britain. In fact there are so many that without the use of sophisticated computers it would be impossible to monitor them all. At the British Telecom satellite station at Goonhilly in Cornwall at any given time there are more than 30,000 separate circuits in use while the new fibre-optical cable laid across the Atlantic in December 1988 can handle up to 40,000 separate conversations. The simplest way to program the NSA's computers at Morwenstow and Menwith Hill is to have them watch for specific names, addresses, telephone and telex numbers, as in the case of Kinnock's call to Turnbull.

Exactly how many calls are monitored in this manner is not easy to discover. Naturally neither the NSA nor GCHQ will discuss the subject since such telephone tapping is illegal but in 1976 the NSA's Harvest computer system[36] intercepted 75 million individual telephone conversations alone around the world, of which 1.8 million were considered sufficiently interesting to require further human analysis, although what happened to the information the NSA had collected and how it was shared and used remains a mystery. But as we know that MI5 taps telephones and keeps files on people simply to pass on political information to the government, one can assume that Kinnock's call to Turnbull is not the only piece of politicised telephone tapping that goes on.

In London itself GCHQ operated the Joint Technical Language Service (JTLS), sometimes called the London Processing Group (LPG). Both these titles were cover-names for the department responsible for eavesdropping on foreign embassies and trade missions in London. Monitoring was done from offices at 4–9 St Dunstans Hill, in the City of London, and the upper floors of the Empress State Building in Earls' Court.

It is, of course, no secret that all diplomatic missions not only operate a massive communications system using local telephone and telex lines but are also in direct radio contact with their foreign ministry. The roofs of every embassy and legation in London are draped with aerials of every size and shape. Equally, the embassies know perfectly well that all their signals traffic is monitored.

Day after day reels of tape slowly turn, recording every word uttered along these lines of communication. This produces pages of transcription which are carefully scanned in the hope that for one brief second some minor indiscretion may have taken place.[37] Not surprisingly the other side does its best to complicate matters by deliberately holding meaningless conversations that defy analysis. This is all part of the game.

But the range of ground surveillance systems, no matter how sophisticated, is inevitably restricted by the curvature of the earth's surface. To overcome this America's intelligence services began to think up other ways of delving right into the heart of Russia and China. Over a period of 30 years a number of surveillance systems were produced: first the U-2 spy aircraft, followed by the incredibly fast SR-71 (both of which are still in service today), and then a whole generation of satellites culminating in *Rhyolite*[38] (see page 28).

America was a late starter in the intelligence game, but today it boasts the most powerful and expensive agencies in the world. The four most important are the CIA, which handles overseas espionage and is therefore similar to Britain's MI6; the NSA which, like GCHQ, handles Sigint, Elint (Electronic Intelligence), and codebreaking; the National Reconnaissance Office (NRO), which controls the surveillance satellites launched into space; and the Defence Intelligence Agency (DIA), which coordinates the intelligence operations of the US Army, Navy, and Air Force. Counter-intelligence operations within America are handled by the Federal Bureau of Investigation (FBI).

The American intelligence agencies (excluding the FBI) are funded from two secret budgets. One is called the National Foreign Intelligence Program and contains about $12 billion and the other, controlled by the Secretary of Defense, is called the Tactical Intelligence and Related Activities Budget and contains a further $12 billion. So there is some $24 billion available for intelligence operations which cover a vast spectrum of activities ranging from the covert and illegal to the overt and legal. None of these funds are subject to any scrutiny or accountability by Congress.

Both the US Navy and Army had run their own intelligence departments since the early 1880s while the FBI had been in existence since 1910 and had been responsible for collating foreign intelligence. When World War II began in 1939 America had no proper espionage organisation operating abroad. In a rather haphazard fashion, and greatly encouraged by the British, Roosevelt finally agreed in 1942 to set up the Office of Strategic Services (OSS) under the command of Colonel William Donovan.

With unlimited enthusiasm for cloak-and-dagger activities and equally unlimited funds, OSS had many remarkable successes throughout the war.[39] One reason for this was that its officers were not bound by past conventions or the class structure that so dominated MI6. At the end of the war OSS naturally expected it would be allowed to continue in some peacetime role but the FBI, which was jealous of the way OSS had taken over its role of supplying the president with foreign intelligence, pressured President Truman into terminating OSS's activities, which he did in 1945.

Although OSS was no more, the idea of having some form of intelligence agency to operate abroad had taken root and only a few months later Truman changed his mind. On 22 January 1946 he agreed to the formation of the Central Intelligence Group (CIG), which was to be a small organisation simply collating all forms of foreign intelligence and reporting back to the president through the National Intelligence Authority (NIA). Nothing of the sort happened. No sooner had the CIG started work than it began to chafe at its restrictions and sought authority to start operating espionage networks abroad. In 1947 the National Security Act was passed creating the Central Intelligence Agency. From that moment onwards America was in the intelligence game.

A great deal of CIA activity has been concentrated in Britain where America has a huge investment in military and intelligence establishments. Since the war the CIA has been very alarmed at some of the left-wing British governments, many of whose politicians it regards as friends of Moscow.[40] Because British intelligence has been reluctant to spy on a legitimately elected government and has also been forbidden from keeping ministers under surveillance, MI5 has welcomed the CIA's intervention and given it a free rein in its British operations, always provided that it can share the resulting information.

Despite the vast amount of money it has squandered the CIA has been remarkably unsuccessful in warning America about genuinely important hostile acts by Russia and her allies. It failed to warn of Russia's ability to build an atomic, and later a nuclear, bomb. This omission the CIA conveniently blamed on a handful of spies. It failed to anticipate the Korean war. The 1968 Russian invasion of Czechoslovakia came as a surprise. So too did the Russian invasion of Afghanistan. And yet the CIA has consistently over-estimated Russia's military strength and fighting capabilities simply to enhance its reputation and to frighten politicians.

Looking at the world, and in particular Europe, today it is hard to see how anything the CIA has done in the past 40 years has significantly affected the map of freedom.[41] The great post-war stabilising factor in war-torn Europe was not covert intelligence but the sensible use of economic aid via the Marshall Plan. Bribing corrupt politicians and propping up rotten governments has not enhanced America's reputation amongst the world's poorer people and nations. Quite the reverse. The name CIA is now synonymous with everything that is corrupt and has certainly turned more people towards Communism than would have been the case had American foreign policy been more open and honest. If ever there was an example of counter-productive intelligence the CIA is it.

One of the most worrying aspects of the CIA's morality is the special brand of patriotism it bestows upon itself. During the 1987 Iran/Contra hearings in Washington the most frightening witness was Colonel Oliver North, who, though not a direct employee of the CIA, had been inextricably associated with it in this sordid affair.

There he stood before the official inquiry in his crisp, bemedalled marine uniform, his voice breaking with emotion as he lectured the assembled politicians on what was in the nation's interests as if he himself had just invented patriotism. North, the zealous visionary, besotted by his lone struggle against Communism, was so blinded by right-wing hubris that he saw nothing wrong in breaking the laws of the country he so devoutly wished to defend.

The tale he told was incredible. A mere colonel on the White House staff, he had involved himself in forgery, false testimony, the illegal shredding of incriminating documents, the illegal shipment of arms to America's enemies, the opening and operation of secret numbered bank accounts in Switzerland involving tens of millions of dollars, shady illegal deals with dishonest arms dealers, and the use of secret funds to support terrorist operations in Central America in direct contravention of Congress. What was even more alarming was that the American president believed North to be some sort of hero. On 25 March 1988, after North had been charged with a number of criminal acts, Reagan said:

I still think Ollie North is a hero. I just have to believe [he's] going to be found innocent because I don't think [he was] guilty of any lawbreaking or any crime. I've got to take a second to tell you the whole so-called Iran scandal, I think hard to think of as a scandal. I have no idea who got that extra money or where it came from.

As North's tawdry tale unfolded one was reminded of the 1962 novel *Seven Days in May*[42] which tells how a group of disaffected American generals plan to overthrow what they see as a weak and ineffective president by a military coup. To support their plan the generals secretly subvent large sums from the Chiefs of Staff's contingency fund in order to build a secret airbase in the Texas desert from which they will launch their coup. The plot is frustrated, ironically, by a colonel in the US Marine Corps who alerts the president and his advisers just in time. In the book the generals see themselves as the heroes anxious to save America. Perhaps North is not alone in this curious twisted world of loyalties.

From time to time, following a particularly embarrassing CIA fiasco, the American president plucks up enough courage to clip its wings. What then follows is usually a change of director and various public pronouncements about the CIA's future activities. After a quiet period the CIA begins to peddle new scenarios, warning of terrible impending disasters facing America if the agency is not allowed to restart its clandestine operations.

The National Security Agency was founded on 4 November 1952.[43] The terms under which Truman created the NSA and what it was meant to do are still supposed to be secret even today. At present, the NSA employs over 20,000 people, with a secret budget of anything up to $4 billion a year. It is far larger than the CIA but much less well known.

The NSA came about as a direct result of the Allied wartime successes in breaking the coded messages of both the Germans and the Japanese. After the war Truman very wisely saw the value of continuing this Anglo/American cooperation with the signing of the UK-USA Treaty in 1947. Because of the NSA's vast budget, which makes GCHQ look like toytown, it is the senior partner by far.

Like GCHQ the NSA has two functions. First, it looks after the security of America's signals traffic by developing new cryptographs and operating procedures. Second, it intercepts every communication it can, from friend or foe, and tries to decrypt it. The NSA is not officially allowed to operate within America. Nor is it supposed to intercept communications entering and leaving America. But it does so all the same.

The NSA has a huge operation in Britain which it regards as one of its most important listening posts, being strategically placed to eavesdrop not only on East Europe but West Europe as well. GCHQ allows NSA to operate in Britain for two reasons. First, the Americans pay for the construction and running costs of Sigint stations such as Menwith Hill and Morwenstow, saving GCHQ a lot of money. Secondly, as we have seen, by allowing the NSA to eavesdrop on British communications (as it does from the Morwenstow station in Cornwall which scoops up everything passing in and out of British Telecom's ground station at Goonhilly), it allows British ministers to claim that GCHQ does not monitor calls within Britain. Likewise the NSA station at Menwith Hill monitors the major domestic trunk networks of the British telephone system.

The Menwith Hill station employs over 1,200 staff, most of them Americans. A recent article in the *New Statesman & Society*[44] listed some of the current operations at Menwith Hill, including those that involve eavesdropping on Russian and West European telephone calls. Evidently Menwith Hill's operations have been so successful that a $26 million expansion programme has been approved as part of the Project P415 programme. Already teams from GCHQ have been out to America to be trained in the use of the new equipment.

All this confirms that the NSA and GCHQ are again becoming bolder and starting to blatantly ignore supposed guidelines, intercepting any transmission they wish. Both the American and British governments are cloaking these new operations in a shroud of secrecy though it is unlikely any politician has the slightest idea what the two agencies are planning to do or that they even care if laws are broken as they have been in the past.

In 1969 the NSA began *Operation Minaret*.[45] The plan was to monitor communications of American organisations and individuals who in the eyes of the NSA wanted to foment civil disturbance or otherwise undermine the security of the United States. Specifically mentioned were those connected with anti-war movements, especially those demonstrating against American involvement in Vietnam. Included in this domestic surveillance programme were well-known names such as Jane Fonda, Joan Baez, Dr Benjamin Spock, Dr Martin Luther King and many others who, at the time, had been outspoken critics about matters like civil rights and the Vietnam war.

Associated with Minaret was another programme called Shamrock. This was a joint Anglo/American affair whereby GCHQ would make available to the NSA all its intercepts of British communications, particularly those with America.

The NSA had naturally taken enormous trouble to keep Minaret and Shamrock secret since they were quite illegal even though they had the tacit approval of President Nixon, another Henry II Syndrome casualty (see Chapter 3). Unfortunately, on 7 June 1973, the *New York Times* revealed details of what the NSA was doing and, faced with the possibility of having to admit to an illegal act in open court, the NSA swiftly terminated the operations. It now seems that it and GCHQ are about to restart them.

The NSA operates many other satellite stations around the world. Typical is the Pine Gap installation near Alice Springs in Australia,[46] a huge project that sucks up communications in the Far East and Pacific. It is a controversial establishment because it is entirely staffed by NSA personnel and there has been much local discussion as to whether the station operates in the interests of Australia or only America. To try to make sense out of the vast amount of raw material intercepted each day the NSA uses computers that are programmed to search for key 'trigger' words, names, and numbers amongst the hundreds of thousands of circuits being continuously analysed. In theory this should sort out the wheat from the chaff but the definition of wheat in the intelligence world is so wide that even with the best filter the net volume of material is of such staggering proportions that it is beyond any useful human assessment.

Once again one comes back to the fundamental question of how much use all this is and whether the NSA really provides good value for money. Statistically the NSA is very impressive. But statistics do not necessarily make for good intelligence. All experience shows that the best intelligence comes from small, well-run agencies, not huge sprawling empires. The NSA is now so large, so complex, and so secret that no one in America, least of all the president or Congress, has any idea what it is doing or how sensibly the taxpayers' money is being spent. Any attempt to impose some sort of external watchdog that might apply a degree of accountability is rejected as compromising its secrecy. Effectively the NSA is defeating itself and its original purpose by its size.

This endless chase for super-technology and an almost reverential reliance on its findings is an extremely dangerous foundation for a nation's intelligence operations. The idea that huge computers can by themselves produce all the necessary facts and warn when danger is near is an extremely fallacious thesis straight out of Hollywood. During the last war intelligence experts came to rely upon Ultra so heavily that if Ultra intercepts told them nothing they automatically assumed the Germans were doing nothing. This resulted in several disasters.[47] Like every other intelligence agency the NSA is very good at giving politicians what they want to hear in peacetime but it has no wartime experience at all. There is no substitute for good, sound interpretation based on personal knowledge of the facts. It will take a second Pearl Harbor for the Americans to realise how inefficient the NSA really is, just as it took the Falklands War of 1982 to reveal the deficiencies at GCHQ.

The National Reconnaissance Office (NRO) is responsible for America's intelligence space programme.[48] Founded on 25 August 1960, it does not officially exist. Its headquarters are in Department 4C-956 in the Pentagon, Washington, DC, where it is known only as the Office of Space Systems. Although a virtually unknown organisation, its $6 billion a year budget is actually larger than that of either the CIA or NSA. In the last ten years it is estimated that the NRO has spent more than $50 billion, none of it accountable. Over this period the NRO has put into orbit over Russia and other countries a wide variety of satellites designed to bring back all kinds of visual and electronic intelligence. As technology has improved so the scope and quality of material recovered has increased dramatically.

One of NRO's most advanced projects was the *Rhyolite* satellite programme.[49] The codename was chosen because rhyolite is a volcanic rock containing colourful pieces of quartz set in a mass of crystals. First launched in complete secrecy on 19 June 1970, the programme placed in geostationary orbit 22,300 miles above the equator an eavesdropping satellite developed by the TRW Corporation of California for the NSA. It could listen continuously to every type of Russian and Chinese signal including telephone conversations on their domestic microwave network. On 6 March 1973 another *Rhyolite* satellite was launched. This, incidentally, is officially referred to as the first launch of the programme although it was the second. A third was launched on 23 May 1977.

Information from these satellites was brought back to earth at the NSA stations at Menwith Hill in Britain and Pine Gap in Australia. Unfortunately all this marvellous technology was wasted because not long afterwards Boyce and Lee at TRW and Prime at GCHQ gave all the details to the Russians (see Chapter 4) who, as happened with the 1955 Berlin Tunnel (see Chapter 2), proceeded to spoof Western intelligence for several years with false information. But because so much money and technical faith had been invested in the project no one thought to check the information elsewhere or suspect that the system might be fallible. So once again technology had taken over from old-fashioned human intelligence.

After *Rhyolite* came the *Argus* and later the *Keyhole* series of satellites. The *Keyhole* KH-11, which has vastly improved visual sensors, is said to have the ability to see objects only six inches long on the ground and to be able to read number plates on cars driving along Russian streets or identify one *mullah* from another in Iran by measuring the size of their beards. It would be nice to think that all this is true. But the intelligence fraternity has a long track record of trying to fool others and in the process usually ends up fooling itself. It would also be wise to assume that by now the Russians know all about this technology and can, when necessary, not only match it but confuse it.

The Defence Intelligence Agency (DIA), has to get along with an annual budget of only $1 billion. Its task is to coordinate the intelligence efforts of the US Army, Navy and Air Force, mainly in assessing the armed strength and fighting capabilities of other countries. Not surprisingly the DIA and CIA frequently cannot agree. This is because both agencies are fighting for a larger share of the available budget and seek to create a good impression by producing the most frightening scenario. As a result most forecasts made by the DIA about the Russians are wildly inaccurate.

Much of America's apparent lead in intelligence technology and the vast sums it spends each year on these organisations has been negated by the large number of spies and traitors continually found within them. Although from the way the Americans complain one would imagine such treachery is solely a British disease, more than 30 American citizens have been recently convicted of serious espionage offences.

Aside from Boyce and Lee, these include Edward Howard, a CIA employee who finally defected to Moscow taking with him a hoard of secret information about his work; the Walker trio who for 17 years handed over details of US Navy cryptograhic equipment to the Russians in exchange for $750,000; Bruce Ott, a USAF airman who tried to sell the Russians a copy of the SR-71 spy plane operating manual; Robert Miller, an FBI agent who passed on secret documents to the Russians; Ronald Pelton, a communications expert with the NSA who for five years gave the Russians details of his work; Clyde Conrad, a retired US Army sergeant who for five years is alleged to have handed over top army contingency plans to the East; and Jonathan Pollard, a US Navy counter-intelligence analyst who was paid $50,000 by Israeli intelligence for top naval information, a particularly embarrassing incident. There are surely more yet to be exposed.

As so often happens, Russia's intelligence agencies have changed names several times. At the end of World War II Lavrenti Beria ruled over two separate organisations. One was called the People's Commissariat of Internal Affairs, *Narodnyi Kommissariat Vnutrennikh Del*, (NKVD), and the other the People's Commissariat of State Security, *Narodnyi Kommissariat Gosudarstvennoi Bezonasnosti* (NKGB). In 1946 these were renamed the MVD and MGB and later changed yet again to their present titles of the *Komitet Gosudarstvennoi Bezopastnosti* (KGB), and the *Glavnoye Razvedyvatelnoye Upravleniye* (GRU).

The headquarters of the KGB is 2 Dzerzhinsky Square in the heart of Moscow, close to the Kremlin, and incorporates the site of the notorious Lubyanka prison where so many opponents of the Russian regime have been tortured and murdered. The Square is named after one of the orignal Bolshevik revolutionaries, Felix Dzerzhinsky, who founded Russia's first secret police force called the *Cheka*.

The KGB has three main tasks: maintaining state security within the country, guarding Russia's borders and conducting foreign espionage operations. It is therefore a mixture of MI5, Special Branch and MI6. The KGB is a vast organisation with at least 100,000 staff officers, 350,000 border guards, 100,000 clerical workers, diplomatic guard, and special troops. But some experts believe the KGB's true total workforce is nearer two million and includes any Russian visiting or working abroad such as journalists, airline personnel and trade representatives, since every Russian is expected to spy for his country and upon other Russians too.

The KGB is certainly the largest intelligence organisation in the world and is divided into five separate directorates. Three of these deal with internal security, one with overseas espionage and the fifth with Russian dissidents. It is so large and bureaucratic that like all such hierarchies it defeats itself. The KGB is answerable to no one and does not even need to attempt to justify what it does or how it does it, therefore there is no incentive for it to become more efficient. Unfortunately some people in the West, notably the intelligence community, deliberately bestow upon the KGB an incredible reputation for efficiency and prowess. Hopefully the Russians believe this. In truth the KGB spends most of its time and resources, rather like the NSA, scooping up large amounts of trivia that it evidently believes are extremely valuable. As a result it is overwhelmed by a mass of material that defies useful analysis and, to make matters worse, unlike the West does not have access to unlimited computer capacity.

A job with the KGB is much sought-after by young Russians because it pays well, offers many special privileges such as housing and foreign goods denied to the ordinary citizen, and also gives the chance of foreign travel. Bearing in mind the size of the KGB's foreign operations it would be surprising if it did not have some successes. But if it was as clever and efficient as we in the West say it is, then one might expect it to have achieved much more.

It is hard to think of many foreign governments the KGB has overthrown

as, for example, the CIA did in Chile. Nor has the KGB conducted many privately organised invasions as the CIA did against Cuba at the Bay of Pigs. Certainly Russia has openly intervened with military force to control its satellites like Hungary and Czechoslovakia when it thought they were stepping out of line and also supported the introduction of martial law in Poland to curb industrial unrest. But these were not covert intelligence operations. Overall the KGB has achieved little in international terms.

As to the political secrets that the KGB has gathered by the basketful over the last 40 years, few seem to have made much impact on the monolithic structure of Russia's political machine. It is hard to think of many instances where Russia has been able to outsmart the West politically as the result of its intelligence operations. The fiasco at the Gorbachev/Reagan summit at Reykjavik seems more likely due to a lack of understanding on the part of Reagan and his advisers and the fear they might go too fast for their NATO partners.

In the future the KGB will face two serious challenges, both from within Russia. First are demands for more autonomy by the minority ethnic groups and quelling the inevitable unrest that these demonstrations bring. Throughout 1988 there were reports of growing unrest in Armenia which eventually erupted into major clashes, with tales of large-scale rioting and murder with tanks and troops on the streets.

The other is coming to terms with a more liberal society where dissent and public protest are no longer automatically met with assault and arrest. Assuming Gorbachev can continue with his reforms the KGB will be in the same position as would MI5 were a Labour anti-nuclear government suddenly returned to power. It will be fascinating to see how the KGB copes with this sudden reversal of the old traditions.

The GRU is the military counterpart of the KGB. It operates through military attachés at overseas diplomatic missions and also runs its own network of spies such as, for example, the Portland spy ring, which are quite separate from the KGB. Because it is far smaller than the KGB with a staff of around 6,000 the GRU is more efficient. Inevitably there is considerable friction between the two agencies but in the past defence needs in Russia had sufficient priority to give the GRU a lead over the KGB.

Once again changes are in the wind. Gorbachev has already taken the West by surprise by agreeing to a reduction of intermediate nuclear weapons and then suggesting further reductions in long-range missile systems. In December 1988 Gorbachev took the United Nations by storm and wrong-footed the American administration, then impotent during the hand-over of power from Reagan to President-elect George Bush, by announcing a unilateral reduction of 10 per cent in Russia's conventional forces. Plainly Gorbachev is hoping to achieve several different things by these radical plans.

First he wants to wind down Russia's huge military spending in favour of diverting resources to create a competitive domestic economy where private enterprise will compete with state industries.

That is easier said than done. At the moment Russia's economy is quite incapable of producing the goods that ordinary people want and falling oil revenues preclude any large-scale purchases of foreign expertise. As a result Gorbachev is in danger of raising people's expectations beyond anything that can be achieved. Military conscription has always been a useful way of soaking up young people and even though Russia is suffering from a decline in the birthrate the sudden release of a large number of men on to the civilian labour market might be difficult to absorb at a time when Gorbachev is trying to raise productivity.

On the diplomatic front Gorbachev is hoping to persuade European countries that Russia is no longer a threat. This comes at a time when some Western governments are questioning the standard hard-line attitude always taken by British and American leaders and certainly in West Germany there is a growing feeling towards more direct contact with Moscow and less reliance on America's nuclear stockpile.

It all adds up to some very big changes, not only in direction but also in the whole philosophy of Russia's attitude to the West. Certainly neither the KGB nor the GRU are going to stop spying, for that would leave them as exposed to criticism as if the CIA suddenly stopped spying on Russia. As a result both agencies have to continue claiming that Russia is facing terrible threats from the West and therefore that their existence is essential despite the fact that Gorbachev is busily telling the Russian people that co-existence is not only possible but desirable as are many aspects of capitalist society. At the moment Gorbachev is like a juggler with a lot of balls in the air at once. Provided he is not forced to drop them it may be that Gorbachev, ironically, could be the first world leader to actually reduce a country's intelligence agencies on the grounds that there is less for them to do.

Both the KGB and GRU spend a lot of time and energy seeking the West's technical secrets. Much of this is done quite legally and openly because the information is freely available. East European military attachés and trade missions spend much of their time buying up every sort of book and technical journal and visiting every trade fair around Europe and America. Russian scientists attend every relevant international meeting and seminar at which there is inevitably a continuous exchange of views and opinions.

As a result it is hard to think of any technical innovations, whether in the military or civilian field, that Russia does not know about. This does not necessarily mean, however, that all Russia's technical achievements are the product of espionage, although Western intelligence would have us believe this. It is claimed, for example, that Russia's ability to produce an atomic and later a nuclear bomb was entirely a result of information given by British spies.[50] By the same token Russia's nuclear submarines are the direct product of information obtained from spies in Britain and America. Even the new silent propulsion system seen on some new Russian submarines was not their own invention but came from Toshiba of Japan. All this creates convenient mythology.

One story told against the KGB is that it tried to steal the design secrets of the Anglo-French supersonic aircraft Concorde.[51] The KGB managed to infiltrate an agent into the British factory who was discovered by MI5 (a rare achievement indeed). It arranged with the manufacturers that he would be allowed to see technical data that had been carefully doctored to include major errors. This information was passed back to Russia, and incorporated into their own copy of Concorde, the Tu-144. As a result the aircraft proved a failure and following a spectacular crash at the Paris air show in 1964 was withdrawn from service altogether. It certainly is a good story but it is hard to believe that a designer as experienced as Tupolev[52] would casually use such information without first carefully checking it out, particularly if one considers the history of the Russian aircraft industry which over the years has sprung many surprises upon the West and will doubtless do so again in the future.

Russian designers have certainly taken advantage of anything they could learn from the West. In 1947 the president of the Board of Trade in Attlee's Labour government, a young and aspiring politician called Harold Wilson, agreed to grant special export licences to Russia for two Rolls Royce jet engines, the Nene and the Derwent. At the time these were two of the world's most advanced designs and the subject of much secrecy within Britain. The Air Ministry's intelligence staff strongly objected to this arrangement yet it went ahead. There was certainly no question of any spying here. Why the Russians were allowed to buy the engines is another matter.

Russia's space programme has matched, and more recently eclipsed, that of America. And Russia's post-war naval building programme produced some startling new warships for a country that had little previous maritime experience. The Russian tank industry has a record of producing some formidable designs over the years. As there is no public debate about Russia's defence spending no one in the West knows what sort of value it gets for its money. When one considers the huge cost overruns the West has on each new fighter, tank and warship, it is hard to believe that the same does not happen in Russia. And Russia must also have its share of design disasters where equipment fails to perform properly in service. Nor do we hear much about Russian military equipment that cannot be used due to a shortage of spares.

Many people in the West fondly believe that if Russia is denied high technology its future political activities will somehow be constrained. In fact, quite the reverse is true. The more high technology the Russians acquire the greater are the production difficulties and delivery backlogs. It must be very galling for the KGB and GRU, having secured some seemingly important technical secret from the West as the result of a long, complex, covert operation, to see it wasted simply because Russian industry is quite incapable of utilising it.

Back in the early 1970s the KGB was busy stealing the secrets of the IBM 360/S and 370/S computers. With the help of the East German Robotron computer factory in Dresden the Russians produced a copy called Ryad-1. But 20 years later this computer is still not fully in use simply because Russia cannot produce enough electrical cable and connectors to link the equipment.[53] The more Gorbachev tries to switch Russia's economy away from the military to the production of domestic goods, the greater will be his peoples' expectations, resulting in ever-increasing technical problems from Russia's outdated industry.

France's two intelligence organisations are the *Direction Général de Sécurité Extérieur* (DGSE), which, like MI6 and the CIA, is responsible for espionage operations abroad, and the *Direction de la Surveillance du Territoire* (DST), which looks after counter-intelligence at home like MI5.

Given the very complex nature of France's post-war politics, especially with regard to Algeria in the late 1950s, it is hardly surprising that the SDECE, as the DGSE was then known, has found itself embroiled in numerous scandals. Having survived these and further political turmoil at home today's DGSE has emerged remarkably unscathed. It is greatly helped by a pragmatic government who, as it showed over the *Rainbow Warrior* affair,[54] is quite prepared openly to back its security services even when they have been caught red-handed in a straightforward act of overt terrorism.

Within France the DST has been reasonably successful in countering Russian and other East European intelligence operations although, as in Britain, spies have been discovered in the highest levels of government. One advantage the DST has is that most French people accept a far greater degree of personal documentation and registration of their whereabouts than would be acceptable in Britain or America. As a result the DST is able to operate a huge computerised identity-card system associated with equally large and efficient telephone-tapping centres which the French appear to tolerate without concern about their civil liberties.

In recent years the DST has had to cope with a conflicting number of loyalties amongst those political refugees France has allowed to enter its country, especially from the Middle East. Pragmatism has also played a part here and when convenient the DST has been willing to do deals with other countries trading off information it has obtained from opposing factions in the Middle East. It has also been willing to bargain over the release of French hostages held by Arab groups in the Lebanon even though the government pays lip-service to the official declarations that no such deals should be made. The Iran/Contra scandal gave the French much cause for amusement.

Israel occupies an unique place in the world of intelligence. It has two organisations, *Mossad Le Aliyah Beth* (Institution of Intelligence and Special Services), responsible for external espionage, and *Shin Beth* (the Security and Counter Espionage service), which looks after internal security.

Israel's uniqueness stems from the fact that it considers itself to be in a perpetual state of war with its Arab neighbours which, together with the Nazi barbarities of the last war, is somehow supposed to make the rest of the world feel permanently sorry for Israel and give it the right to carry out any intelligence operations it likes.

As a result Mossad involves itself in any type of operation that it feels helps Israel or at least deters its enemies. Henry II has never been heard of in Israel (see chapter 3). If something needs to be done, like a murder or a retaliatory bomb outrage, those in charge do not conceal their wishes behind fine phrases. Morality and accountability are conspicuously absent. In 1973 a Mossad hit squad went to Norway and murdered an innocent Moroccan mistaking him for an alleged Arab terrorist. The world was shocked but did nothing. Mossad agents stole the plans of the French Mirage fighter from Switzerland. A West German ship with a cargo of uranium concentrate bound from Antwerp to Genoa disappeared and its cargo later turned up in Israel. An Israeli nuclear technician, Mordechai Vananu, who came to London and gave away details of Israel's nuclear weapon plant at Dimona in the Negev desert, was lured from London to Rome by an attractive Mossad agent, then kidnapped, brought back to Israel and put on trial. In 1986 when Shin Beth murdered two Arab terrorist suspects they had taken into custody there was some local outcry but in the end the agency was protected by the government.

In December 1988 controversy ensued when Yassir Arafat, chairman of the Palestine Liberation Organisation, was refused a visa to go to America and address the United Nations in New York. The American State Department argued that because Arafat represented an organisation that used terrorism he should not be allowed to enter America. If one was to draw up a balance sheet of terrorism and murder involving innocent people it is likely that Mossad, the Israeli government and the CIA would easily exceed Arafat's record depending, of course, upon how you choose to define terrorism. To a family in the Lebanon whose house has been bombed by Israeli jet aircraft or destroyed by a CIA-backed bomb the definition probably does not matter much. The fact remains that while Mossad is the honoured guest of the American government in Washington, especially at election time, the entire UN General Assembly had to be air-lifted to Geneva to hear what Arafat had to say.[55]

Western agencies are very envious of Mossad because it relies not on huge arrays of computerised technology but on a small group of efficient and dedicated men and women who are not bothered by any form of morality so long as Israel benefits. It is considered justifiable to let off bombs in Britain and kill innocent people, blaming Arab countries, if that helps Israel. Furthermore, Mossad has the advantage that Jews the world over, rich or poor, owe an ethnic loyalty to Israel that enables them to be called upon to help even in quite minor ways. No other country enjoys such a network of unofficial agents.

Despite the fact that over the years America has been Israel's guardian, both politically and militarily, and continues to give Israel $3 billion-worth of aid annually, that does not stop it from falling victim to Mossad's activities. In 1985 Jonathan Pollard, a US Navy analyst, was paid $30,000 by Mossad in return for handing over thousands of pages of top-secret material. As part of the same operation Mossad is credited with the theft of enough uranium from a plant in Pennsylvannia to make six nuclear weapons. The ease with which this theft was carried out and the incompetent way in which it was investigated makes one wonder if America is not secretly pleased that Israel has become a nuclear power in the Middle East so that it can act as tripwire in any conflict.

In order to placate[56] Washington Israel officially claimed this was all an unauthorised operation but in the intelligence world an unauthorised operation is simply one that is too hazardous to handle by normal channels in case something goes wrong.

Because it is so efficient Mossad is courted by other agencies who are anxious to trade off information, particularly about Arab terrorism that affects their own countries. Mossad is always willing to cooperate provided it will benefit. Mossad also makes available to the West various examples of Russian and East European military equipment captured in various Middle East wars. One way and another Mossad has a lot to offer and makes certain that it gets the best of the bargain.

Following the Sowan affair the Foreign Office expelled the five-man team of Mossad agents that Britain had permitted to work unofficially in London.[57] But in a few weeks they were allowed to return because Mossad had threatened to stop giving MI6 any more information about Arab terrorism. So the Foreign Office, which with so much contrived anger and publicity expelled Cuban diplomats in September 1988 for firing a gun in a British street,[58] is quite willing to have in Britain an intelligence organisation that was planning bomb outrages. Considering the long anti-semitic history of the Foreign Office which always shares the Arab viewpoint this demonstrates a curious pragmatism.

There are, of course, many other players in the game. As one might expect, West Germany has inherited the ability to maintain vast dossiers on people within its borders and, bearing in mind that some 8,000 spies working for East Germany and Russia are said to be operating in West Germany, there is certainly plenty for them to do. The problem is that since West Germany also spies on its neighbour, a great deal of time is taken up with swopping convicted spies back and forth across the border. Middle-aged women working in the West German government have also been a favourite target for East German spies and several have passed over supposedly valuable information for a number of years before being caught. Whether any of this espionage achieves much is a matter of opinion but West Germany is never slow to publicise the capture of a few spies as being a serious breach of national security.

In the end a nation tends to get the intelligence organisation it deserves. Americans like their billion-dollar computerised organisation, believing that big is beautiful, and now these monoliths are out of control. The British stumble after the Americans trying to copy their technology but waste their limited resources because their agencies are run by an amateurish élite who are too highly politicised and target the wrong enemies, allowing the real spies to go free. The Russians are so bureaucratic that any gems of intelligence they might cull are lost in a mass of trivial dross. The French are pragmatic to the point of openness over their illegal activities but in the end it is the smallest and most immoral of them all, Mossad, which is the most efficient.

Whether any intelligence does much good or actually enhances a country's security is doubtful. After all, despite the success of Mossad, Israel still lives in a perpetual state of fear and terrorism. But the intelligence game is now an international affair where winning and point-scoring is the most important thing. No one dares ask whether any of it is worthwhile or could be done far more cheaply. The king must not be seen without his clothes.

CHAPTER 2

THE WASTELAND OF TRUTH

Listening to your enemy illicitly is one of the fundamental functions of intelligence. Indeed, it is probably the single most important source of information. Eavesdropping takes many forms. For over 400 years, for example, the British Foreign Office has been opening people's mail, reading their telegrams and, more recently, listening to their telephone calls.

It is easy to do this in your own country. Listening to your enemies is more difficult. Certainly anything they send by radio or by microwave circuit within their country can be intercepted. But what every intelligence chief longs to do is somehow to tap into the very heart of the opponent's communication system and listen to his most secret messages without him being aware. Bearing in mind the geographical locations of the superpowers, this is easier to contemplate than achieve.

At the end of World War II, Europe lay divided under the control of the four Allied powers – America, Russia, Britain and France. The divisions were arbitrary, mainly depending upon who happened to be where when the fighting stopped. The city of Vienna ended up under the control of all four occupying powers. The city was not actually physically divided, as is Berlin today with a wall, and therefore all the city's utility services operated throughout the four zones.

Vienna at this time has been immortalised in Carol Reed's brilliant 1949 film *The Third Man*[1] based on Graham Greene's novel in which a drug trafficker, played by Orson Welles, manages to elude the police by crossing from one zone of the city to another via the network of underground sewers. Perhaps the film caused someone in MI6 to do a little thinking as to whether drugs were not the only thing that crossed the zonal boundaries. The Vienna telephone system, which had not been greatly damaged in the war, most certainly did and each of the four occupying powers used it.

In 1950 the Russians had their headquarters in what had been the Imperial Hotel, a fine baroque building which the Russians had quickly turned into a slum as they found it hard to understand the intricacies of a modern plumbing and toilet system which few of them had ever seen before.[2]

In order to communicate with military headquarters in Moscow Russian engineers had simply diverted some of the multicore trunk circuits from the main Vienna exchange so that they terminated in the Imperial Hotel. By Russian standards the availability of such circuitry seemed remarkable and since their traffic was being sent eastward they saw no reason to suspect interception.

MI6 had discovered that the trunk cable from the Imperial Hotel passed along a main road and it acquired a shop from which a tunnel was dug towards the cable duct and the trunk circuits were then tapped one by one. The project was a complete success in that the Russians never suspected that their Moscow traffic was being read. Exactly what it told us that has made any marked difference to Europe, or even Austria, as we see it today is another matter. But it was an intelligence coup that certainly fired the imagination of both MI6 and its partners in the CIA. Not surprisingly, everyone looked around for a similar opportunity.

This was not hard to find. An even more bizarrely divided city was Berlin. Here the four powers had carved themselves out oddly shaped zones amongst the rubble and devastation left by the Allied bombing. The Berlin intelligence scene was dominated by one of the most charismatic figures in post-war espionage – General Reinhard Gehlen. Gehlen's army career had begun in the late 1920s and as a staunch Nazi supporter he had enjoyed rapid promotion until he became military intelligence chief of Hitler's *Wermacht* Foreign Armies East.[3] Gehlen knew more about Russian intelligence than anyone else in Germany and on several occasions had outwitted Russian intelligence completely. He had turned captured Russian officers and allowed them to 'escape' and make their way back to Russia where they became his agents. Gehlen had even managed to plant an agent in Stalin's war council and in Marshal Zhukov's headquarters.

As Nazi Germay started to crumble into dust during the final battles of 1945 Gehlen realised that it was time to change sides. He had no intention of staying by Hitler's side in his Berlin bunker and instead set off for his own headquarters. Here Gehlen collected up the thousands of spools of microfilm that over the years he had painstakingly amassed as part of his record of Russian intelligence. Then, with a small group of his best experts, Gehlen set off for Bavaria to await the arrival of the Americans.

After some initial difficulties Gehlen was able to explain who he was and what he had to offer. He was taken to see General Rush Patterson, the US 7th Army's intelligence chief who, without any fuss, took Gehlen to see General Eisenhower. Then Gehlen, together with his vast hoard of microfilms, was flown to America. It did not require much effort on Gehlen's part to convince the Americans that the real enemy was Russia and with his help they could have a ready-made intelligence organisation. In return the Americans quietly overlooked Gehlen's record with the Nazis.

Thus re-established Gehlen returned to Germany on the winning side to head up the CIA's new Cold War against Russia. Initially all Gehlen's funding came from the CIA but later, in 1954, when the German Federal Republic was established as a sovereign state, Gehlen took over the running of the Federal German Intelligence Service.

When the CIA and MI6 approached Gehlen with the idea of tapping into Russian communications in Berlin he responded warmly and at once started to prepare a list of suitable sites where the zones ran close together, and offering opportunities for driving tunnels from one to another. The first attempts in 1953 were not very successful.[4] One of Gehlen's assistants, Major Werner Haase, who was a wartime electronics expert with the German Army, volunteered to take a cable across the Heidenkamp Canal on the night of 13 November 1953. As soon as Haase reached the other side of the canal he was arrested by East German police. Although sentenced to death by the Supreme Court of East Germany his sentence was commuted to one of life imprisonment, but he has never been heard of again.

Another attempt by a Gehlen agent called Christopher Komarek to lay a similar cable across the Jungfern Lake also ended in failure. He too was arrested and later convicted of treason and executed. It transpired that both had been betrayed by a Russian agent, Hans Geyer, who using the alias 'Henry Toll' had infiltrated Gehlen's organisation and passed on all the details of his plans to Moscow.

Despite these setbacks MI6 and the CIA were still anxious to tunnel into the Russian sector and Gehlen was keen to assist. After much research of possible sites Gehlen suggested that a tunnel could be driven into the Russian sector from the suburb of Rudow in the American sector. The area was deserted and still devastated from the wartime bombing and seemed an ideal starting point. The plan was sent to London for consideration by MI6 and the CIA in December 1953. The secretary of the planning committee that examined the project was an MI6 officer called George Blake who had recently returned to England after a long spell of captivity in Korea.

Operation Gold, as it was called by the CIA, was approved and the first task was to establish a suitable cover story. The US Military Commandant in the American sector notified his Russian counterpart that the US Air Force intended building a new radar station at Rudow to control flight movements in and out of the American airfield at Buckow. This work went ahead, although rather slowly, and allowed the tunnelling to begin at the same time. It was a massive operation with the tunnel 24 feet below ground level stretching 1,800 feet into the Alt Glienicke area of East Berlin. The tunnel was seven feet in diameter and made up of cast-iron segments with its own air-conditioning plant, lighting and heating. The entire operation cost around $25 million.

The tunnel ended at the Schoenfelder Autobahn alongside which ran the trunk telephone cables connecting the main East German government offices, the Russian intelligence (KGB) headquarters at Karlshorst and the Russian Army headquarters with Warsaw and Moscow. The tapping equipment was supplied by Britain. Most of the basic equipment came from the British General Post Office, then responsible for Britain's telephone system. Its equipment, though somewhat antiquated, was strong and designed to withstand heavy use under harsh working conditions with minimum main-tenance. This was particularly important because the Americans wanted as few people as possible working in the tunnel in case it was suddenly discovered.

The tape recorders were supplied by the British Ferrograph Company of South Shields, who made an extremely high-quality and tough recorder capable of operating for long periods without attention. The final connections into the East German telephone cables were made by John Wyke, MI6's top technical expert,[5] who had to carefully splice in the connections so that the East German operators would not notice any change in line quality or impedance. All this was done with great success and without any suspicions being aroused. On 25 April 1955 the recorders began to turn.

And turn they did. The volume of material they produced was staggering.[6] Reel after reel of voice recordings and intercepted teleprinter messages were recovered daily. The voice recordings were shipped to London where MI6 had to set up a totally new department of 250 specially recruited Russian-speaking experts to slowly work their way through the material. Even then it piled up far faster than they could analyse it. Other raw material was flown back daily to the CIA in America and here too a special department had to be set up to cope with the volume. Each day the fear was that a perfectly normal fault might develop in one of the trunk circuits that would require physical inspection by an East German repairman who might notice the MI6 taps. But this never happened.

On the morning of 15 April 1956 watchers on duty at the Rudow watchtower saw a group of East German engineers begin digging alongside the autobahn near where the tunnel ended. At first it looked like a perfectly routine maintenance operation but as a precaution those in the tunnel were evacuated and the heavy steel doors at the eastern end barred and locked. Then East German police began to arrive and shortly afterwards they burst into the tunnel. From that moment onwards *Operation Gold* was at an end. The East Germans and Russians were furious at the discovery. Their innermost secrets had been at the mercy of the West for a year. During the next few weeks over 15,000 East Germans visited the tunnel to see what the 'capitalist warmongers' were up to.

Though naturally disappointed MI6 and the CIA were not downhearted. They had had a good run for their money and there were still thousands of reels of tape to be analysed and matched against other intelligence sources. They could well imagine the panic that would now ensue at Russian military headquarters once it was realised that all their previous secrets had been lost.

George Blake, the MI6 officer who had been secretary of the committee that had planned *Operation Gold* in 1953, had joined MI6 shortly after the war. Blake was not in fact English by birth nor was Blake his original name.[7] Born in 1922 of Dutch parents in Rotterdam, Blake began life as George Behar. He grew up in Holland until at the age of 13 he was sent to live with his uncle, Henri Curiel, in Egypt, where he studied at the English school. His uncle was a leading member of the Egyptian Communist Party.

Blake, or Behar, returned to Holland at the start of the war in 1939 and played a minor part in the Dutch resistance. In 1943 he managed to leave Holland and travelled across France to Spain and thence to England. On arrival, like all refugees, he was taken to the Patriotic School at Wandsworth where he was interrogated and his background checked. Fortunately, his work with the Dutch resistance, though relatively unimportant, was enough to prove his loyalty and he was released. Then he had the good fortune to meet Commander D. W. Child RN who had been an intelligence officer in Holland and who Blake had met there. It was Child who suggested that Behar volunteer for the Royal Navy which he did in November 1943, having first changed his name to Blake.

Because of his knowledge of languages Blake was recommended for a commission and was sent on to an officers' training course at HMS *King Alfred* which in the spring of 1944 he passed and was appointed a sub-lieutenant in the RNVR. For a while he was seconded to work with the Dutch Section of SOE but in May 1944, during the preparations for the Normandy landings, Blake was posted to naval headquarters at Portsmouth as an interpreter with Supreme Headquarters Allied Expeditionary Force (SHAEF).

The end of the war found Blake in Hamburg on the naval intelligence staff of HMS *Albert* where he was attempting to collate as much technical information as possible about the defeated German Navy. Additionally, Blake was involved in checking Communist infiltration into the British sector and as part of these duties he began to learn Russian and had some officially approved contact with the Russians as part of a plan to see whether any of them could be persuaded to become British agents. Exactly when Blake became a Russian spy is hard to determine. He may have been influenced by his early days as a teenager in Cairo with his uncle or during his time in Hamburg.

Blake left the navy in 1947 with an excellent report on his work, a copy of which was sent to General Gerald Templer, Director of Military Intelligence at the War Office. Nothing much came of this until he was summoned to an interview at the Foreign Office with Kenneth Cohen, an MI6 officer he had known in Hamburg. It was arranged that on leaving the navy he would go to Cambridge University to study Russian. Blake arrived there in October 1947.

By all accounts Blake was a very quiet person who did not join in any of the usual university activities and spent most of his time reading about Russia and its people. He evidently studied hard and by Easter 1948 had completed his course and joined MI6. Blake was then posted as an MI6 officer to the British Legation in Seoul, Korea where in 1950 he and other members of the legation staff were captured by the North Koreans and held prisoner until the spring of 1953.

Exactly what took place, as far as Blake was concerned, during his period of captivity is unclear, but certainly none of his colleagues ever voiced any suspicion that Blake was in any way pro-Communist at the time or after- wards. Indeed, the Minister of the Legation, Captain (later Sir) Vyvyan Holt, was later to say that he would not have survived one of their many forced marches in intense cold had it not been for Blake's courage and help. During their captivity, in late 1951, a member of the KGB called Gregory Kuzmitch arrived at their internment camp and attempted to convert them to Communism.

By a curious twist of fate[8] Kuzmitch later defected to the CIA by which time Blake had been convicted of spying, one of the charges being that he contravened the Official Secrets Act in November 1951 while still in captivity. But Kuzmitch alleged that Blake told him nothing about his work for MI6 nor did he give any indication that he was ardently pro-Communist. Kuzmitch did mention that Blake had been unimpressed by the American and British intervention in South Korea but so too were a lot of other people. Either Kuzmitch was lying (and defectors often do), or Blake was a very clever spy who, despite the temptation to confide in Kuzmitch and thus get better treatment, maintained his role as a long-term sleeper agent.

Blake returned to London a hero in the eyes of MI6 but the secret nature of his work precluded any official recognition. For a couple of years he worked in London with MI6, mainly bugging diplomatic premises and illegally opening diplomatic mail. Blake's own description of his work matches that given many years later by Peter Wright in his book *Spycatcher*. Blake also took part in the joint planning meetings that were held between the CIA and MI6 during one of which, in December 1953, the Berlin tunnel operation was approved. During all this time Blake was passing back to Moscow full details of his work, including *Operation Gold*, so the Russians knew all about the plan two years before the tunnel was actually finished.

On 23 September 1954 Blake married his secretary Gillian Allan and on 14 April 1955 he was posted to West Berlin, just about the time that the Berlin tunnel became operational. When the tunnel was 'discovered' by the

Russians in 1956 an inquiry was held within MI6 and also the Gehlen organisation to determine if there had been a leak to warn the Russians. The results were inconclusive but Blake's name did not feature in the report.

Blake's work for MI6 included not only gathering intelligence from the Russians but tracking down and watching Communist spies sent over into the West.[9] In the autumn of 1955, some six months after he had been in Berlin, Blake approached his superiors with the suggestion that he should pretend to become an agent working for the Russians. Double agents are quite commonplace in the world of espionage. The idea is that they feed the other side with what appears to be genuine material so as to establish their credibility and then the other side asks them to do things for them on their own home ground.

One of the great arts of intelligence work is to find out how the other side thinks and what interests it. A double agent is, therefore, well placed to achieve this. But running doubles is a tricky business. Obviously the Russians are not fools. And when someone indicates his willingness to work for them they naturally suspect he is a plant. In Blake's case there was a further complication in that Blake was already a Russian agent. What Blake did was to set up a very clever cover story which would pre-empt any subsequent accusations that he was in touch with the Russians. He could now say that this was with the approval of his superiors. Effectively, therefore, Blake became a triple agent.

Blake told his superiors at MI6 that in order to win the confidence of the Russians he would need to give them enough genuine information to convince them of his sincerity. MI6 agreed and produced numerous impressive documents for Blake to pass over which, although largely faked, did contain enough facts to confirm their authenticity. The Russians played along with this charade and gave Blake similar information with which to impress his superiors so that the arrangement appeared to be working in favour of MI6. The Russians even sacrificed a few of their less important informers in the West so that Blake could claim further success.

Between 1955 and 1959 Blake betrayed numerous agents in the East. What is unclear is how many of these betrayals were the work of Blake's original direct links with the Russians and how many were part of the officially authorised game of double bluff. As we saw in World War II when SOE agents in France were deliberately sacrificed in order to plant deception schemes upon the Germans,[10] espionage is a very brutal game in which human lives are of no more significance than pieces on a chess board. The Blake case is still extremely sensitive because Blake was authorised to do some very terrible things in the East-West espionage war without MI6 being aware that all the time he was one of Russia's most important agents.

In April 1959 Blake and his family returned to London. By this time he was regarded by MI6 as one of its most trusted officers who was very adept at handling the most complex and dangerous operations. For the next 16 months Blake commuted daily between his house in Bickley, Kent and MI6's headquarters in London. During this period he remained in regular touch with his Russian controller, giving him details of all the work he handled.

In September 1960 Blake and his family arrived in Beirut where MI6 had enrolled him at the language school known as the Middle East Centre for Arab Studies. Since leaving Berlin Blake had had one or two scares when various West Germans had been arrested for spying and made allegations about him. Fortunately, because of his seemingly impeccable record with MI6, they were not believed.

In December 1960 Blake's luck ran out.[11] A high-ranking Polish military intelligence officer, Colonel Michael Goleniewski, who had been in charge of Polish military intelligence in East Berlin, defected to the CIA in West Berlin. Goleniewski had been in touch with the CIA since 1958 during which time he had passed on to them a considerable amount of information that had led to the arrest of several important spies. In late 1959 Goleniewski had given MI5 enough information to identify Harry Houghton, who worked at the Admiralty's underwater research laboratory at Portland, which eventually led to the exposure of the Portland spy ring. Goleniewski was immediately flown to America, and taken to a CIA safe house called Ashford Farm in the heart of Talbot County, in Maryland.[12] Here he was carefully debriefed and given the codename Sniper, while MI5 codenamed him Lavinia.

Goleniewski had left behind in Warsaw copies of some 300 important intelligence documents which were retrieved by the CIA and brought to America. Amongst the information they contained was a vital piece of evidence that a senior MI6 officer in Berlin was, in reality, a Russian agent and had betrayed numerous MI6 agents behind the Iron Curtain. Goleniewski then came to London and was carefully interviewed by MI6 about his evidence. Very reluctantly MI6 was obliged to accept the terrible fact that Blake was a long-time Russian spy.

It was decided to recall Blake to London in a manner that would not arouse his suspicions so a message was sent to Nicholas Elliott, chief of MI6 in Beirut, who got in touch with Blake and said that London would like to discuss a chance of promotion and a new job with him. Blake flew to London on 3 April 1961. He was not immediately arrested at the airport but kept under close surveillance. The next morning he reported to Sir Dick White, then head of MI6 (having taken over from Sir John Sinclair after the Crabb fiasco – see Chapter 3). Blake was then confronted with the allegation that he was a Russian spy and eventually he confessed, was arrested, formally charged and appeared for trial at the Old Bailey in London on 3 May 1961.

Blake pleaded guilty to the five charges against him under the Official Secrets Act which referred to him having passed on information since November 1951. The British public was not allowed to know what Blake had actually done. The Russians knew. The East Germans knew. The CIA knew. But when it came to the British people, who it was claimed he had so dreadfully harmed, the court went into secret session. Why? Plainly national security cannot have been at stake since that had already been damaged. Knowledge of the details could do no further harm. What was at stake was acute government embarrassment. What it did not want the public to know was that Blake had been authorised to do shady deals with Russian intelligence, including the betrayal of MI6 agents in East Germany, and the whole plan had backfired because he was a spy already.

The other embarrassing fact was that MI6 never suspected for one moment that Blake was a spy. Had it not been for Goleniewski's information, which the court could not be told about, Blake would never have been caught and because Goleniewski could not have given evidence without Blake's confession he could not have been brought to trial. Blake was told by his MI6 interrogators that if he cooperated this would be taken into account when sentence was passed.[13] The purpose was to encourage other spies to confess since obtaining proof of spying without compromising sources of information is almost impossible.

But the Lord Chief Justice, Lord Parker, evidently had other ideas. After intoning the usual statements about the harm done to the nation's security, the judge sentenced Blake to a total of 42 years' imprisonment. He did this by making three of the sentences, each for 14 years, run consecutively instead of concurrently. The sentence was the longest ever passed in modern British criminal history.

Blake collapsed with shock and was taken to the Wormwood Scrubs prison hospital. The public was bewildered as to what Blake had done to deserve such a draconian sentence. The press could provide little enlightenment because all newspapers had received a D-Notice asking them not to print any details about the background to the case. Nor was parliament any better served. The prime minister, Harold Macmillan, took refuge behind the usual claim that he could say nothing for fear of damaging national security. Then, under pressure, Macmillan offered to brief the leader of the opposition, Hugh Gaitskell, and a group of Privy Councillors on a confidential basis, provided nothing was disclosed in the House of Commons.[14] It later transpired that Macmillan claimed that he had deliberately delayed answering questions in the Commons in order to give time to withdraw MI6 agents from East Europe. This was obviously untrue since Blake's arrest had been known to the Russians for several weeks.

Speculation continued until Blake's appeal was heard on 19 June 1961 and was rejected. By this time MI6 and the government had got their act together and decided to leak a false version of events to the public. The vehicle used, as on many occasions in the past, was Chapman Pincher, the defence correspondent of the *Daily Express* who on 19 June entertained George

Brown,[15] the ebullient and unpredictable Labour politician, to lunch at the Ecu de France restaurant. Brown was one of the Labour opposition Privy Councillors who had attended a confidential briefing by Sir Norman Brook, the Cabinet Secretary, at which Macmillan was present.

Brown proceeded to tell Pincher the government's version of events including the allegation that Blake had betrayed over 40 British agents, hence the claim was born that Blake was sentenced to one year in prison for every agent. But Brown did not tell Pincher that some of those agents had been betrayed with the knowledge and authority of MI6, as part of Blake's supposed role as a double agent, because the government had suppressed that part of the story just as it had Blake's part in the Berlin tunnel affair. Even Pincher was surprised at the nature of this scoop and when he got back to his office telephoned Admiral Thomson, the secretary of the D-Notice Committee, in case Brown had become over-tired during lunch.[16] But despite the fact that Brown had passed on Privy Councillors' information, Thomson assured Pincher there was nothing to stop publication. As a result the following day, 20 June 1961, the *Daily Express* carried the government's story in full on its front page, giving the impression that Blake had betrayed all these agents on his own. It was a very neatly packaged piece of disinformation planted on Pincher that carried added credibility since it did not come from a government source but from an opposition Privy Councillor.

While the press and public contemplated the truth about Blake, at MI6 and the CIA there was total dismay. Since 1955 both had been swamped with material from *Operation Gold* and even six years later MI6 was still transcribing voice tapes from the tunnel operation. All of a sudden they realised they had been tricked from the very beginning. The East Germans and Russians had known all along that the tunnel was going to be built. They knew that the story of the radar station at Rudow was a blind. They had probably listened to the sound of the tunnel being carefully pushed into their zone. And they knew perfectly well when the connections had been made. From that time onwards they simply diverted their genuine traffic through other circuits and then arranged to send carefully prepared disinformation over the tapped lines.

No wonder MI6 and the CIA had been swamped with material.[17] That was exactly what the Russians intended. The entire operation had been a waste of time. All the carefully prepared summaries and analyses were not worth the paper they were printed on. And then there was Blake's complex double-agent operation in Berlin. Now that too turned out to be fake. The Russians had known all along that the information Blake was officially giving them was fake. The real information was coming direct from Blake anyway. And what about the agents Blake had been allowed to betray in order to prove his sincerity? They too had been wasted. No wonder MI6, the government and the court had tried every means to suppress the facts of the story.

But although the case, and particularly the sentence, shocked the public at the time it was soon forgotten. After all, despite what the judge had said Britain still went on much the same, Berlin was still a divided city (and was later to become even more so) and Russia seemed no more or less secure. If there were any winners or losers in Blake's games with MI6 they were not readily apparent.

Blake began his sentence in Wormwood Scrubs prison in West London. Although he was a first offender and there was no suggestion he might try to escape, because of the nature of his offence the governor, Thomas Hayes, decided that Blake should be placed on the escape list.[18] This meant that Blake was allocated a special cell which was changed at irregular intervals, that had to be examined every day, and Blake and the cell completely searched at least once a fortnight. At night a light had to be on all the time and Blake's prison clothes had to be placed outside his cell while, during the day, the clothes he wore had distinctive patches of coloured cloth on them to show that he was on the escape list.

Five months later, on 3 October 1961, Hayes removed Blake from the escape list, allowing him a more normal life although some minor restrictions still applied. During these initial months Blake was intensively interrogated by MI6 and when they had finished in November 1961 the question arose as to where Blake was to serve his sentence. The 1966 official report into his subsequent escape has some incredibly tedious and unconvincing arguments as to why Blake was not moved to a high, or at least a higher, security prison such as Birmingham. One excuse given was that the authorities did not want Blake to associate with another spy which would have happened if he had been transferred to Birmingham prison. Another equally banal excuse was that it would be a hardship for Blake's wife to visit him if he was moved away from London.

None of this makes any sense because one of Blake's fellow prisoners in D block of Wormwood Scrubs was the Russian spy Gordon Lonsdale (whose real name was Konon Molody), a key figure in the Portland spy ring who, ironically, had also been exposed by the defector Goleniewski. He had been sentenced to 25 years' imprisonment in March 1961. On 20 April 1964 Lonsdale was exchanged for a British businessman, Greville Wynne, who had become involved in espionage and been imprisoned in Russia. Plainly on his return to Moscow Lonsdale was able to brief the KGB on security at Wormwood Scrubs. Why two such important Russian spies should have been placed in the same cell block so that they could freely meet and talk together is a mystery. So too is the reason why, when the matter of their being able to meet was raised in parliament (after an article about it had appeared in the *Sunday Times* in May 1964), the Home Secretary, Henry Brooke, denied that the pair had ever met which was plainly untrue.[19]

The most generous excuse one can make is that Brooke was deliberately misled by his advisers. The official report avoids the whole issue of how and why Blake and Lonsdale were able to meet so easily and relies entirely on what it was told by MI5. As MI5 had already misinformed the Home Secretary there is no reason why Lord Mountbatten's inquiry was treated any better.[20]

During 1964–65, Hayes received a number of reports that attempts would be made to free Blake. All these were investigated by MI5, Special Branch and Scotland Yard. Some of the stories were pretty fanciful and involved helicopters and mercenaries but at least one claimed that Blake would be helped to escape by another prisoner and once free would go to East Germany and thence to Russia. MI5 claimed to have carefully investigated each of the stories and told the inquiry that no evidence to support them was ever found. In each case, MI5 alleged that those who had reported such stories were either mentally unbalanced, or seeking publicity, which was a convenient way of denigrating them and the tales.

Towards the end of 1965 special high-security accommodation had been built at Durham, Leicester and Parkhurst, prisons. In early 1966 Hayes was asked to nominate any prisoners he felt should be transferred to these new secure prisons. Hayes submitted three names one of which, not surprisingly, was Blake. But Blake was not moved. Instead a child murderer was transferred to Parkhurst. The 1966 inquiry plodded its way through an incredible number of excuses as to why Blake had not also been transferred and concluded that if Blake had been moved, and the child murderer left at Wormwood Scrubs had then escaped (rather than Blake), there would have been great public criticism. In fact there was plenty of room for both at Parkhurst.

Although Blake may have given the impression to the prison authorities that he had accepted his sentence and settled down to serve it (it would surely have been odd had he done otherwise), in reality neither he nor the KGB had any intention of him remaining in prison a day longer than necessary. Blake had been a very good agent and the KGB always looks after its own. Quite apart from enhancing its reputation, it also reassures other agents that they will not be forgotten. Ideally, the KGB would have liked to have swopped Blake. But Blake was British, unlike Lonsdale and the Krogers, the other couple caught in the Portland spy ring. If Blake could not be exchanged the only alternative was to get him out of prison.

Between 1964 and 1966 Blake, together with the KGB, made plans to escape from Wormwood Scrubs. Unless Blake chooses to make the details public they will never be known for certain.[21] In the meantime all we have is the popular version that Blake was befriended by a 32-year-old Irishman, Sean Bourke, who at the time was coming to the end of a seven-year sentence and was living in the prison hostel just inside the perimeter wall of the prison but allowed to go out to work each day on parole.[22] With the aid of £700, a few friends, some two-way radios, a car jack and a ladder made out of knitting needles, Bourke got Blake out of prison, over the wall and across the Channel to East Germany.

Bourke, who died in 1982, was a colourful person who over the years gave a number of different versions of how he helped Blake escape, progressively embroidering each one with more fanciful figments of his imagination. That Bourke was involved there is no doubt. But it is impossible to accept that he acted alone in such an amateurish manner.

There are a great number of anomalies in the accounts he gave. Blake and Bourke are supposed to have talked together each evening via two-way radios with Blake in his ground-floor cell and Bourke outside the walls. Apart from whether the weak transmissions[23] from a pair of £25-sets operating on the American Citizens' Band FM frequency could have penetrated the thick walls of Blake's cell,[24] which were reinforced with cast-iron segments, with no external aerial and close to the 17 feet-high perimeter wall, there is also the question of how Blake managed to keep a radio in his cell without it once being noticed over six months during which he and his cell were regularly searched.

Furthermore, if Blake had this two-way radio which he used nightly, how did he manage to obtain a supply of batteries to power it? Bourke also claims that another prisoner in the same wing picked up part of their nightly conversations on his radio. But prison regulations then (and now) permit prisoners to have only radios that operate on the medium and long waves.[25] Sets with FM bands are not allowed.

It is perfectly true that Blake did have a battery-operated radio in his cell which worked on medium and long waves only. Blake left this behind after he escaped and it was examined by experts.[26] They found it had not been modified in any way and could not operate on the 27–28 MHz frequency (the FM Citizens' Band). They told the inquiry that if a particularly strong FM transmission was made very near the radio it might be possible for it to pick up the sub-harmonic at around 14 MHz but that such a signal could not have emanated from a low-powered, hand-held type of two-way radio. One can only conclude that the story about the two-way radios is entirely false.

There are in existence some brief audio recordings of alleged two-way radio conversations between Blake and Bourke which are said to have been made in October 1966.[27] Bourke had been discharged from prison on 4 July 1966 and was living in rented accommodation in Perryn Road about a mile away from the prison. From this distance Bourke says he was unable to contact Blake by radio and therefore he would drive to Old Oak Common Lane, park his car and then walk across Old Oak Common with his radio to a point close to the north side of the prison from where he could re-establish contact, lying down in the grass so that he would not be seen. Bourke had to do this every time he spoke with Blake up to the time of the escape in October.

If Bourke recorded some of these conversations with Blake in October he would have had to take a battery-operated audio recorder with him across the common, as well as the two-way radio, and link the two together while lying in the grass talking to Blake. This is certainly not impossible – battery-operated recorders existed in 1966 – but it does seem an unnecessary complication to add to an already hazardous operation. Bourke claimed that Blake brought his two-way radio with him when he escaped and both radios were left at Bourke's flat in Highlever Road where they must have been found by the police when they raided the flat on 1 January 1967. But no mention of two-way radios appears anywhere in the official report, so either the police concealed the details from the inquiry or they never existed.

Then take the matter of the car jack which, according to Bourke, he smuggled in to Blake who used it to prise away the window bars in order to make his escape from D block. How did Blake manage to keep this in his cell undetected for so many months?

The official facts[28] surrounding Blake's escape are as follows. On the evening of Saturday, 22 October 1966, there was a period of free association between 5 p.m. and 7 p.m. in D hall. Of the total number of 317 inmates, 210 had gone to watch a film in another part of the prison. Blake was not one of these. Most of the remaining inmates were watching wrestling on television. There were only two warders on duty.

At about 5.30 p.m. Blake spoke to one of the warders, which is the last time anyone can remember seeing him. Blake then went up to the second floor of the block and along to the main window. This had small panes of glass set in a large cast-iron frame. Blake apparently broke one of the cast-iron sections of the frame, creating a space through which he could crawl, and then dropped down to the ground below, a distance of 22 feet, which was broken by the roof of a covered passageway. The official report states that the broken piece of window bar was later found to have adhesive tape wrapped around each end, suggesting that it had been severed beforehand.

Blake was then only 60 feet from the prison wall. It was raining heavily and visibility was poor. Although this section of the wall was under constant surveillance by two warders, one of whom had to patrol the perimeter wall on foot taking about eight minutes, Blake was able to reach the foot of the wall unobserved where he found Bourke's ladder, with which he made his escape, hanging over the wall. The fact that Blake was missing was not discovered until 7.20 p.m. and the first call to the police did not occur until 7.43 p.m. so Blake had roughly two hours' start. There then followed a long period of muddle and confusion not helped by the fact that no one had a recent photograph of Blake and that it was a Saturday evening.

As Blake jumped down from the wall he fell heavily and broke his wrist. Bourke says that he then drove Blake to new accommodation that he had rented a few days earlier at Highlever Road in north Kensington. Bourke found a doctor who came and put Blake's wrist in plaster. During the next few weeks Bourke and Blake moved to several different apartments in London owned by friends who Bourke claimed were members of CND and named as Michael Reynolds and Pat Porter.

However, on 4 October 1987, Barrie Penrose, a very experienced journalist with the *Sunday Times*, identified these two as Michael Randle and Pat Pottle, members of the left-wing radical group, the Committee of 100, not CND, and in February 1962 both were sent to prison for 18 months for offences under the Official Secrets Act. Penrose also claimed that most of the money needed for Blake's escape had not (as Bourke had claimed) come from Blake's mother.

The same article also claimed that the late Tom Driberg, who worked at various times for both MI5 and the KGB, was also involved in getting Blake out of prison and back to Russia. This is much more credible than Bourke's story and suggests that in reality Bourke was no more than a go-between because he had been in prison with Blake.

Most of the final parts of this story cannot be independently verified but events appear to have run as follows. In late November 1966 Bourke and his friends bought a second-hand Dormobile camper and converted it so that there was a hidden compartment under the bed where Blake was to lie concealed. On 17 December 'Reynolds' and his wife 'Anne', with Blake safely hidden away, left Britain on the Dover ferry to Ostend, drove across Belgium to West Germany and thence to a border crossing-point with East Germany where they arrived on 19 December. Here Blake left them, identified himself to the surprised border guards and a few days later was flown to Mosow for a triumphant reunion with the KGB.

Travelling on a false passport made out in the name of James Richardson, Bourke travelled by train from London to Paris (apparently without encountering any problems with the police who were searching for him), and thence by air to Berlin where he crossed into the eastern sector and shortly afterwards was flown to Moscow to be reunited with Blake. Bourke did not enjoy his time in Russia and on 23 October 1968 returned to his native Ireland. The British government attempted to extradite Bourke for his part in helping Blake escape but after a long legal wrangle this was rejected by the Irish courts. Thereafter, Bourke enjoyed the notoriety of his escapades and even wrote a book about them. On 26 January 1982, at the age of 49, Bourke collapsed in the street and died. Blake, now aged 67, has been well looked after by the KGB and lives in considerable comfort with his second wife Ida and their son Mischa.

The more one studies the facts of Blake's escape the more questions remain unanswered. Mountbatten's report makes it plain that MI5 and MI6 believed that the KGB would attempt to keep in contact with Blake. A large section of the report is devoted to explaining how Blake's mail, visits and his Arabic correspondence course were all carefully vetted by MI5 in case they contained coded messages from the Russians. If the security services were so concerned about this then it clearly suggests that they had good reason to believe that Blake had not been forgotten by the Russians. What the report does not mention is whether MI6 received any overtures from the KGB to exchange Blake, nor does it consider the possibility that the KGB might want to free an agent who served it so well. But evidently the idea that Blake might escape from prison with the help of the KGB was very much in the minds of MI5 and MI6. It is, therefore, surprising that all the reports that plans were afoot to free Blake were so quickly denigrated by the police and MI5.

Even more puzzling is why, throughout the five and a half years Blake was in Wormwood Scrubs, no action was taken to move him to a more secure establishment. The explanations in the official report are so naive that they cannot be taken seriously. What is particularly interesting is that the report implies that it was MI5 who endlessly delayed any decision rather than the prison authorities. It seems as if MI5 wanted Blake to remain in London.

All this suggests that Blake's escape was the result of a deal between MI6 and the KGB. MI6 was very shocked at the severity of Blake's 42-year sentence. They saw it as a betrayal of their promise that by making a full confession Blake would be more leniently treated and felt that such a heavy sentence would deter any future traitors from confessing.

There was also another reason. The KGB wanted Blake safely home in Moscow. If the KGB released those agents Blake had betrayed then in return MI6 and MI5 would unofficially assist in aiding Blake's escape. Lonsdale was allowed to remain with Blake despite all the assurances to the contrary given to the Home Secretary. Special Branch would look the other way. Reports of escape plans were denigrated by MI5. What form other help took will never be known but there was certainly no need for two-way radios or car jacks.

In December 1987 Kim Philby, the Russian agent who defected to Russia in 1963, agreed to be interviewed by the journalist and author Phillip Knightley at his flat in Moscow.[29] Knightley asked Philby how Blake escaped from Wormwood Scrubs. Philby refused to give any details claiming it involved 'operational matters'. When Knightley further asked if Blake was helped by the KGB, IRA, or activists in the Committee of 100, Philby interrupted to suggest that SIS (MI6) may have been involved. Obviously, one cannot accept anything that Philby says since he would have a vested interest in causing mischief amongst the British security services, but it is interesting that he did volunteer the suggestion that MI6 was involved.

If one accepts the idea that there was a deal between MI6 and the KGB then at the end of the day everyone was satisfied. Blake was back in Moscow where he could do no more harm. Presumably the KGB kept its side of the bargain and freed the agents he had betrayed. The KGB owed MI6 a favour which might come in handy one day. Deals of this nature are not uncommon because, for example, the CIA and KGB give each other the right to approve the appointment of their station heads and can use their veto if the opposition proposes someone unacceptable.[30] The draconian 42-year sentence had been negated. A sort of honour had been restored.

But disasters like Blake and the Berlin tunnel do immense damage to the morale of intelligence agencies. Inevitably doubts begin. If that was false what else was? And if he was a traitor who else was and still is? Like a chain reaction, such suspicions quickly breed upon themselves and in the convoluted world of intelligence find ready ears because there is always someone willing to denigrate another person's opinions. One of the most fascinating aspects of *Spycatcher* is how Wright describes the enormous amount of time wasted on petty departmental quarrels and jealousies with each person guarding his little private empire.

Those who work in intelligence live in a very bizarre world totally removed from normality and very often morality too. Most of what they do and others do to them is illegal, deceitful and untruthful. The intelligence game is a mixture of doubt, hope, elation, disappointment and despair. There are a hundred different ways of evaluating every piece of intelligence gathered so it is not hard to come to the wrong conclusions. Working in the secret world of espionage places enormous mental strains on individuals, often leading to delusions of grandeur, paranoia, and personal obsessions, over specific objectives that are either non-existent or unattainable.

This leads to senior officers and their departments becoming increasingly secretive about their work and refusing to discuss it with others who might offer a better sense of judgement. In turn, this creates even more secret cabals which go off on their own and carry out unauthorised operations, firmly believing that their plan is the only way to make progress. One of the most frightening aspects of all intelligence agencies is the manner in which they create a totally false brand of patriotism in order to further a particular cause on the spurious grounds that only they understand what needs to be done and should not be asked to account or explain for any of their actions which must remain secret for all time. It is often said that anyone who works in intelligence for more than ten years becomes slightly crazy.

Nowhere is this paranoia more evident than over the question of defectors. Every intelligence agency believes that their defector is the best. And equally every defector wants to be the best. In truth defectors are far more trouble than they are worth. Of course some are useful in identifying spies who would have otherwise gone on undetected but often this is not all it seems, as the Russians may have decided to expose one or two spies who have served their purpose in order to protect a more important one still at work. Nor is the exposure of a hitherto unknown spy by a defector well received because it shows that the counter-intelligence section responsible has not done its job properly and gives those who are controlling the defector the opportunity to boast about their success. It also throws up endless suspicions about anyone who was friendly with the spy and about those in charge who recommended his promotion.

The exposure of long-term spies like Blake, Vassall and Prime had a terrible effect on morale amongst staff in MI5 and MI6, who were made to look like fools. The Royal Canadian Mounted Police were equally upset by Igor Gouzenko's revelations that a large Russian spy ring existed right under their noses about which they knew nothing. Governments have an ambivalent attitude towards defectors because although they recognise their information is of value, even though it may prove highly embarrassing, they dislike having to deal with traitors. But the main problem with defectors is that they quickly run out of crown jewels and then inevitably resort to inventing what they think their new-found paymasters want to hear in order to extend their usefulness and avoid being discarded to end their days washing dishes in a Hungarian restaurant in downtown Washington.

One of the earliest defectors to the West was the Russian Igor Gouzenko who with considerable difficulty sought asylum with the Canadian authorities in September 1945, bringing with him a vast amount of information about Russian espionage activities in North America.[31] It has been said that Gouzenko's defection was the start of the Cold War in that it convinced people that Russia was not benign and friendly but busily spying on its wartime allies by any means at its disposal. Gouzenko's defection alerted the West to these dangers and caused certain countries, particularly Canada, to tighten up their own security and counter-intelligence procedures. As the direct result of Gouzenko's information 21 people were charged with various offences of whom 11 were convicted, two had charges withdrawn, and eight were acquitted.

Unfortunately his value to the West went to Gouzenko's head and he quickly became paranoid, demanding endless attention and claiming to have saved Canada and indeed the West from disaster. He started living lavishly and tried to extort more and more money from the government who were paying him a tax-free pension of $1,050 a month. Eventually Gouzenko ran up debts of $153,000 which were partly settled by the sale of his book and film rights. He also engaged in endless litigation against the media which he considered was misrepresenting him. By April 1954 Gouzenko had become a 'problem child partly because of his insatiable desire for publicity and remuneration from papers and partly because he has been ready to exploit present hysteria among the new administration in the United States'.[32]

Gouzenko's involvement in the allegations against Sir Roger Hollis was the result of statements he made during the lengthy debriefing following his defection when he claimed there were two Russian spies both with the codename Elli. The first was quickly identified as a Kay Willsher. But all

Gouzenko could say about the other Elli was that he was in 'department five of Military intelligence' and had been told this by a colleague called Lubimov, or possibly Liubimov,[33] who had worked with him in the GRU code room in Moscow. Over the years Gouzenko's story about the second Elli varied considerably. One theory advanced was that Gouzenko had misunderstood his colleague and the other Elli was really an acronym for Guy Liddell who had run MI5's 'B' Division in World War II and some people believed had also been a spy for the GRU.

The main problem was that everyone seemed to assume that Gouzenko was an expert on every facet of Russian intelligence operations. In truth Gouzenko's knowledge was extremely limited but no one appreciated that until Gouzenko had become part of the folklore of intelligence mythology. Gouzenko had obvious reasons for perpetuating this myth and was always astute enough to embroider his story with whatever facts the listener wanted to hear, eventually becoming so vain that even he did not know what was truth or fiction. Towards the end of his life Gouzenko went blind but the news was kept so secret that in 1973 MI5 sent an agent to show him some photographs in the hope that he could recognise Hollis.[34]

Another pair of defectors who caused endless headaches were the Petrovs who changed sides amidst bizarre publicity in Australia in 1954.[35] Although the Petrovs did not bring quite as many gifts as Gouzenko they were very useful in showing the extent of Russian penetration in Australia. Mrs Petrov had been a senior Russian agent in Sweden and after her defection Swedish intelligence visited Australia and obtained much useful information from her about the networks she had established in their country.[36] But once the Petrovs had given up all their secrets they became difficult to please, claiming that their true value was not being appreciated.[37]

Defection is, of course, a two-way trade but there is no reason to think that those who go from the West to the East are any more valuable or enjoy a rewarding lifestyle. The original defections of Burgess and Maclean in 1951 naturally came as a great shock to the British establishment and were embarrassing because of the inept way MI5 handled the matter. Although it was a great coup for the KGB, once the pair got to Moscow it is hard to see what they could have told the Russians that was not already known or made any great difference to East–West relations. Life in Russia for Western defectors is a severe cultural shock, although for George Blake it was better than 30 years in a British prison. At one time Prime considered defecting to Russia where he had been promised a KGB colonel's pension for life. Even for a paedophile, life in Russia might be better than a cell in Long Lartin prison.

The Russians provide good accommodation (by their standards), a car, chauffeur, and access to special food stores where Western goods can be bought. But once the defector has been squeezed dry of all useful information he will end up sitting in a bare office in Dzerzhinsky Square, the KGB headquarters, with nothing to do but sift through material from his country. Before long he will be so out of touch with technical matters that he has nothing new to contribute. To the Russians he will always be a traitor and therefore suspect and under surveillance in case he tries to re-defect so he cannot leave Russia, his letters will be censored, and telephone calls bugged.

Donald Maclean's wife Melinda joined her husband in Moscow but soon found life bleak and dismal. They parted and Melinda married Philby briefly but this did not work either and she eventually returned to America. Guy Burgess had an even worse time. His homosexuality made him an outcast, he had no job to do, very little money to live on, and ended his days in an alcoholic haze clinging desperately to his Old Etonian tie as the last link with his sordid past. According to Phillip Knightley, Philby had done rather better and was enjoying the comfortable lifestyle of a retired KGB general with his wife Rufa, had built up a library of 12,000 books, saw Western newspapers regularly and was able to maintain contact with his family in the West.[38] But despite these comforts and the fact that he was fully accepted by the Russians as a patriot, it seems doubtful that he found life very rewarding.

The more senior the defector the greater the difficulties. Oleg Gordievsky, who defected in 1985 after several years as an in-place MI6 agent, was head of the KGB mission in London and as such enjoyed a very privileged lifestyle both abroad and in Russia. Although the money MI6 has provided has given him access to Western luxuries, they cannot compensate for the fact that he will never see his motherland again. Initially Gordievsky was treated as a very important person and briefed Mrs Thatcher before her first meeting with Gorbachev.[39] He was also flown to Washington to see Reagan before his meeting with the Russian leader in Geneva. However as Gorbachev managed to outsmart Reagan at every meeting it does not seem that Gordievsky's advice was particularly useful and Reagan would probably have got on better without him. At best Gordievsky was tolerated by the authorities but still regarded as a traitor and untrustworthy. Once his immediate knowledge had been used up his value, particularly after the Cyprus spy fiasco, was a fast-diminishing asset. He is now a forgotten man who will while away his twilight years alone and insecure in an alien land, longing to return to Russia.[40]

The KGB has not been slow to remind its senior intelligence personnel of the isolated lifestyle that awaits them in the West should they be tempted to defect, pointing out the benefits of enjoying a relatively luxurious and secure existence in Russia. It has also sent the West numerous doubtful and bogus defectors to muddy the waters. One of the earliest was Oleg Penkovsky, a lieutenant-colonel in the GRU, who approached MI6 in 1960 with offers of information after having been twice rebuffed by the CIA. A businessman called Greville Wynne was asked to act as a freelance MI6 contact and for the next two years Penkovsky provided an incredible wealth of intimate detail about the Russians' innermost plans including the period of the 1962 Cuban missile crisis.

So perfect was his information that it enabled President Kennedy to call Khrushchev's bluff over the Cuban affair. Despite giving Wynne this non-stop array of almost magical material it was not until late 1962, after the Cuban crisis was over, that both Penkovsky and Wynne were arrested by the KGB. At a four-day show trial in May 1963 Wynne received an eight-year prison sentence but in April 1964 was conveniently exchanged for Konon Molody, or 'Gordon Lonsdale', the professional KGB spy and member of the Portland spy ring who had been in prison with George Blake. Penkovsky was sentenced to death with enormous publicity about his espionage activities. But other reports say he lived happily in retirement on a generous KGB pension. In the years that followed endless analyses were made to try and determine whether Penkovsky had really been what he seemed. One school of thought argued that he was too good to be true and his information was deliberately fed to the West by a faction within the Kremlin who opposed Khrushchev's plan to send missiles to Cuba.

Another bogus defector was codenamed Fedora, possibly in reality Viktor Lessiovski, who used his work at the United Nations as a cover. For 12 years from 1962 he successfully fed Edgar Hoover at the FBI a mixture of tantalising bits of fact and rubbish, including false information about Russia's space-rocket programme which led the Americans to think they were ahead of the Russians. In order to enhance his credibility Fedora was allowed to expose John Vassall who by then had outlived his usefulness. Fedora returned to Russia in 1974. Another fake defector operating at the same time was Top Hat (whose real name remains unknown), who also planted a lot of false information on the West through the Americans but did in 1965 expose the spy Frank Bossard, who worked in the Missile Guidance Branch at the Air Ministry[41] and had been selling secrets to the GRU for some while. Bossard was sentenced to 21 years' imprisonment and once again it seems that the Russians were willing to sacrifice an agent, probably because Bossard had given them all the details he could of the American rocket-guidance systems, in order to enhance the credibility of Top Hat so that he could continue peddling disinformation.

In 1969 Josef Frolik of the Czechoslovakian intelligence service defected to the CIA with his wife and proceeded to give some startling information about numerous British Labour Party politicians and trade union officials who he claimed were working for the KGB. Frolik certainly did expose some real spies including Nicholas Praeger, who had given the Czechs details of the RAF's electronic counter-measures equipment codenamed *Blue Diver* and *Red Steer*. As a result Praeger was sentenced to 12 years' imprisonment in June 1971. But the rest of Frolik's information was not particularly valuable except in that it convinced the CIA that Britain's Labour Party was riddled with Communist sympathisers and thus untrustworthy, and helped lead to the suspicions against Prime Minister Harold Wilson.[42] It is now generally accepted that Frolik was a plant designed to waste MI5's resources while important spies remained undetected and to sow seeds of distrust between MI5 and the CIA.

In 1971 Oleg Lyalin, a KGB officer working at the Russian trade mission in London, defected to MI6 and gave enough information about Russian espionage activities to justify the prime minister, Edward Heath, expelling an unprecedented 105 Russian diplomats from Britain. Lyalin also gave MI6 bizarre details of what he claimed were Russian plans to sabotage military establishments in Britain prior to the outbreak of World War III.

Lyalin said his personal task was to destroy the early-warning radar station at Fylingdales while other agents would flood the London underground system. He also alleged that the KGB had recruited hundreds of British traitors who were only waiting for the signal from Moscow to begin destroying Britain's communication system and military establishments around the country. Like most defectors, Lyalin was suffering from delusions of grandeur and it was hard to judge whether he had been reading too much of Pincher's material or books by Le Queux dating from the turn of the century. But because he told MI5 and MI6 what they wanted to hear he was automatically believed and suitably rewarded. It must sometimes puzzle the Russians how easy it is to plant such nonsense on British intelligence but what they do not appreciate is that if defectors did not invent such silly tales MI5 and MI6 would do so themselves anyway.

Two more recent bogus defectors were Oleg Bitov and Vitali Yurchenko. Bitov went to Venice in 1983 for the KGB, using as cover his work for the *Literary Gazette*, and then approached the British asking for asylum. He spent a year in Britain during which time he was commissioned to write numerous articles criticising Russia which earned him a considerable amount of money, some of which he spent on a very comfortable lifestyle.

Then quite suddenly he disappeared and turned up in Moscow at a news conference, claiming that he had been kidnapped by MI5 in Italy, drugged, and taken to Britain and held in captivity until he managed to escape. Bitov said that he had been interrogated by Lieutenant-Colonel James Westoll at Flat 4, 34 Redcliffe Square, Earls Court, London, and 118 Sheen Court, Richmond. Other members of MI5 that looked after him included Colonel George Hartland, Michael Wilmont, Peter Haylor, Captain Charles MacNott, and a clerk, Rose Prince. He was given two telephone numbers to contact MI5, 01-222 5471 and 01-637 7319.[43] Not surprisingly, after Bitov's news conference both numbers were not answering.

Yurchenko contacted the American Embassy in Rome in August 1985, having already worked for them as an agent in place. He was flown to

America and during his debriefing exposed two Russian spies, Edward Howard, who worked for the CIA,[44] and Ronald Pelton, who had worked for the NSA.[45] Both had given away vast amounts of top-secret material without their employers being aware. Howard evaded the FBI and managed to escape to Russia but Pelton was arrested and sentenced to life imprisonment in 1986. Everything seemed to be going well[46] and Yurchenko was about to provide more useful information when, on 2 November 1985, he eluded his CIA colleagues at a restaurant in Washington and made his way back to the Russian Embassy and thence to Moscow. Once there he held a much-publicised news conference during which he ridiculed American intelligence and claimed he had been held in captivity by the CIA. Nothing happened to either Bitov or Yurchenko on their return to Russia so obviously both were planted in the West to cause confusion and also to show their colleagues back home how badly they were treated by the Americans and British.

But without doubt the most contentious defector to reach the West was Anatoli Golitsin, who arrived at the office of the CIA's station chief in Helsinki in Finland in December 1961 and asked for asylum for himself, his wife and daughter. From the moment he arrived Golitsin split the Western intelligence fraternity into two camps. At first he exposed a number of Russian agents and thus established his credentials. But then he embarked on his main thesis, which was that the entire Western intelligence system in Britain, France, Germany and America had been deeply penetrated by the KGB and systematically manipulated with clever disinformation put out by Moscow. According to Golitsin everything the West believed about Russia was wrong and they needed to start all over again with his help and interpretation of the truth.

It was a grandiose theme so radical and ridiculous that it naturally appealed to many intelligence officers living in their secret world of fantasies who saw it as a convenient excuse for all their previous problems and disasters. Others rejected it as nonsense. One of those who became a Golitsin addict was James Angleton,[47] head of counter-intelligence operations at the CIA, whose conversion unfortunately spread across the Atlantic to some members of MI5, including Peter Wright, with disastrous results as a hunt began for this highly placed mole that Golitsin was so sure existed. By carefully selecting pieces of so-called evidence, in reality negative evidence, these Golitsin disciples were able to construct cases against all manner of people including, of course, Sir Roger Hollis.

As with other defectors, the glory went to Golitsin's head and he was soon proposing that he be allowed to establish a world-wide intelligence research organisation with unlimited funds so that he could play out his fantasies against the KGB. Whether Golitsin was a KGB plant or simply a fraud is irrelevant. Either way he successfully wrecked the morale of Western intelligence by encouraging ludicrous molehunts and sowing seeds of discontent and suspicion that remain to this day. Everything Golitsin claimed could be proved or disproved according to which set of arguments one wishes to accept. It has even been suggested that some of Golitsin's claims were based on CIA files that Angleton had allowed him to inspect. If this is true then it would be the supreme irony that the CIA were being fed with their own information. But in the crazy world of intelligence that would not be out of place.

If defectors stayed at home the intelligence world would be much better off as a result. Perhaps there ought to be an intelligence extradition agreement that all defectors are immediately put on the first aircraft back home.

The stories of Blake and the various defectors show how easily the intelligence fraternity fools itself. Living in such a cloistered world such operations are never looked at objectively but simply as a means of gaining personal kudos for one small group within an agency. Time and again intelligence organisations chase after these grandiose projects only to find themselves lost in the wasteland of truth created by their own stupidity.

CHAPTER 3

HENRY THE SECOND

One of the greatest dilemmas facing intelligence agencies in the West is the Henry II syndrome. This occurs when a politician, perhaps so senior that he is notionally responsible for the agency itself, makes it known that he would be very pleased if some particularly sensitive and hazardous intelligence coup could be attained, usually in order to enhance domestic political popularity. Such wishes are carefully expressed in a manner that neither leaves a permanent record for posterity nor gives the impression that illegality was ever suggested.

For many years the East had no such problems. The KGB and GRU were so powerful that there was no need for them to behave in such an opaque manner. If the head of the KGB wanted something done then he simply demanded action. If an operation went wrong and resulted in a scandal because one of their agents had been caught in the act there was no one in Russia who would criticise. Not for them the worries of an investigative *Panorama* or *Insight* team of reporters. No question of civil rights or legal experts poking amongst the debris of the fiasco.

'Who will rid me of this turbulent priest?' asked Henry II.[1] His knights took him at his word. The problem for any intelligence agency, East or West, is whether to take a politician at his word when he is publicly declaring a desire for greater friendship and understanding with the very same people against whom the covert operation is intended. Politicians have to be all things to all people. On the home front they need to seek domestic popularity as election time comes round and talk the way the nation expects to hear them. Abroad they must be seen as great statesmen anxious to build peace-making bridges between East and West.

Both President Reagan and Mrs Thatcher came to power on a platform of military rhetoric with Reagan calling Russia an evil empire and Mrs Thatcher earning herself the title of the Iron Lady. Yet during their tenure of office both have had to deal with a Russia now run by an apparently liberally minded head of government who has come to the conference table willing to reduce arms at a rate that the West sometimes finds embarrassing. Reagan and Mrs Thatcher claim that their tough stances have forced the Russians into this compromising attitude. But others would claim with equal sincerity that Mr Gorbachev is a pragmatic leader who is giving the reconstruction of the Russian economy a greater degree of priority than have his predecessors. For the intelligence agencies a dilemma emerges. Is the Cold War still on, despite the sudden benevolent behaviour of the superpowers? Will the CIA and MI6 suspend operations against the East? Are the KGB and GRU likely to emulate Gorbachev's friendly approach?

It is not a new problem. During a naval review off Portsmouth in October 1955, British naval intelligence had their first sight of the new, post-war Russian Navy when the heavy cruiser *Sverdlov* arrived to take part. Considering that Russia had not engaged in naval warfare for some 50 years and that its industrial economy had been almost totally destroyed during the war, it came as a considerable shock to discover that it was capable of building such a strikingly graceful, and powerful, class of warship.

The *Sverdlov*-class of cruiser,[2] of which 22 were to be built, was an extremely versatile type of warship. Its loaded displacement was 19,200 tons, with a length of nearly 700 feet. Each was equipped with twelve six-inch guns, in four triple turrets, twelve 3.9-inch guns in twin mountings, and over 30 37-mm anti-aircraft guns. There were also ten 21-inch torpedo tubes, and it possessed the ability to lay up to 240 mines. The vessels were remarkably fast, and on sea trials had reached a speed of over 34 knots. The crew numbered 1,050, and the ships' operating range was more than 5,000 miles. Clearly, the *Sverdlov* posed a new and totally unexpected threat to the sea defences of Europe.

Naval intelligence, with the help of MI6, immediately mounted a major operation against the *Sverdlov* and sent frogmen to inspect her hull in order to try to find out as much as possible about her underwater design, the shape of her propellors and any sonar equipment. Later, MI6 arranged that a wartime midget submarine, known as an X-Craft, would attempt to penetrate the Russian naval base at Leningrad.[3] These vessels were fitted with a 'wet chamber' through which a diver could leave the submarine and, it was hoped, make an underwater inspection of the Russian ships in the harbour. But the operation was not a success, because security at the naval base was far too good and, rather than risk being caught in the act, the plan was dropped.

By 1956, East–West tensions had reached breaking point. Both sides were spying on each other quite openly in the course of which many aggressive situations had occurred with loss of spy aircraft and their crews. The new British prime minister, Sir Anthony Eden, who had finally managed to take over the reins of power from Churchill only in 1955, was determined to try to moderate the hostility between Britain and her former wartime ally after the death of Joseph Stalin in 1953. Accordingly, in 1956, Eden invited the Russian leaders – Communist Party Secretary Nikita Khrushchev and Prime Minister Marshal Nikolai Bulganin – to make a goodwill visit to Britain. The invitation was accepted and, on 18 April 1956, the two Russian leaders arrived at Portsmouth in the cruiser *Ordzhonikidze* (sister ship of the *Sverdlov*), accompanied by the destroyer *Smotryashcy*. Both vessels moored alongside the main jetty in the Royal Navy dockyard, and Eden was there to greet his guests on what he hoped would be an historic visit.

Having been Foreign Secretary for so long, Eden was well aware of the likely activities MI5 and MI6 would deploy against their Russian visitors. He therefore issued a written directive[4] to both MI5 and MI6, and the three armed services, banning any intelligence operations against the Russians. It is hard to know now whether Eden was really being serious, or merely protecting himself for posterity. Certainly the intelligence services did not take him seriously. For a start Claridges Hotel, in London's Mayfair, where the Russians would be staying, was fully bugged by MI5 on a permanent basis[5] (because so many 'interesting' foreign guests stayed there) and it was certainly not going to miss the opportunity of eavesdropping on the two leaders.

In fact MI5 was wasting its time because Khrushchev and Bulganin were well aware of this and spent much of the time in their suite holding nonsensical conversations that appeared to include tantalising references to important matters but were in reality pure rubbish. Doubtless MI5 translators wasted hours pondering over these supposed gems of intelligence.

The Director of Naval Intelligence, Rear Admiral John Inglis, was particularly anxious to know more about the *Ordzhonikidze*'s propellor design since the ship was able to travel much faster than British naval experts had calculated. The Naval Intelligence Division (NID) contacted Nicholas Elliott, who was then head of MI6's special naval section (known as the Merchant Navy section),[6] with offices in London's Vauxhall Bridge Road.

Elliott was a long-serving and extremely experienced MI6 officer. Before the war he had been stationed in Holland, during the war he had served with MI6 in Turkey and, in mid-1944, had been appointed head of MI6's operations in Berne, in Switzerland. After the war, Elliott had been responsible for the interrogation of the Russian spy Kim Philby before he defected.

Elliott agreed to mount the operation and, as is often the custom with intelligence agencies when engaged in hazardous operations, decided to use a freelance agent so that, if anything went wrong, MI6 could distance itself from the affair and deny any knowledge of it. To make this very difficult underwater inspection, MI6 approached one of the Royal Navy's most experienced wartime frogmen – Commander Lionel 'Buster' Crabb GM OBE RNVR.

Crabb had served with distinction as an expert in the newly developed art of underwater warfare in the RNVR. In post-war years, Crabb had taken part in the salvage operation following the loss of the submarines HMS *Affray* and HMS *Truculent*. He had retired from the Royal Navy in April 1955 at the age of 46, but had maintained informal contacts with the intelligence fraternity. However, despite his undoubted experience, Crabb's health was not good, and he had become a heavy smoker and drinker. Nevertheless, when approached by MI6 to carry out an underwater inspection of the *Ordzhonikidze*, he agreed without hesitation.

During the planning stages of this operation MI6 approached MI5 for some peripheral help, and a meeting was arranged between John Henry, MI6's Technical Officer, and the Deputy Director of MI5, Roger (later Sir Roger) Hollis. MI5 agreed to give what help was necessary so it is fairly obvious that none of the security services took Eden's directive seriously.

On 17 April 1956 Crabb travelled by train to Portsmouth with his fiancée, Mrs Patricia Rose. Mrs Rose left him at the station and returned alone to London. Evidently, during the journey, Crabb told Mrs Rose something about his mission and appeared to have some misgivings about the whole affair. At Portsmouth, Crabb was met by a local MI6 officer, using the cover name 'Bernard Smith', and together they booked in at the Sallyport Hotel where 'Smith' gave his address as 'c/o Foreign Office, London'. Crabb used his real name. Once in the hotel, Crabb and 'Smith' were joined by another MI6 officer, Edward Davies.

Crabb then made his way to HMS *Vernon*, the Royal Navy's diving establishment, where, together with NID officers, he put together all his equipment and tested it. Unlike civilian frogmen, who use compressed air, Crabb was using the naval closed-circuit oxygen diving equipment which leaves no trail of tell-tale bubbles to disclose a diver's presence. Crabb was also going to wear a black rubber one-piece diving suit made by the Avon Rubber Company.

The next day, 18 April, saw the arrival of the two Russian ships and their distinguished guests and, from a convenient vantage point, Crabb, 'Smith' and Davies watched the official ceremony. The following morning, 19 April, at about 7.30 a.m., Crabb and 'Smith' made their way to the dockyard where Crabb changed into his diving gear and, with the aid of some officers from NID, entered the water near the south-west jetty. After a few minutes Crabb returned to the jetty for some extra weights to overcome his buoyancy and, having fitted these to his satisfaction, set off for the Russian cruiser.[7]

Crabb was never seen alive again. When he failed to return, NID made a search of the dockyard area in case he had been forced to come ashore elsewhere. When this proved negative it seemed obvious that Crabb had drowned.

'Smith' returned to the Sallyport Hotel, paid both their bills, and collected Crabb's belongings. Davies, the other MI6 officer, had, unfortunately, suffered a mild heart attack that morning,[8] but he insisted on giving 'Smith' a hand to clear up any traces of Crabb's visit. MI5 was then advised that Crabb had presumably drowned and was asked to help provide a suitable cover story. However, before any of this could happen, Rear-Admiral Kotov, from the *Ordzhonikidze*, went to see Rear-Admiral Philip Burnett, Chief of Staff of the Portsmouth naval base, complaining that his sailors had seen a frogman near his ships that morning, and demanding an explanation.

As Burnett had been told nothing about the MI6 operation, he simply rejected Kotov's complaint as a typical piece of Russian propaganda. However, later that evening, the First Lord of the Admiralty, James Thomas, was entertaining some Russian officials including the captain of the *Ordzhonikidze*, who casually asked Thomas what the frogman had been doing near his ship that morning. Thomas, who also knew nothing about the affair, was highly embarrassed and could only say that he would make enquiries. It later transpired that the Russians knew perfectly well what had happened, but were obviously enjoying the confusion their seemingly naive questions were provoking.

Matters were further complicated when MI5 decided to take it in hand. Through Special Branch it arranged for Inspector Lamport, of the Portsmouth CID, to visit the Sallyport Hotel two days later, on 21 April, where, in front of the astonished manager, Edward Richman, Lamport tore out from the hotel register the pages bearing the signatures of Crabb and 'Smith', and threatened Richman with prosecution under the Official Secrets Act if he told anybody anything about the affair.

At this point the whole incident could, perhaps, have been kept from public view, but plainly the Russians had no intention of abiding by normal protocol and were determined to alert the British press. This Nikita Krushchev did at his press conference at Central Hall on 27 April when, in his usual ebullient style, he started making references to 'underwater rocks' hazarding the goodwill of his visit. It didn't take journalists long to catch the drift of Krushchev's remarks and reports started to circulate that a British frogman had tried to spy on the Russian ships. Two days later, on 29 April, in a vain attempt to deflect speculation, MI5, MI6 and NID persuaded the Admiralty to issue a seemingly casual press statement to the effect that Commander Crabb was missing, presumed dead, 'having failed to return from a test dive in connection with trials of certain underwater apparatus in Stokes Bay'. Not only was this untrue but it was a very foolish piece of disinformation, since Stokes Bay is a good three miles away from where Crabb was last seen alive. Far from stemming speculation, it did quite the reverse, and the press soon descended on the Sallyport Hotel to inspect the hotel register with its missing pages.

The Russians watched all this with much amusement, and then sent an official protest note (which the Foreign Office managed to lose for five days) demanding an explanation. Very belatedly the Foreign Secretary was forced to admit that the frogman seen by the Russians had been Crabb and, as a result, on 10 May the subject was aired in parliament. Eden took refuge behind the usual claim that it would not be in the national interest to disclose how Crabb had drowned. What he really meant was that it was not in his interest or that of the intelligence services involved. National interest did not come into it at all. The opposition leader Hugh Gaitskell pressed the point and eventually, on 14 May, Eden was forced to admit that an underwater spying operation had been carried out against the Russian ships by Crabb but that it had been done without official approval.

MI6's mistake was not to have a convincing cover story ready as soon as Crabb failed to return. The sensible thing would have been to say that Crabb had been diving in the area to test out equipment and had got into difficulties, surfaced near the Russian ships and then drowned. This would have pre-empted any Russian protest. But the fear that nagged MI6's mind was that the Russians had captured Crabb alive and might produce him to tell the full story.

Having obliged Eden to make an embarrassing statement in parliament the Russians lost interest in the affair. In fact they had known all about Crabb's venture before they arrived at Portsmouth and their frogmen were waiting for him as he approached the cruiser. Exactly what happened is not known for certain, but the most likely scenario is that Crabb was intercepted by Russian frogmen and taken on board the *Ordzhonikidze* through a 'wet chamber'.

Many years later Harry Houghton, one of the members of the Portland spy ring sentenced to 15 years' imprisonment in 1961, claimed that his Russian controller (who was, incidentally, somehow tipped off about the impending arrest of the spy ring and never caught), told him during a meeting at the Crown Inn, at Punknoll in Dorset (not far from the underwater research laboratory where Houghton worked), that the Russians had been warned of Crabb's plan. According to Houghton's controller, Crabb had been brought on board the cruiser in a state of collapse from oxygen poisoning and later died in the sick-bay. A similar tale was also told by the Russian defector Anatoli Golitsin who arrived in the West in late 1961. One of his main claims was that MI5 had been fully penetrated by Russian intelligence which led to the allegations that Roger Hollis was himself a Russian mole. Hollis had been present during the planning of the Crabb operation.

On 15 May Patricia Rose left London to escape the attention of reporters and went to stay with her brother and sister-in-law at Biot, in France. While there, it is alleged, a neighbour called Kessler told her that a photograph of her and Crabb had appeared in an East German newspaper. When shown a copy of this Mrs Rose is said to have identified the photograph as being one of her, Crabb and her sister-in-law, of which only three copies existed. Two of these Mrs Rose could trace but the third had been with Crabb when they said goodbye and was not amongst his personal possessions returned to Crabb's mother by 'Smith'. About two weeks later, while still at Biot, Mrs Rose began receiving strange messages by telephone purporting to come from Crabb which were according to Mrs Rose supposed to have contained personal phrases and nicknames which only the two of them knew. Mrs Rose was clearly given to understand that Crabb was still alive. Since Mrs Rose is dead these stories cannot be verified.

Then, just over a year later, the story was back in the headlines again.[9] On 9 June 1957 a fisherman found a body, with the head and hands missing, clad in a black rubber suit, floating off Pilsey Island at the mouth of Chichester Harbour.

Crabb's ex-wife saw the body at Bognor mortuary but was unable to confirm that it was that of her husband.[10] Another naval diver[11] and a close friend of Crabb who knew him well, Sidney James Knowles BEM, also saw the body and was quite definite that it was not Crabb. Crabb had had hammer toes and this body did not. Knowles claimed that he was interviewed by two security oficers who asked him to change his story on 'patriotic grounds' and say the body was Crabb's. Knowles alleged that one of the officials told him: 'I know it's not Crabb's body, but you must swear to me if you're asked in court if it's the body, you're to say it is – for Queen and country.'

Knowles reluctantly agreed and on 26 June 1957 the Chichester coroner, Mr Bridgman, recorded an open verdict as to the cause of death, but said he was quite satisfied the body was that of Crabb. On 5 July the body, whether it was Crabb's or not, was finally laid to rest in Portsmouth cemetery.

Although the body may have been buried, the story was not. The verdict satisfied no one, particularly as it was obvious that the authorities were keen to prove the body was Crabb's when, plainly, the evidence was not there. The body was badly decomposed and had been in the water for a long time. Tidal experts agreed that the body could not have been off Pilsey Island for more than 24 hours. Furthermore, a body lost in Portsmouth Harbour a year previously would have washed out to sea long ago and, in any case, would be unlikely to have turned up in Chichester Harbour.

However, another fisherman later claimed that he had dredged up the same body a few months earlier and, in the process of trying to recover it, the head had come off in his hands. The fisherman was so shocked that he let the body slip back into the water and, though he reported it to the police, no action was taken by them. It is impossible to know if this story is true since the police have no record of the event.

Who put the corpse into the water in Chichester Harbour so that it could be so conveniently found? Had the Russians dumped Crabb's body into the sea off the mouth of the harbour as they steamed past, suitably weighted with ropes that would rot in due course? Or did British intelligence produce an unidentifiable corpse simply to bring the whole affair to an end?

On 1 June 1981, Mrs Rose received a letter which read:

For what it's worth, I was a schoolboy visiting the [Russian] cruiser that afternoon after school, and was on the main deck looking over the side next to the quay, when I saw a diver (with full deep-diving headgear) being pulled beneath the surface by two frogmen. At the same time a klaxon sounded and Russian sailors cleared the deck.

The problem with this letter, apart from the fact that the only copy available is unsigned,[12] is that it does not agree with the timescale of events. We know that Crabb entered the water before 8 a.m. The writer talks about being on board the cruiser after school in the afternoon or, say, around 4 p.m. Obviously, Crabb would have been caught, and was probably dead, by 10 a.m. Therefore the letter is either a fake, or the diver the writer saw was a Russian still inspecting the ship for other British frogmen. Either way it is irrelevant.

The legend that Crabb was taken back to Russia alive continued to circulate for several years and indeed still does, helped by a number of books claiming to be based on secret information from the East.[13] One of the tales was that Crabb had agreed to join the Russian Navy where he became Lieutenant Korablov, and a very poor-quality photograph was even produced supposedly showing Crabb in Russian naval uniform. Many interviews were quoted with contacts in East Europe, all of whom claimed to have proof that Crabb was still alive, but not a shred of evidence was ever produced to support any of these bizarre allegations. At best it was either a publicity stunt designed help sell third-rate books or a neat piece of disinformation put out by the Russians in order to sow confusion amongst the West's intelligence agencies.

The real truth about Crabb will never be known, but it does seem that he was expected by the Russians, was caught and either died of a heart attack or was murdered, and his body dumped over the side as the ships left Portsmouth. The body later found in Chichester Harbour was almost certainly not that of Crabb.

Whatever the facts may be the Crabb affair, even after more than 30 years, remains intensely embarrassing and many important documents relating to the incident are still withheld from public scrutiny. It was one of those rare occasions when a covert operation could be examined in the full glare of publicity and it showed what a foolhardy idea it was from the start for, even if Crabb had returned safely, it is unlikely he could have brought back enough information to have justified the risk in the first place. It is an excellent example of the pointlessness of so much intelligence work, often conceived in the looking-glass world of make-believe where no one seems to be in touch with the real world outside, or to even consider the consequences of their ludicrous ideas.

The most important point to come out of the Crabb affair was that it showed that the intelligence services were prepared to carry out operations contrary to the direct orders of the prime minister who was in charge of them. In order to try to distance themselves from this operation they employed a freelance, just as they tap telephones illegally or burgle property by using freelances. The Crabb incident is a salutary reminder that one should never believe anything a government says about an incident involving intelligence. Nothing is impossible and the more unlikely the allegation the more likely it is to be true.

The outcome of the Crabb affair was equally bizarre. Eden was so angry at having been made a fool of that the Director General of MI6, Sir John 'Sinbad' Sinclair, was obliged to retire prematurely and was replaced by the head of MI5, Sir Dick White. Ironically, White's successor at MI5 was Roger Hollis, so if Hollis was a long-term Russian spy as has since been alleged (but never proved), then his command of MI5 came about because someone leaked details of a MI6 mission to the Russians that led to the downfall of the head of MI6. Was that someone Hollis? If you believe that Hollis was a Russian agent then the Crabb affair fits neatly into the jigsaw but, as so often happens in the intelligence world, the same set of facts can be tinkered and tailored with so as to fit any preconceived belief.

But the Crabb affair is of interest for another reason. Had the Russians not decided to make the facts public the truth would still be hidden. If some investigative journalist had claimed that Crabb died while making an unauthorised underwater inspection of the Russian cruiser he would have been ridiculed on the grounds that he had no proof. If that journalist had attempted to inspect any files relating to Crabb's 'accident' he would either be told that no such files existed or, if they did, were classified in the interests of national security. We can also see how the press were deliberately misled by the official statement put out by the Admiralty which was a pack of lies.

Even if Crabb's next-of-kin had been dissatisfied with the official explanation and had made such a fuss that the government was forced to hold some sort of inquiry the truth would still not have been told. Some learned judge would have been appointed to head it and his only access to the facts would be to ask the Cabinet Secretary, the Admiralty, the Director General of MI5 and MI6 what they knew.

The Cabinet Secretary would have said that the prime minister had issued a specific directive that no intelligence operations were to be mounted against the Russians during their visit. The Director General of MI5 could truthfully say that he knew nothing. And because the Crabb operation was unauthorised the Director General of MI6 could also honestly tell the inquiry that he too knew nothing about such a plan. The Admiralty would probably say something to the effect that Crabb was testing highly secret equipment that could not be discussed in detail and had unfortunately drowned. Anything Crabb's fiancée, Mrs Rose, might claim would be quietly denigrated by a smear campaign alleging she was hysterical, mentally disturbed, or anxious to make money out of the affair by selling her story to the press.

In the end a brief report would be published. Most of it would be devoted to Crabb's bravery and service to his country during the war, the fact that he was an underwater expert and that he was always willing to test the latest equipment, some of which work was inevitably hazardous. On this occasion Crabb was carrying out experiments in which the Admiralty had a peripheral interest, but it would not be in the national interest to detail them, and unfortunately he drowned and his body was swept out to sea. The report would conclude that there was no evidence that the intelligence services were involved. On any future occasion when the subject was raised the government of the day would always quote this report as the fountain of truth. It is not hard to see why official inquiries concerning matters like spies or telephone tapping very rarely tell the truth.

From every point of view, therefore, the Crabb affair was a classic example of how not to carry out a dangerous covert operation.

The French handle such operations rather differently. At 11.38 p.m. on the night of 10 July 1985,[14] agents of the French General Directorate for External Security, DGSE, the equivalent of Britain's MI6 and America's CIA, blew up and sank the Greenpeace ship *Rainbow Warrior* in Auckland harbour in New Zealand with two limpet mines, killing a member of the crew, a Portugese photographer called Fernando Pereira.

This was no unauthorised operation carried out by a bunch of freelance hotheads. It was a carefully planned attack by France's secret service with the full backing of President Francois Mitterand. The reason for the attack was very simple. France was a nuclear power and, more important, a proudly independent one. For several years France had been carrying out nuclear weapons tests on the remote Pacific island of Moruroa in the Pacific.

During these years there had been routine protests in places like the United Nations, which France ignored, and around the island of Moruroa itself involving the Greenpeace organisation. In 1981 and 1982 the group had visited the test site with their ship the *Vega* and on the last occasion had been attacked and arrested by the French Navy as they attempted to enter the 12-mile territorial limit. Quite apart from the publicity such incidents provided, they also tied up a lot of ships and manpower. By 1985 Greenpeace was better organised and French intelligence had learned that it was planning to send out to Moruroa its larger 420-ton *Rainbow Warrior*, together with the *Vega*, and then to launch a number of small boats in which its members would try to elude the French Navy and penetrate the test area. The whole plan greatly alarmed the French for the small boats would be impossible to detect on radar and if any of the occupants were affected by radioactivity after a test they would automatically become worldwide martyrs.

The French Navy passed the problem to the DGSE who at first suggested that the simplest course of action was to tow the *Rainbow Warrior* out to the test area. But this pleased neither the defence ministry nor the navy who pointed out that it would merely sail back again. The DGSE then decided that the only other option was to destroy it. The simplest method would have been for a French submarine to wait for the *Rainbow Warrior* somewhere on the high seas and sink it with a torpedo but that posed the problem of what to do with any survivors. Even the DGSE might have baulked at letting them drown or shooting them in cold blood.

Funding an operation of this kind required the authorisation of the office of France's prime minister, Laurent Fabius, and he was certainly not going to give that without the president's approval. Mitterand was a proud man who agreed with Fabius and his defence chiefs that no boat-load of lunatics, probably under Russia's influence, was going to stop France's nuclear programme. 'Who will rid me of this troublesome boat?' he asked. DGSE had the answer. Mitterand was too clever a politician to put anything in writing but nevertheless his seal of approval was clearly on the operation.

To find out more about the Greenpeace operation the DGSE infiltrated a 34-year-old agent, Christine Cabon, into their New Zealand office. Using the alias Frederique Bonlieu, Cabon wrote to Greenpeace claiming she shared their views, and when she arrived in Auckland on 3 April 1985 offered to work for the organisation without salary. Although neither very efficient nor popular with the other staff, Cabon made herself useful and soon had the run of the office and was able to look at all the files, amongst which she found one relating to the proposed voyage of the *Rainbow Warrior* into the nuclear test area. On 24 May Cabon told Greenpeace she had to leave and returned to Paris where she was able to report fully on its plans.

On 29 May 1985 Petty Officer Gerald Andries of the DGSE flew to London and bought a French-made Zodiac inflatable dinghy and outboard motor for £1,400 from the Barnet Marine Center in North London, paying in cash. This action was very strange because Andries not only attracted a lot of attention to himself by the manner of his purchase but also the dinghy had a serial number on it which made it instantly traceable. One possibility is that the DGSE somehow hoped that by buying the dinghy in London blame for the operation would be placed on MI6, although in this case it would have made more sense to buy one made in Britain. Alternatively, the DGSE may have unoffically told MI6 what it planned to do in New Zealand. The idea of destroying the *Rainbow Warrior* would have pleased both MI6 and the British government since they dislike organisations like CND and Greenpeace who hold very vocal anti-nuclear views, and already had their members listed on MI5 files and regularly tapped their telephones.

By the last week in June the DGSE had arrived in New Zealand – Major Alain Mafart and Captain Dominique Prieur, posing as honeymoon couple Alain and Sophie Turenge, using false Swiss passports, who arrived at Auckland airport on the Air New Zealand flight from London. They had booked a Toyota camper van and told the hire company they intended spending the next three weeks touring New Zealand.

Three DGSE frogmen, Roland Verge, Gerald Andries and Jean-Michel Bartelo, had arrived off the northern New Zealand coast in the French yacht *Ouvéa* using false names and passports. They pretended to be the crew of Dr Xavier Maniguet, who was playing the part of a rich playboy who had chartered the vessel from a French travel agency for a winter cruise in the Pacific. The *Ouvéa* made its way south, eventually arriving at Whangarei on 28 June.

Exactly what happened between this date and 10 July is not known precisely and it is possible that in addition to the group of six already identified there were other DGSE agents involved. The *Ouvéa* sailed from Whangarei on the morning of 9 July, 36 hours before the *Rainbow Warrior* was blown up, arriving in Norfolk Island 625 miles to the north on 13 July, thus providing Maniguet and his 'crew' with a seemingly perfect alibi. In fact, after leaving Whangarei, the yacht turned south and made landfall under cover of darkness on 10 July somewhere north of Auckland where it was met by Mafart and Prieur. They loaded the Zodiac dinghy, outboard motor, and the limpet mines into the camper and drove south, reaching Auckland around 7.30 p.m. where witnesses living at Stanley Point on the northern shore of Auckland Harbour saw two men take an inflatable dinghy out of a camper van and carry it down to the water's edge.

The two bombs were attached to the hull of the *Rainbow Warrior*, berthed at Marsden Wharf, at around 8.30 p.m. and at about 9.30 p.m. a man wearing a red woollen hat was seen abandoning a Zodiac dinghy near the Outboard Boating Club in Hobson's Bay and then climbing up the embankment to Tamaki Drive where he was picked up and driven off in a camper van. Because there had been a recent spate of thefts from boats in the area the Club had formed its own teams of vigilantes who patrolled the moorings and by chance one of these noted down the camper's registration number. The identity of the person who abandoned the Zodiac dinghy and therefore presumably planted the bombs has never been discovered but from the descriptions it seems fairly certain it was Bartelo from the *Ouvéa*, while the man who helped him get the dinghy into the water was Mafart.

The following morning, after the attack, the police were told about the abandoned Zodiac dinghy and also given the number of the camper van. They discovered it had been hired by a Swiss honeymoon couple and they put out an alert for them. Quite unexpectedly, at 9.00 a.m. on 12 July, the couple turned up at Auckland airport and told the hire company's office there that they had to return early to Europe and were planning to catch the 11.30 a.m. Air New Zealand flight to London. Had Mafart and Prieur simply abandoned the camper and boarded the flight they would have left the country undetected because at the time the police believed they were still driving around the country. Instead they asked the company for a refund on their hire agreement and when the airport office checked with the Auckland office they discovered the pair were wanted by the police.

The couple were taken to police headquarters for questioning where they admitted they had picked up a man on the night of 10 July by the harbour but did not know him and had only given him a lift into town. The police soon traced the couple's movements and found they had made a number of telephone calls to Paris. The French police said the number they had called did not exist but in fact it was a special number allocated to the DGSE. Finally the New Zealand police established through Interpol that the two Swiss passports were forgeries and were able to arrest Mafart and Prieur.

The police were also told about the yacht *Ouvéa* and its four-man French crew and on 15 July officers flew to Norfolk Island to interrogate them, although Maniguet had left the island for Australia that morning. The police questioned the three 'crew', who were far too well trained to give anything away, and although forensic samples were taken from the *Ouvéa* it was impossible to examine them on the spot. At 8.00 p.m. on 16 July the trio were allowed to sail for the French island of New Caledonia. They never arrived. Somewhere en route the *Ouvéa* met up with the French nuclear submarine *Rubis* and after the trio of DGSE agents had boarded her the yacht was sunk. Maniguet was questioned by the police on his arrival in Sydney but again they were frustrated by lack of evidence that would have allowed them to detain him. Reluctantly Maniguet was allowed to leave for Paris.

For a while the French government maintained a stony silence about the affair, claiming it was beneath its dignity to comment on allegations that the DGSE had been involved. But as the French press produced one embarrassing revelation after another, including leaks from the DGSE itself, it was decided that 65-year-old civil servant Bernard Tricot should carry out a rigorous investigation and that the French government would cooperate fully with the New Zealand police. Tricot had investigated intelligence fiascoes before including the kidnapping by French intelligence agents in 1965 of Ben Barka, an Algerian left-winger, who was never seen again and was presumably murdered by them. Tricot delivered a report of stunning mediocrity similar to those so often produced by pompous security commissions in Britain investigating spies, traitors, and telephone tapping. In fact the report was so useless that it did more damage than had Mitterand kept silent.

While the story rumbled on in France, the New Zealand police prepared to place Mafart and Prieur on trial facing a charge of murder. But if the French government had been inefficient in Paris it had certainly been busy in New Zealand. France made it clear to New Zealand that it would allow more imports of lamb and dairy products into France if New Zealand reduced the charge against the couple to manslaughter and then deported them. Quite apart from blackmail the New Zealand police had no proof that either Mafart or Prieur had planted the bombs so when the two appeared in court in Auckland on 4 November 1985 the prosecution announced that they had accepted a plea of manslaughter. Three weeks later they were sentenced to ten years' imprisonment.

This was plainly not part of the agreement and not only was the French government furious but it used the sentence as an excuse to generate public support for Mafart and Prieur on the grounds that they were being unfairly treated by the New Zealand government. Suddenly all the political quarrels were forgotten and the French people decided that France's honour was at stake and the two agents were not terrorists but national heroes. Ironically this change in public opinion came at a time when Arab terrorists were letting off bombs in Paris, which French people thought quite terrible. It evidently did not occur to them that the people of Auckland felt the same.

Encouraged by this sudden surge of perverted patriotism, the French government blocked the import of New Zealand agricultural products into the Common Market, including its EEC daily import quota to Britain, over the next two years by a protracted series of legal wrangles. Throughout this period both Britain and America remained strangely silent. New Zealand was an old ally of Britain, a member of the Commonwealth, who had been attacked by terrorists using bombs. Both Mrs Thatcher and President Reagan were constantly reminding people that the world must stick together to fight the threat from such attacks. Yet not a word was said condemning France or defending New Zealand against France's blackmail at the EEC. The reason was not hard to find. Both Britain and America, being nuclear powers, supported France in its attack on the *Rainbow Warrior*, particularly as Greenpeace had been active around the shores of Britain drawing unwelcome attention to the discharge of radioactive waste from nuclear power-stations. Furthermore the New Zealand prime minister, David Lange, was a Labour politician. So while it was wrong for the IRA to let off bombs in

Northern Ireland it was quite all right for the DGSE to let them off in New Zealand.

The dispute was only resolved in July 1986[15] when Senor Perez de Cuellar, Secretary General of the United Nations, arranged a package deal whereby France paid the New Zealand government £4.5 million in addition to what it had privately paid to Pereira's family and the £5 million it also had to pay Greenpeace in October 1987.[16] In return Mafart and Prieur had their sentences commuted to three years which were to be served in exile at the French military base on the Pacific island of Hao.

By now the French government had become quite brazen about the whole affair and the new French prime minister, Jacques Chirac, publicly stated that France had good reason to be proud of what Mafart and Prieur had achieved, a view that was evidently shared by most people in France. In December 1987 Mafart was allowed to return to France[17] in defiance of the agreement because it was alleged he was ill, although the French government refused to allow a New Zealand doctor to examine him. A few months later Prieur became pregnant and she too returned to France.[18] Mafart's illness cannot have been very serious because he was well enough to sit the entrance examination to France's élite School of War where he won a place in March 1988.[19]

Like the Crabb affair, this fiasco teaches quite a few lessons. First, the operation was pointless because the destruction of the ship did not affect Greenpeace's continued opposition to the tests. Second, it was badly planned and not enough thought was given to how the team would make their escape from a remote island like New Zealand. Third, it would have been better to use freelances whose connection with the DGSE could have been denied, whereas both Mafart and Prieur made telephone calls to DGSE numbers in France when first arrested. And fourth, having been caught out it would have been wiser to brazen it out immediately, as do the Israelis, rather than go through the tedium of Tricot's inquiry. Although the project was a disaster, costing France £10 million, and counter-productive in giving Greenpeace much-needed publicity about France's nuclear tests, it at least gave the DGSE some confidence that if in the future it accepted another Henry II-type command it would have the backing of its politicians.

But not every intelligence agency is as fortunate as was the DGSE. In America all presidents are acutely afflicted by the Henry II syndrome because so much American foreign policy is controlled by their intelligence organisations. As a result, many actions that presidents allow to happen are covert and frequently illegal, usually concealed under a cover of wanting to help another country defeat Communism. Even President Jimmy Carter, who came to office in a house-cleansing operation after the shambles of Richard Nixon's resignation, indulged in a variety of covert operations around the world, including the supply of weapons by the CIA from America and other sources to Afghan rebel forces fighting against the Russians.

By the time President Reagan came to office on 20 January 1981 he had plenty of reasons for wishing to emulate Henry II. Carter's presidency had ended disastrously. In November 1979 the Iranians had taken over the American Embassy in Teheran and held the staff hostage for 444 days, only releasing them 30 minutes after Carter had left office. During the long drawn-out hostage crisis the American people had watched impotently, wondering how it was that a nation with the supposed military capability to wipe Russia off the map at the push of a button could do nothing. Then in the spring of 1980 came the disaster of the rescue mission, with agonising pictures of wrecked helicopters and charred bodies across the pages of every newspaper and on every television channel.

One of the first things Reagan did upon becoming president was to name Iran as an enemy of America and to ensure that no trade of any kind went on between the two countries, either directly or indirectly, imposing draconian penalties for anyone caught doing so. On the face of it such legislation seemed unnecessary; after all, who in America would want to trade with a country like Iran? Although Reagan's knowledge of foreign affairs was non-existent, to the point where if he was not prompted he often had no idea which country he was talking about, he needed little convincing by the American intelligence agencies that now was the time for America to start waging a secret war against its enemies. To Reagan there were only three sorts of enemies: Communists, Libyans and Iranians. This made things much simpler for his advisers because they knew exactly the sort of information Reagan wanted to hear.

Within three months of taking office[20] he had authorised secret funding for moderate Christian Democrats and military officers in El Salvador. By the end of 1981 Reagan had authorised the covert supply of weapons and other military equipment through the CIA to help the Contras overthrow the Sandinista government of Nicaragua. In theory this action was to stop arms shipments from the Sandinistas being sent to El Salvador to support the left-wing rebels there. In practice it was a straightforward piece of CIA terrorism designed to overthrow by force a legitimately elected government that America did not like. The person in charge of coordinating these covert activities between the White House and the intelligence agencies was Colonel Oliver North of the US Marine Corps.

Those working around Reagan soon discovered that he was a very lazy president. He could not be bothered to read anything longer than a single sheet of paper, and even that with great difficulty, and got so bored when any detail was explained to him that he often fell asleep. Like any actor who has to play many different parts, all Reagan wanted were a few good lines written for him on cue cards that he could quote without having to tax his own abilities. Reagan was therefore a perfect example of an elderly Henry II. He wanted things done but was neither interested in nor concerned with the way they were achieved.

Although the American Embassy hostage crisis in Iran had been settled, the situation in the Middle East grew steadily worse. Aside from the stalemated Iran-Iraq war, Lebanon continued to tear itself apart in continuous internecine struggles. On 6 June 1982 Israel invaded Lebanon in order to drive out Palestine Liberation Organisation (PLO) terrorists from the southern part of the country, who they claimed had also attempted to murder the Israeli ambassador in London three days earlier. In fact the ambassador had been attacked by members of the Abu Nidal faction, who had long severed connections with the PLO, but a small detail like that was not enough to deter the Israelis.

While the world criticised Israel, America made only its usual token gestures of condemnation because it was supporting the CIA-backed Phalangist leader Bashir Gemayel to the tune of more than $4 million. Gemayel was also a good friend of Israel and the CIA was hoping to get him elected as president of Lebanon. Gemayel had been in the pay of the CIA like King Hussein of Jordan who had been on the CIA's payroll for 20 years. Gemayel became president of war-torn Lebanon on 23 August 1982, while the Israeli army were still occupying large parts of the country right up to the outskirts of Beirut. On 14 September 1982 Gemayel planned to meet with a group of Mossad officers, but was killed when a bomb planted by Syrian intelligence exploded in the local Phalangist party offices where he was speaking.

Once again the American's plans for the Middle East were in disarray and then the Israelis allowed Phalangist units to enter the Palestinian refugee camps at Sabra and Shatilla and massacre everyone within reach. Reagan responded by sending in 1,200 US Marines on a peace-keeping mission which, although it sounded all right and looked good on television, had no particular purpose. On 18 April 1983 the American Embassy in Beirut was car-bombed and collapsed like a pack of cards, sixty-three employees, including a team of senior CIA agents holding a meeting at the time were killed. By 17 October 1983 six marines had been killed by snipers but Reagan claimed that their presence in the Lebanon was 'vitally important to the security of the United States and the Western world'. On 23 October a truck containing 12,000 pounds of explosives was driven into the US Marine's barrack compound and detonated with the driver still at the wheel, killing 241 servicemen. Both these attacks were attributed to Iranian terrorists. A stunned nation watched the coffins brought home and wondered what had been achieved.

While all this was going on a number of Americans, including the head of CIA operations in Beirut, William Buckley, were kidnapped by Islamic Jihad and other terrorist organisations which had tenuous links with Iran. Then on 14 June 1985 TWA Flight 847 was hijacked and forced to land at Beirut where, before the world's television cameras, it was held for 17 days. During this time an American sailor, Robert Stethem, was murdered but all the remaining passengers, including 39 Americans, were released unhurt. By now public anger in America was mounting and there were demands for Reagan to turn his cosy rhetoric into action. The problem was that although Iran was identified as the villain there was no way of selectively pinpointing any particular group or location that could be attacked without causing enormous innocent civilian casualties.

For Reagan it was a frustrating time. The problems mounted whichever way he turned. Yet despite being the most powerful man in the world, in command of some of the most deadly and sophisticated weaponry ever designed, there seemed to be nothing he could do. Not only did he quite genuinely want to ease the distress of the hostages' relatives but Reagan was well aware of the damaging analogy to his own political fortunes when comparing this hostage crisis to that suffered by Carter. To try to rejuvenate his fading presidency Reagan wanted to be seen on prime-time network television across America greeting each hostage in turn as they stepped safely back on to American soil. This is what presidents, particularly ex-Hollywood actors, dream about. Ideally Reagan would have liked a more dramatic scenario whereby his armed forces, especially the US Marines, stormed the hostages' hideout, killed their kidnappers and returned in glory with the stars and stripes held high. Common sense and logistics ruled this out. Whether Reagan actually said: 'Who will rid me of this turbulent problem?' is irrelevant. Those around him anxious to please and do his bidding were in no doubt as to what he wanted and desperately sought a solution at any price that would satisfy their commander-in-chief.

According to Ali Akbar Rafsanjani, the powerful speaker of the Iranian parliament, 'The Americans started contacting us through scores of channels begging us to help them in the Lebanon; through Japan, our neighbouring countries like Pakistan, our embassies, the United Nations and numerous arms brokers.'[21] The first positive response came, not surprisingly, from the Middle East's most efficient intelligence agency, Mossad. It was an open secret that following the overthrow of the Shah and throughout the Iran-Iraq war Israel had supplied Iran with weapons to the value of more than $500 million, mainly paid for in oil. Another supplier was South Africa whose huge Armscor factory in Johannesburg had supplied Iran with all the 120-mm guns that it fruitlessly fired across the desert in this never-ending conflict, and much else besides. They too had been paid in oil to get round the world trade boycott. Everyone knew this was going on but the vast profits involved generated a convenient blanket of economic hypocrisy.

Israel's plan was actually that of an American businessman now under arrest in the United States charged with trading with Iran. He claimed that Iran badly needed TOW anti-tank missiles and in return for them would get the American hostages being held in Beirut released. Mossad proposed that to conceal the plan they would send TOW[22] missiles to Iran from their own stocks and America would ship them replenishments.[23] In this way, if anything leaked out about the deal, the Americans could claim they were not supplying Iran directly. The person selected to control this illegal operation was Oliver North, the ubiquitous US Marine colonel so closely involved in the Central American covert actions. He was provided with a false passport in the name of William Goode.

To complicate matters further Israel was using an intermediary,[24] an Iranian businessman called Manucher Ghorbanifar, who was already well known to American intelligence for having fabricated tales. In 1981 he had told the CIA that Colonel Gadaffi, Reagan's pet enemy, had sent assassination squads to America to kill the president. This story had been used extensively by the Americans to drum up support against Gadaffi in the tame sections of the Western media even though they knew it was untrue. Ghorbanifar had also offered to provide the CIA with intelligence about Iran in return for being allowed to smuggle drugs. It is an indication of the panic induced by the Henry II syndrome that those advising the president could even consider having contact with a person like Ghorbanifar, let alone do business with him. Since Iran refused to pay for the TOW missiles until they were delivered a Saudi Arabian middleman called Adnan Khashoggi, whose social lifestyle and divorce proceedings help fill the pages of the tabloid press, put up a bridging loan of $5 million. Iran received 508 TOW missiles for that price and the Reverend Benjamin Weir, one of the American hostages, was released on 15 September 1985.

Reagan was ecstatic and Weir was paraded before the media at the White House to demonstrate how the president's firm Middle East policies were paying off. It is impossible that Reagan was unaware that Weir had been released only because the American government had sold 508 TOW missiles to Iran for $5 million. The deal was so simple that even Reagan could understand it.

The Russians had also had some problems in Beirut when four of their diplomats were abducted by the radical Hizbollah movement.[25] One of the four was murdered so the KGB sent a hit squad to Beirut who kidnapped a relative of those holding the three remaining hostages, castrated and killed him. They dumped his body outside the Hizbollah's offices with a note saying that the rest of them would die in a similar fashion if the three diplomats were not released. Two days later the hostages were freed unharmed. On this occasion at least the KGB were more efficient than the CIA.

By now North, flushed with success at the release of Weir in exchange for the TOW missiles, was getting into his stride. He established a dummy Swiss company, Lake Resources Inc, through which he laundered vast sums of cash from shady middlemen and arms dealers, right-wing American bigots, and the enormous profits out of the arms' shipments to the Iranians, who had paid twice the going rate for what they bought. In November 1985 North shipped out of America two Boeing 707-loads of Hawk anti-aircraft missiles, ostensibly for Israel although by now the pretence was wearing thin and they were simply transferred to Israeli cargo aircraft and flown straight on to Iran.

By the beginning of 1986 two major problems faced Reagan: further arms sales to Iran and a pre-emptive strike against Libya following several terrorist incidents the Americans believed were Libyan-backed. The first was a continuation of the earlier sales because Iran had now promised that within about two months it would be able to arrange the release of the remaining five American hostages. This idea was proposed by Admiral John Poindexter, the president's national security adviser, at a meeting at the White House on 6 January attended by Reagan, Vice-President George Bush, Secretary of State George Shultz, Defence Secretary Caspar Weinberger, head of the CIA William Casey, the White House chief-of-staff Donald Regan, and Edwin Meese, the president's legal adviser.

How much the meeting was told about the previous shipments to Iran is unclear but it is hard to believe that those present were not aware of them. Shultz and Weinberger opposed Poindexter's plan, pointing out that it undermined America's much-stated policy, usually made in conjunction with Mrs Thatcher, that no deals must be made with terrorists and that there could be no question of bargaining to get hostages released since this would inevitably lead to more abductions. Poindexter and Casey claimed they were in touch with moderate elements within Iran that America should exploit, otherwise the Russians would. In fact neither Poindexter nor Casey had any evidence of this other than some vague promises made to Poindexter's predecessor, Robert McFarlane, who had met Iran's foreign minister, Ibrahim Yazdi, in Washington. Exactly what Reagan said remains a mystery, but the very fact that he did not dismiss the idea out of hand as quite contrary to all his public statements about Iran certainly left those at the meeting in no doubt that he wanted the deal to go ahead.

In February North arranged a further shipment of 1,000 TOW missiles directly to Iran using Ghorbanifar as intermediary and without bothering to use the Israelis. No hostage was released, the excuse given by Ghorbanifar being that Iran did not really need the TOW missiles so they were not counted in the exchange deal.

Meanwhile Reagan's other major concern, the plan to attack Libya, was gathering momentum. On 22 March an armada of 45 US Navy warships, *Operation Prairie Fire*, complete with aircraft carriers, 200 aircraft, and nuclear submarines, appeared off the Libyan coast in the Gulf of Sidra and deliberately trailed their coats until the Libyans reacted by firing two SA-5 missiles at the American aircraft. In retaliation the US Navy sent in A-7 attack aircraft launching stand-off Harm missiles which neatly homed in on the Libyan radar stations and destroyed them, killing over 70 Libyans. A month later, on 14 April 1986, F-111 bombers from bases in England attacked Tripoli and Benghazi, dropping 32 laser-guided 2,000-pound bombs.[26] Two F-111s were lost and there were considerable civilian casualties among the Libyans.

The Libyan attack occupied both the minds of Reagan and the public around the world, although from very different viewpoints as to the morality of the action. Reagan continued to assert that direct action was the only way to deal with terrorist countries like Libya and Iran and that he would not countenance any other approach. But meanwhile North had discovered that the secret shipments of arms to Iran were generating upwards of $15 million which he proposed diverting to fund the American-backed Contra forces fighting in Nicaragua for whom Congress had refused to provide any further financial aid on the grounds that Reagan was involving America in an operation to overthrow by force another country's legitimate government.

That a mere colonel in the White House would have taken it upon himself to engage in such duplicitous and totally illegal operations without the president's knowledge and authority is quite impossible to believe. Throughout 1985–86 North continued shipments of arms to Iran in a series of complex deals involving sleazy arms dealers, shady middlemen, Swiss numbered bank accounts, suitcases stuffed with dollar bills, and all the trappings of dishonest behaviour one would associate with drug smugglers and the Mafia rather than a member of the White House staff. On 26 July 1986 Father Lawrence Jenco was released after being held hostage for 18 months.

But during this period the CIA began noticing that North's sales of weapons and monies received from Iran did not add up. A sum of $3.5 million had gone missing from the first shipment of TOW missiles in 1985 and a further $24 million could not be accounted for from one of North's Swiss bank accounts. The more the CIA tried to investigate the more inconsistencies they turned up. Eventually the CIA stumbled on the fact that North was privately diverting these missing millions to the Contras.

To add to the confusion North had started dealing directly with the Iranians cutting out Ghorbanifar, who was threatening to sue the American government in the courts for breach of contract. In September 1986 the Iranians paid $7 million direct into one of North's three Swiss bank accounts and North drew out $2 million to pay for 500 TOW missiles that were flown direct from America to Iran (which shows the true price of TOW missiles compared to what Iran was being charged). At the same time two giant Lockheed C-5A Galaxy transport aircraft flew from Clarke air-force base in the Philippines to Teheran with spare parts for Iran's F-4, F-5 and F-14 aircraft and some much needed radar equipment.[27] Both deliveries reached

Iran at the end of October when North was in Cyprus with large sums of cash, at the same time as the Archbishop of Canterbury's envoy Terry Waite was on the island.[28] These two arms shipments to Iran resulted in the much-publicised release of David Jacobsen to Terry Waite on 2 November 1986 which at the time was said to have been made on humanitarian grounds following Waite's appeal to the Iranians. It is now clear that Waite's involvement was peripheral and that he was used by North as a cover to conceal the true reason for Jacobsen's release. When asked how his release had been arranged Jacobsen and Waite both charged reporters with being irresponsible and endangering the lives of the remaining hostages.

In Iran Rafsanjani had come under strong attack from Khomeini supporters who accused him of siding with America by accepting arms from the Great Satan and helping to get some of their hostages released. In order to extricate himself Rafsanjani gave details of the entire American arms-supply operation to the Lebanese magazine *Al-Shiraa* which published them on 3 November, the day after Jacobsen's release. Jacobsen flew back to Washington for the ritual photocall with the president at the White House on 7 November and when reporters asked Reagan about the arms deal story the president said it had 'no foundation'.

But it was too late. At a White House meeting on 10 November Reagan argued that he had not been dealing with terrorists in Iran but only moderates. It was only then that George Shultz, Reagan's secretary of state, learned the president had actually signed an order authorising the arms shipments on 17 January and that he had not been consulted or told. A week later, on 17 November, Reagan told the American people on network television that 'We did not – repeat, did not – trade weapons or anything else for hostages. Nor will we.' The president claimed that only defensive weapons had been supplied to Iran and that it had all been legal. Reagan said nothing about the diversion of money from these sales to the Contras.

Although the American people had long realised that Reagan's administration was one of the most corrupt in the nation's history, even the most hardened supporter was amazed by these revelations.[29] But across the Atlantic the news stunned the British government. Reagan was their great friend and ally, with whom they had this supposed special relationship and who shared Mrs Thatcher's much-publicised belief that no deals of any kind should be made with terrorists or governments that supported terrorism. Indeed, Mrs Thatcher had risked her personal reputation by allowing American F-111 aircraft to attack Libya from British bases in April 1986. (Though in reality she had had no choice. It was repayment of the long-standing debt she owed the Americans from the 1982 Falklands War). In its usual puppet-like manner the British government went along with the White House, initially ridiculing the suggestion that America would have supplied arms to Iran. When the details began to trickle out it was reluctantly conceded that perhaps two Boeing 707 shipments might have been made. As the rest of the tawdry tale emerged the Foreign Office and Downing Street lapsed into embarrassed silence.

The French and Germans watched the whole affair with much amusement. During the same period both countries had done deals with Iran and paid ransoms to terrorist groups to get their hostages released and had been strongly criticised by Mrs Thatcher and President Reagan for breaking Western unity.

As the revelations gathered pace in America strenuous efforts were made to distance the president from the facts, while North busied himself with his office shredder. The stories came out one by one until eventually the diversion of funds to the Contras became known. Finally Americans and the rest of the world witnessed on television unbelievable scenes as a US Marine colonel and a US admiral both invoked the Fifth Amendment so that they need not tell the truth about their dishonest dealings. It was the first time in American history that serving officers did not dare say what their commander-in-chief had told them to do.

The inevitable scapegoats were found. Casey of the CIA died, taking his secrets to the grave; Poindexter resigned; and North went into a bizarre media limbo reserved for bogus patriots. Of all the participants Reagan came out best of all. With his junior staff loyally taking the blame and trying to pretend he knew nothing about it (despite his signature on the 17 January presidential order), Reagan began to believe he had known nothing about it and it is possible that he did not know what he was signing. But it is hard for an old actor to separate fact from fantasy. When Robert McFarlane was charged with withholding information from Congress about diverting arms sale funds to the Contras, Reagan openly joked that he had done the same and withheld information from Congress.[30] When North was charged with a number of very serious offences Reagan publicly announced that North was innocent and a hero.[31]

It will be interesting to see how President Bush deals with the continuing hostage/Contra problem, particularly as he was once head of the CIA. That Reagan managed to escape public disgrace was probably only because Americans found it very hard so soon after Nixon to see another president fall from grace, since the presidency is the last moral totem pole the nation possesses. To many observers Reagan had long ceased to be a president and become a king-like figure who communicated with his people in platitudinous homilies. Reagan may well have been the reincarnation of Henry II.

CHAPTER 4

SECRETS FOR SALE

In the early evening of 27 April 1982,[1] two officers from the Hereford police knocked on the door of Laburnum Cottage, a detached chalet-style house on the corner of Pittville Crescent Lane, Cheltenham. It was opened by a tall, balding, rather gaunt-looking man called Geoffrey Prime who worked as a sales representative in the area for the Peiroth Wine Company.

The officers explained that they were investigating a series of sexual assaults on young children in the Cheltenham area over the previous two years, and wanted to interview every owner of two-tone brown and cream 'S' registered Ford Mark IV Cortinas, since one had been seen in the vicinity of some of these assaults. Prime invited them into the house and answered their questions. The two policemen said they would return later when Prime's wife, Rhona, returned from shopping. When Rhona arrived, Prime explained that the police had called, what it was about, and that they would be back. Prime then said he must go out for about an hour, which he did. Some two hours later the two officers returned and asked Prime to give an account of his whereabouts on the date of the last assault, 21 April, to which he replied that he had been at home that day.

After the police left the Primes sat together in silence. Then Geoffrey told his wife that he had been responsible for the series of attacks in the area. Whatever passed between the two as the twilight gathered, one thing is certain. Rhona's strong Christian beliefs overcame any repulsion she may have felt at this terrible revelation and she immediately offered to support her husband. As a result Geoffrey Prime decided to unburden himself completely and told Rhona that he had been a Russian spy for fourteen years.

The next morning Prime telephoned Hereford police station and admitted to Detective Chief Inspector Smith that he was the person responsible for the assaults. The police said they would come round in about an hour and, in the meantime, Prime gave his wife £600, part of the money he had been paid by the Russians, and they drove into Cheltenham to settle all their outstanding bills. Shortly after they returned to the house the police arrived and Prime was arrested and charged with three indecent assaults. On 29 April he was remanded in custody by Hereford magistrates. To the police, it seemed a highly successful conclusion to a long search for a dangerous and sordid pervert.

Meanwhile Rhona still could not believe that her husband had been a Russian spy. But as she started to search through his belongings she came across what was obviously a complete spy's kit: a briefcase with a false bottom, sheets of secret writing paper, pre-addressed postcards to East Berlin, a small Minox-B camera, equipment for making microdots, and curious little books of five-figure numbers printed on cellulose, known in the intelligence profession as one-time pads.

For three weeks Rhona fought with her conscience, her Christian beliefs and her loyalty to her husband. She sought advice from her doctor, her priest and her solicitor. Of the three, the last was the most pragmatic. If she kept quiet she would have her husband home again quite soon. If she told the police that he was a spy she would be unlikely to have him home again for at least 20 years.

In the final days of May 1982 Rhona instructed her solicitor to ask Smith at Hereford police station to come and see her. After an interval of several days Smith and a colleague arrived at her house where her solicitor handed over Prime's spy kit together with a statement from Rhona. Smith was not very impressed and told Rhona not to worry as some people liked to fantasise that they were James Bond. However, after Smith inspected the items more carefully back at the police station, he soon changed his mind and hastily called Special Branch. One look was enough for them. They called MI5. The assembled intelligence officers stood round the table looking at Prime's spy kit in stunned horror.

For Prime had been no ordinary spy. From 1968, he had worked at the Government Communications Headquarters (GCHQ) in Cheltenham, and though he had officially resigned from GCHQ in 1977 it was clearly evident that his spying activities had not ceased then.

MI5 immediately contacted GCHQ to find out what sort of work Prime had been doing there. As the shock waves rippled through GCHQ at the news their worst fears were confirmed. This was not a case of some junior employee passing on the odd photocopy here and there. Prime had worked on the most secret and sensitive projects known to GCHQ, including one called *Rhyolite*. What was worse, it was an American project. Now GCHQ had to tell its transatlantic partners that everything had been compromised to the Russians by a spy who had been stumbled upon by accident.

Prime was born on 21 February 1938, at Stoke-on-Trent in Staffordshire, in the manufacturing north of England. Prime had an unhappy childhood. At school he was very much a loner, could not make friends easily, and even feigned illness and played truant to avoid attending. He was later to claim that he had been the victim of sexual assault by an adult relative.

In 1956, at the age of 18, Prime began his national service (then compulsory for every male in Britain) with the Royal Air Force.[2] He had hoped to be selected for air-crew duties but discovered that he was colour blind. Believing he had some aptitude for languages Prime applied to take a course in Russian. First, however, he had to sign on for a nine-year engagement after which, in September 1956, he was posted to a special services college, RAF Crail, in Scotland.

Although Prime failed the first Russian course he passed the second one in April 1957. He was then promoted to acting sergeant and sent to London University for an advanced Russian language course. Evidently Prime did not do very well, because after only three months he gave up the course and returned to his unit. Losing the acting rank of sergeant Prime became a storeman and served as such from 1957 to 1963. In April 1962, after a tour of duty in Kenya, Prime returned to Britain and reapplied for a Russian language course. This time he did rather better and by May 1964 he had qualified in Russian to GCE O-level.

Prime had his first introduction into the world of intelligence when that same month he was posted to RAF Gatow, in West Berlin, as a voice radio Sigint operator. For the next four years his duties were quite simple and involved monitoring Russian voice transmissions in East Berlin and East Germany. Clearly, Prime did his work well and in May 1968 was promoted to the rank of sergeant.

Five months earlier, in January, Prime had decided to become a spy for the Russians. What prompted him to make this decision is unclear. The official report was later to make vague references to Prime having been disturbed by the sight of poverty while serving in Kenya and that the British government's support for the white minority Rhodesian government, plus the American involvement in Vietnam, had all contrived to make him believe that capitalism was corrupt. Prime was also said to have been affected by Communist propaganda while serving in Berlin.

Much more likely is that Prime had already developed his perverted interest in young girls and this had come to the notice of Russian or East German intelligence agents who would, as a matter of course, target odd lonely servicemen like Prime working in military intelligence in West Berlin. These agents are very experienced at striking up what appear to be chance friendships and then detecting, and apparently encouraging, deviant sexual behaviour, such as homosexuality and paedophilia. The odd thing is that while the East European intelligence agencies are so good at detecting these behaviour patterns in Westerners, our own counter-intelligence agencies like MI5 never seem able to recognise them. It is, therefore, highly probable that Prime was lured into a situation where his paedophiliac activities entrapped him so that he was blackmailed by the Russians into becoming a spy. Prime's own version of events was that he simply handed a note to a Russian officer at one of the checkpoints stating that he would be willing to spy for the Russians.

The Russians arranged a meeting with Prime at the Friedrichstrasse subway station in East Berlin and, after satisfying themselves that he was not a plant, gave him a small Minox camera and showed him how to use it to photograph documents. During the next six months Prime had regular meetings with his Russian controllers in East Berlin and on each occasion he handed over rolls of film containing photographs he had taken of documents, for which he was paid £40. Some of the documents were not particularly secret but others were and Prime was also able to tell the Russians which of their transmissions particularly interested RAF intelligence and which codes were being read. Furthermore, whatever his role at that time, Prime was a small and very cheap acorn in the intelligence game that might one day grow into a large, productive tree.

Prime's engagement with the RAF was due to end in August 1968 and the Russians suggested he apply for a job with GCHQ. First, however, he needed to be trained as a professional spy. On his way back to England from West Berlin, Prime made a detour via Amsterdam back to East Berlin. Here he was taken to the KGB headquarters at Karlshorst and for a week underwent intensive training.

He was shown how to identify 'allo messages' on short-wave radio.[3] These are voice broadcasts reading out lists of five-figure code numbers. He was taught the art of secret writing, how to encrypt a message and reduce it in size to a microdot that can be placed in the text of an ordinary letter, further instruction with the Minox camera, and how to leave and collect material at dead-letter drops in Britain. Above all, Prime was shown how to use the one-time code. These are small pads containing columns of five-figure groups. Only two identical pads exist. As each page of numbers is used it is destroyed, hence the expression 'one time'. Because the code groups are completely random and unique, the system cannot be broken.

At the end of his week's training Prime was given a set of one-time pads, some secret writing paper and £400, all concealed in a briefcase with a secret compartment. Any future meetings would be held in Austria. Prime then continued his interrupted journey to Britain where he applied to join GCHQ. He was exactly the sort of person GCHQ liked to recruit for their routine duties[4]: a good service background, excellent knowledge of Russian, especially military and technical expressions, ability to adhere to a strict daily routine, and an unblemished character. But before Prime could join he had to be positively vetted.[5]

Positive vetting had begun in Britain in 1951. It had come about as the result of the decision by the Labour prime minister, Clement Attlee, in March 1948, that known Communists or Fascists would no longer be allowed to work in any job which was vital to the security of the state. In the past it had been up to MI5 and Special Branch to offer any information it might have on an applicant. The new procedures required all civil servants and members of the armed forces who had regular and constant access to the most highly classified defence information to be positively screened.

Everyone in this category was given a questionnaire in which they had to detail their antecedent history, declare any past or present sympathies or connections with Communism or Fascist organisations, and then give the names and addresses of two character referees. Ideally, these referees should have known them for many years, perhaps going back to their school days, and could testify as to their character and attitudes. All this was in addition to checks made with police and MI5 records to see if the individual had any criminal or extreme political connections.

The idea was excellent in theory. But, in practice, it was not successful at preventing spies and traitors from getting their hands on secret information. The obvious flaws in the scheme were that spies and traitors were unlikely to admit their true sympathies while referees were reluctant to pass on some odd bit of gossip about a person that might have happened many years ago. Positive vetting has never managed to catch a single spy or traitor.

Prime had first been positively vetted in May 1966 while with the RAF in Berlin. For GCHQ's new vetting, Prime gave three referees; two colleagues who had worked with him in the RAF, and a Mr Bowers who had known him since childhood. None had anything adverse to say about Prime so on 9 September 1968 Prime's security clearance was approved and on 30 September he joined GCHQ as a Linguistic Specialist Grade IV.

In fact, while Prime was being positively vetted for his new job with GCHQ he was in East Berlin undergoing his spy training from the Russians.

Prime began his training at the Joint Technical Language Service (JTLS) at St Dunstan's Hill, in the city of London. The work was very boring and consisted of listening to hours of tape recordings of intercepted telephone calls, telex and radio morse messages sent by the various East European diplomatic and trade missions in London, and then transcribing summaries to be sent to GCHQ at Cheltenham. On 30 June 1969 Prime passed his language examination and became a fully fledged civil servant and transcriber. The official report on Prime naturally plays down his spying activities at JTLS and, while the information he was handling may not have been of top-grade sensitivity, it was extremely useful to the Russians.

Prime was able to tell them which circuits were being monitored, what information was being obtained from them, whether any telephone scramblers had been penetrated, whether MI5 had managed to place any bugging devices inside various buildings, and, of course, a mass of information about the internal workings of the JTLS itself. All this would have enabled the Russians, and their East European allies, to send disinformation over these circuits whilst ensuring that really important information went by other routes.

Whatever Prime told the KGB during his first year at the JTLS it was wise enough to encourage him. In October 1969 Prime picked up an 'allo message' in one-time-pad code on his new, powerful short-wave receiver. This sent him to a dead-letter box in the Esher area where he found a letter of congratulations and £400. It is worth noting that the sums of money Prime is said to have received from the KGB are based on what Prime later told MI5 after his arrest. Not surprisingly most spies, when they are caught, tend to denigrate the value of what they handed over and what they were paid.

Prime's new job and extra income had a marked effect on his previously solitary social life. In March 1969 Prime contacted a marriage bureau and was introduced to Miss Helena Organ, a teacher. After only three weeks they became engaged and on 9 August 1969 were married. From the start it was not a happy relationship. Prime felt inferior to Helena who because of her teaching qualifications earned more than he did. The marriage was not sexually successful because Prime was continuing with his paedophiliac activities, keeping notes about young girls, some of whom he telephoned. It is highly likely that his KGB controllers were aware of this.

Despite these personal problems Prime continued to work and spy at the JTLS using his Minox camera to photograph anything of interest that came his way. In 1969 he paid a visit to Vienna, ostensibly on holiday, in order to contact his KGB controllers and hand over the films he had accumulated. They told him how pleased they were with his work, encouraged him to go on as before without attracting any attention to himself and gave him more money. By May 1970 Prime had more to pass on and left his films in a dead-letter box in the Abbey Wood area of London. Later in 1970 Prime visited Dublin where he met his controller and handed over yet more films in return for money.

Throughout 1971 the same pattern continued. Prime again met with his KGB friends in Rome,[6] and also left other material at dead-letter drops in Britain. From a dead-letter box near Banstead railway station, in Surrey, he collected fresh supplies of one-time pads, secret writing paper, and a further £400. During 1972 Prime visited Cyprus where he again met his controllers but later that year also managed to lose his set of one-time pads. He wrote a secret letter to East Berlin explaining what had happened and received an acknowledgement via an 'allo message'. But the KGB were in no hurry to reactivate Prime, since he had given them all the useful information they needed about the JTLS, and they decided to let him become a sleeper.

In 1973 two important things happened. In April, his wife Helena found a large sum of money in their flat. How much is not known but it was sufficiently large to arouse her suspicions. This raises the question as to whether Prime told the truth about the sums of money he received from the KGB. According to Helena, Prime told her that the money had been paid to him by the Russians in return for information. Helena then subsequently told a close friend, a Miss Barsby, that Prime was a Russian spy. Miss Barsby was later to tell the official inquiry that she had threatened to tell the police but Helena then said she would deny the story.

What makes all this so bizarre is that also during 1973 Prime's regular positive-vetting check fell due. One of the referees he gave was Miss Barsby. Unfortunately, Miss Barsby took an instant dislike to the security officer who interviewed her (because he asked so many personal questions about her rather than Prime), and as a result she decided not to tell him about Helena's revelation.

It is hard to know what to make of this weird tale. Why should Prime so readily confess to being a spy when Helena had found nothing that suggested this? He could easily have explained away the money with any number of plausible excuses. Helena was an extremely intelligent and responsible person whose marriage to Prime had proved a disaster, and was now seeking a divorce. She must have known the importance of Prime's work, yet made no attempt to contact the authorities. Miss Barsby's attitude is even stranger unless, of course, she feared that by going to the police she might somehow implicate Helena. Inevitably, one wonders if a certain amount of hindsight has influenced these stories. What it does seem to show is that although Prime was later to be described as inadequate with women he evidently generated a remarkable degree of loyalty from his two wives.

On 18 November 1973 Prime's security clearance was reconfirmed and in the following year, by which time Prime had agreed with Helena to a divorce, it was again confirmed, then again in February 1976. In all Prime was positively vetted six times.

In December 1974 the Russians gave Prime a briefcase with a secret compartment, in which he found a letter inviting him to Vienna the next year (1975), new sets of one-time pads, more secret writing material, some pre-addressed postcards to East Berlin addresses and £400. The KGB had decided to wake their sleeping agent.

This was because by 1975 the JTLS had been moved from London to Cheltenham and due to his excellent steady work Prime was to be promoted. The official report on the Prime affair goes to enormous efforts to play down the importance of his new work, merely stating that he became a Higher Linguist Specialist. In fact, Prime had been given *Byeman* clearance to work in GCHQ's J Division where he would have access to the most secret material being received from the CIA's *Rhyolite* satellite programme. Later he was also told about the even more secret, and more powerful, versions to be launched called *Argus* (for *Advanced Rhyolite*) and *Pyramider*, and a satellite system developed by the US Navy to detect Russian nuclear submarines when they surfaced anywhere in the world.

As soon as he had been fully briefed about his new work in J Division, Prime took a package holiday to Vienna in the summer of 1975 where he met his KGB friends once more. He took with him photographs of all the documents he could find about the *Rhyolite* project. The official report claims that Prime could not have had a detailed discussion about the material he had taken with him because the KGB agents lacked the necessary technical knowledge. This is absurd. Apart from what his photographed material revealed Prime would have been able to explain what *Rhyolite* was able to do without difficulty as he spoke perfect Russian. At this meeting Prime claims to have been given £800.

Prime did well in J Divison and by November 1976 was made section head and given the additional responsibility of Personnel Security Supervisor. This role allowed him to talent spot other potential agents for the KGB and it is alleged that Prime passed on to them the names of 140 such people, none of whom have ever been identified.

While Prime was handing over the innermost secrets of GCHQ's J Division to the KGB, the same was happening to the NSA across the Atlantic.[7] On 29 July 1974, 21-year old Christopher Boyce joined the Classified Material Division of TRW in California, having been cleared by the FBI to handle top secret material. Boyce was a drug user and university drop-out who associated with other drug addicts, was deeply hostile to United States institutions and values, and particularly despised the CIA. Yet by 15 November 1974 Boyce had been given *Byeman* clearance to work on the *Rhyolite* project for which he had been required to sign the CIA clearance Form #2441 – Special Project Secrecy Agreement.

In January 1975, Boyce met 23-year-old Andrew Lee who he had previously known at the Palos Verdes High School back in 1966. Lee was also a drug addict and dealer and since 1971 had been arrested several times, serving a jail sentence in 1974. Boyce now told Lee of his secret work at TRW and suggested that together they could sell this information to the Chinese or Russians for a large sum of money. Lee agreed to work with him. In March 1975, Boyce gave Lee some NSA *Okana* computer programming cards, and some lengths of key tapes used with the NSA's KG-13 and KW-7 crypto-graphs which Lee then took to the Russian Embassy in Mexico City with a note from Boyce offering to provide more material.

The Russians were only too delighted to accept and over the next 18 months Boyce gave Lee a continuous stream of *Rhyolite* and similar material to pass on for which the KGB paid over $60,000. The amount of material they handed over to the Russians, both in Mexico City and later in Vienna, was of embarrassing proportions since it included every technical detail of the entire operations handled by TRW on behalf of the NRO, CIA and NSA.

Effectively, therefore, from the moment Prime, Boyce and Lee began their espionage activities, *Rhyolite* was finished. The Russians knew exactly what it was capable of doing (and therefore could judge what it had scooped up since it was first launched), and could now send carefully doctored disinformation over those circuits vulnerable to its prying antennae.

One of the first things they did was to programme their on-board computers to transmit false telemetry which they knew *Rhyolite* would pick up.[8] This purported to show that the Russians were having problems with their rockets, leading the Americans to believe that they were far ahead of the Russians in space technology. Only later did the Americans discover that they had been well and truly tricked and that the Russians were able to send large payloads into space without difficulty while the Americans fumbled with their Challenger space project.

Had Boyce and Lee not fallen out over the amount of money they were sharing they would never have been discovered. Certainly no one at either TRW or the NSA suspected there was a leak of such massive proportions. In January 1977, entirely due to their own stupidity, both were caught by the FBI and later that year sentenced to long terms of imprisonment with Boyce receiving 40 years. In theory Boyce is now due for parole but it seems most unlikely he will get it although two Australian government ministers, Peter Staples and Peter Duncan, together with several other Labour MPs, are busily campaigning on Boyce's behalf to have him released on the grounds that he was not a criminal but a conscientious objector who revealed American violations of Australian sovereignty at the NSA's Pine Gap intercept station.[9] Whatever Boyce's conscience may have told him to do, he certainly did not overlook the opportunity to accept large payments from the KGB.

The arrest of Boyce and Lee caused a good deal of smugness within GCHQ. It also gave Prime much cause for thought even though it was obvious no one had any suspicions that there was a leak of equal proportions at GCHQ. Meanwhile, Prime's social life was on the up again. On moving to Cheltenham from London Prime had taken lodgings in a house owned by Mrs Rhona Ratcliff, a very attractive 33-year-old divorcee with three young children. The chemistry of affection turned to love and on 18 June 1977 they were married. Whether because of the new responsibilities of a wife and three stepchildren, or the news of Boyce and Lee's sentences, Prime decided that he had had enough of spying.

On 28 September 1977 Prime resigned from GCHQ. Bearing in mind that he had provided the KGB with a steady flow of GCHQ's most secret material and that there was every reason to believe he would rise to even more senior positions,[10] the fact that the Russians allowed him to resign means that by this date Prime was not their only spy inside GCHQ.[11] Had he been then there is no doubt the KGB would have forced him to stay.

The KGB realised that not only was Prime becoming a worried spy but his paedophiliac activities were making him a liability. It decided to let him resign but kept him on its payroll so that he could act as an adviser inspecting material brought out of GCHQ by other spies, and be compensated for his loss of income. To this end, Prime needed a suitable cover.

He found it by becoming a taxi driver. The official report is very uninformative about this period of Prime's career. It claims that he resigned because he was nervous about giving lectures. This is untrue. Other GCHQ staff have confirmed that had this been the case it would have been a simple matter to revise Prime's duties and excuse him from lecturing.[12] The report is also remarkably vague as to whether anyone at GCHQ made any inquiries as to why a senior and well-paid employee, who had had access to some of the most sensitive information and was obviously destined for further promotion, suddenly left and became a taxi driver just at the time he had taken on the added financial responsibility of a wife and three stepchildren. None of this makes any sense and the stark truth is that no one at GCHQ bothered to make any inquiries at all.

What Prime did for the KGB between September 1977 and April 1982 is completely ignored in the official report. Prime claims that for over two years, until April 1980, he heard nothing further from the KGB. Then he was asked to come to Vienna, which he did on 16 May 1980, when he handed over 15 rolls of film he had taken prior to his resignation. For this he was paid £600.

But the KGB behaved very strangely on this occasion.[13] Instead of meeting Prime secretly the agents took him about Vienna quite openly, dining him at the best restaurants where they knew Austrian and Western intelligence agencies would recognise them as KGB agents and soon identify Prime as being an ex-GCHQ employee. Clearly the KGB had decided Prime had outlived his value and decided to sacrifice him to British intelligence so as to distract attention from its other, more important, spies still working within GCHQ. As it turned out, however, Western intelligence agencies failed to notice the KGB or Prime.

Eighteen months later, Prime claims he was invited to East Berlin, where he arrived on 16 November 1981. At this meeting he was given a fresh supply of one-time pads, secret writing paper and £4,000.

It hardly requires an intelligence expert to see that Prime's account (if it is his account and not a piece of MI5 disinformation) is absolute nonsense. If Prime had really finished spying in 1977 the KGB would hardly have invited him twice to Europe and given him fresh spying equipment and £4,600 which is far more than he claims he was paid in all the previous years. Nor is it likely that Prime would have held on to 15 rolls of film containing vital intelligence for more than two years before handing them over to his controllers.

Obviously, Prime continued working for the KGB by acting as an adviser checking over material brought out of GCHQ by other less experienced spies. Prime's taxi would have been excellent cover, allowing someone to drive around the countryside while Prime examined the material and photographed it. His knowledge would have enabled him to advise as to what other pieces of information to look for and bring out for him to inspect. Even if the other spies were not as highly placed as Prime had been, with his help even the most lowly placed spy could have found the right material.

This would explain why, five years after his resignation, Prime still had in his possession an active spy kit complete with sets of one-time pads, microdot instructions and current radio frequency lists. At the time of his arrest he was also in possession of a copy of a top-secret internal GCHQ report that had only been published a few weeks earlier. It would also explain why on the evening Prime was first visited by the police he left the house for an hour on an unexplained mission. The most obvious reason was that he went to warn his controller, probably through some intermediary, that he was under police suspicion and likely to be arrested for a crime unconnected with his spying.

One other question that also remains unanswered is whether Prime had access to a radio transmitter.[14] Certainly no transmitter was found at his house but Prime might have buried it in an adjoining building plot which was part of the garden of his house before he bought it and having lain undisturbed for many years is only now being built on. When the two Russian spies Peter and Helen Kroger were arrested at their Ruislip bungalow in January 1961, MI5 and Special Branch discovered a hoard of espionage equipment including a transmitter. But a second, even more powerful, transmitter was accidentally discovered by the bungalow's new owners buried in the garden in 1980.

Prime was such an important spy that it is hard to believe that the KGB relied only on occasional dead-letter drops and visits to Vienna. The one-time-code pads could, of course, have been used for outgoing as well as incoming messages. If there was a transmitter, then it would suggest that the GCHQ spy ring involved more people than just Prime alone. And that might explain why, several weeks after Prime's arrest had become public knowledge, the same 'allo broadcasts' were still reading out lists of five-figure groups on the frequency Prime had used.

As the full extent of Prime's version of his activities was revealed, MI5 and GCHQ were appalled at having to confess to their American partners. Fortunately, because of the Boyce and Lee scandal, the NSA were in no position to make too much of a fuss. Nevertheless, they did want to know how Prime, with all his character defects, had managed to pass no less than six security checks. GCHQ countered by pointing out that Boyce had even worse character defects yet in less than six months had received a top secret clearance from the Department of Defence, a *Byeman* strategic intelligence clearance from the CIA, and a high-level cryptographic clearance from the

NSA, yet had managed to avoid any suspicions. His arrest, like that of Prime, had been accidental.

The truth of the matter was, and still is, that many people who work in the closed, secretive world of intelligence develop all manner of peculiar habits. Some people would say that after ten years of this work they go slightly crazy. In World War II GCCS had some very odd people on its staff at Bletchley Park. One wonders how many would have survived today's positive-vetting check and, perhaps, the polygraph (lie-detector). For example, Alan Turing, a brilliant mathematician who designed one of the earliest computers to break the Enigma keys, was not only a homosexual (which would bar him from working at GCHQ today), but possessed many weird obsessions[15] and ended up committing suicide by biting into an apple he had coated with potassium cyanide.

While GCHQ and the NSA argued about the matter, the next important task was to see that the British public did not learn the truth of what had happened. The fact that the Russians had been privy to GCHQ's innermost secrets for years was beside the point. If the taxpayers discovered that years of supposedly secret work had been wasted, they might start asking questions as to whether GCHQ was really efficient and giving good value for money, and whether a much smaller and cheaper organisation might do the really necessary work better.

Fortunately the British media was legally prohibited from commenting upon the case until after Prime stood trial at London's Old Bailey on 10 November 1982 before the Lord Chief Justice, Lord Lane, when he pleaded guilty to the charges of spying and indecent assault. As soon as the court started to hear evidence of what Prime had done it went into secret session, so that the British public was not able to know what the Russians already knew. Prime was sentenced to 35 years' imprisonment for spying, and three years for the indecent assault. One can now see what sort of sentence Prime would have received had Rhona not told the police that he was a spy.

With the trial complete, and Prime safely locked away in Long Lartin prison, the media and parliament could indulge themselves with the luxury of hindsight. Mrs Margaret Thatcher, the prime minister, as head of the security services, came under the usual ritualistic attack from the Labour opposition although, when they were in power, similar spy scandals had occurred. The prime minister made the conventional defence of the intelligence fraternity by asserting everything was under control although she was unable to tell parliament how she knew this. When asked if there should be some control by parliament over the security services, Mrs Thatcher caused considerable amusement by stating:

I believe the present arrangements are the most appropriate and, if we went further, we would undermine the efficiency of the intelligence services.

In reality, of course, the term 'present arrangements' is meaningless. The security services all operate as they wish, spend what they can squeeze out of frightened politicians, and are accountable to no one because, they claim, their work is so secret. However, to placate parliament it was agreed that an inquiry would be held into the Prime affair by the Security Commission, headed by Lord Bridge.

Inquiries of this nature are a British way of deflecting attention from any embarrassing incident. They have two immediate advantages: that the impression is given something is being done, and that while the inquiry is taking place ministers can avoid answering any further questions. The inquiry began on 11 November 1982 and completed its report by May 1983. The part of the report the public was allowed to see was not worth the paper it was printed on. None of the members of the Commission had any first-hand experience of intelligence operations so they had to rely on what they were told by others and, looking at the list of people they had interviewed, it is hardly surprising that they were given a version of events that suited the intelligence fraternity and GCHQ rather than the truth. The one person the Commission did not interview was Prime himself, so the inquiry was like *Hamlet* without the prince.

Throughout the report the Commission deliberately plays down the extent and value of Prime's spying. He is depicted as a sad, solitary, inadequate man who did a little bit of spying on the side. In fact, Prime was a very clever and extremely important spy. His work with the RAF in Berlin is brushed aside as unimportant. So too is his later work at the JTLS. Although the report lists the large number of dead-letter box drops Prime admitted making, and the frequent foreign trips to meet the KGB, the Commission did not consider this confirmed the enormous amount of information he had passed on. The report casually mentions Prime's transfer to Cheltenham and his subsequent promotion to J Division without giving any indication of the sort of work he was doing.

When it comes to Prime's sudden resignation from GCHQ in September 1977 the report is incredibly naive and accepts Prime's version (or more likely MI5's) that in the following five years he simply worked as a taxi driver, and later a wine salesman, who went on visits abroad to meet the KGB (who gave him £4,600), and somehow had need of microdot equipment and one-time-code pads.

Much of the report is concerned with finding excuses for the abysmal lack of security within GCHQ that allowed Prime to remove thousands of top-secret documents from supposedly secure vaults during his lunch hour and copy them on GCHQ's own photocopiers. The report concludes that these security lapses were quite unusual and that no one was to blame. But the report does not mention that as long ago as 1973 Jock Kane, who had worked for GCHQ at Cheltenham, Hong Kong, Singapore, Turkey and Aden, had sought to expose what he believed were very serious security weaknesses and corruption within GCHQ.

Jock Kane had joined GCHQ as a radio operator straight from the RAF in November 1946. Over the next 25 years he worked his way up through GCHQ serving in virtually every section so that he came to know a great deal about how the organisation worked. In 1973, Kane discovered that there was a great deal of fraud going on within GCHQ connected with bogus payments for subsistence allowances. Members of staff sent on training courses at Bletchley Park, or on detachment to other GCHQ outposts like Edzell in Scotland, were claiming their full allowances over periods like the weekend when they had in fact returned home. The frauds had come to light because one GCHQ employee supposedly at Edzell had been involved in a traffic accident near his house in Cheltenham which had been reported to the police.

When Kane went out to Hong Kong in the mid-1970s he uncovered even worse frauds. Each GCHQ employee was then being paid £600 per month rent allowance. Kane discovered that local Chinese landlords, who seemed to know far too much about the inner workings of GCHQ, were renting apartments to GCHQ employees at lower rates, then rendering bogus invoices for £600 a month and sharing the difference. As the GCHQ staff in Hong Kong totalled 600 the amount of money being defrauded was very substantial. Kane also discovered that some senior GCHQ officers were apparently involved in this fraud by authorising the allocation of apartments with dishonest Chinese landlords.

It has to be said, of course, that cheating on allowances and expenses is one of the great British traditions and is euphemistically known as an 'old Spanish custom'. Such practices are commonplace in all kinds of industries. Over the years, these frauds are tacitly allowed to continue until they form part of an employee's untaxed salary. Not surprisingly, therefore, Kane became most unpopular when he tried to draw attention to these malpractices and he found it impossible to interest senior management within GCHQ, perhaps because they too were involved and a full inquiry would have been very embarrassing. Kane argued that frauds of this nature could easily lead to GCHQ personnel being blackmailed, particularly as espionage was a serious problem in Hong Kong where a spy ring had already been discovered in the GCHQ station at Little Sai Wan, and more than 150 people were arrested for spying in the colony between 1970–76.

Kane also alleged that security within GCHQ was very lax, mainly because the Security Division was staffed by elderly people on the point of retirement who lacked the necessary initiative and authority. Kane found that there was no proper control of photocopiers and anyone could run off documents without having to record the number of copies in a register, nor was any record being kept of the daily totaliser readings of each copier. Far too many people had access to highly classified material and it was commonplace to find staff wandering around high-security areas without proper clearance. On one occasion, in Turkey, Kane found the setting instructions for the Typex cipher machines lying around unchecked and even being read by the local cleaners.

When Kane complained about such matters he was chided by his colleagues for taking security too seriously. But Kane persevered and over the next few years had meetings with the Special Branch, the Director of Public Prosecutions, the Security Commission, and eventually Kenneth Warren MP. Warren took the matter up with the then prime minister, James Callaghan, who in 1978 asked a Home Office minister, Sir James Waddell, to investigate Kane's complaints. By the time he had finished in April 1979 Mrs Thatcher was in Downing Street and Waddell's report was never published.

On 20 May 1980 Mrs Thatcher told parliament that Kane's allegations were unfounded although, as she spoke, Prime was in Vienna handing over GCHQ's top secrets to the KGB. On 27 May 1980 Waddell had a long telephone conversation with a television journalist[16] in which he said he was not anxious to embarrass the prime minister but tacitly inferred that her assertion that Kane's allegations were 'unfounded' was not what his report had concluded. Plainly, Waddell's report was suppressed by the prime minister because it contained far too many embarrassing revelations about GCHQ that she did not wish the public to know.

Having retired from GCHQ in November 1978, four years later Kane tried to publish a book about corruption and lax security within GCHQ,[17] but this was seized by Special Branch and the publishers, Robert Hale, were injuncted to prevent it from seeing the light of day. Kane himself was interviewed at length by Special Branch but was not prosecuted, doubtless because the government knew that a trial would only serve to publicise his complaints. As Robert Hale decided not to fight the injunction, Kane wrote a second book, *The Hidden Depth of Treachery*, which contained much of the information from his earlier book, and Transworld Publications Ltd agreed to handle this. When the government heard of this second book, further injunctions were served on Transworld to stop publication. However, on this occasion, the publishers decided to fight the case and the matter is now before the courts.

Kane was not interviewed by the Prime inquiry despite the fact that he could have explained his specific concerns over security from years of first-hand experience which were directly relevant to the case. Why wasn't he interviewed? Because he would have given far too truthful an account of what went on inside GCHQ and that might have obliged the inquiry to publish the truth, which would have exposed that the government ignored Kane and misled parliament, and GCHQ's inefficient management.

The inquiry devotes a great deal of space to the idea of introducing the polygraph, often called the lie-detector machine, to GCHQ.[18] This is popular in America but, as its growing list of spies and traitors shows, is not necessarily infallible. Prime had become so used to living a triple life of lies, as a married man with three stepchildren working as a senior analyst in GCHQ, an important and well-paid Russian spy, and a determined and calculating paedophile, that he would probably have defeated the polygraph anyway. Prime had no difficulty in concealing his complex lifestyle because so many people in places like GCHQ behave oddly that it is very hard to differentiate between eccentricity and genius.

But the most important aspect of the entire Prime affair was overlooked, not only by the Security Commission but also by the media and parliament. This was that although Prime had been spying inside GCHQ from 1968 to 1982 and passing on to the Russians the most sensitive and important secrets from the very heart of American and British Sigint, not a single whisper about his activities ever leakèd back to the West through GCHQ's and the NSA's own Sigint activities, MI6's operations, or any of the various Russian defectors during those 14 years.[19] This is quite incredible. Virtually every other major traitor in our midst has been exposed by a defector. This means that Prime's information was so valuable that the KGB over all those years protected his identity so carefully that no one, outside a tiny group, knew where the information was coming from.

Following Prime's trial MI6 began an intensive inquiry to try to establish why none of its contacts had ever heard of a leak of such a magnitude within GCHQ, and whether there were any signs that other spies were still operating there. Unfortunately, in the intelligence world, the more you search for something the more risk you run of people telling you what you want to hear. Eventually, in late 1983, Oleg Gordievsky, a senior KGB officer who defected on 12 September 1985 and had been a double agent for several years, told MI6 that the Russians had a spy in Cyprus who was passing sensitive Sigint information back to the KGB.

Cyprus was an ideal choice because GCHQ operates there, with the Ministry of Defence, an important eavesdropping station[20] run by the 9th Signals Regiment, based at Mercury Barracks near the village of Ayios Nikolaos about 25 miles from Larnaca. As soon as MI6 received this news from Gordievsky it alerted MI5 and military security who descended upon the Cyprus base in early 1984 and started looking for the spy. To their delight they found not just one spy but eight; five members of the Royal Air Force and three from the Army. It seemed that MI6's information was right and that this nest of spies had handed over more than 2,000 top-secret documents to glamorous Russian agents in bars and exotic nightclubs on the island, and had also been involved in deviant sexual orgies.

The eight servicemen were brought back to Britain and held in custody for over a year until their trial began at the Old Bailey on 10 June 1985, at which they all pleaded not guilty. As is the rule with trials involving spying and national security, all the potential jurors were carefully vetted by Special Branch and MI5 to ensure that they were from the right sort of backgrounds, likely to support the state and that none of them had ever held any controversial political or social views. Any who failed to satisfy Special Branch were automatically excluded. The defence at that time (the rules have since been altered) had the right to challenge four jurors without giving cause so, as there were eight defendants, that gave a total of 32 potential challenges.

The trial lasted four months until 28 October 1985. Most of it was held in secret so, as usual, the British public was unable to judge the facts. However, from the officially inspired leaks that somehow found their way into sections of the media sympathetic to the government, it looked as if the Crown had an open-and-shut case and the verdict would be a triumph for British intelligence. But much to the horror of the government, the Ministry of Defence and the intelligence services, one by one each of the eight defendants was found not guilty and walked free from the court.

Denied their great intelligence triumph, the government and MI5 began an intensive disinformation campaign through their usual collection of tame journalists[21] and instant experts who blamed the acquittals on the defence lawyers who, by using their right to challenge, had got rid of all the respectable, upper-class, decent, right-wing jurors and packed the jury with left-wing woolly-minded liberals from the uneducated social classes who were automatically anti-government and favourably inclined towards the defendants.[22] The fact that Special Branch and MI5 had vetted all potential jurors to ensure that no liberally minded people were included was quietly forgotten.

The truth of the matter was far simpler. There never was a spy in Cyprus. Gordievsky had been misled by a clever in-house cover-story prepared by the KGB to protect a far better-placed spy or spies. All intelligence agencies use this technique so that secrets do not leak from one department to another and possibly into the hands of someone who is later captured or defects. By saying it had a spy in Cyprus the KGB was able to explain away a good source of intelligence with a plausible cover. As with so many defectors Gordievsky was trying to please MI6 by telling it what it wanted to hear.

Because the military police were so certain there must be a spy, or spies, in the 9th Signals Regiment they made the classic error of interrogating suspects to the point where they will say anything the questioner wants. And that was what the eight servicemen did. The confessions they gave were false, so false in fact that one of the accused even admitted passing over documents to a Russian agent in a hotel that was not built at the time. Apart from the confessions there was no other evidence to put before the jury. For example, the prosecution sought to prove that over 2,000 secret documents were missing. But in the end they were obliged to concede that security within the base was so lax that no one knew exactly how many documents were unaccounted for nor was it possible to show if they had been destroyed in the proper manner, given to the Russians or mislaid. Quite sensibly the jury was not impressed by the Crown's case and threw it out. It is not hard to see why the trial was held in secret for had the public been able to witness such a ridiculous event it would have lost all confidence in MI5, MI6 and Special Branch.

As a result of this fiasco, which cost the taxpayer £5 million, the government attempted to hide its embarrassment by holding yet another inquiry,[23] this time into how the defendants had been treated while in military custody. The report of this inquiry wended its tedious way through over 100 pages and, with staggering naivety and a lot of legal hairsplitting, concluded that the eight servicemen had been unlawfully detained for part of the time but that none had been subjected to any threats of violence, torture or degrading treatment. Sensibly the eight accused refused to have any part in this charade.

The affair ended on a sordid note. Greatly upset at having wrecked the original investigation, the Ministry of Defence vented its anger on the eight acquitted servicemen and withdrew their security clearance, preventing them from returning to their Sigint work. Very reluctantly the Ministry was obliged to pay a total of £19,000 compensation to six of the defendants, which was but a fraction of what they would have received had they been civilians.

The Cyprus spy saga provided the KGB and GRU with great entertainment. A lot of counter-intelligence time and energy was wasted in chasing after non-existent spies and endless false trails while the Russians got on with their espionage operations elsewhere. All the evidence surrounding the Prime case clearly shows that there were, and still are, other spies working within GCHQ. Naturally, after Prime's exposure they were told to lie low and may not have been reactivated for some while. As a result the Prime case remains a very sensitive issue. On 15 November 1987, Rhona Prime took part in a BBC television *Everyman* programme[24] in which she very courageously explained the Christian beliefs that gave her the strength to stand by her husband in the long years ahead.[25] GCHQ was so alarmed at Rhona's participation that it insisted on seeing the video tape of the programme before it was transmitted[26] and, surprisingly for an organisation that claims to be independent, was allowed to do so by the BBC even though it contained no references to intelligence matters or GCHQ.

The legacy of what Prime did, who he recruited, how easily he got away with his treachery and for how long, and that he was only caught by accident, will haunt GCHQ for many years to come. How many other spies are sleeping as they rise up the promotion ladder?[27] Why are 'allo messages' still being broadcast?[28] Are they real and being received and acted on by other agents, or are they fake messages designed to keep MI5 searching for non-existent spies? The game of bluff and double-bluff is a long and convoluted one, often with no clear answer outcome.

Prime was able to spy for so long without being detected because security was so lax within GCHQ that no one bothered to make the simple checks on his background that would have immediately revealed grounds for suspicion. But because organisations like GCHQ are so secret they are able to conceal their misfits by claiming it would damage national security to have the organisation accountable to external checks. Exactly the same happened within MI5 in the case of Michael Bettaney, who managed to join MI5 despite being unsuitable in every possible way. How he slipped through its supposedly improved vetting procedures is, of course, something that must be hidden from the British people who are forever being assured that everything is all right with our intelligence services.

Bettaney was an unstable drunkard from a humble background who, after receiving a public-school and university education, became a Marxist. It is doubtful whether Bettaney had the slightest idea what Marxism meant since at about the same time he wanted to be a Catholic priest. He also showed great interest in Nazi right-wing style politics. One would imagine that with their vast computerised filing systems and abilities to spy on anyone they chose MI5, together with Special Branch, would have been able to detect something odd about Bettaney the first time he applied to join MI5 in 1975, particularly as he had a criminal conviction for fare dodging in 1970.

But, just as with previous misfits, Bettaney's behaviour patterns did not seem out of place. In 1982 he appeared in court again, charged with using an invalid ticket, and shortly afterwards was arrested for being drunk and disorderly wherepon he abused the policeman, shouting, 'You can't arrest me, I'm a spy'. None of this caused any worries when reported to his superiors at MI5. They evidently thought it quite normal behaviour for one of their officers because Bettaney was described by his MI5 colleagues as being intelligent, articulate, agreeable, and with a bizarre sense of humour. This included telling his colleagues that he was working for the Russians and they should 'Come and see me in my *dacha* when I retire'. For an organisation that can without difficulty find subversives in CND it is truly amazing that MI5 was unable to detect a misfit of this order under its very nose. Bettaney was positively vetted twice and, as with Prime, nothing adverse was reported about his background or personal lifestyle with the result that he was promoted to the Russian desk where security was so lax (just as Jock Kane found at GCHQ) that he could take secret files home and copy them whenever he wanted. When Bettaney's house was finally searched by Special Branch it was found to be packed with piles of secret documents taken from MI5, none of which had been missed.

Having decided to become a spy Bettaney chose the absurd method of hand-delivering a letter on 3 April 1983 to 42 Holland Park, the private residence of Arkady Gouk, second secretary at the Russian Embassy, giving details about the recent expulsion of three Russian diplomats.[29] When Gouk, not surprisingly, failed to show any interest, Bettaney pushed some highly secret papers through his letter box giving MI5's estimate of the KGB's London operation. Naturally Gouk thought he was being set up in a trap, which is an indication of how highly the Russians value MI5's efforts, and again failed to respond. The Russians soon tired of the nonsense and decided to blow Bettaney to MI5. Some reports say it was Gordievsky who did this in which case he was probably fed the Bettaney story as bait.

Despite the fact that Bettaney had been unable to give the Russians anything of value his trial in April 1984 (at which he was sentenced to 23 years' imprisonment) was held in secret, not to protect national security but simply so the British public would not learn of yet another MI5 scandal. As usual there was an inquiry which published its report in May 1985.[30] This stated that MI5 had detected Bettaney's treachery itself which was totally untrue. Until Gordievsky passed on the details of Bettaney's activities no one in MI5 had suspected anything, so once again the public was deliberately misled by those in authority attempting to hide their own inadequacies. Ironically, it was the government's lies over the Bettaney case that stirred Peter Wright far away in Tasmania into action to try to bring the public's attention to his long-held belief that MI5 was riddled with spies and incompetents, in turn leading to the *Spycatcher* affair.

For many years it was always assumed that these sort of problems were entirely a British disease and the Americans, with their huge resources and the use of the lie-detector, were able to weed out undesirables from their secret agencies. In truth exactly the same problems plague the NSA. With its vast organisation and its 20,000 employees, together with hundreds of civilian contractors working for the NSA on highly secret projects, how can it be sure that others like Boyce and Lee do not exist? It is tempting to think that the American armed services, with their highly controlled and disciplined lifestyle, would be able to control espionage activities in their midst more easily. But this is not so.

One evening, in early February 1968, Warrant Officer John A. Walker Jnr USN walked into the Russian Embassy on 16th Street, Washington, DC[31] and offered for sale a copy of a KL-47 cryptograph[32] key card for the current month.

Walker was born in 1938, joining the US Navy in October 1955, and after completing his basic training at the Bainbridge Training Centre in Maryland was sent to the Naval Schools Command, in Norfolk, Virginia, for training as a radio operator. After successfully completing the course, Walker applied to serve in submarines and in October 1960 was posted to the USS *Razorback*. Walker had married on 4 June 1957 and, by April 1960, he and his wife had three children, all girls, which placed a considerable strain on Walker's finances. In 1962, Walker was promoted to supervisory radio operator and posted to the newly commissioned nuclear submarine USS *Andrew Jackson*. Three years later he was promoted to senior operator on the *Simon Bolivar*, another nuclear submarine. By now Walker's wife, Barbara, had a fourth child, a son called Michael.

Together with a shipmate, William C. Wilkinson, who was also a chief radio operator, Walker decided to open a restaurant and bar near Charleston, in Virginia. It is an odd facet of US Navy life that servicemen are allowed to run civilian businesses on the side. Despite their high hopes it was not a success and Wilkinson soon pulled out of the partnership, leaving Walker with even greater financial problems. Also at this time the Naval Investigative Service ran a routine background check on Walker similar to the positive vetting system in Britain, but despite all Walker's problems his security vetting was approved. In April 1967, having been in the navy for 12 years, Walker was suddenly promoted to warrant officer and posted to the headquarters of submarine command, COMSUBLANT, at the Norfolk Naval Base in Virginia.

During the next year Walker's private life went from bad to worse. He had constant rows with his wife and children, the restaurant continued to lose money, his debts were mounting, and the Internal Revenue Service was demanding large sums in unpaid back taxes. And so it was that Walker rang the bell at the Russian Embassy and offered the US Navy's secrets for sale. Not surprisingly, the Russians were cautious. It might have been a trick. Nevertheless, a meeting was arranged in a Washington suburb three weeks later and Walker was to bring with him a list of the secret material he had access to.

All this was very similar to what had happened in Britain back in early 1970 when Maureen Bingham, the wife of a sub-lieutenant in the Royal Navy, called at the Russian Embassy in London and said that her husband would like to sell some secrets for cash. Like the Walkers, the Binghams had been living beyond their means and had substantial debts. Here too the Russians suspected a trap but just to see what was to be planted on them pretended to go along with Mrs Bingham. However, her visit had not passed unnoticed by MI5 watchers who with the help of naval intelligence quickly identified her as the wife of an electronics warfare officer serving on HMS *Rothesay*.

As a result all the papers Bingham had access to were carefully doctored so as to provide bogus information.[33] Bingham passed over what were supposed to be operational details of tactics used against Russian submarines and also technical information about American nuclear depth charges then in use with the Royal Navy. In all he was paid £2,800. The Russians were quite certain Bingham was a plant and that the information was false. They let the game go on for some while and then, tiring of the charade, told the CIA via a double agent that there was an important spy in the British Navy handing over secrets of their nuclear weapons, giving just enough information to identify Bingham. The CIA were naturally horrified and told MI5, who assured them they knew all about Bingham and were running him with false information. The CIA did not believe this and assumed MI5 were covering-up yet another leak in the sieve-like British security system.

In order to appease the CIA Bingham had to be arrested and on 13 March 1972, true to form, Mr Justice Bridge said 'the damage you have done is incalculable' and sentenced Bingham to 21 years' imprisonment. This convinced the CIA that Bingham had been a very important spy and MI5 had not told them the truth, all of which greatly amused the Russians. The irony was that this was one of the few occasions that MI5 actually managed to catch a spy on its own and then no one believed it. Although Bingham was certainly a spy he was kindly treated and freed on parole after only seven years.

Evidently the FBI was not watching the Russian Embassy in Washington as carefully as MI5 does in London otherwise Walker's visit would have been noticed. Three weeks later Walker kept his appointment with his Russian contact, the Russians in the meantime having carefully checked out his background and found out all about his lifestyle and debts, while in Moscow cryptanalysts experimented with his key card to see if it decrypted KL-47 intercepts which were used on the US Navy's fleet submarine broadcast channel. Walker told his contact all about the KL-47, KWR-37, KL-7 and KG-26 cryptographs, and the various frequencies used by the navy. Depending upon what Walker provided the Russians agreed to pay him between $2,000 and $4,000 a month in cash. Walker had sole access to the safe where the new sets of key cards were kept, and was able to break open the sealed packs, copy them in the same office and put them back in the safe without anyone noticing. It was so easy. So easy in fact that for a while the Russians could not believe that US Navy security was so lax.

Walker's new-found wealth enabled him to move his family into a luxurious apartment which cost far beyond his naval pay but he explained this away by claiming the restaurant was now extremely profitable. His wife had by now become a heavy drinker but was sufficiently curious to look through her husband's desk one day, where she found enough evidence to confront him with the accusation that he was selling naval secrets to the Russians. Walker did not deny it but, like Prime's first wife, Barbara could not bring herself to tell the police.

Throughout 1968 and 1969 Walker continued passing on cryptographic material to the Russians, earning himself around $4,000 a month. In the autumn of 1970 he recruited another spy, Petty Officer Jerry Whitworth, who was also a radio instructor at the naval school. Whitworth was already defrauding the US Navy by continuing to draw his marriage allowance when he had been divorced for four years, so the idea of making money by selling naval secrets for yet more cash attracted him. It is an indication of the quality of the US Navy's vetting procedures that they did not even know Whitworth's true marital status after four years.

In 1972 Walker's routine positive vetting check was due and because of his new and more sensitive work he feared there would be a thorough investigation of his marital life which might cause his wife to expose him. Walker therefore forged a fairly good copy of the official stamp used by the Naval Investigative Service, typed up his own background clearance on an official form, stamped it and placed it in his service record so that it would seem that he had been vetted. The forgery was accepted without question.

By now Walker and Whitworth were regularly passing on cryptographic material in huge quantities. Indeed, Walker took so many photographs that he actually wore out the shutter on his Minox camera and had to buy a new one. On 22 June 1976 Walker divorced Barbara, agreeing to pay her $10,000 in cash and monthly maintenance of $500. A month later, on 31 July 1976 he retired from the US Navy after 21 years' service with an apparently impeccable record. He continued to run Whitworth and then, amazingly, recruited his own son, Michael, as a spy when he joined the navy.

Walker's spy network continued unchecked for another eight years until on 23 November 1984, alone, depressed and bitter, Barbara called the FBI and told them her ex-husband was a long-time Russian spy. It was eleven days before the FBI called to see her. Barbara was nervous and bolstered her courage with vodka. The FBI listened politely, saw the level in the bottle fall, and filed a report recommending no further action be taken.

Three months later, in February 1985, Barbara's statement was routinely checked and something caught the attention of the FBI supervisor, who sent it back for further investigation. The FBI put Walker, Whitworth and Michael Walker under surveillance and on 20 May 1985 was rewarded when Walker kept an appointment with Aleksey Tkachenko, a Russian diplomat and KGB agent. Later that evening Walker was arrested at a hotel nearby and so too were Whitworth and Michael Walker, then serving on board the USS *Nimitz*. Their trial lasted from March until July 1986, cost $1 million, and all three were given multiple terms of life imprisonment and heavily fined for failing to report the payments they received from the Russians for tax purposes. The KGB had paid Walker $750,000, Whitworth $332,000, and Michael Walker a mere $1,000. It was a bargain.[34]

When the extent of Walker's spy ring's activities became public knowledge the US Navy and Department of Defence were quick to claim that irreparable damage had been done to the navy's communications systems and at least $100 million would be needed just to re-establish immediate security. In reality, the US Navy was horribly embarrassed by the exposure of the three spies and was desperately trying to divert public attention away from its own security lapses. What was particularly galling was that if Walker had treated his ex-wife better Barbara would probably never have turned him in so the spy ring could have gone on for another generation. And, of course, if the US Navy's security vetting system had done its job properly Walker would have immediately been suspect and never allowed to hold high security-risk jobs.

In 1968 Walker, then a petty officer, was heavily in debt, owned a civilian restaurant that was a financial failure, was borrowing large sums of money and was in trouble with the tax authorities. His wife and four children were eking out a miserable existence in a caravan. Yet within a few months he had moved his family into a luxury flat and was living far beyond his naval salary. Although he boasted that his new found wealth came from his restaurant it would have been a simple matter to establish that this was untrue. A check of Walker's bank account would have shown he was regularly paying in large amounts of cash in $50 notes. Walker's marriage was far from satisfactory, he physically assaulted his wife and children and openly boasted of his womanising.

Any one of these facts should have alerted Walker's immediate superiors that his lifestyle warranted investigation. Yet not a single comment about Walker's profligate lifestyle appeared on his service record despite the fact that he was constantly being given access to more and more sensitive material, nor did investigators notice that his 1972 security clearance had been forged. Exactly the same could be said about Whitworth's lifestyle, which was even more lavish than Walker's.

Security in the various ships and shore stations where Walker's spy ring worked was appalling. Considering the care with which the NSA produced and hand-delivered the key cards it was quite incredible that only one person could have access to the safe where they were kept. In all the years Walker was spying no one ever noticed that the seals on the unissued packs of key-cards had been broken which clearly shows that no random security inspections were ever made on the safe where they were kept. As at GCHQ, there was no control on the photocopiers or who used them. Equally, it transpired that there was no proper check kept on material sent for destruction because when Walker's son Michael was finally arrested on board the USS *Nimitz* his locker was full of key cards, tapes and messages, all of which were listed as having been destroyed.

What did the Russians get for their $1 million? During the 17 years from 1968 and 1985 they were obviously able to read all the radio traffic compromised by the key cards Walker, and later Whitworth, handed over. All of this would have been retrospective decryption, particularly when Walker was serving in Vietnam on the USS *Niagara Falls*, because his material took six months or more to reach the KGB in Moscow. Even when he was based at shore stations Walker only handed over material every three months. Effectively, therefore, the Russians were not doing as well as the Americans in 1940–41 with their Magic decrypts of Japanese diplomatic signals, nor the British with their Ultra decrypts at Bletchley Park between 1940–45, which were often read within an hour of being sent.

Without an intimate knowledge of the US Navy's cryptographic system it is impossible to know how many different networks existed for each separate naval command during the period the Walker spy ring was in operation. Military organisations usually divide their cipher traffic into a variety of different networks, each with its own key, so that if a cryptograph is stolen or captured in time of war, or an operator defects (as did Igor Gouzenko from the Russian Embassy in Ottawa in 1945), the damage is limited to only a certain amount of traffic. Further cipher security can be provided by using double encipherment, requiring two sets of key cards, one set being held by an officer. In World War II some Enigma messages used an 'officer key' so that while the radio operator could decrypt the first encipherment an officer had to use his own key to decipher the second. Much the same system was used by the US Army and Air Force in World War II, when certain coded messages required decipherment by two officers.

Although Walker and his spy ring compromised the main US Navy's submarine broadcast network using the KL-47 cryptograph, even given the US Navy's abysmally lax security this would not have necessarily exposed all KL-47 traffic throughout the world. It follows, therefore, that despite the outpouring of anger by the US Navy and Defence Secretary Caspar Weinberger the Walker spy ring did not betray all the US Navy's secrets and, without a continued supply of stolen key cards, Russian eavesdropping ceased immediately following the spy ring's arrest.

Although Walker and his team spied for 17 years and are supposed to have given away the crown jewels of the US Navy it is worth noting that, as in the Prime case, not once during this period did any Russian or East European defector who arrived in the West ever hint that the KGB enjoyed an unrestricted flow of such top-secret naval information. Nor during this same period did the CIA or naval intelligence ever detect the slightest indication that the Russian Navy was outsmarting the Americans because it had some unexpected intimate knowledge of the US Navy's operational and technical plans. Furthermore, as there were no Pearl Harbors or Midway Battles to fight during these 17 years, the Walkers' information was never put to use.

Weinberger was to claim that the Walkers betrayed over a million messages but this type of hyperbole, designed to influence public opinion, has to be judged in its proper context. The vast majority of these messages would have been of a very routine nature and their intelligence value (if indeed it ever existed) highly perishable after a matter of days or weeks, so decoding them three or six months after they had been sent was not much of an achievement. As to the story that the Walker spy ring gave the Russians secrets of the West's silent magnetic pump-propulsion system that is to be fitted to Britain's *Trident*-carrying *Vanguard*-class submarines and the US Navy's *Seawolf* hunter-class submarine, this is pure fantasy and just another excuse to try to pretend that anything designed in Russia is always based on the fruits of espionage in the West.[35]

Hardly had the dust from the Walker case settled when in August 1988 yet another spy ring was discovered, this time at the West German headquarters of the US Army's 8th Infantry Division at Bad Kreuznach.[36] Clyde Conrad, a 41-year-old retired army sergeant, had served for five years as administrator of the unit's secret records. He has now been charged with systematically selling to Hungarian intelligence (acting for the KGB) everything that passed through his hands during this period, including the 8th Division's wartime contingency plans, details of supplies and reserves, and technical information about nuclear missiles. For this he was paid $1.1 million.

Like Prime, Walker and Bettaney, Conrad's security checks were minimal and he had not been properly vetted for seven years despite having sole access to the highest classified material. Conrad was a devoted family man living a simple life matching his army pension of $800 a month so what he did with his espionage income is a mystery. He did, however, travel a lot around Europe and one theory is that he may have recruited other spies, as did Walker.

As to the information Conrad gave the Hungarians, this would have been of very fleeting value since contingency plans are constantly being changed. In any case there are no great mysteries about how World War III might be fought in Europe so it is hard to see what the Hungarians got for their $1.1 million that could not have been found in a few military books and magazines. Oddly enough, Conrad's spy ring was first detected when a colleague of his was seen in Vienna with a Hungarian intelligence agent, again similar to the Prime affair when the KGB tried to expose him to the West.

Throughout all these cases the one self-evident central theme is that these vast and expensive Western intelligence agencies who are constantly worrying about unseen enemies from the East are, in reality, so poorly staffed and organised that they cannot detect the misfits and traitors within. If one believes that people like Prime, Walker, Bettaney, and all the others not yet exposed, have done so much damage to the security of the West – although there is no evidence to support this – then the danger lies not with the Russians but in our own intelligence services who hide their inefficiency behind this web of unnecessary secrecy.

CHAPTER 5

THE SCRAMBLE FOR THE THIRD WORLD

The end of World War II left behind a trail of local wars and many confused loyalties and ideals about the future. The Far East in particular had seen the overthrow of the British, French and Dutch colonial empires and in the battle to defeat the Japanese many Communist-backed guerrilla organisations fought alongside the allies, having become respectable following the invasion of Russia by Germany in 1941. Throughout the war the Americans had made no secret of their dislike of colonialism and tacitly promised many of those who had supported the fight against the Germans and Japanese that when peace came they would not have to return to this paternalistic and élitist style of government.

Paradoxically the Japanese thought of this first and in some of the ex-colonies they captured – notably Vietnam, Indonesia and Burma – transferred a limited amount of political power to nationalist parties during 1942–45 as a reward for their cooperation. The defeat of Japan and the sudden and unexpected end of the war left a political vacuum which the pre-war colonial rulers, exhausted by the war, were in no position to fill.

Communism was not new to the Third World. During the 1930s Russia had embarked on a policy of exporting its political creed throughout the Far East, India and Africa, but enjoyed little success simply because the colonial rulers had efficient police forces able to negate any discord and prevented Communist views being publicised. Before the war, therefore, Communism was tolerated with a certain amount of amusement since it seemed clear that the vast mass of illiterate people in the Third World were happy to live under benevolent colonial control which, although now much maligned in history books, kept opposing tribal communities together in cohesive nations thus ensuring economic stability, developed mineral and agricultural resources, controlled disease and disaster, and provided a reasonably fair system of law and judicial order.

111

The whole future of post-war colonial rule in the Third World was therefore affected by several factors: Russia's emergence as a major world power having already dominated Eastern Europe and now evidently anxious to export its ideologies, America's decision to free its foreign policy from the shackles of pre-war isolationism, and the economic problems faced by Britain, France, Belgium and Holland. As wartime alliances soured and the Cold War began the West was afflicted by the belief that all the emerging liberation movements were under the direct control of either Russia or China. In fact this was not so. Most of these movements were autonomous (often fuelled by tribal rivalries that had long been held in check by colonialism), and copied Communist rhetoric and principles only out of convenience.

While Britain adopted a fairly pragmatic attitude towards its post-war role, granting independence to India in 1947, France sought to regain control over its possessions in Indo-China in 1946 and found itself involved in an eight-year war against a Communist-controlled peasant army who in 1954 forced the French to accept a humiliating surrender at Geneva. This was a new type of warfare unknown in the West that was to have a dramatic effect on American foreign policy.

The role of intelligence in all this was both ambivalent and confused mainly because after the war there were so many small agencies competing against each other with no clear idea of what they were trying to achieve. With no previous experience, America automatically assumed that money alone would dazzle the natives who could be bribed into accepting the West's philosophies. Russia, which also had no experience, took the simplistic view that Communism would automatically appeal to the Third World and any remaining white minority governments, such as those in Africa, would easily be overthrown by classic socialist revolutions. The initial role of the intelligence services was therefore to watch for subversion from the other side while targeting those in power who could be blackmailed and bribed.

Intelligence agencies like the CIA and KGB have also been closely involved in operations throughout the Third World in what are known as Low Intensity Conflicts (LIC). These are covert forms of guerrilla warfare and counter-insurgency or terrorism, financed by the agency in question, using secret and unaccountable funds and frequently using surrogate forces in the form of hired mercenaries who bolster the government forces of the regime the agency wants to keep in power.

The birth of the CIA in 1947 coincided not surprisingly with the start of the Cold War. As a result all post-war American overseas intelligence operations have been seriously flawed by their rigid obsession that everything to do with Communism is bad and anything claiming to be anti-Communist is good. It has never occurred to the Americans that there are forms of Communism that might prove a far better style of government for some poor countries. As a result the CIA has invariably backed the wrong horse and ended up on the losing side. Time and again the CIA has squandered hundreds of millions of dollars' worth of taxpayers' money propping up corrupt and bestial regimes in faraway places, often using dubious and dishonest intermediaries, on the pretext that they are anti-Communist.

Shortly after its formation the CIA began covert operations in Korea, a sad and much fought-over country that had been arbitrarily divided at the 38th parallel at the end of the war leaving two equally corrupt and inefficient governments, in the north backed by China and in the south by America. Exactly what the CIA's purpose was has never been explained but its operations served to generate a great deal of hostility from the North Koreans who in June 1950 launched a full-scale attack upon South Korea. So badly organised was the CIA that it was unable to provide Washington or the South Koreans with any warning of the attack and also incorrectly judged that China would not come to the aid of the North Koreans. The war ended inconclusively – and the countries remain in turmoil today, 36 years later – and has resulted in two equally undemocratic governments remaining in power.

The intelligence disaster in Korea should have been a warning to the CIA but it went unheeded. In 1954, when the French withdrew from South Vietnam after the Geneva armistice, the Americans took over the training of South Vietnamese forces much as they had done in South Korea, once again propping up a rotten regime only because it claimed to be anti-Communist. Throughout the late 1950s the CIA maintained a steady stream of reports alleging that if the Communists in North Vietnam were not stopped there would be a domino effect as one Far East country after another fell under their control. Coming so soon after Korea, the Berlin Blockade, and all the hyperbole of the Cold War, this was exactly what the American administration wanted to hear and consequently suitable tales were peddled to the American people and compliant allies.

Eventually the Americans started sending in small numbers of advisers, totalling only 9,000 in 1962, but by 1968 there were over half a million US troops in the country and America was bogged down in a vicious war against an army of peasants in black pyjamas who moved through the jungle on bicycles and eventually defeated the might of the American military machine. A great deal of the fighting in Vietnam and neighbouring Laos and Cambodia was done in a covert manner by the CIA so that the president of the day could claim that American forces were not involved.

Throughout the Vietnam war American leaders deluded themselves by believing their own intelligence agencies who as usual merely gave them the information they wanted to hear.[1] Vietnam was certainly a case of the blind leading the blind, although ironically the end came when a few notable sections of the American media shook themselves free of planted stories and started reporting the truth. If any dominoes fell as the result of Communism in

South East Asia they were the American presidents who succumbed one after another to this folly.

The Vietnam war should have made people realise how bankrupt are the philosophies of agencies like the CIA, but they have continued to invent new enemies whenever old ones disappear. In order to justify these bizarre, costly and useless operations, the CIA constantly plants on gullible presidents and the media misleading and distorted reports proving that its work is vital to stop the spread of Communism in that particular part of the world which, if unchecked, would become a direct threat to America itself. In reality all that happens is that the bulk of the CIA's injected money ends up in the pockets of corrupt politicians who cling to power on the coat-tails of America and then manage to flee the country, cushioned by their swollen numbered bank accounts, shortly before their rotten regimes collapse under their own dishonesty. America is then left as the villain of the piece.

President Marcos of the Philippines was propped up by the CIA for many years, not only because he offered the US armed forces suitable bases in the Far East but also because he claimed to be fighting Communism. Since he fled with a large slice of the country's wealth, most of which came from the American taxpayer, the CIA has been trying to ingratiate itself with the fragile government of Mrs Cori Aquino which replaced him.

In Iran exactly the same thing happened. The CIA argued that the Shah was supporting a vital bastion of democracy on the very borders of Russia. The CIA conveniently ignored the fact that the Shah's brand of democracy was an insult to human decency. That in return for America's approval and support the Shah was willing to allow the NSA to base eavesdropping Sigint stations along Iran's borders and to permit the US Air Force to fly electronic intelligence (Elint) missions from its airfields was enough to satisfy the CIA. It totally failed to monitor the political pulse of the country and ignored local intelligence warnings about the truth of the Shah's insecurity, as these did not agree with what the CIA wanted to believe. The rise of Ayatollah Khomeini was also completely misread by the CIA and even after his triumphal return to Iran it still believed the Shah was safe on his tinpot throne.

An almost identical situation currently exists in Saudi Arabia where the CIA is advising support for a monarchist regime that is totally isolated from its people. Once again we see the Saudi leaders surrounding themselves with billions of dollars' worth of the very latest sophisticated weaponry which they cannot operate and have to hire surrogate experts to maintain, whilst their own safety is secured by bands of imported mercenaries recruited from supposedly loyal Arab neighbours.

The CIA has survived and continues to grow more or less unchecked because over the years it has scared successive presidents and administrations into allowing it to interfere with America's foreign policy, both overtly and covertly, on the grounds that it alone knows what the Communists are up to. The CIA's answer to any foreign problem has been, and remains, to spend money. Thought and expertise have never been high on the CIA's list of priorities.

Since it began the CIA has created its own private armies and air forces, invaded foreign countries, and destabilised and overthrown by armed intervention democratically elected governments that it disapproved of. It has bribed and blackmailed politicians around the world to the tune of billions of dollars in order to try to influence the outcome of supposedly free elections, financed a variety of front organisations including newspapers, magazines and radio stations to peddle propaganda, taken part in assassinations and terrorist operations, and even illegally sold arms to America's enemies. All this has been done by the CIA in the name of the security of the American people and in defence of democracy.

Another continent that naturally attracted much attention after World War II was Africa whose vast area, although largely underdeveloped, was also rich in important materials. Russia's first foray into Africa had been during the Boer War of 1899–1902 when Czar Nicholas II sent Russian troops to fight with the Boers against the British. Soon after the Bolshevik revolution of 1917 the Communist International was founded, one part of its task being the spread of its views in Africa, and early links were established with African National Congress (ANC), which had been founded in 1912 and later with the Communist Party of South Africa (CPSA), founded in 1921. After 1941 Russia established diplomatic relations with South Africa for the first time but these only lasted until 1956 when Eric Louw, South Africa's Minister of External Affairs, expelled all the Russian diplomats for allegedly furthering the aims of Communist organisations, since when there have been no diplomatic relations between the two countries.

By the early 1950s changes were already beginning to reshape the political power of Africa.[2] One of the first countries to be affected was Egypt, then racked with internal dissent under the corrupt leadership of King Farouk. In an effort to deflect attention from his country's problems Farouk encouraged attacks on the British garrison in the Suez Canal zone and in October 1951 arbitrarily renounced the 1936 Anglo-Egyptian Treaty and laid claim to the Sudan which had long been the responsibility of a joint Anglo-Egyptian agreement. It was at this point that the Americans decided to involve themselves and the CIA in Cairo began bribing dissident army officers to overthrow Farouk in the belief that a military government would halt the spread of Communism in Egypt.

At a cost of some $3 million (worth around $50 million today)[3] paid by the CIA into Swiss bank accounts, General Mohammed Neguib was persuaded to organise a coup on 22 July 1952. Without bloodshed King Farouk was ousted and fled the country in his yacht with his collection of pornography and as much of Egypt's gold as he could steal. The CIA and the British were delighted with this intelligence coup but it soon emerged that the CIA had been completely misled and Neguib was only a front man for Colonel Gamel Nasser, who took over from Neguib in February 1954.

Far from being a friend of the West Nasser turned out to be a left-wing firebrand who immediately embarked on a massive campaign of anti-imperialist propaganda, broadcast on the 'Voice of the Arab' radio station from Cairo, urging countries throughout Africa and the Middle East to stage coups against their pro-Western leaders. One of the early victims of Nasser's rhetoric was the Baghdad Pact, a NATO-type organisation fostered by Britain as a means of maintaining pro-Western military links in the Middle East.[4] The Egyptian broadcasts aroused so much nationalist fervour on the streets that the Pact soon fell apart and the Iraqi monarchy was overthrown in a very bloody coup in 1958.

Nasser also embarked on grandiose plans for modernising Egypt's tattered Army and Air Force, which had suffered badly at the hands of Israel in 1948, and also for the expansion of Egypt's economy. In September 1955 Nasser arranged a $400 million deal through the Russian Foreign Ministry, theoretically to be paid for in cotton, and bought 300 tanks, 200 MiG-15 fighters, 50 Ilyushin bombers, two destroyers and four minesweepers from Czechoslovakia. This greatly alarmed the Israelis, who now had a formidable foe on their borders, while the CIA were still upset at having been outsmarted.

On the economic front one of Nasser's first projects was the construction of the Aswan High Dam. In 1955 Nasser asked America for help with this scheme and America's foreign secretary Foster Dulles and the CIA's Kermit Roosevelt flew to Cairo to try to persuade Nasser to reverse his pro-Russian stance in return for them financing the dam. When Nasser refused the Americans declined to help him, so Nasser approached the Russians who immediately agreed to build the dam, seeing it as an opportunity to gain an important propaganda victory. By now America, Britain, France and Israel, for differing reasons and without any integrated political strategy, had become greatly alarmed at Russia's growing influence in Egypt.

This precipitated Nasser's nationalisation of the Suez Canal on 26 July 1956, resulting in the ill-fated invasion of Egypt by British, French and Israeli forces[5] whose leaders, unknown to the public at the time, were involved in an inept intelligence operation to make it seem that Egypt had attacked Israel and that Britain and France had invaded only to secure the international freedom of the Suez Canal. At the time, also unknown to the British public (as is so often the case with ailing leaders), Prime Minister Anthony Eden was desperately ill and not fully in command of his senses. Eden had become so obsessed by Nasser that he saw him as some personal enemy who had to be destroyed at all costs.[6]

1   The *Rainbow Warrior* submerged after attack.

2 and 3   French agents Dominique Prieur and Alain Mafart who sank the *Rainbow Warrior* and were imprisoned in New Zealand for manslaughter, but have since returned to France as heroes.

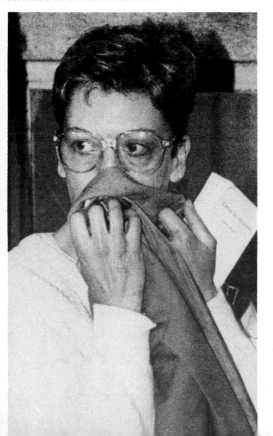

4 Commander 'Buster' Crabb, the frogman who lost his life inspecting a Russian cruiser for MI6.

5 George Blake, the triple-agent who escaped from Wormwood Scrubs in 1966.

6 and 7   The Berlin Tunnel, or *Operation Gold*, the $25 million project that was compromised by George Blake from the start.

8 GCHQ, Cheltenham, the centre of Britain's signals intelligence operations where Geoffrey Prime spied for fourteen years.

9 Geoffrey Prime: was he allowed to resign because the KGB had other spies in GCHQ?   10   Prime's home, Laburnum Cottage.

In London, MI5 bugged the telephone in the cipher room at the Egyptian Embassy[7] as part of *Operation Engulf* so that GCHQ was able to listen to the cipher clerks calling out the daily settings for the Hagelin cryptographs which GCHQ copied on to its own machines at Cheltenham. As a result the British government, and of course the NSA with whom GCHQ shared the decrypts, was able to read all the exchanges between Egypt and Russia throughout the protracted Suez crisis. Eventually a cable was read which indicated that the Russians were prepared to confront Britain on a military basis, with nuclear weapons if necessary, if the invasion of Egypt continued, which significantly influenced Eden's decision to halt the operation.[8] Peter Wright believes that the Russians knew GCHQ was reading the Egyptian Embassy cipher traffic in London so the cable may have been a piece of disinformation designed to scare Eden and the Americans. Either way the entire invasion was a fiasco, both in military planning and political reality.

America's ambivalent attitude towards the operation was based on its ability to read Eden's own intelligence via GCHQ (which Eden did not realise at the time[9]), its historical distrust of British and French colonial policies, its wish to help Israel, and the CIA's belief that it could control Nasser more successfully through bribes and blackmail than military action. Although Eden had to accept defeat on the battlefield he avoided it in the political arena by pleading ill-health and resigned, leaving Harold Macmillan to clear up the mess. The entire episode was the result of the CIA blundering into the situation and offering bribes to the wrong people. Had it kept Farouk on the throne, paying him off with a million dollars or so, and then sensibly channelled economic aid instead of military hardware into Egypt to help its people, then the entire Suez fiasco could have been avoided.

Although at the time of the Suez invasion Russia was far more preoccupied in putting down the Hungarian anti-Stalin uprising, the complete disarray of Western policy not only encouraged her to try elsewhere in Africa but also helped create the mythology of Russia's expertise in subverting Africa's diplomatic affairs which exists to this day. For many years afterwards Russia and the KGB lavished attention on Nasser and by the time of his death in September 1970 had provided him with over $2.5 billion-worth of military equipment, the bulk of which was lost fighting the Israelis[10] and was of no value to the Egyptian people whose plight worsened during these years. Both the KGB and the GRU had built up huge operations in Egypt, and Moscow believed they had established a secure base in Egypt for the subversion of the rest of Africa.

But the Russians had underrated both Nasser and the Egyptian people. Despite his apparent pro-Russian stance Nasser remained independent and had the complete support of the Egyptian people. Frustrated by its lack of progress the KGB started to recruit agents who might one day overthrow Nasser and all seemed to be going well when Nasser unexpectedly died and was replaced by Anwar Sadat, who the Russians believed was a colourless, mediocre bureaucrat. But the KGB miscalculated with Sadat just as the CIA had over Neguib and Nasser a decade earlier. Sadat turned out to be a very shrewd and courageous president who on 22 May 1971 arrested and deported the entire KGB network and its agents in Egypt, including the Russian ambassador Vladimir Polyakov. At one stroke the entire Russian intelligence network was in ruins. It was an act of bravery that sealed Sadat's fate and on 6 October 1981 Sadat was assassinated by KGB-backed dissident soldiers while he was reviewing a military parade outside Cairo. Sadat was succeeded by Hosni Mubarak who, though he studied in Moscow, remains fiercely independent of either East or West although, paradoxically the success of any economic progress for Egypt relies heavily on outside aid.

At the moment the Americans are back in favour in Egypt while the KGB worries about problems nearer home and counts the cost of its expensive and futile operations there over the past 35 years. Both sides have poured money into Egypt which, with the skill of a bazaar trader, has played one off against the other. At the end of the day neither America nor Russia has anything to show for all its effort and expense. Egypt remains perilously balanced between wanting peace with Israel yet having to placate the ever-increasing demands of political and religious fanaticism. Meanwhile its 50 million people become poorer,[11] oil revenues have fallen, housing is in short supply and so too are basic foodstuffs.

Another major intelligence confrontation in Africa occurred in June 1960 when the Belgian government suddenly and without any preparation granted independence to the Congo. The result was a predictable collapse of authority and economic chaos throughout this country rich in much-wanted strategically important minerals. With Belgian control gone the area swiftly reverted to tribal conflicts with Patrice Lumumba, the prime minister of the newly created state, trying to maintain order only to be confronted by the breakaway leader Moise Tshombe who formed the independent state of Katanga. Lumumba and his president, Joseph Kasavubu, appealed to the United Nations for help in ousting Tshombe and ending Katanga's secession but little was done and Lumumba turned to Russia for help.

On 26 August 1960 about a hundred Russian technicians arrived in ten Iluyshin IL-18 transports. The CIA station chief in the Congo, Lawrence Devlin,[12] sent a typically exaggerated report to Washington stating that the Congo was about to be taken over by the Russians and that America would lose control of the Congo's vital uranium deposits. Devlin concluded 'there may be little time left in which to take action to avoid another Cuba'.

The mention of Cuba was enough to galvanise the CIA into action because it had disastrously miscalculated Fidel Castro's overthrow of the American-backed corrupt dictator General Fulgencio Batista just a year earlier in 1959 and at the time was planning an invasion of Cuba using Cuban exiles with covert CIA support. As a result Devlin was authorised by CIA headquarters to plan Lumumba's murder. On 5 September 1960 the CIA bribed Kasavubu to sack Lumumba and appoint Colonel Joseph Mobutu in his place. But even then it feared some Russian backlash and eventually had Lumumba arrested and on 17 January 1961 he was murdered. The affair caused considerable disquiet in America and the Church Commission was set up to investigate American involvement. It concluded that:

> The testimony is strong enough to permit a reasonable inference that the plot to assassinate Lumumba was authorised by President Eisenhower.

In fairness to Eisenhower, he probably never realised he was agreeing to Lumumba's murder either because he was not told the whole story by his intelligence advisers or because he was not clever enough to ask the right questions. In fact the Russians had no plans to interfere in the Congo, or Zaire as it later became known, and with the help of the Americans Mobutu has now become one of the world's richest dictators leading a regime that is continuously criticised for its atrocious human rights record. This is typical of the CIA's and the State Department's moral attitude towards other countries. But of course America succeeded in maintaining access to Zaire's vital uranium ore exports for its own nuclear programme. Certainly the KGB had no success here.

Another African country that received early attention from the KGB was Ghana, which used to be the British colony of the Gold Coast until its independence in 1957.[13] A very poor country whose only significant export is cocoa, it suffered from having a bizarre lader, Kwame Nkrumah, who, having become president, then frittered away the country's fast-dwindling resources on grandiose projects including luxury yachts and palaces while demanding more aid from the West.

In 1962 Nkrumah survived an assassination attempt but fearing for his own safety asked the Russians for help. The KGB obliged and offered to organise a special bodyguard to protect him. Nkrumah accepted and soon Ghana was flooded with hundreds of Russians, Chinese, East Germans, Czechs, Poles, North Koreans and Cubans. The KGB chief in the capital Accra was Issakovich Akhmerov who established a secret police force called the National Security Service and arranged that Ghanaian officers and NCOs be flown to Moscow for special training with the KGB. Akhmerov also trained a special bodyguard of some 300 selected Ghanaian soldiers to protect Nkrumah.

By now Nkrumah was so deluded with his own grandeur, preoccupied with promoting himself to field-marshal and giving himself bogus honours and status that he completely overlooked the real situation; that he was now a prisoner of the KGB in his own country. The KGB had meanwhile drawn up elaborate plans to use Ghana as a base where they could train terrorists for guerrilla operations in other African states. Unfortunately for the KGB they kept themselves so far removed from the ordinary Ghanaian people that they failed to appreciate the contempt the population had for Nkrumah who had surrounded himself with sycophantic supporters giving the impression that he was very popular.

In February 1966 Nkrumah set off on one of his regal visits to China and while he was away anti-Communist army forces stormed his headquarters at Flagstaff House where after a ten-hour battle they found eleven KGB officers, who they lined up against a wall and shot. The National Liberation Council then formally deposed Nkrumah. Since the KGB did not want to admit that they had officers in the presidential palace the deaths went unreported. The new regime quickly uncovered hordes of KGB files which showed the extent of the subversion that had been planned and the CIA arrived hot-foot on the scene to assist and spread the word. Over the next few weeks some 1,500 Russians and Chinese left Ghana and the entire KGB operation was destroyed. It was probably one of the worst defeats suffered by the KGB in the history of its African operations and showed its incompetence in judging the African character which is hardly surprising given Russia's complete lack of colonial experience.

Having failed in West Africa, Russia then turned its attention to Rhodesia (now Zimbabwe), which in 1965 had unilaterally declared its independence from London under the white minority government of Ian Smith.[14] This seemed to be an excellent opportunity to stir up trouble and the Russians backed Joshua Nkomo's Zimbabwe People's Revolutionary Army (ZIPRA) only to find that China was supporting Robert Mugabe's Zimbabwe African National Liberation Army (ZANLA). The KGB helped train Nkomo's guerrillas in Russia and neighbouring Zambia and supplied them with weapons and explosives, including surface-to-air missiles, to carry on their fight against the Smith regime.

Russia supported resolutions at the United Nations imposing an international economic blockade against Rhodesia while at the same time Moscow was buying large quantities of Rhodesian chrome ore and tobacco through South Africa and then reselling the products on the open market with false certificates of origin. A large tonnage of Rhodesian chrome ore was shipped to the United States in this way and although the State Department knew perfectly well where the ore had come from originally, American companies were allowed to buy it because it was so vital to the country's armament programme.

Eventually the two rebel leaders joined forces and formed the Patriotic

Front and in 1979 talks began at Lancaster House in London to negotiate a settlement of the Rhodesian problem. MI5 bugged all the hotels used by the various delegations and intercepted their communications back home so the Foreign Office was fully apprised of their negotiating strategy before each morning's session began. The final agreement resulted in Lord Soames being appointed governor to oversee the disarming of the guerrillas and the holding of elections. Russia wanted Nkomo to boycott the conference but he ignored their advice and then, much to the Russian's dismay, was heavily defeated by Mugabe who became Zimbabwe's first black prime minister. Once again the Russians had backed the wrong horse.

Not surprisingly Mugabe had no affection for the Russians and did not even invite them to the Independence celebrations in 1980. It was not until 1981 that they were allowed to establish an embassy in Harare (formerly Salisbury) and even then Mugabe naively insisted that the treaty of diplomatic recognition included a clause that Russian diplomats would not interfere in Zimbabwe's internal affairs, which the Russians must have signed with considerable amusement. At first Mugabe continued showing a strong preference for the Chinese and even turned down an invitation to visit Moscow. But the then Russian ambassador, Gheorghy Ter-Gazariants, bided his time and slowly cultivated a better relationship between the two countries, signing a number of meaningless cultural and trade agreements.

It was not until 1985 that Mugabe finally met Gorbachev in Moscow and opened an embassy there the following year. Throughout these years the Russians have encouraged any anti-American attitude on the part of Mugabe, such as the famous diplomatic walk-out by President Carter and his diplomatic colleagues from the Fourth of July celebrations in Harare in 1986 after America had been publicly criticised for its attitude towards South Africa. This led to the Americans cutting off $13.5 million-worth of aid for 1986 and ending further economic assistance, but Russia was not in a position to step in and make up the loss.

In 1987 it was reported that Zimbabwe had bought a squadron of MiG-29 fighters from Russia for $324 million but Russia seems in no great hurry to supply them. Quite apart from the fact that Zimbabwe hardly has $324 million to spare the MiG-29 is a very sophisticated aircraft, never before supplied to any African country, and as well as highly skilled pilots would require equally sophisticated ground-support services to keep the aircraft operational and protected from a pre-emptive strike. This would mean the Russians becoming directly involved in military operations that threatened South Africa which they would not wish to do. Mugabe is also well aware that his country's exports depend upon South African rail links so there is a limit to which he can risk upsetting his relationship with Pretoria, quite apart from inviting pre-emptive strikes against military targets that the South Africans believe threaten their security.

During this period the KGB has kept a very low profile because Mugabe's government lives in a continuous state of paranoia about external threats of subversion and espionage and has already arrested and imprisoned many members of Nkomo's party and others suspected of collaborating with South African intelligence. Effectively therefore the Russians have come to a dead end in Zimbabwe.

The two southern African countries that have received most attention from the Russians have been the ex-Portugese colonies of Mozambique and Angola. In Mozambique from 1963 Russia and China supported Samora Machel's rebel movement FRELIMO and when Machel became president in June 1975 at the end of Portugese rule he entered into a treaty with Russia.[15] This resulted in the Russians supplying him with a variety of military hardware including some outdated MiG-17 aircraft together with several hundred instructors and members of the KGB to help reorganise and train the army. Later more experts from East Germany and Cuba arrived and set about converting Mozambique into a Marxist state and creating an internal security police on the lines of the KGB.

However South Africa had other ideas and backed a rebel movement called RENAMO, or the National Resistance of Mozambique (MNR), which embarked on a bloody campaign of terrorism designed to destabilise Machel's regime. On several occasions South African troops and aircraft crossed into Mozambique and carried out attacks against selected targets alleged to house supporters of the African Nation Congress (ANC). Machel appealed to the Russians for help and the Russian ambassador to Mozambique warned the South Africans that any further incursions would result in either Russian or Cuban troops being sent to help Machel. But the American State Department issued an equally blunt warning to Mozambique, and indirectly to Russia, not to allow foreign troops into its country. The Russians backed down leaving Machel to deal with the problem on his own, evidently deciding that Mozambique was not worth the fuss, and since the early 1980s Russia has scaled down its operations and economic investment in the country.

As a result Mozambique had to turn to Portugal, Zimbabwe and Britain for help in training its army to fight the MNR and by 1983 had entered into direct negotiations with South Africa that culminated in the Nkomati Treaty signed between Prime Minister P. W. Botha and Machel on 16 March 1984. This was supposed to lead to an end of South African support for the MNR but the attacks continued, leading Machel to accuse the South Africans of reneging on the treaty. Machel then sought help from the Americans and visited Reagan in September 1985. Although an economic aid package of $40 million was agreed, the CIA successfully lobbied against any military aid to Machel because he was a Communist and instead recommended covert aid to the MNR because they were anti-Communist.

On 19 October 1986 Machel's Russian-built Tu-134 aircraft with a Russian crew crashed into a mountain on the South African border killing him and ten of his closest aids. The investigation into the incident was far from conclusive and many believed that South African intelligence, perhaps acting without government approval, had deliberately lured Machel's aircraft off its correct flight path by using a decoy navigational beacon. This would be an extremely easy thing to do. Machel was succeeded by Joaquim Chissano, the foreign minister, and Russia immediately tried to re-establish better relations with the new administration, but Chissano preferred to look to the West – mainly Portugal, France and Britain. In 1987 Chissano visited Moscow and met Gorbachev but the latter was far too preoccupied with internal problems to offer more than rhetoric and Chissano returned home empty-handed. The Russians seem to have concluded that Mozambique is yet another country not worth chasing after.

Angola is a very different matter and over the past decade has become a major battleground between East and West at enormous cost in terms of human life and military hardware, though with remarkably little result.[16] Its early history was similar to Mozambique's, with Russia providing limited support to the MPLA, the supposedly Marxist guerrilla movement that operated in the northern part of the country around the capital Luanda. Portugal's prime minister, Antonio Salazar, kept the MPLA contained by a series of bloody attacks against their strongholds. The Americans criticised Salazar for this and advocated a peaceful transition to black majority rule and in 1961 the CIA began covertly supporting Holden Roberto, head of the exiled rebel group GRAE then based in the Congolese capital of Leopoldville (now Kinshasa).

But Salazar threatened America with the closure of its military bases in the Azores if it continued to support Roberto, with the result that the State Department authorised the supply of American aircraft to Salazar for his counter-insurgency campaign while the CIA continued secretly supporting Roberto. As usual the CIA wasted its money because Roberto was quite content to sit in Leopoldville making the right sort of anti-Communist statements that the CIA likes to hear but had no intention of doing any fighting. As a result Jonas Savimbi, a member of Roberto's GRAE, set up his own organisation, UNITA, which operated in the south of Angola near the South African border while Roberto renamed his organisation the FNLA. In 1970 Salazar died and his successor, Marcello Caetano, contacted both UNITA and the FNLA in 1971 and offered them recognition if they would help destroy the Russian-backed MPLA.

But before anything could happen Caetano was overthrown in a left-wing military coup in 1974 and Portugal effectively gave up control of Angola (and Mozambique), leaving it to the MPLA, UNITA and FNLA to fight it out amongst themselves. US President Ford and Secretary of State Henry

Kissinger authorised the CIA to spend $32 million secretly supporting UNITA and the FNLA to stop a Communist-backed take-over. Most of this money was paid to Roberto's FNLA through the CIA's office in Zaire since having put Mobutu in power after the murder of Lumumba they were able to operate there without restriction. Naturally the bulk of it ended up in the pockets of Roberto, Mobutu and their friends, all of whom became extremely rich at the expense of the American taxpayer. CIA money was also poured into UNITA via South Africa.

On 11 November 1975 Agostinho Neto, president of the MPLA, announced the creation of a People's Republic of Angola which was soon under attack from Roberto's CIA-backed forces in the north and UNITA and South African troops from the south. Neto appealed to Russia for help and between November 1975 and March 1976 more than 12,000 Cuban troops, equipped with T-34 and T-54 tanks, armoured personnel carriers, MiG-21 fighters, anti-tank missiles, BM-21 rocket launchers, and SAM-7 missiles, arrived in Angola in a massive sea and air supply operation. As a result the MPLA was able to defeat both UNITA and the FNLA, inflicting heavy casualties on both as well as the South African contingent. However the MPLA could not hold on to its gains and eventually only controlled the capital Luanda and the surrounding area. In an effort to bolster its forces UNITA used some of its vast CIA funds to recruit mercenaries from Britain with the tacit approval of the government but most were either killed, or captured and suffered a humiliating and embarrassing trial in Luanda.

In America reports of the cost of the CIA operation began to emerge and led to a Senate Select Committee on Intelligence investigation in 1977. This concluded:

> Certain covert operations (in Angola) have been incompatible with
> American principles and ideology and, when exposed, have resulted in
> damaging this nation's ability to exercise moral and ethical leadership.

Congress also stated that the 'Communist threat' used by the CIA as the excuse for their intervention was over-dramatised to the point where genuine grass-roots freedom movements were automatically considered suspect so that they eventually turned to Moscow for help.

Although the CIA officially terminated its support for UNITA and the FNLA (which greatly upset South Africa), it was too late to prevent America coming under strong attack from other black African states who saw the CIA's association with South Africa as justifiable cause for Russian involvement and eventually the MPLA was recognised as the legitimate government of Angola.

In the aftermath of this costly fiasco Roberto and his FNLA movement quietly disappeared, doubtless to enjoy the fruits of their Swiss bank accounts stuffed with CIA money while the CIA and South Africa continued to covertly support Savimbi's UNITA. During the subsequent decade Russian and Cuban involvement has increased substantially and by 1988 there were 28,000 Cuban troops in Angola and over 1,000 Russian military advisers together with large units of the KGB. Military hardware has also become more sophisticated and now includes MiG-23 fighters, Mi-24 *Hind* attack helicopters, SAM-8 missiles and an air-defence radar network. This has required an investment of some $2 billion which, ironically, has been paid for by the sale of Angolan oil to the Gulf Oil Company of America.

Throughout these years sporadic fighting sometimes of great intensity has continued between the MPLA and UNITA. In 1985, Russian General Konstantin Shaganovitch, the highest-ranking Russian officer ever posted outside Europe or Afghanistan, arrived in Angola to take charge of operations against UNITA with General Mikhail Petrov. After two years of preparation a huge force of some 12,000 Cuban and MPLA troops slowly marched south with armoured support and air cover to destroy UNITA positions. But UNITA was clever enough to melt away into the miles of uncharted bush and make swift hit-and-run strikes at the long supply columns, finally inflicting over 1,000 casualties and causing the Russian-led forces to withdraw in confusion back to the safety of Luanda. UNITA's success was largely the result of massive South African aid and the Reagan administration's decision in March 1986 to supply them with *Stinger* surface-to-air missiles and TOW anti-tank missiles together with a further $20 million-worth of covert assistance approved by Congress in September 1986.

This was all part of Reagan's publicly stated policy to counter Russian imperialism in Third World countries by any means, which had included $250 million for covert military aid to Afghanistan rebel groups and $27 million non-lethal aid for the Contras. However Reagan's policies suffered a severe setback after the Iran/Contra scandal and it is doubtful if Congress will be willing to become further involved in these operations with the dubious political motivations of Savimbi's UNITA, and at a time when there is growing opposition to America's continued support for the South African government.

Similar criticisms are to be heard within Russia too. After the débâcle of Afghanistan questions are being raised as to whether it is worth continuing to carry the enormous burden of Angola. Even though the cost in human lives is mainly being borne by Cuba the financial cost for Russia over the last decade has been in excess of $5 billion, money badly needed at home. Furthermore there is no indication that Russia is any more popular in Africa than America, nor can the KGB point to any greater success than the CIA. Both sides have frittered away billions chasing ideological shadows in a backward country the only concern of whose people is daily survival against the elements while their leaders live in obscene luxury. Naturally Gorbachev has to be seen to maintain Russia's position and during Angolan President Dos Santos's visit to Moscow in May 1986 stated: 'We are standing and will continue to stand firmly and unswervingly by our commitments to Angola. No one should have any doubts on this score.'

Since then Gorbachev has found himself embroiled in far more important and far-reaching changes in his own domestic policies and though a settlement in Angola is still some way off there is no doubt he would like to extricate himself from this hopeless situation. Any settlement in Angola will have to involve South Africa which neither Russia, America, nor indeed the rest of Africa, can afford to ignore.

South Africa has been the primary target for Russian subversion in the whole of its African intelligence operations. Quite apart from being the most economically advanced country in the continent, possessing huge reserves of vital minerals, South Africa also controls the sea routes around the Cape of Good Hope into the Indian Ocean and beyond, along which nearly 30,000 vessels pass each year, over 8,000 of them oil tankers plying between the Middle East and Europe and America. Nearly 70 per cent of Western Europe's oil and 30 per cent of America's imported oil together with 75 per cent of all strategic materials used by the West uses the Cape route.

During the mid-1960s Russia began deploying naval units in the Indian Ocean using ports in Ethiopia, Mozambique and Angola as bases.[17] Since then the Russian Navy has continued to fly the flag, making visits to friendly African countries. The presence of these warships has little strategic importance because if a world war was really likely they would be in a very exposed position and unable to maintain a blockade of Western shipping in the Indian Ocean. Meantime the Russians are certainly not going to involve themselves in any direct military conflict in southern Africa. Nevertheless America has become greatly alarmed at this naval presence and as a result the CIA and South Africa's intelligence agency the National Intelligence Service, still usually referred to as the Bureau of State Security (BOSS), have worked closely together and the NSA have experts working at Silvermines, a Sigint installation near Capetown which shares information with Fort Meade in America and GCHQ at Cheltenham.

Russia takes a great interest in these activities and also South Africa's highly secret nuclear programme. It was a Russian reconnaissance satellite that in 1977 photographed what was believed to be a nuclear test site in a remote part of the Kalahari Desert and when told about this the Americans put pressure on South Africa to have the site dismantled. In 1979 an American *Vela* satellite operated by the NRO detected two flashes of light over the southern Indian Ocean which were believed to be from a small nuclear test probably carried out jointly by the South Africans and Israel, which also possesses nuclear weapons. South Africa denied any such test had been carried out but was happy to allow the mystery to rumble on as a useful deterrent to its black African neighbours. Like Israel, South Africa undoubtedly has the capability of assembling nuclear weapons if its existence was really threatened but meantime can protect itself with an ever-increasing range of sophisticated home-made weaponry that out-performs anything the surrounding African states can handle on their own.

The KGB has also sent agents into South Africa and recruited others. The three most important have been Edmund Trinka, arrested in 1967, Major Aleksei Kozlov, a KGB major posing as a diplomat and arrested in 1981, and Commodore Dieter Gerhardt, the former chief of the Simonstown naval base arrested in January 1983. Of the three Gerhardt was certainly the most important.

Gerhardt had been spying for the GRU (not the KGB) for over 20 years,[18] having originally offered his services to the Russians while on secondment to the Royal Navy in London. During these years he gave the Russians details of the Royal Navy's shipbuilding programme and after returning to work in South Africa details of the contingency plans to keep oil shipments moving around the Cape in time of war. Gerhardt is also said to have supplied the Russians with details of the French Exocet missile (actually no great secret), and kept them informed about the Royal Navy's operations during the 1982 Falklands War which the South African Navy was monitoring. At the time the Royal Navy used Simonstown as a refuelling base because the Ministry of Defence kept large reserves of oil and diesel fuel there. At Silvermines Gerhardt had access to South Africa's most sensitive secrets, particularly relating to its intelligence links with Britain and America, and passed these on to Moscow. Both Gerhardt and his wife were found guilty of high treason and sentenced to life imprisonment

But naturally the KGB's main effort has been directed at supporting the two black African parties, the African National Congress (ANC) and the South African Communist Party (SACP). Since the mid-1960s the KGB has provided training facilities in Tanzania, Zambia, Angola and Mozambique, all of which have come under attack from South African military units from time to time. In the last five years the ANC has increased its number of bomb attacks in towns and cities but the level of violence still suggests that Russian help is mainly in rhetoric rather than weaponry. One of the reasons for this is that there is a great deal of ambivalence in Russia's attitude towards South Africa.

On the one hand it is prepared publicly to aid those who wish to overthrow the white minority government in Pretoria and give them political support in forums like the United Nations, yet equally Russia is one of South Africa's most important customers (the statistics being falsified by both parties to conceal the extent of the trade), and with certain important minerals like diamonds, gold and platinum, Russia works closely with South African companies to ensure orderly marketing within carefully controlled cartels so that prices remain as high as possible. It is an Alice in Wonderland situation whereby South Africa is attacking Russia's allies in Mozambique and Angola, Angolan oil is being sold to America and helps finance the war against CIA-backed forces, and the KGB is helping the ANC kill and maim white South Africans with car bombs yet maintaining high-level secret commercial contacts between the two countries.

Since Gorbachev's arrival in the Kremlin there has been a sharply pragmatic appraisal of Russia's future participation in African and Third World affairs. Gorbachev no longer believes that the ANC or any of the black African states can ever overthrow the South African government by force and Russia is certainly not going to get involved in any direct action itself. While it may continue its rhetoric to keep up appearances and not upset long-held ideologies, Russia is now far more interested in cooperating with the West to achieve a negotiated settlement between the races that would enable it to extract itself from a very costly and wasteful confrontation while maintaining its trade links with South Africa. Equally South Africa, while having to sustain the hardliners on the right, is also entering into discussions to break the stalemate.

If one examines the entire African scenario over the past 35 years one finds time and again the classical bankruptcy of intelligence operations. Neither the CIA nor the KGB ever understood the ethnic complexities within the various countries they tried to subvert. Instead they both poured money for military purposes into the hands of dubious groups that professed either extreme violence or anti-Communism yet without exception each operation has ended in failure without the original goals being achieved or any advantage for the people it was supposed to help.

Meanwhile, with the exception of South Africa itself, the rest of the continent staggers from one disaster to another, either natural or man-made, with incompetent, cruel and corrupt dictators squandering what little wealth they possess on useless status symbols, or tucking it away in Swiss bank accounts, while the population starves. If one-tenth of the money spent by Russia and America chasing false intelligence idols had been used to give sensible economic aid to the same countries and help them develop sound industries Africa might today be a much healthier and prosperous place. Not only has intelligence and subversion failed in Africa but it has set the continent back at least five decades and caused genocide on a scale unseen anywhere else in the world. The ghosts of the old colonial powers must have much to smile about.

On the other side of the world America has quite naturally always regarded events in Cental and South America as its own special sphere of influence and what it has been unable to dominate by trade has sought to destabilise by undercover means. Nevertheless, it has been no more successful than in South-East Asia or Africa.

An early example was Cuba. The island of Cuba lies less than 100 miles off the southern coast of America. Like that of many Caribbean islands, Cuba's history has been a turbulent one. Early in the sixteenth century Cuba was conquered by the Spanish under whose control it remained for the next 400 years. For one year, 1762–63, it was under British rule, but was handed back to Spain in exchange for Florida. In the closing years of the nineteenth century America developed a colonial paternalism towards Cuba and after a short Spanish-American war Cuba was controlled by America. However by 28 January 1909 an elected republican government had been installed.

The mainstay of Cuba's economy is sugar, a labour-intensive industry often using very primitive equipment, but since there are no alternative crops to absorb employment there is little commercial encouragement to improve things. Because America wanted to ensure a stable supply of sugar close at hand and at the same time help the Caribbean economy, for many years Congress approved a number of special sugar import quotas. One of these was for more than 3 million tons of Cuban sugar which was sold to American refiners at well over 5 cents (US) per pound, or more than three times the average world market price. The fact that Cuba knew that it had this guaranteed outlet for more than half its total annual production was a very important part of its economy and therefore kept the country within the sphere of American political influence.

In keeping with America's foreign policy the State Department believed that this type of economic support was enough to keep the Cubans happy. In truth Cuba was a wretchedly poor country racked by corruption of every kind with wages of only 5 cents (US) per day commonplace for sugar-cane workers until World War II. Americans regarded Cuba as a conveniently cheap playground for holidays, gambling and prostitution. On 4 September 1933, as the result of a military coup, an army sergeant called Fulgencio Batista overthrew the cruel regime of General Machado and became president. By Cuban standards Batista was not too dishonest although by 1944 he had acquired enough wealth to retire. By 1952 corruption had reached such a level that his successor President Martin was accused of stealing $174 million and as a result Batista carried out a second coup and returned to office. However, on this occasion he displayed total disregard for honesty and became deeply involved in every form of corruption, with a great deal of help from American criminals who found Cuba a useful offshore haven.

On 2 December 1956 a totally unknown guerrilla called Fidel Castro landed on the coast of the eastern province of Sierra Maestra from the yacht *Granma* with 81 followers and started to harrass Batista's government from the hills. Castro was so inefficient a leader that no one, especially American intelligence, took him seriously which was not surprising because on his first encounter with Batista's forces Castro was nearly wiped out and left with only 15 supporters. But Batista's response to these attacks was so brutal, with his police allowed to murder and torture at will that many middle-class Cubans began to support Castro. He then began to attack the sugar mills and their crops most of which were owned by American companies.

The CIA still refused to take Castro seriously and was assured by Batista that he had the situation under control. Meanwhile, to be on the safe side and save their crops from destruction, the American mill owners started secretly paying Castro protection money which he used to buy more efficient weapons. The Americans continued to back Batista but on 1 January 1959, like many of America's corrupt protégés, Batista decided he had had enough and fled the country with as much stolen cash as he could amass. A week later a very surprised Castro rode in triumph into Havana at the head of his motley collection of troops and found himself in charge of the country.

To begin with, Castro and his bewildered bearded followers wandered round the streets of Havana not knowing what to do. They settled a few old scores with some of Batista's police, opened up the prisons to let out their supporters and promptly filled them up again with Batista's, with the level of torture and cruelty much the same. They changed a few names – the Havana Hilton hotel became the Havana Libre – but life went on much as before. The poor remained poor, the few remaining rich who had not fled to Florida were still rich. Whether Castro was a Communist at this stage is a matter of opinion. He had received little help from Russia during his fight against Batista. Equally, he had no love for the Americans and not much for the British, who had supplied Batista's regime with some fighters just before he fled. However since Cuba's economy was tied to America in every respect Castro needed to retain good relations with Washington.

For the next year an uneasy calm descended on Cuban-American relations. The CIA knew very little about Castro but assumed he was a simpleton it could keep in its pocket as it had done Cuba's past leaders. The Russians, sensing an opportunity to upset the Americans in their own backyard, began wooing Castro, promising that they could supply Cuba with anything it needed. The current joke at the time was that Castro was like a water melon – green on the outside, red on the inside. By early 1960 it was clear that Cuba and America were on a collision course. As part of Castro's grandiose nationalisation plans, more than 600 American-owned companies in Cuba would be taken over and the three major international oil companies, Texaco, Royal Dutch and Standard Oil, were told that in future they must refine up to 6,000 barrels of Russian crude oil a day.

All this infuriated the State Department which decided to give Castro a warning and as a result, on 6 July 1960, President Eisenhower reduced Cuba's sugar quota by 700,000 tons. Russia immediately announced she would buy this sugar instead.[19] On 16 December 1960 the American ambassador was withdrawn and the remaining American sugar quota cancelled. Once again Russian Prime Minister Nikita Krushchev announced that Russia would buy all this sugar as well so that Cuba would not suffer financially.

The CIA was furious at having been outsmarted by both Castro and the Russians and the American sugar-mill owners, who had lost everything, represented a powerful lobby in Washington demanding action. Florida was by now full of Cuban refugees who had been staunch supporters of Batista and were only too anxious to see Castro overthrown. They fed the CIA all manner of fairy-tales about how the Cuban population would rise up in support of an invasion and because this was what the CIA wanted to hear, it was believed.

In the meantime an election had taken place and John F. Kennedy arrived in the White House in January 1961. Kennedy was a young president, full of great ideas as to how he would reform the CIA after the embarrassing fiasco when a U-2 spy aircraft operated by the NSA and CIA had been shot down by the Russians on 5 May 1960. At first the Americans had claimed it was a weather reconnaissance aircraft that had strayed off course but then President Eisenhower publicly admitted that he had sanctioned the flight, handing Krushchev an enormous propaganda victory.

Even though it was in disgrace the CIA handled Kennedy cleverly and, playing on his love of adventure, briefed him with some details of a proposed Cuban invasion that had been prepared during Eisenhower's term of office. Naturally the CIA only told Kennedy the best bits of the plan and, perhaps because he had only just taken office, he did not seek any other opinion. The Bay of Pigs invasion went ahead in April 1961 and was a disaster with every invader either killed or captured. Once again the CIA had completely misjudged its intelligence and presented Castro with a magnificent propaganda victory that drove him into the open arms of the Russians. Ironically, Gorbachev's new ideas are considered far too radical and advanced for today's Cuba where Castro prefers to keep his people in a 1960 Marxist time-warp awaiting the next CIA invasion. It will be interesting to see how long Castro's magic can work in the face of this new style of Communism being propagated by Russia itself.

Although America was able to cut Cuba off from the rest of the world with the exception of Russia and Mexico, it could not stop the ideals of a Castro-style revolution from spreading to other Central and South American countries. The first causes for alarm occurred in Chile where during the 1964 elections the CIA provided half the financial support for Eduardo Frei in order to stop Salvador Allende, heading a coalition of left-wing parties, from being elected. On this occasion it succeeded, and when Allende stood as a presidential candidate in the 1970 elections President Nixon ordered the CIA to stop his victory, while the CIA and various American companies with factories in Chile provided funds to bribe electors.

Nevertheless Allende won 36.3 per cent of the votes and became president. The CIA was then ordered by the president to get rid of Allende by force and on 11 September 1973, during a CIA-backed military coup, Allende was killed. Since then Chile has been ruled by a military dictator, General Augusto Pinochet, whose undemocratic behaviour and abandonment of civil rights has not worried successive American presidents because he is anti-Communist. The CIA's overthrow of the Chilean government cost the American taxpayer about $20 million and was done in the name of democracy.

The next country to suffer the attentions of the CIA was Nicaragua which since 1933 had been under the control of the pro-American Somoza family. In the late 1970s this regime came under attack from the Sandinista National Liberation Front which in 1979 forced General Somoza to resign. Elections were then held and a non-aligned government elected. When Reagan took over the US presidency from Carter in the wake of the Iranian hostage affair he was told by the CIA that the Sandinista government was secretly shipping weapons to El Salvador to support left-wing guerrillas there. All this was quite untrue but Reagan immediately authorised the CIA to supply weapons and military equipment to the Contra rebels in an attempt to overthrow the democratically elected government of Nicaragua. When Congress belatedly found out about this and cut off funds for the operation the president's go-between Oliver North secretly diverted profits from the illegal shipments of arms to Iran (see Chapter 3).

When one looks at the CIA's involvement in other countries' affairs it is hard to find a case in which it has actually improved the lifestyle of those it claims to be helping. Life in Cuba today may not be wonderful but it is a lot better for most people than it was under Batista. Throughout the rest of the world wherever the CIA has interfered the effects in terms of human rights have been disastrous. By comparison the KGB has been positively dull and though its record on human rights is no better at least it does not pretend to be the saviour of democracy as does the CIA. It is difficult to judge which threatens the Third World most: inherent incompetence and corruption or interference by the intelligence agencies of the superpowers.

CHAPTER 6

DIRTY TRICKS

Despite the glamour bestowed upon it by fiction writers the intelligence world is a sordid twilight place of twisted moralities where many unpleasant and illegal actions regularly occur and are taken for granted. Members of the intelligence fraternity do not consider that breaking the law is wrong. They believe that their work is so important that laws do not matter and that the end justifies the means. The dirty tricks carried out by the intelligence world come in many different forms. At their simplest they may be nothing more serious than peddling propaganda through sycophantic journalists smearing the characters of those who dare disagree with them, right the way up through burglary and forgery to the ultimate crime of mass murder.

In wartime sacrifices have to be made. But even then unnecessary deaths and suffering are caused due to quarrels and jealousies. A typical example of this occurred in 1943 when Britain's Special Operations Executive was infiltrated by an MI6 agent, Henri Déricourt, who in order to plant false information about a non-existent invasion was told to collaborate with the enemy and thereby sent 400 SOE agents to their deaths.[1] Because he was protected by MI6 he was never punished.

In peacetime one might expect intelligence operations to be less dramatic and draconian as far as human life is concerned. But this is not necessarily so. George Blake was authorised by an unsuspecting MI6 to play the role of a double agent in West Berlin and pretend to be willing to help the Russians (see Chapter 2). Blake was allowed to expose a number of MI6 agents in the East, who were subsequently executed, in order to establish his credentials with the Russians. This was a totally futile exercise because Blake was a Russian spy anyway. Likewise the Russians have often let a minor spy be captured in the West in order to protect a more important agent.

Human life is also not highly valued by the intelligence services when dealing with terrorism. One favourite dirty trick of the intelligence services is to murder people or explode bombs in public places and leave behind clues to suggest that it was the work of a terrorist organisation. This is done in the hope that it will bring further public condemnation of the terrorists themselves and cause a rift within their leadership.

In 1988 a 28-year-old Palestinian, Ismael Sowan, a research assistant at Humberside College of Higher Education, was discovered by British police to be in possession of a large quantity of arms and explosives. At first it was assumed he was an Arab terrorist. But it subsequently transpired that Sowan was working for Mossad, the Israeli intelligence service. Sowan was sent to prison for 11 years. Mossad's plan was that Sowan would let off bombs in Britain that would leave sufficient forensic clues to suggest that they were the work of Middle East countries and thus damage Anglo-Arab relations. At the time there was talk of Britain re-establishing diplomatic links with Syria and Britain had also just concluded a very lucrative contract to sell Saudi Arabia £10 billion-worth of sophisticated aircraft and military equipment and as a result Israel was anxious to show that Arab countries were untrustworthy and closely involved in terrorism.

Sowan had been run by a five-man Mossad team[2] operating in Britain under the cover of a private company with the tacit approval of the Foreign Office and MI5 because in return Mossad was giving MI6 useful information about Middle East terrorist groups and hostages held in Lebanon. But the Sowan affair was too much even for the Foreign Office who expelled Arie Regev and Jacob Barad, both attachés at the Israeli Embassy, and ordered the Mossad undercover team to leave.

Israel retaliated by telling MI6 that their exchange of information about terrorists and hostages was at an end.[3] MI6 was horrified and warned MI5 that it was getting far more from Mossad than it was giving the Israelis. MI5 put pressure on the Foreign Office who quietly agreed that a Mossad undercover team could return to Britain.

While all this was going on the Foreign Office found itself embroiled in a typical CIA dirty trick in the heart of London. The story began back in 1982 when two Cuban intelligence agents frm Cuba's *Direccion General de Inteligencia* (DGI), Antonio Sanchez and Luis Garcia, were arrested on their arrival at Gatwick airport. Both were found to be in possession of spying equipment including a radio that was designed to pick up transmissions from Cuba. Since neither made any statement to the police before being sentenced to eight years in prison their mission was never exposed other than the fact that one possessed a forged passport in the name of Maria Rodruigez. Both enjoyed full remission on their sentences and were expelled from Britain in August 1986. It is noteworthy that the Cuban DGI is just as inefficient as other intelligence agencies and allowed two of its agents to arrive in a foreign country on an espionage mission with their spying equipment easily detectable.

On 6 June 1987 Aspillaga Lombard, a major in the DGI, defected from his post in Czechoslovakia[4] and presented himself at the American Embassy in Vienna together with his girlfriend, 23-year-old Martha Palsencia.[5] Lombard had brought several gifts for the CIA including names of Cuban agents working in America, some posing as double agents and actually working for the CIA. Lombard also identified a number of Cuban diplomats that he alleged were potential defectors. One of these was Carlos Perez, the 32-year-old commercial counsellor working at the Cuban Embassy in London.

The CIA brought Lombard to Britain with the agreement of MI5 and proceeded to shadow Perez who recognised him and his team of CIA and MI5 minders and feared for his own safety. Given the CIA's record of bombings and assassinations Perez had good reason. 'I knew that the CIA had a plan to use that miserable traitor to induce or to force me to defect,' Perez later explained, 'because of that I decided ... to carry a weapon, something I never did throughout the time I spent in Britain.'[6]

On 12 September 1988 Lombard and a team from MI5 and the CIA confronted Perez near his flat in Sussex Gardens.[7] Perez drew a gun and fired at them, injuring one man. The MI5 and CIA teams fled the scene leaving the puzzled police to cope with what appeared to be a straightforward shooting incident. Perez identified himself as a diplomat and told police he had believed he was about to be attacked. As usual MI5 was protected by Special Branch and the police would not even identify the person wounded by Perez.[8]

The Foreign Office had not been told what MI5 and the CIA were up to and was obliged to go through a charade of protests to divert attention away from yet another MI5 fiasco. Fortunately the Foreign Secretary was out of the country visiting Africa and there was only a very naive junior minister, Timothy Eggar, in charge. Normally Foreign Office ministers only meet the press under carefully controlled conditions but on this occasion Eggar came out on to the steps of the Foreign Office and willingly gave an impromptu news conference, declaiming in a display of outrage that Britain would take strong action to rid the streets of diplomats who used guns. As a result of the incident both the Cuban ambassador and the luckless Perez were expelled by Eggar. During the next few days a few Pincheresque journalists published planted MI5 stories claiming that Perez was the head of a Cuban spy ring (which he probably was but not a particularly good one), without mentioning the role of MI5 or the CIA.[9] MI5 leaked tales blaming the incident on the CIA and the CIA blamed MI5.

Thrilled by being suddenly thrust into the limelight Eggar warmed to his theme and the pro-government press gave him endless coverage[10] on his strong action to rid Britain of diplomats who abused our laws. But not a word was said about what MI5 or the CIA had been doing on our streets to antagonise Perez. Nor was any mention made of the Mossad hit team responsible for the Sowan affair which had blackmailed its way back into Britain. Apparently, for Eggar, a Mossad bomb is different to a Cuban bullet.

The whole incident was a classic example of a bungled CIA and MI5 operation based on false information supplied by a dubious defector who was anxious to impress his new paymasters. It is worth adding that had the government's new secrecy laws been in force the media would have been unable to report any aspect of the affair, particularly MI5's incompetence, so the public would have been left with the belief that the shooting was all the fault of the Cuban diplomat. This is how secrecy favours an inefficient intelligence service involved in illegal activities.

His master still absent, Eggar became deluded with his own importance and summoned various diplomats to the Foreign Office to hear more of his tirades. But by now the diplomatic corps was tiring of his behaviour[11] and held its own meeting at which one commented, 'Eggar was just using the occasion for his own local political ends and we refuse to help him in such an enterprise'. A senior member of the corps later complained to Sir Geoffrey Howe on his return about Eggar's absurd performance.

Another popular dirty trick is to leak bogus stories to the media about the origin of terrorist attacks so as to influence public opinion against certain countries. One such target is Libya. That Libya is involved in international terrorism is not in doubt. It was responsible for the murder of policewoman Yvonne Fletcher on the streets of London in April 1984. But American intelligence has gone much further in attempting to link Libya directly with specific terrorist attacks.

On 5 April 1986 a bomb exploded in the La Belle nightclub in West Berlin killing three people and injuring 230 others. The Reagan administration claimed that it had 'irrefutable proof' that Libya was directly involved in this outrage. Stories were then carefully leaked to certain sections of the American media claiming that the NSA had intercepted and decrypted coded messages from Tripoli to eight Libyan diplomatic missions, including that in East Berlin, specifically ordering this attack. To make the leaked information seem more authentic, once the stories appeared the American government strongly criticised the newspapers for revealing such secrets.[12]

According to West German intelligence, the BND, it supplied the cipher key that enabled the NSA to decrypt these messages and the BND was sent copies of the original raw intercepts.[13] Its analysis of the codes was quite different. According to Reagan the NSA version of the message intercepted on 4 April contained the phrase that 'the attack would be carried out the following morning'. But the West German version was that 'something will happen when Allah wills'. There were also important discrepancies between the West German and American versions of the subsequent messages which Reagan claimed contained specific congratulations from Colonel Gadaffi about the attack.

Nevertheless, using these alleged intercepts as justification, ten days later the Americans bombed Tripoli and Benghazi. Other Western governments were given summaries of the CIA's and NSA's intelligence about Libya but even the Foreign Office, who had no love for Libya, did not believe that the Libyan connection had been proved. What happened was that the intelligence had been carefully massaged to please Reagan and produce the sort of information the American people wanted to hear.

Subsequently West German police arrested 27-year-old Christine Endrigkeit in connection with the La Belle bombing.[14] They claimed that she was a friend of Ahmed Hasi, a Jordanian, who in November 1986 had been sent to prison in West Germany for a bomb attack on the German-Arab Society in West Berlin using explosives supplied by the Syrian Embassy in East Berlin. Hasi is a brother of Nezar Hindawi who was sent to prison by a British court in October 1986 for 45 years for attempting to blow up an El Al airliner at Heathrow airport.[15] Hindawi was said to have been working for Syrian intelligence and Britain broke off diplomatic relations with Damascus as the result of his trial. The Libyan connection with the La Belle bombing was the product of Imaginint which no one queried at the time because people had been encouraged to believe that Libya was responsible for all such attacks.

In the autumn of 1988 American intelligence leaked stories to the media that Libya had built a chemical weapons factory 35 miles south-west of Tripoli. No evidence was provided to substantiate the claim which Libya denied. In December, during a Christmas television interview on the ABC network, Reagan revealed that a new military strike against this factory was being discussed between America and her NATO allies.[16] This incredible revelation brought an immediate correction by State Department officials who said that such military action was 'not under active consideration' but there had been consultations 'with our allies to establish what we know about this plant and to establish whether it is a menace to world peace'. The Arab League pointed out that Libya had already denied having such a factory and in any case Israel's nuclear weapons plant was a far greater threat to peace.

Terrorism presents the security services with an acute dilemma over how far to go in protecting the public against horrific attacks without breaking the law. Nowhere is this better demonstrated than in Northern Ireland. Terrorism in Northern Ireland goes back to the late nineteenth century but the present troubles began in 1969 as the result of civil-rights protests by the Catholic minority about housing, employment and electoral rights. This led to prolonged violent demonstrations starting on 12 August 1969 in which seven people were killed, 750 injured, and 275 buildings were destroyed, forcing 1,505 Catholic and 315 Protestant families to leave their homes. On 14 August units of the British Army were called in to help the exhausted police. Since then to all intents and purposes there has been civil war going on between Protestant and Catholic paramilitary organisations with the Royal

Ulster Constabulary (90 per cent of whose members are Protestant) and the army standing somewhere in between. During the period to September 1988 there were 31,872 shooting incidents and 8,665 explosions with 2,695 people dead as a direct result of the conflict.[17] The scale of the fighting is best demonstrated by the recovery of 9,759 guns, over a million rounds of ammunition, and nearly 100 tons of explosives by the security forces during the same period.

Successive British governments have never made it clear whether they are fighting an all-out war in Northern Ireland or simply trying to maintain the standards of law and order that exist in the rest of Britain. The official line is usually very dismissive,[18] claiming the IRA is a small group of murderers numbering no more than 100 with perhaps 200 active supporters who are detested by the Catholic population, cannot get support at the ballot box, have achieved nothing and are on the point of defeat.[19]

Unfortunately fighting this type of terrorism is not as easy as fighting a conventional enemy. There is no question of the IRA surrendering as did the Germans in Occupied Europe in 1945 and then being shipped off back to their homeland. Northern Ireland is the homeland of most members of the IRA. Furthermore, as SOE demonstrated in the last war, a small number of trained men and women armed with modest amounts of weaponry and explosives can tie up enormous numbers of highly trained soldiers with sophisticated military hardware. Although the IRA is not as well-trained or supplied as was SOE, nevertheless it is proportionately doing rather better by tying up 12,000 regular army personnel, 6,500 members of the Ulster Defence Regiment (UDR), members of the Special Air Services (SAS), 8,500 full-time members of the RUC plus 4,500 reservists, a large contingent from MI5, MI6 and GCHQ (who spend much of their time quarrelling amongst themselves), plus a vast array of military hardware in the form of helicopters, armoured cars, Sigint equipment and all the paraphernalia of a modern army.[20]

Although most of the capital and running costs of these units would exist even if the IRA did not, the security operation in Northern Ireland remains extremely expensive. It is estimated that the extra cost of deploying the army to assist the RUC is £175 million a year while the RUC itself costs nearly £400 million a year.[21] This is in addition to the compensation paid by the government for personal injuries which between 1969 and March 1988 totalled £134.7 million, and damage to property totalling £518 million, and the £1.5 billion a year subsidy Whitehall provides to keep Northern Ireland's tottering economy alive.

On the mainland the threat of the IRA has turned government offices and military bases into miniature fortresses and the prime minister cannot venture out of Downing Street except in an armoured convoy. After the IRA nearly wiped out the entire Cabinet at Brighton in 1984 it is claimed that

security for Mrs Thatcher's three-day visit to the Conservative party conference in Brighton in October 1988 cost £1.5 million[22] and required the
services of 1,400 police, members of the armed services, and even the SAS.

Yet as the Germans found in France, defeating this sort of terrorism is
impossible. Although they rounded up hostages and shot them in public,
hanged suspects from lamp posts, used torture as a matter of course, and
even burned down entire villages, SOE and the resistance movements went
on harassing them. In Northern Ireland the army and the RUC used torture
which backfired on them. They tried bribing people to give false evidence in
court and all that did was to bring the judicial system into disrepute. And
they tried detention without trial which simply produced political prisoners
for propaganda purposes. If the Israeli Army was running Northern Ireland
things would be much simpler. They would beat and shoot suspects on the
streets,[23] round up others and place them in concentration camps without
trial, blow up houses belonging to suspects' families (an idea they have copied
from the Germans who in 1942 destroyed the Czechoslovakian village of
Lidice as a reprisal for the murder of Richard Heydrich), and send armoured
columns across the border into Ireland to attack suspected IRA bases.
Whether this would be any more successful is doubtful, since it has not
worked in the Israeli-occupied territories on the West Bank of the Jordan
river, but at least it would pass without comment. If the British Army did the
same there would be worldwide condemnation – a good example of how
attitudes towards terrorism vary around the world.

In an effort to try to get more terrorists convicted the British government
has changed the judicial rules in Northern Ireland on a number of occasions.
The police have powers to detain people for interrogation and hold them
incommunicado for up to a week without having to bring them before a
magistrate and inevitably this has led to complaints that confessions have
been forced from suspects under duress. In December 1988 the European
Court of Human Rights ruled that this procedure was unlawful and that four
days should be the maximum period of detention before bringing a suspect to
court to obtain permission for a further period. On 22 December the Home
Secretary told Parliament that the government intended temporarily to
ignore this ruling, claiming it needed more time to consider the matter.[24]

Because of intimidation juries were done away with in Northern Ireland in
1973 and instead a single judge sits in what is known as a Diplock Tribunal.
One of the problems here is that the judge hears all the evidence whereas a
jury is frequently excluded from the courtroom while legal submissions are
made as to whether a particular piece of evidence can be put before them.

A more controversial change was made in 1988 when it was decided to
abolish the principle of a suspect's right to silence so that if a suspect refused
to answer questions put to him by the police the tribunal would be told this
and it would be assumed that he had something to hide. All these changes

would make perfectly good sense was there any goodwill prevailing in Northern Ireland but unfortunately, because the RUC is predominantly Protestant, a large section of the Catholic population trusts neither it nor the courts. In fact this is unfair because despite all the problems that beset the judiciary, the tribunals and appeal courts have dismissed numerous cases involving very serious offences on grounds of tainted, corrupt and insufficient evidence and the accused have been freed even though the police know they are closely involved with terrorist organisations. What obscures this impartiality is the time suspects have to spend on remand in custody, often as long as two years, only to have the case against them collapse in court for lack of evidence.

Another thorny issue created by the terrorist situation in Northern Ireland is extradition, particularly when it involves the Republic of Ireland. While there may not be much overt support for the IRA in Ireland (where it is a banned organisation), there is even less for the British government, and while this may be largely based on history a great deal of hostility has been generated as a result of boorish and insensitive behaviour by the RUC and army against the Catholic population which the British authorities refuse to investigate. Further antagonism has been created by a series of convictions involving Irish men and women for alleged terrorist offences in Britain which the Home Office has been remarkably slow to review when new evidence has come to light, with the result that some have already spent many years in prison. The impartiality of the appeals is not helped when someone as prestigious as Lord Denning is on record saying that even if an injustice has been done in some of these cases, it would be wrong to overturn the verdicts and free those involved because it would lower respect for the British police and courts.

In the last two years there have been a number of bungled extradition applications for suspects wanted in Britain but the worst example occurred following the arrest of Patrick Ryan in Belgium on 5 July 1988. Ryan's name had been mentioned in reports about the IRA leaked to British newspapers in January 1988, following the Gibraltar shootings (see p 146). But after his arrest in July a host of new stories appeared, all apparently based on 'official sources' which claimed amongst other things that Ryan was the IRA's leading banker, arms supplier and bomb maker. Ryan was also credited with planning an IRA attack on the Queen during her visit to Holland and being involved in shipments of Libyan arms to Ireland.

However when Britain sought Ryan's extradition from Belgium (where he had been close to the point of death as the result of a hunger strike), none of these exotic claims were mentioned, and having rejected Britain's application the Belgian government allowed Ryan to fly in a military aircraft, carefully avoiding British airspace, to Ireland on 25 November. The British pro-government press naturally vented its anger on the Belgians with emotive headlines accusing them of cowardice[25] but then a few days later switched its wrath to the Irish government when Ryan discharged himself from a Dublin hospital and went into hiding. More carefully leaked stories about Ryan's guilt appeared in the press and in Parliament Conservative MP Michael Mates demanded to know why 'one of the most wanted terrorists has been let free'. During an EEC meeting at Rhodes Mrs Thatcher lectured the Belgian and Irish prime ministers about their responsibilities but was met with stony silence.

On 13 December John Murray, the Irish attorney-general, issued a statement that Ryan would not be extradited because comments by the British government and media had made a fair trial impossible.[26] The following day in Parliament Sir Patrick Mayhew, the attorney-general, was loudly cheered by Conservatives when he said that the Irish claim was an insult and British juries act 'with the fairness one expects in the ordinary men and women of our country'.[27] This was certainly an odd remark because in recent years there have been many allegations from Conservatives and right-wing newspapers that our juries are inept, biased, easily manipulated and frequently bring in wrong and perverse verdicts.[28]

The question then arose as to whether Britain would ask the Irish government to have Ryan tried in the Republic under its Criminal Law Jurisdiction Act but it was then suggested that witnesses from Britain would not feel safe going to Ireland to give evidence.[29] The Irish naturally regarded this as an insult.

The government could well be accused of acting hypocritically over the Ryan affair. And indeed, on 16 December Patrick Haseldine, a second secretary in the Foreign Office, wrote to the *Guardian* accusing Mrs Thatcher of being soft on terrorism in connection with the case of four South African businessmen charged in 1984 with evading the ban on military exports to South Africa.[30] They had been released on £400,000 bail put up by the South African Embassy and then left the country, refusing to return to stand trial. Haseldine alleged that Mrs Thatcher deliberately allowed them to return home because she did not want them on remand in prison during her talks with the South African president and foreign minister in June that year. Whether the two cases are really similar is irrelevant to the fact that a member of the Foreign Office was willing to go public with a criticism that would almost certainly lose him his job and career.

A more serious case involved four Italians, all members of a Fascist terrorist organisation linked to the bombing of a train outside Bologna in 1980 which killed 85 people.[31] All four fled to Britain and were tried in their absence in Italy, found guilty and sentenced to long terms of imprisonment. The Italian government tried to have them extradited but magistrates refused and the four continue to live openly in London with at least one actively engaged in politics. The Italians have every reason to feel as upset about this case as Mrs Thatcher does about Ryan.

Such political limitations and anomalies have long frustrated the army and RUC fighting vicious terrorists who are able to hide behind legal loopholes and thus create synthetic sympathy for their non-existent cause. Between 1969 and 1986 the security forces in Northern Ireland killed 166 civilians, none of whom had any connection with paramilitary organisations. In the same period republican groups killed 524 innocent people and loyalists 587. The British Army did learn one thing from the Israelis and that was to ignore the courts when it suited them. In August 1983 22-year-old Private Ian Thain shot dead 22-year-old Thomas Reilly, an unarmed civilian in Belfast. He was charged with murder and tried in Northern Ireland. Pleading not guilty, Thain claimed he had twice shouted a warning that he would open fire. But the judge did not believe Thain's evidence and found him guilty, sentencing him to life imprisonment. Incredibly, while Thain was in prison, he remained a serving soldier which must be unique in the history of the British armed forces.[32] In February 1987, after serving just 26 months, Thain was released on parole and returned to his regiment.[33]

The army claimed it was only being a 'caring employer' but to many in Ireland it seemed clear that the army was placing Thain above the law, as did the French when protecting their agents who blew up the *Rainbow Warrior*. On 26 September 1988 the army paid a substantial sum in compensation to Reilly's parents,[34] unfortunately coinciding with a decision by the Director of Public Prosecutions not to prosecute another soldier, 18-year-old Private David Holden of the Grenadier Guards, for unlawfully killing 23-year-old Aidan McAnespie in February 1988 following the accidental discharge of a machine gun at a border crossing-point.

Every time a particularly horrific outrage occurs there is a knee-jerk reaction in Whitehall usually resulting in the deployment of SAS units. But even then politicians are ambivalent as to what role the SAS is supposed to play.[35] On the one hand they are happy to leak stories to the media that the SAS is to be used because it makes it look as though they are taking positive action, yet when the SAS ambush and kill members of the IRA there is an immediate embarrassed blackout on the details. If the SAS is a good deterrent[36] against terrorists, why be coy about admitting its role?[37]

Emulating Henry II, politicians constantly demand that something must be done about the terrorist situation in Northern Ireland that has hung like an albatross round the neck of every government these past two decades. Each in turn has devised some new 'initiative' only to find it falter in the wasteland of the province's polarised politics. Mrs Thatcher has always insisted that Britain stays within the rule of civil law in fighting terrorism.[38] But in 1982 a high-level decision was taken to target certain terrorist suspects in Northern Ireland and entrap them into situations where they could be killed, faking the evidence surrounding their deaths so that it would appear the security forces had only been returning fire in self-defence.

By 1984 there had been a series of suspicious shootings in Northern Ireland[39] and RUC officers had admitted in court that they had been ordered to lie about their role in these incidents. As a result the expression was coined that a 'shoot to kill' policy existed in Northern Ireland. Like most headline material, it was meaningless. If you shoot someone with a modern high-velocity weapon, especially in automatic mode, you will almost certainly kill them. A more sensible expression would be a 'shoot not arrest' policy.

The government had a choice of how to react to these allegations. It could either deny them, claiming they were IRA propaganda, or admit they were true and that it was in the national interest that suspected terrorists should be killed whenever possible, irrespective of whether they were armed or not. Some people believed the latter was the correct approach. During the trial of three RUC officers accused of the murder of three unarmed men shot dead at Lurgan on 11 November 1982 the judge, Lord Justice Gibson, acquitted the three officers and congratulated them for having brought the three dead men to 'the final court of justice'.

But the government decided to do neither of these things. Instead they invoked that old British favourite, an inquiry, and in May 1984 the Deputy Chief Constable of the Greater Manchester Police, 47-year-old John Stalker, was asked to go over to Northern Ireland to take charge of it. It was never intended that the inquiry would achieve anything. What the government expected was that Stalker would go over to Belfast, look through some RUC files, ask a few routine questions and after a suitable interval publish one of those nice bland reports like the ones that regularly appear on sensitive matters like spies and telephone tapping. Most of the report would be taken up with detailing the history of Northern Ireland, the atrocities committed by the IRA, the innocent people it had murdered and the number of RUC policemen and soldiers that had been killed on duty. The report would then briefly state that there was no evidence that there had been a policy of shooting people instead of arresting them but that some minor operational errors had occurred which had now been corrected. Anything important or sensitive would be placed in an appendix to the report which would not appear in the version available to the public. At some convenient date in the future Stalker would be rewarded by promotion to Chief Constable and be awarded the Queen's Police Medal.

Unfortunately someone made a terrible mistake. Stalker was an honest policeman, and thought he was going to Northern Ireland to carry out a genuine inquiry. And despite lots of hints that he was treading on too many toes Stalker did just that. At the end of two years he had reached the point where he was about to confront the RUC with specific allegations against certain officers when, on 29 May 1986, he was suddenly removed from the inquiry and suspended from duty following allegations of improper conduct.[40] On 23 August 1986, the allegations against him having been rejected, Stalker returned to work with the Manchester police and encountered considerable hostility from his immediate superior the Chief Constable, James Anderton, and a bill for £21,980 for defending himself against the allegations. On 13 March 1987 Stalker left the police force a bitter and disillusioned man, having been caught up in a web of deception and dirty tricks.[41] On 23 March 1987 his successor eventually produced a watered-down version of Stalker's report which recommended that a number of RUC officers should be prosecuted.

The government, the RUC and MI5 were appalled. If these prosecutions went ahead it would mean the appearance in court of junior and middle-ranking RUC officers who might in their defence reveal all sorts of unsavoury and embarrassing details about the instructions they had received from very senior officers, and in particular the shadowy and possibly illegal role played by MI5. The first task was to refuse to prosecute anyone in the RUC and on 25 January 1988 the attorney general, Sir Patrick Mayhew, told Parliament that in the interests of national security no prosecutions would take place. The second was to confuse the issue by setting up yet another inquiry, and the third was to denigrate Stalker's character.

The smear campaign was orchestrated by MI5 with stories in pro-government newspapers that Stalker was an inexperienced and naive police-man, politically motivated and pro-Catholic. Even worse, like Peter Wright, Stalker had blossomed into print with his account of the affair which went straight into the best-seller lists and, ironically, was serialised in the strongly pro-government *Daily Express*. Based on the government's much-stated attitude towards *Spycatcher*, Stalker ought to have been prosecuted under the Official Secrets Act and the book subjected to numerous injunctions to stop it being published. Stalker revealed far more intimate details about the dirty world of Special Branch and MI5 than had Wright and Stalker's information was about current operations whereas Wright's had been 25 years old. Furthermore, Stalker was making a considerable profit out of retailing details of his official police work. But on 11 February 1988 the government decided that prosecuting Stalker would not be in the public interest.[42] The government had at last learned a thing or two from the Australian trial. Ironically the more MI5 tried to smear Stalker, the more copies of his book were sold.

At the end of the day the central question of Stalker's inquiry remains unanswered, providing marvellous opportunities for the IRA to exacerbate relations between the Catholic community and the RUC with propaganda. The families of those who had been shot had to wait for six years until in November 1988 the inquest into the first shootings began. Exactly why this delay was necessary was not explained but all it served to do was to reawaken old enmities against the RUC. In any case coroners' courts in Northern Ireland are of little value because they can only consider how, when and where a person met their death and bring in 'findings', not a verdict. They are not allowed to express any opinion on matters of civil or criminal liability, are unable to bring in a verdict of unlawful killing, and witnesses who might incriminate themselves cannot be compelled to give evidence. These restrictions were introduced in 1980 after there had been a number of embarrassing revelations from RUC and security forces' witnesses about undercover operations and the use of rubber and plastic bullets that had caused death.

The first inquest had hardly begun when the lawyer for one of the dead men challenged the coroner's ruling that the RUC officers involved should not give evidence but merely have their statements read out. When the coroner refused to change his mind the lawyer sought a ruling from the Appeal Court which, surprisingly, in December agreed that the police officers should be called even though they did not have to answer questions that might incriminate them. The lawyer, Patrick Finucane, paid for his high-profile involvement when he was murdered in February 1989.

It is hard to understand why the government continues with these elaborate charades. Plainly it does not want the truth about the shootings to be publicly revealed and one can only assume that this is because the six men were deliberately shot instead of being arrested. If this is not true then there can be nothing to hide.

The ultimate losers in the whole affair are truth, objectivity, respect for the RUC in Northern Ireland and the attorney general in London, some members of the police in England, the security services and, of course, the next of kin of those who have been killed, since no one has been brought to justice. All this does is to perpetuate the hatred in Northern Ireland for a little longer and alienate law-abiding members of the Catholic community from the government because they can see no difference between the policeman and the terrorist.

In October 1988, as part of a government drive to try to stop people discussing events in Northern Ireland, Tom King, the Northern Ireland secretary, announced a ban on television interviews with terrorist organisations in the province although their statements could be quoted secondhand and newspapers were unaffected by this ban. Questions were raised in legal circles as to whether King had the power to enforce such censorship, since his powers over broadcasting are intended for use only during a national emergency, and plans were made to challenge his ruling in the High Court. Mrs Thatcher went even further than King and stated (in Australia on 5 August 1988) that anyone who interviewed a member of a proscribed organisation would be guilty of an offence but on 24 October the Crown Prosecution Service stated that such interviews were not illegal. Meanwhile the BBC started warning viewers that interviews from Northern Ireland had been compiled under the new government restrictions, a term hitherto only used for reports from South Africa. King's announcement backfired and gave enormous publicity to the IRA and also a useful weapon for them to use abroad. Bearing in mind that the IRA has been in existence for over 60 years, longer than television has been around, the ban is unlikely to have any effect.

What is happening in Northern Ireland precisely mirrors the situation in South Africa where the police are dealing with the terrorist activities of the African National Congress, similar in military terms to the IRA although, of course, with considerably different moral considerations. In April 1988 the image and morale of the South African police suffered badly when following a sensational murder trial two white police officers were found guilty of murdering two black drug dealers in Johannesburg and were sentenced to death.[43] This was the first time such a sentence had been passed on a white policeman.

In court both policemen stated that they hated members of the ANC, especially after the car-bomb attack in the centre of Johannesburg in 1987, and believed that senior police officers in Pretoria wanted ANC terrorists eliminated whenever the opportunity arose. In the policemen's defence, it was claimed that there was a 'sub-culture of violence' prevailing in the ranks of the South African police and, it was pointed out to the court, when members of South Africa's defence force raided neighbouring countries such as Botswana and killed ANC suspects there they were praised and given medals.

In November 1987 the security services in Northern Ireland intercepted a number of letters passing between members of the IRA in Belfast and Spain.[44] As a result four suspects – Daniel McCann, Sean Savage, Mairead Farrell, and another woman – were placed under close surveillance by the RUC, Special Branch, MI5 and the Spanish police as they travelled to and from Spain. This was made very easy because they were using forged passports which immediately showed up on the Spanish and Irish immigration control computers. While the quartet were in Spain their movements were carefully watched, their telephone calls tapped and hotel bedrooms bugged, and two members of MI5 worked with the Spanish police in Malaga to ensure perfect liaison with Gibraltar. During February the fourth woman, using a passport in the name of Mary Parkin, had twice been followed from Spain across the border into Gibraltar where she was seen watching and timing the guard ceremony that takes place each Tuesday morning. From these observations and the bugged conversations the security services were able to deduce that the IRA's target was the guard ceremony on 8 March 1988.[45]

At 6.30 p.m. on Saturday 5 March 1988 Farrell, using a driving licence in the name of Katherine Smith, went to the Marbessol car-rental firm in Marbella and hired a white Ford Fiesta[46] (in addition to the white Renault 5 and red Ford Fiesta the trio had already hired) which she collected the next morning at around 10.30 a.m. and left in the Marbella underground car-park. Some time that Sunday morning 141 pounds of Semtex explosive,

8o pounds of metal fragments and two electronic timing devices were loaded into the white Fiesta. Whether Farrell drove this car somewhere to meet with McCann and Savage to collect the explosives, or whether they were brought to the underground garage, is unclear but as the car only travelled 10 kms from the time Farrell hired it the latter seems more likely.

Considerable mystery still surrounds the origin of the Semtex. At first it was assumed that the IRA group in Spain had got it from the Basque terrorist movement ETA but this was denied by the Spanish police who stated that ETA had never possessed Semtex. British intelligence sources claimed the Semtex came from Libya and was part of one of the earlier shipments of arms and explosives that entered Ireland undetected between 1984 and 1986. If this were true then it would mean the four suspects carried the 141 pounds of explosive with them into Spain from Ireland. The airport security checks in force and the fact that all four were under surveillance would have made this impossible.

If it was Libyan Semtex then the only source was the shipment on board the freighter *Eskund* intercepted by the French off Brest on 30 October 1987.[47] But since it was claimed that the vessel had been under close surveillance from the moment it left Tripoli it is hard to believe it could have stopped off the Spanish coast and off-loaded the Semtex without being noticed, and it would also mean the explosives arrived in Spain before Savage and McCann made their first visit in November 1987. Previous experience suggests the IRA are not that well organised. The red Ford Fiesta hired by Savage is alleged to have travelled 1,594 kms by the time it was recovered after the shootings and Spanish police claimed it had been driven to Valencia and back, but how they knew this latter fact has never been explained nor whether they were aware this journey was connected with obtaining the explosives. If the Semtex was brought into Spain in early 1988 then that suggests a source other than the *Eskund*. It is possible that another IRA member might have brought it into Spain by car and handed it over in Valencia, but with the trio under such close surveillance all this must have been known to the Spanish police working with MI5.

However the Semtex was obtained, the fact remains that on Sunday morning, 6 March, the Spanish police and British intelligence knew that the bomb was in the white Fiesta which had been left in the underground car-park at Marbella. The trio then drove off to the Spanish frontier in the red Fiesta and white Renault, closely followed by Spanish police cars, a helicopter and observers along the route, so that their progress and arrival at La Linea could be reported by radio to MI5 in Gibraltar. The red car was left at La Linea while one of the gang drove the white Renault over the border into Gibraltar and used it to reserve a parking place in Main Street in which to park the car containing the bomb in two days' time. The other two members followed on foot.

Having parked the Renault all three started to walk back to the frontier. At this point they were intercepted by a group of SAS soldiers and shot dead. Based on official statements issued by the Gibraltar authorities, BBC and ITN news broadcasts that Sunday evening reported that a 500 lb car bomb had been found and that the three terrorists had been killed in 'a fierce gun battle' after which the car bomb had been defused by a controlled explosion. Monday's newspapers all carried similar accounts and on the BBC *Today* programme armed service's minister Ian Stewart talked about the car bomb and its timing for the parade on Tuesday. It was not until 3.30 p.m. that afternoon that the foreign secretary, Geoffrey Howe, told Parliament that there was no bomb and the three terrorists had been unarmed and then set the tone for the government's future attitude towards the affair by stating that the shooting of the three had prevented a dreadful terrorist act. On 8 March the Spanish police discovered the Fiesta car with the bomb in it in Marbella.

The shootings naturally caused much controversy. One section of the media predictably took the view that it did not really matter how and why the trio had been killed so long as they were dead. Others raised the issue of whether the SAS had been deliberately told to kill them.[48] On 10 May the Gibraltar coroner, Felix Pizzarello, announced that he would hold an inquest into the deaths commencing 27 June. But on 23 May Bernard Ingham, Downing Street's press officer, announced that the inquest had been postponed[49] until August although Pizzarello seemed unaware of this. Belatedly he agreed that a postponement had been agreed because the Gibraltar police would be fully occupied controlling an arts festival which started on 24 June, although there had never been an arrest in the festival's four-year history. Sceptics wondered if the postponement was connected with the fact that Parliament would be on holiday in August.

The inquest finally opened on Tuesday, 6 September 1988, amidst much international media interest and a great deal of bizarre security. The court authorities decided to increase the cost of the daily transcripts from the usual charge of 50p to £5 a page[50] which was a considerable financial burden for the defence lawyer who had given his services free to help the relatives of the three victims. Although it was understandable that MI5 witnesses did not wish to reveal their identity it was significant that fear of the IRA was so great the British soldiers felt it necessary to give evidence from behind a curtain. The coroner was given two 'certificates of immunity', one signed by defence secretary George Younger asking that no details of SAS operational methods and equipment be given in court, and the other signed by Home Secretary Douglas Hurd requesting a ban on any details of the information about the IRA plan known to MI5 prior to 6 March.

After the first three days the inquest quickly bogged down in peripheral irrelevances.[51] However Soldier 'F', the senior officer in charge of the SAS team, told the inquest that they had been briefed by MI5 that the IRA gang

11 Miss Hilda Murrell, an elderly anti-nuclear supporter, victim of an opportunist thief or a bungled MI5 burglary?

12 Miss Murrell's car, which was not found by the police until three days after her disappearance.

13   Morwenstow, Cornwall, the American tapping station that eavesdropped on Neil Kinnock's calls to Malcolm Turnbull.

14   Cathy Massiter, the MI5 officer who risked her freedom to tell the public about the illegal activities the agency was involved in.

15 and 16   Sarah Tisdall and Leon Brittan: she leaked state papers and was imprisoned for six months; he leaked state papers yet later received a knighthood.

17   Clive Ponting leaked state papers but the jury did not convict, believing that the public should know the truth.

18, 19 and 20   The leading figures in the *Spycatcher* affair: *above left*, Peter Wright; *above right*, Lord Victor Rothschild; *below*, Chapman Pincher.

was dedicated and ruthless, had left a large car bomb in Main Street, had a radio-controlled triggering device in its possession that required only the push of a button to detonate it, and was armed. Under the circumstances it was hardly surprising that the SAS team took no chances and immediately started shooting at the trio in what a pathologist called a 'frenzied attack', firing as many as 16 shots at each of them.

Many questions were asked of the anonymous SAS witnesses to ascertain whether they had given the trio a genuine opportunity to surrender or if it had always been their plan to kill them. The SAS witnesses told the inquest that they had shouted a warning ordering the suspects to surrender but each had made a suspicious move which the SAS thought was to trigger the bomb. Unfortunately the SAS team were not asked whether, had they been told the trio were unarmed, there was no bomb and no triggering device, they would have acted differently.

The nub of the inquest was therefore whether the SAS had been deliberately briefed by MI5 with false information to encourage them to kill the three rather than arrest them. Had the trio been arrested there was nothing with which they could have been charged since they had committed no offence in Gibraltar other than using stolen passports. At best they could have been extradited to Spain to stand trial for possession of explosives but this might have revealed embarrassing details as to the origin of the Semtex. The head of the MI5 operation, Witness 'O', said that they knew the names of the trio (the question of the fourth member being outside the scope of the inquest), their aliases, that they possessed a 141 pound Semtex car bomb, and that they intended to attack the guard ceremony on 8 March. No one was allowed to ask the witness where the Semtex came from and how he knew so much about it, or why, if he knew so much intimate detail about the IRA's plans, he did not also know the whereabouts of the car bomb that Sunday morning.

The MI5 witness claimed that the trio were not under surveillance in Spain that Sunday and had entered Gibraltar without anyone seeing them until one of them was recognised near Main Street. Unfortunately the Gibraltar police let the cat out of the bag when they admitted they had been forewarned of the trio's identities and the fact they were planning to enter Gibraltar that Sunday. The matter would have been quickly cleared up had members of the Spanish police and security services given evidence, which would have shown the extent of the surveillance carried out by them and MI5 in Spain between November 1987 and March 1988. There were conflicting reports as to why no one from Spain came to the inquest.[52] Some claimed it was because of the long-running dispute between Spain and Britain over Gibraltar. But a spokesman for the Spanish interior ministry, Augustin Valladolid, not only stated that a sworn affidavit giving full details of the surveillance operation had been given to the British Embassy in Madrid in August but also that 'when the terrorists entered Gibraltar, the British authorities knew they were coming. It's logical that they only would have known this if there had been surveillance on the Spanish side'. Somehow this affidavit never reached the coroner so the jury was never told anything about MI5's operations in Spain.

The government did not want the Spanish security services to give evidence because Hurd's certificate of immunity did not apply to a foreign police force. If the Spaniards had told the inquest how MI5 officers had worked with them, monitoring the gang's movements and conversations throughout the previous months, and explained where the Semtex came from it would have become plain that MI5 had deliberately briefed the SAS with false information.

Effectively the inquest was hamstrung in its early stages, as the government had always intended, and then got side-tracked into a lot of detail about the manner in which the trio were shot.

On 30 September, after 19 days, the coroner summed up with impeccable judgement the issues he had been allowed to put before the jury. As expected the jury returned a verdict of lawful killing although this was only with a nine to two majority. The reporting of the verdict was as predictably polarised[53] as are the politics in Northern Ireland, with the government and its supporters jubilant.[54] But even the most pro-government sections of the media remarked on the lack of evidence from Spain that would have supported MI5's claims. The SAS emerged vindicated only in the sense that they had believed the MI5 briefing and acted accordingly. Whether they relish this role of being used as minions of Henry II is doubtful.

So here again a dirty trick that some may have felt was justified backfired and has done nothing to bring peace to Northern Ireland or hasten the destruction of the IRA who, on the contrary, have milked much useful publicity from the resultant controversy. Had France or Israel carried out the same trick they would at least have ensured that weapons were found on the bodies of the trio and that the Renault car did contain a bomb.

But in the world of dirty tricks the Gibraltar shootings are quite a minor affair. During the early 1980s there was a series of attacks on Americans in the Middle East, particularly in Beirut. Both the American Embassy and the US Marine's barracks were devasted by car bombs with appalling loss of life. Israeli intelligence told the CIA that the person responsible for these attacks was Sheikh Mohammed Hussein Fadlallah. The CIA, in collusion with the Saudi Arabian government, decided to murder Fadlallah.[55] They hired a British ex-Special Air Services soldier and paid him to plant a car bomb in a crowded street outside the block of flats where Fadlallah lived. On 8 March 1985 the bomb exploded killing eighty men, women and children and seriously injuring 200 others. Fadlallah escaped without injury. In an effort to cover its tracks the CIA tried to blame Israel for the bombing but no one believed it. The Saudis, ashamed at the carnage they had helped cause, gave Fadlallah $2 million as a bribe to stop attacking the Americans. He agreed.

Apparently no one in the CIA was disciplined for this outrage. The CIA would argue that since Americans had been killed by bombs they were entitled to retaliate in the same way. The fact that the CIA killed large numbers of totally innocent people who had nothing to do with the attacks worried them not at all. The CIA's bombing in Beirut also demonstrates the lack of accountability that surrounds such agencies enabling them to plan and carry out such operations with impunity. The fact that the CIA employed an ex-SAS soldier is not surprising. It is reliably reported that MI6 has close contacts with and may even control a company called KMS, registered in Jersey in the Channel Islands and run by David Walker, himself an ex-SAS officer, who rents out his private armies to foreign governments to carry out dubious undertakings from which they wish to distance themselves.[56]

According to former KMS employees Walker has regular meetings and lunches with senior MI6 officials and his name has also been linked with Colonel North and terrorist operations in Nicaragua. If all this is true (and no one from KMS has so far denied the allegations), it suggests a very hypocritical attitude on the part of the British government in permitting such contacts to continue while berating other governments for not doing enough about international terrorism.

In recent years it has become the practice in Britain and America to smear the characters of those now dead, who have served their country with great distinction, with all manner of allegations about their capabilities and character. Wartime leaders like Churchill, Montgomery and Eisenhower have all suffered from such attacks. In the intelligence world one of the best examples of this has been the ludicrous claims made against Sir Roger Hollis which are based on nothing more than gossip, bad feeling, some odd bits of information that have been selectively rearranged to suit a preconceived answer, and an inability to come to terms with the fact that MI5 is very inefficient.

Another strange story was told about Harold Holt, the Australian prime minister, who drowned on 17 December 1967. In 1983 a bizarre book was published[57] claiming that Holt had been a long-time spy for the Chinese and had not drowned[58] but had been taken off Cheviot Beach near Portsea, about 40 miles south of Melbourne, by a Chinese submarine. The book's author, Anthony Grey, had been Reuter's correspondent in China and was imprisoned there during the cultural revolution for two years. He got the story from Commander Ronald Titcombe, a retired Royal Australian Navy officer.[59] In turn Titcombe claimed to have been told the details of Holt's spying by Chinese contacts who he had met while doing business in that country.

One of the allegations against Holt was that he had communicated with his Chinese controllers by code within the plain text of letters he wrote to his family and friends during the period 1952–1962 when he was travelling abroad meeting other world leaders representing the Australian government.

A retired GCHQ codebreaker, Phillip Chambers,[60] had examined these letters and told Titcombe that there were two hidden codes within the plain text.[61] The first was a tabular code. Chambers claimed that Holt had in certain parts of his letters included details of items like menus, theatre programmes[62] or horses running at a race meeting, and rearranged the text of these so that the exact number of words and punctuation marks in a line gave either a 'yes' or 'no' answer to some question asked him by the Chinese.[63] The second code was based on the descriptions of flowers and fruit Holt had in his room. Chambers claimed that a pineapple might represent a battleship, a banana a submarine, an orange a destroyer, and in this way Holt was able to pass on details of Western fleets to the Chinese.[64]

The same report also contained the weird allegation that because Holt never discussed defence and political secrets in his letters to his friends this proved that he must be passing on the information in code somewhere within them. The more I read this report with all its verbiage the more I wondered what really went on inside GCHQ if this was typical of its work. One could easily imagine a report of this nature surrounded by an aura of secrecy induced by exotic codewords like 'Umbra' or 'Cosmic' arriving on a busy minister's desk who might assume it was true. One can certainly see why no one thought Prime was odd at GCHQ.

Holt's letters,[65] running to some 300 pages of typescript, proved to be very ordinary, chatty accounts of his travels and meetings written in a breezy, extrovert manner that certainly matched his character. Evidently Holt enjoyed his travels enormously and was kept extremely busy with both ministerial and social engagements but, whenever he could, he borrowed a secretary from the Australian High Commission's office and dictated some notes about his journey. As I read through these intriguing letters, I noticed that they had all been typed on an identical typewriter over the ten years, and set out in the same style. Neither Titcombe nor Chambers had mentioned this. It therefore seemed fairly obvious that the rough draft Holt dictated while he was travelling was sent back to Australia, together with theatre programmes and anything else he wanted included in the text, and a secretary there typed up the final letter making the necessary seven copies for distribution to his family and friends.

It followed, therefore, that the manner in which a wine list or theatre programme was included in the final letter was entirely at the discretion of a typist 12,000 miles away from Holt. The fact that the words and hyphens in a particular line added up to an odd or even number was entirely fortuitous and had no significance whatsoever.

The story about the fruit was even more farcical. On arriving in Singapore, Holt was taken as an official guest to his suite at a hotel overlooking the harbour. Holt describes the room, the view and the gift of fruit. Chambers concludes that Holt was passing on to the Chinese details of the naval vessels he saw from his hotel. The only problem is that the naval base in Singapore is 20 miles away on the north side of the island, and Holt never went near it, so he would have seen no warships during his 24-hour stay on the island

Were it not for the distress the allegations caused the Holt family, such a tale might be marginally amusing and deserve a short-lived place on the fiction shelves. But what is most interesting about this story is the manner in which all sorts of vague allegations are linked together and then presented as proven evidence upon which to base the claim of Holt's treachery.

One of the greatest areas of dirty tricks is sexual entrapment. This applies just as much in the East as it does in the West. People working in a foreign country, especially if young and unmarried, are always a target for sexual blackmail. Life in an embassy or military base for such people can be incredibly boring, particularly if they do not speak the language and there is not a lot they can afford to do in their spare time. Western embassies in Moscow and other East European capitals employ a surprisingly large number of local people as interpreters or even just cleaners, all of whom are trained by the KGB to talent-spot new arrivals who may find their lives lonely and dull. The KGB watcher service immediately starts building up a dossier on their private life to see if there are any chinks in their security such as heavy drinking, overspending or any kind of sexual deviation. Because of the rather barren lifestyle in eastern cities these problems often occur.

Sometimes no effort is needed. John Vassall, a sad but obvious homosexual, was posted to Moscow in 1954 in quite a humble position.[66] Apparently no one at the embassy noticed anything odd about Vassall, but the KGB did. A clerk working in the Polish Embassy called Mikhailsky, who claimed to be as bored and lonely as Vassall, soon managed to make friends with him[67] and before long the pair were photographed in bed together and Vassall was blackmailed into passing on classified information. When Vassall returned to London in June 1956 he went to work in the Admiralty and, although still quite junior, contrived to see as many secret files as possible, all of which he photographed. Whatever security checks were made on him evidently did not reveal Vassall's continuing homosexuality nor that he had taken a flat in Dolphin Square, a luxurious address for a clerk, which he proceeded to fill with antique furniture, as well as depositing over £3,000 in the bank. Vassall was finally exposed by a Russian defector called Yuri Nosenko[68] and received 18 years in prison. There were later many doubts as to whether Nosenko was a genuine defector or a plant so it is possible that Vassall had outlived his value to the KGB and was deliberately betrayed in order to establish Nosenko's credentials with the CIA.

But it is not just junior homosexual clerks who get caught this way. In 1968 the British ambassador in Moscow, Sir Geoffrey Harrison, had an affair with a Russian maid called Galya who worked in his official residence and ended up going to bed with her. As one might have expected, Galya turned out to be a member of the KGB who somehow managed to take compromising photographs of the pair together. What made this particular incident remarkable was that even after returning to London and being told that the woman was a KGB agent Harrison continued to correspond with her,[69] his letters being intercepted by Special Branch. Despite this Harrison was not prosecuted because the trial would have been too embarrassing.

Houghton, one of the Portland spy ring, was compromised because of his black-market deals involving a Polish girlfriend who, of course, turned out to be a member of Polish intelligence. Geoffrey Prime's interest in young girls was probably noticed by East German intelligence officers when he was serving in West Berlin and led to him being recruited as a spy. East German intelligence has also been remarkably successful in seducing middle-aged women[70] working in sensitive areas of the West German government and persuading them to hand over all secret material passing across their desks.

In Western capitals there are far more temptations for Eastern bloc diplomats although usually they are rather too expensive for their foreign currency allowances. Nevertheless, MI5's D4 section, in conjunction with Special Branch, has a number of prostitutes on its books (in return for not prosecuting them), who can be used to set up entrapments for unwary diplomats. The idea of running a brothel in order to blackmail people is not new. In Berlin before and during the war the German equivalent of MI5, the SD, or *Sicherheitsdienst*, ran a brothel in the west of the city on the Giesebrechtstrasse, called Salon Kitty.[71] All the rooms were bugged and some of the women were not prostitutes but had volunteered to act the part with selected clientele. This might be a more productive and financially rewarding extension of MI5's activities in London.

Western businessmen visiting Eastern Europe are always warned against getting involved in sexual entrapment although, from my own experience of many years visiting these countries, glamorous Mata Haris seem in very short supply. There is the apocryphal story of the businessman who having been lured to bed by a beautiful KGB female agent was then confronted the next morning with explicit photographs of their activities and promptly ordered two dozen because they were so good.

Not all such incidents are as funny. Commander Anthony Courtney, a former naval officer and Member of Parliament, who was a persistent critic of Russia and her allies, was trapped into a scandal in 1961 when on a visit to Moscow he went to bed with a woman, Zinaida Volkava, who was supposed to be an Intourist travel guide but was actually a KGB agent.[72] Photographs were taken and Courtney was threatened that they would be publicly distributed if he did not stop his anti-Russian attacks in Parliament. In the end they were sent to Western newspapers and as a result Courtney's political career suffered. At the time Courtney had separated from his first wife and was engaged to another woman so perhaps if he had copied the apocryphal businessman and ordered copies of the photographs he would have done better.

The only occasion I was arrested in Eastern Europe was in the early 1960s when I had driven to Bulgaria for a very short holiday on the Black Sea at the then very small and unknown resort of Varna.[73] What I did not know was that the area had been sealed off for a visit by the Russian premier, Nikita Krushchev, but my car had been mistakenly waved through the checkpoints.

The hotel I eventually reached was most surprised to see me because apart from a couple of British engineers from the Dunlop Rubber Company working in the Varna shipyard it was empty. The next day I drove over to the port of Balchik where I discovered one of the first Russian nuclear *Hotel* class submarines had arrived to be inspected by Krushchev. At this point I was arrested and taken back to my hotel where I and my room were carefully searched. My colour films were flown to Vienna for processing to the first monochrome stage but proved innocuous. Then two KGB interrogators arrived and warned me that if I did not confess to being a NATO spy I would never see my wife and children again or my lovely house in Eastbourne. Sadly, I had to explain I had neither a wife nor children and did not live in Eastbourne. It then dawned on the Russians that they had not arrested my brother who was then in the Royal Navy and involved in the positive vetting of Polaris submarine crews. But at least it showed they had done most of their homework properly, even if they got the wrong member of the family.

The Russians, like MI5 and the FBI, devote an enormous amount of time and effort collating useless information about people. One evening in Moscow I was royally entertained by senior officials from the state agricultural organisation v/o Prodintorg to thank me for having secretly disposed of a large quantity of unwanted Cuban sugar Krushchev had obliged them to buy to help Castro's ailing economy. In the course of the relaxed atmosphere the conversation turned to old age and Madame Gaidamashko, a very clever and charming woman in charge of the sugar division, remarked that her mother was over 90 years old. At this one of her colleagues who by then was a little over-tired remarked, 'But Mr Rusbridger, your mother is over 75 years old'. As it happened this was true, but I had never even mentioned her existence.

An even more bizarre incident occurred when I had invited some guests from Eastern Europe to our London office to see how the commodity markets worked. As usual they brought with them their equivalent of a KGB minder. A day or so after they had arrived the senior member of the party told me with some embarrassment that their luggage had been broken into at the hotel and this was obviously the work of British intelligence. I thought this unlikely because I could not see that they would be of any interest to MI5. I made a few discreet inquiries and was assured that no one from MI5 or

Special Branch had been near their hotel. In the end it transpired that it was their security minder who had done it so as to make them suspect the British and prevent them from becoming attracted to Western life. This shows how the Cold War is encouraged by both sides.

The dividing line between propaganda and dirty tricks is often hard to define. In the West we expect to be told bad things about the Russians and their allies just as we assume they are being told bad things about us. We hear a lot about them spying on us but far less about what we do to them. Russia argues that America poses just as great a threat to world freedom itself and can point to the overthrow of elected governments as in Chile, the mining of harbours in Nicaragua, supporting Contra 'freedom fighters' who daily murder other people, invading Cuba, letting off car bombs in Lebanon and a host of other CIA-inspired blackmail and terrorist operations costing many billions of dollars a year. Indeed, since the turn of the century, America has intervened with force in foreign countries on 28 occasions compared to the Russians' four.

The head of the KGB, Viktor Chebrikov, recently stated that despite all the talk of better relations over 20 spies, including some KGB officers working as doubles, had been caught and more than 50 NATO diplomats expelled for spying, while the Russian Navy had found newly placed underwater listening devices attached to Russian telephone cables in the Okhotsk Sea off the Russian coast. Although these accusations too could be part of the propaganda game.

The American government accuses Russia of being a secretive country where debate about its defence spending is not allowed, yet the Russians could argue that the Americans distort their own defence spending by giving totally misleading claims of Russian superiority and, as the Iran/Contra hearings showed, are equally adept at concealing the truth from their own people.

The war of words has gone on for so long and both sides have now entrenched themselves so deeply that when a new Russian leader actually agrees to some aspect of mutual disarmament, signs a treaty, and then offers more, the West falls apart in disarray as if it hardly wanted the Cold War to stop. As Russian foreign minister Eduard Schevardnadze put it, 'My country has done a terrible thing. We have deprived you of an enemy.' It was almost comical to watch the embarrassment of the Americans and British as the first Cruise missiles were taken out of Britain back to America for destruction and how eager officials were to explain that this will not weaken NATO because the warheads will soon return to Europe on other missiles. If the Russians said such things it would be proof that they were not sincere about disarmament. Meanwhile the idea that Russia is the enemy, poised to invade America, is perpetuated by films like *Red Dawn*, *Top Gun*, and *Amerika*. Similar films are shown in Russia.

Intelligence is a do-it-yourself profession where any crisis situation can be created to support the current version of the truth. But at the end of the day both East and West spend more of their time fooling themselves than the other side. The use of dirty tricks often seems a clever way of putting the blame on others or defeating an enemy without regard to the law but more often than not such practices are found out and the subsequent public exposure is always far more damaging than had there been a straightforward admission of the facts from the start. Dirty tricks are a sign of inefficiency which is why they are used so often by intelligence agencies that have nothing better to offer.

CHAPTER 7

THE CURZON STREET WATCHERS

If international intelligence operations are uncontrolled and unaccountable, much the same applies to the relatively mundane domestic operations of Britain's security service MI5 where there is no concern for the law despite the elaborate set of guidelines laid down in 1952. For this reason no sensible home secretary would want to inquire too deeply into what MI5 gets up to. The less he knows the fewer awkward questions he may be called upon to answer in Parliament. Does MI5 break the law? The answer is that it most certainly does. A former home secretary, Merlyn Rees, confided in a television interview[1] that he was aware that MI5 broke the law but did nothing about it. Much of the fuss about Peter Wright's book *Spycatcher* is because it describes in detail numerous cases of MI5 burgling premises and planting bugs. In the past such claims were officially brushed aside on the grounds that there was no evidence to substantiate them, but in Wright's case that could not be done. So here at least we have a benchmark of illegality with which to judge MI5.

Has MI5 the right to break the law? There are varying views about this. Rees has said that there is no legal basis for claiming that MI5 enjoys some form of royal prerogative enabling it to act outside the law, but it is noteworthy that he never made any inquiries about such activities when home secretary. Lord Denning has stated:

> Officers of MI5 have no prerogative to justify any of their actions. If they break into premises or seize documents, they are breaking the law and can be brought before the courts and punished accordingly.

This is precisely what Lord Denning said about MI5 in his 1963 report on the Profumo affair: 'The members of the security service (MI5) are, in the eye of the law, ordinary citizens with no powers greater than anyone else.'

On the other hand, Sir John Donaldson, Master of the Rolls (and Lord Denning's successor), takes a different view:

> It is silly for us to ... say that the security service (MI5) is obliged to follow the letter of the law; it isn't real. Of course there has to be some control. Probably the best yet devised is to say the security service is bound by a strict rule of law, but always to bear in mind a prerogative power not to pursue criminal proceedings and a statutory power in the Director of Public Prosecutions to stop criminal proceedings. It was essential in the public interest for MI5 officers to break the law in some ways and that such breaches could, or would, never be prosecuted. Murder is an entirely different matter.[2]

James Callaghan was home secretary from 1967–70, foreign secretary 1974–76, and prime minister of Britain from 1976–79. Yet when he was asked about the accountability of the intelligence services he could only waffle.

> I am not sure what its accountability is to Parliament ... I find it a difficult question to answer. I really do. They [MI5 and MI6] are run as separate departments. Some ministers do not want to know a lot ... I am going to give you a very unsatisfactory answer. I do not know ... I am very, very, mixed up about this. I do not think I can help you with this.[3]

If a senior politician who at various time has been in direct control of MI5 and MI6 and also head of the nation's intelligence operations does not know what is happening then it shows that these agencies are out of control. It is hardly surprising MI5 feels free to break the law as and when it chooses, when even if its officers are caught in the act they run no risk of being prosecuted. In all the years that MI5 has been in existence not one of its officers has ever been charged by the police with any sort of criminal offence associated with his work. Yet MI5 has a special section called A1A (Technical Operations) whose only work is breaking and entering private property, often done with the vast collection of keys it keeps, as was vividly described by Wright in his book.

MI5 maintains contact with the police through Special Branch.[4] Founded in 1883 to deal with Irish republican terrorism, it is the nearest thing Britain has to a political police force. Until 1958 Special Branch was a small unit controlled by the Metropolitan Police but since then it has grown much larger with 2,000 officers, 25 civilian staff, a nominal budget of £25 million per year and departments in each provincial police force. The headquarters of Special Branch is at New Scotland Yard in London and in theory it is supposed to be quite independent of MI5 and just a normal part of Britain's police force. Some chief constables like to pretend they control their area's Special Branch activities[5] but in fact Special Branch is a law unto itself.

MI5 needs close links with Special Branch because MI5 has no legal powers and in the unlikely event it ever finds a spy a Special Branch officer is needed to make the arrest. Special Branch officers also help to smooth over any embarrassing incidents, such as MI5 officers being seen burgling premises by members of the public who call the police or incidents involving firearms, as occurred with the Cuban diplomat.

MI5's activities are neatly protected whatever the legal position may be. Ministers in charge do not inquire. The police take no action. Thus the courts get no cases of MI5 lawbreaking before them. As a result everyone can say with perfect honesty that they have no proof that MI5 breaks the law.

Under the new Security Service Bill all this will change. MI5 will operate within 'a framework of regulations welded into legislation'[6] that will require it to confine its activities only to the protection of national security. It would not be permitted to act against any person or organisation just because they campaigned against the policies of the government of the day. Home Secretary Douglas Hurd told Parliament on 15 December 1988:

> For the first time ever this Bill makes the political neutrality of the service a statutory requirement. The service could not get involved in lesser objectives. Nor could it take action intended to further the interests of any political party, including the party of the government of the day. These were strong safeguards set down for the first time by statute.

For all practical purposes there is no difference between what Hurd is proposing now and what Maxwell Fyfe set out in 1952. Interestingly, Hurd uses the expression 'for the first time ever' which plainly suggests he is aware that MI5 has consistently ignored the 1952 directive. Yet Hurd does not explain why, if he and previous home secretaries knew this, they did nothing about it. Until now home secretaries have always refused to discuss allegations of malpractice by MI5 and that this new legislation has been forced upon the government only due to the embarrassing revelations from Wright, Cathy Massiter and others, who worked in the organisation and despite attempts to smear their characters could not be ignored. If these revelations had never occurred it is unlikely that the government would have introduced this new Bill.

In the past, home secretaries have refused to comment on MI5's responsibilities beyond quoting the Maxwell Fyfe directive, giving the impression that this bestowed some statutory obligation upon the security service. Hurd now implies this directive was valueless, which is what many people have always believed. The Maxwell Fyfe guidelines failed because there was no system of external accountability and MI5 knew it could ignore them with impunity. This new Bill does not provide external accountability, so it is stretching credulity to its limits to believe that MI5 will be any more likely to obey these rules than it was the previous ones simply because they are now enshrined in legislation.

As far as burgling and bugging premises are concerned the new Bill requires MI5 to obtain a warrant in the same way as it does currently for telephone tapping, which certainly gives no cause for satisfaction. MI5 will presumably submit a 'short reason' of why it wants to burgle a particular house or office and submit this through the Home Office to a judge. Although the judge could ask to see the complete file relating to the case, if he is busy – as most judges are – and MI5 insists the matter is urgent,[7] it is more likely he will approve the warrant without further comment, which is what happens with telephone-tapping warrants.[8] Judges are not known for rigorous investigation into technical matters and it is safe to assume that the judge chosen for this chore will be one who has a good track record of supporting government policies.[9]

Furthermore MI5 is unlikely to be so foolish as to submit a request for a warrant that is any way controversial or doubtful.[10] For these operations it will use, as in the past, freelance burglars and engineers whose work is not only illegal but unrecorded anywhere within MI5. So despite all the majesty of the new legislation MI5 will carry on as before.

The next point to consider is who is worthy of attracting the attention of MI5 and Special Branch? MI5's charter says that it should only concern itself, on the domestic front, with subversives. But interpretation of the word subversive has changed over the years. Back in 1963, Lord Denning described a subversive as 'someone who would contemplate the overthrow of the government by unlawful means and, in particular, violent means'. But by 1978 Rees described a subversive as 'those I think are causing a problem for the state'.

Exactly what causing a problem for the state might mean is open to wide interpretation but it is not new. Between 1947 and 1950 Labour Prime Minister Clement Attlee authorised MI5 to tap the telephone of a respected *Financial Times* journalist, Paul Einzig, because he had written a number of embarrassingly accurate articles about the Labour government's plans to nationalise the British steel industry. No question of national security here.

When Mrs Thatcher came to power she defined a subversive as someone who:

Is or has recently been a member of a Communist or Fascist organisation or subversive group acknowledged to be such by the minister, whose aims are to undermine or overthrow parliamentary democracy in the United Kingdom by political, industrial, or violent means.
Is or has recently been sympathetic to or associated with members or

sympathisers of such organisations or groups in such a way as to raise reasonable doubts about his reliability.

Is susceptible to pressure from such organisations or groups.

This definition is so broadly based that it could affect anyone. Who is able to say whether another person who they have never met is susceptible to pressure or not? And what criteria does a minister use in judging that someone, or some organisation, falls within this category? Inevitably he will have to rely on what he is told by MI5.

In August 1985 Leon Brittan, then home secretary, said:

> Both elements of the definition must be met before an activity may be regarded as subversive, i.e., there must be a threat to the safety or well-being of the state and an intention to undermine or overthrow parliamentary democracy. The definition therefore imposes strict tests which ensure ordinary political or trade-union activity cannot be taken to constitute subversion.

Like the 1952 Maxwell Fyfe guidelines for MI5, these are fine-sounding words. But once again, as there is no mechanism for impartial accountability, they are meaningless. Only two chief constables have ever publicly spoken out about the definition of subversives. One was John Alderson, former chief constable of the Devon and Cornwall police. He said:

> The terms of reference of the Special Branches leave much to their discretion. To some all 'activists' may be subversive and both individuals and groups critical of the established order are marked out for surveillance and recording.[11]

The other was Harold Salisbury, former chief constable of the York, North and East Riding police, who said:

> I would say anyone who's decrying marriage, family life, trying to break that up, pushing drugs, advocating the acceptance of certain drugs, homosexuality, indiscipline in schools, weak penalties for anti-social crimes ... a whole gamut of things ... that could be pecking away at the foundations of our society ... if a chap doesn't like a file being kept on him ... that's just the kind of chap we should be keeping files on.[12]

As a result of attitudes like this millions of people totally innocent of any crime have dossiers kept on them by MI5 and Special Branch. Much of the information is totally inaccurate and slanderous based on gossip and tittle-tattle and is frequently used to denigrate the person's character and frustrate their career. Because such files are secret and there is no way of checking their contents it is usually impossible for individuals to prove they are being smeared. But sometimes there is a slip up and the facts become public.

A good example of this was the case of Jan Martin, a freelance television producer, whose husband was mistakenly identified by a Dutch border guard in September 1978 while they were on the continent as being a member of the Baader-Meinhof gang.[13] This information was sent back to Special Branch, who opened a file on her without checking the facts and then warned several of her clients including Taylor Woodrow, the civil engineers, not to use her services because she was a security risk connected with terrorism.

Fortunately Jan Martin's father was a retired police officer, Superintendent John Robertson, who was able to establish that a file did exist at Special Branch. Eventually Superintendent Peter Phelan of Special Branch confirmed to Jan Martin that the file was based on inaccurate information and said it would be destroyed. Martin was lucky to have someone with the right connections to help her. Had she not then she could have been blacklisted for the rest of her life, as indeed are many others who find themselves on an MI5 list which stops them from getting work or promotion. At the BBC Brigadier Ronald Stonham liaises with MI5 and Special Branch and advises the corporation on whether or not to employ someone. There are numerous cases where producers and writers have been prevented from working on a film because MI5 has branded them as a security risk. In all these instances the individual is not allowed to know what allegations are being made and therefore has no opportunity of challenging their accuracy.

In cases where MI5 or Special Branch are unable to directly affect a person's character or career they leak information from their records (police computers are as secure as a rusty colander) to private organisations who maintain private files and blacklists of people which they supply to their members. Many retired police officers join security firms or set up their own investigation agencies, often indulging in very dubious practices, and have no difficulty in getting information off police computers from their previous colleagues, often for quite large sums of money. The Home Office and senior police officers pretend to be terribly upset by such leaks but in reality turn a blind eye. Special Branch also liaise with tame journalists around the country to whom they give bits of unsavoury gossip about people and in return are given names and addresses of people who have written letters criticising any aspect of government policy.

The government's hypocritical attitude is shown by an answer given by former home secretary, Leon Brittan, to a House of Commons Home Affairs Committee in January 1985. It had asked if members of CND were considered subversive within the guidelines laid down for MI5 and Special Branch surveillance. Brittan replied:

There is no doubt that peaceful political campaigning to change the mind of the government and of people generally about . . . nuclear disarmament, whether unilateral or otherwise, is an entirely legitimate activity which does not fall within the very strict criteria.

The most generous conclusion of this ridiculous statement is that Brittan did not know what MI5 or Special Branch had been, and was, doing.

But another home secretary, Roy Jenkins, commented:

I took the view . . . that MI5 should be pulled out of its political surveillance role. I had been doubtful of the value of that role for some time. I am convinced now that an organisation of people who lived in the fevered world of espionage and counter-espionage is entirely unfitted to judge between what is subversion and what is legitimate dissent.[14]

One person who knew perfectly well what Special Branch and MI5 were up to was Mrs Madeline Haigh, a 38-year-old mother of two children who lived at Walmley Road, Sutton Coldfield, in the West Midlands. Mrs Haigh was concerned about the siting of American Cruise missiles in Britain and in 1981 wrote a letter[15] to her local newspaper expressing her fears. The letter was noted by Special Branch and MI5. Two months after the letter appeared a Special Branch officer called at her house claiming to be a representative of the mail order firm Grattans. He said he was investigating a £20 fraud that had taken place from her address. When he started asking Mrs Haigh personal questions about her political views, she became suspicious and contacted her local police station. They assured her that her caller had not been a police officer.

Still unhappy, Mrs Haigh wrote to her MP. This happened to be a Cabinet minister, Norman Fowler, who the police could not easily ignore. Fowler contacted the chief constable of the West Midlands police, Sir Philip Knights, who assured Fowler that neither the police nor Special Branch had been involved. Unfortunately Fowler was not convinced. After two years and five more inquiries Knights finally told Fowler that he had discovered that Special Branch were involved all along. His excuse for not finding out at the first inquiry was that some of their files had been destroyed.

The Special Branch officer concerned was not disciplined nor was the file on Mrs Haigh destroyed and Knights justified his action by claiming that:

Mrs Haigh had written to a newspaper in terms which were interpreted as indicating that she might be a person prepared to support or get involved in public protests, and the responsibility of Special Branch is analysing and assessing information of that kind.

In other words Special Branch and MI5 make the interpretation that suits them and then act as they wish. This shows that guidelines and criteria are of no value in protecting innocent people because there is no way of enforcing them, nor is there any method by which those involved can obtain redress.

Despite what Brittan and other ministers may claim Special Branch and MI5 compile dossiers on the following:

Those who belong to any form of protest group.

Homosexuals and lesbians.

Owners of cars parked near selected political meetings and demonstrations.

Owners of vehicles seen parked near houses owned by suspected or controversial people.

Victims of crime.

Alleged associates of criminals, subversives and controversial people.

Parents and other members of such families.

Anyone who makes a complaint about the police.

Anyone who writes controversial letters in the newspapers criticising government policy on sensitive issues like nuclear weapons.

Anyone who writes letters to newspapers criticising the security services.

Anyone who makes inquiries about matters like civil defence.

In view of the wide range this covers it is not surprising that MI5's computer needs storage capacity for 20 million individual names. Of course some controversial people do not get listed. Anyone who held a rally or wrote letters and articles advocating more Cruise missiles and nuclear power-stations would not find themselves visited by Special Branch officers posing as mail-order representatives. This clearly shows that, despite the 1952 Maxwell Fyfe directive, both Special Branch and MI5 are highly politicised in their targetting.

The new Security Service Bill is supposed to do away with all this and as Hurd told Parliament: 'The security service was not interested in the normal and proper doings of the trade unions or other groups which might campaign against government policy.'

This is a repetition of what Leon Brittan said four years ago but it plainly had no effect on MI5 who continued targetting organisations like CND, the NCCL and trade unions during wage negotiations.

In theory the new legislation provides for a system whereby someone who believes MI5 has them under illegal surveillance can complain to a tribunal. But how would they know? For many years CND believed its telephones were being tapped, its offices and members' homes burgled, and files kept on them by MI5, but could not prove it because successive home secretaries refused to admit or deny the charge. Only when Cathy Massiter broke ranks and went on television to say that MI5 had indeed done such things, not only to CND but others too, did the truth come out. No minister has ever denied what Cathy Massiter said was true.

Under the new legislation anyone who suspects they are being similarly treated can go to the tribunal and lodge a complaint. If the tribunal is as efficient as the police complaints system then they will probably have a long wait. And however prestigious the tribunal may appear to be on paper it can only ask MI5 whether the complaint is true.[16] If MI5 says it is not then there is nothing more the tribunal can do. It has no power to enter Curzon House or MI5's computer centre at Mount Row, to demand access to its records or question its staff.

So if the cases of Jan Martin and Madelaine Haigh occurred under the new Bill they would fare no better than under the previous system where they were told deliberate lies to frustrate their inquiries. The only way they could learn the truth would be if another Cathy Massiter went public, but the government has ruled out this possibility by making it an offence to give away such information even when the law is being broken by MI5. So despite all the hyperbole about making MI5 more accountable, in fact it will be less so under the new Bill.

There is also the question of what will happen to all the files on people and organisations MI5 has accumulate over the past 35 years which will be illegal under the Security Service Bill. Will they be destroyed under independent supervision or simply allowed to stay even though Hurd assures people that the information in them is no longer of interest to MI5?

In September 1978 a young Reading student, Guy Smith, was visited by Detective Constable Mooney of the Reading police.[17] Mooney told Smith that he was investigating a wages robbery that had occurred on Friday 8 September at 8 a.m. during which a motorcycle similar to that owned by Smith had been involved. Mooney claimed that Smith was one of twenty people who owned such motorcyles and was being interviewed because the number of his machine had been given to the police by a witness.

Smith thought this was a bit odd because his motorcycle was only a 125cc Honda lightweight and it was still registered at his old London address. He explained to Mooney that he had been having breakfast at the time of the robbery. When he asked Mooney for more information about the wages robbery, which Smith had not seen reported in the local press, Mooney said it was being kept out of the papers for security reasons.

Having satisfied Mooney about the robbery Smith was then questioned about his private life and Mooney asked him why he was interested in emergency planning. For a moment Smith was nonplussed and then remembered that a few weeks earlier he had written to the local police asking for information about emergency plans for dealing with a nuclear attack as part of a research project. Only that morning he had received a letter from the police regretting that they could not help him. After Mooney had left Smith telephoned Reading police station and was told that Mooney was not with the CID but Special Branch.

Smith then made a formal complaint to the Thames Valley Police and eventually received a letter from the assistant chief constable who admitted that he had been interviewed by Mooney on an entirely fictitious pretext since the robbery had never taken place. The ACC apologised for the method used by Mooney but added that it was necessary to probe the authenticity and intentions of people like Smith who asked questions about civil defence. The reply was remarkably similar to that given in the Haigh case.

In 1982 I was also researching material on Britain's civil defence and wrote to the Home Office[18] asking what arrangements had been made to provide television transmitters with emergency power supplies to enable them to continue operating if normal electricity supplies were disrupted by air attacks or sabotage. In fact the answer was quite simple. There are no arrangements.[19] The Home Office declined to confirm this and several weeks later two men called at my house claiming to be BBC engineers.

They asked why I was interested in the subject, which I explained, and they then started to ask me other more personal questions. Realising they were from Special Branch I asked them some simple technical questions about one of our local transmitters which of course they could not answer. In the best traditions of Fleet Street they made their excuses and left. A subsequent check with the regional BBC engineering department showed that none of its engineers had been in the area that day.

Telephone tapping in Britain by MI5 and Special Branch has always been, and remains, a very sensitive issue. There are two issues involved: the official tapping done under a warrant and the unofficial tapping and bugging of premises done at the whim and fancy of the department concerned. Concern over telephone tapping goes back many years. One of the earliest inquiries into the whole question of the interception of communications was the Birkett Committee report of 1957. It accepted there was no legal power, either in statute or common law, to sanction the interception of communications. However, it agreed that the government was able to invoke a prerogative authority to intercept letters and telegrams. When it came to telephones, all the committee could say was:

> It is difficult to resist the view that if there is a lawful power to intercept communications in the form of letters and telegrams, then it is wide enough to cover telephone communications as well. If, however, it should be thought the power to intercept telephone messages was left in an uncertain state that was undesirable, it would be for Parliament to

consider what steps ought to be taken to remove all uncertainty if the practice is to continue.

Removing uncertainty was the very last thing either the security services or the bureaucrats wanted in a matter like this. Far better to go on muddling along in a grey world of legality using the talisman of national security to obscure the facts and muzzle debate. And that is what happened. Parliament has never approved telephone tapping. The official line taken by all post-war governments is that tapping only occurs, insofar as MI5 and Special Branch are concerned, when the security of the state is endangered but this is quite untrue.

If there is too much of an outcry on the subject, the tried and tested response is to hold an inquiry. Some prestigious judge is produced who, after a suitable pause, publishes a short report which always says that he is perfectly satisfied that any telephone tapping is being properly carried out within the official guidelines. The annual review of telephone tapping for 1987[20] shows that only 252 warrants were in force at 31 December 1987[21] and the commissioner, Lord Justice Lloyd, mentions that he visited Special Branch, MI5 and MI6 to see these warrants. But he did not visit any of the tapping centres themselves nor talk with the special British Telecom staff who carry out the interceptions.

The report goes into absurdly elaborate detail with childlike naivety, describing how three numbers got tapped by mistake because the engineers connected up the wrong number in two cases, and in the third tapped the suspect's old number which had been changed. Lloyd's only comment was that this shows that things sometimes go wrong. A more pertinent conclusion is that MI5 must still be remarkably inefficient if it listens to the telephone calls for a month of someone who is supposed to be a subversive or a serious threat to national security and fails to realise it is tapping the wrong number.

Ex-MI5 employees tell a very different story. Cathy Massiter explained how the telephones of trade-union officials were tapped during wage negotiations so that the relevant government department could be told of their intimate discussions in advance of the next meeting.[22] This is in direct contravention of Paragraph 5 of MI5's guidelines which specifically states that MI5 should not pass on information to another government department unless the security of the state is involved. Since the government department which received and used this information must have known it had been illegally obtained the fact that they did not report MI5 to the home secretary shows that neither the government nor civil servants take the regulations relating to MI5 seriously.

In a 1981 television programme[23] a freelance engineer told how he had frequently been employed by MI5 and Special Branch to illegally tap telephones and bug premises, quoting a figure of more than 500 operations in a year. Asked if this meant that the home secretary was lying to Parliament when he stated that the total number of telephone taps in a year was only 457, the engineer replied that the home secretary was only repeating what he had been told by his civil servants and would have neither the wish nor ability to make more detailed inquiries himself. If MI5 and Special Branch are going to do something illegal they will hardly leave a trail of evidence around for others to find.

The account in *Spycatcher*[24] also gives a far more alarming picture. Wright casually mentions that all the telephones in Claridges Hotel are tapped by MI5 because so many interesting foreign visitors (such as official guests of the British government) stay there. One wonders if Lloyd asked about that, or had he prudently not read Wright's book? Whatever learned judges and governments may claim, most people in Britain believe that a great number of telephones are tapped without any form of a warrant or accountability simply to suit MI5 and Special Branch. Since previous home secretaries have admitted that they knew this went on, but did nothing about it, one must assume that the present incumbent knows about it too.

During the hunt for some drug traffickers in October 1976 called *Operation Julie*, Detective Inspector Richard Lee of the Thames Valley Police wanted to tap the telephone of one of the suspects, Henry Todd, in London.[25] Instead of getting a warrant and having the line officially tapped Lee got in touch with a private security firm who did it for him illegally. Lee's excuse was that he believed police officers in Scotland Yard were being bribed by the drug traffickers and if he used the official monitoring system the suspects would be tipped off. So far as is known Lee was not disciplined for tapping telephones illegally nor were his accusations of bribery and corruption within Scotland Yard ever investigated. What is interesting about this incident is that Lee evidently knew where to find private engineers to tap a subscriber's line and had no difficulty in persuading them to do it. One wonders how Lloyd would deal with that sort of situation.

Lloyd's report also makes no mention of the numerous occasions that Special Branch and MI5 ask British Telecom to give them a list of the numbers called by a particular subscriber. This is done by a print-check meter normally used to log a subscriber's calls when there has been a complaint of overcharging. The printer produces a list of all calls made, their time, destination and duration. But because the conversation is not monitored this is not considered to be an interception. Nevertheless, it provides the security services with a great deal of personal information when building up a dossier on someone. When British Telecom finally complete their installation of the electronic System-X exchange every subscriber's calls will automatically be listed in this manner for computerised quarterly billing and will also be readily available to the police and security services without any need for a warrant.

To get a warrant to tap a telephone officially MI5 sends the permanent secretary at the Home Office a summary called a 'short reason', and this is passed to the home secretary for signature. In theory the home secretary can ask to see MI5's complete file on the person, persons or organisation concerned but in practice he never does. Those telephones that are tapped, whether officially or unofficially, have their conversations recorded at a number of different centres.[26] It is unlikely that Lloyd or any other inquiry judge has ever visited any of these centres or British Telecom's R12 Division at its research centre at Martlesham Heath, near Ipswich, which works closely with GCHQ devising new ways of bugging its own equipment to suit the security services. Lloyds review also made no mention of the wholesale tapping that GCHQ does at places like Palmer Street, Menwith Hill and Morwenstow.

In March 1983 defence secretary Michael Heseltine set up a propaganda unit[27] within his ministry called DS–19 to counter the effect of CND's campaign to stop Cruise missiles being stationed at Greenham Common. DS–19 then approached MI5 for information about members of CND which Heseltine could use during the forthcoming general election. As Cathy Massiter explained, 'It did begin to seem that what the security service was being asked to do was to provide information on a party political issue.'[28]

Here again MI5 was breaching its own guidelines by disclosing material that it had (illegally, as it happened) gathered and passing it on to another government department for political purposes that had nothing to do with national security.

Even the National Council for Civil Liberties (NCCL) is considered a legitimate target by MI5. The official excuse is that MI5 consider some of its members to be Communist sympathisers but the real reason is that the NCCL upsets MI5 and Special Branch by publicising cases of corrupt and illegal practices by the police.

Despite the 1952 directive that MI5 should be free from any political bias it can open a file on any organisation it chooses simply by claiming it is subversive when what it really means is that it is anti-government or controversial. As the bulk of MI5's staff are right-wing by political definition it follows that anything left-wing is automatically suspect. Edward Heath, Conservative prime minister from 1970–74, who was responsible for the expulsion of the 105 Russian diplomats in 1971, commented:

I met people in the security services who talked the most ridiculous nonsense and whose whole philosophy was a ridiculous nonsense. If some of them were on a tube [underground train] and saw someone reading the *Daily Mirror* they would say 'That is dangerous, get after him find out where he bought it'.[29]

Another ex-MI5 officer remarked:

> Some officers live a very sheltered life and never work in the real world
> ... and the overall tone is right-wing ... some of them thought people
> who wore jeans were potentially subversive.[30]

If MI5 consists of people like this, living in their twisted twilight world, one can see how easy it is to plant ridiculous stories on them, like that about Roger Hollis, and why they find it so difficult to catch even very stupid and obvious spies in their midst. It is hard to believe that these attitudes will change, although MI5 will have to be more careful how they keep their records.

It is perfectly possible that the British electorate might one day return a Labour government to power and this would present MI5 and Special Branch with a difficult problem if suddenly being against nuclear weapons was the official government line and no longer a subversive activity. One wonders what would happen to the files of those who had been illegally targeted for such beliefs during the tenure of Conservative governments and whether a Labour government would have the courage or ability to destroy them. One can assume that MI5 has anticipated such an eventuality and has duplicate computer tapes carefully hidden away which could await the return of a right-wing government.

One obvious target of MI5's interest has always been the Communist Party of Great Britain (CPGB), although its value to Moscow is miniscule. Nevertheless in 1955, during *Operation Party Piece*,[31] the Mayfair flat of a senior member of the CPGB was burgled by MI5's A2 division who stole the records kept there, microfilmed them and returned them undetected. As there were 55,000 individual cards it must have been quite a complex operation and one can only assume that the police were not very observant in Mayfair that night. MI5 claims that since the CPGB is dedicated to the overthrow of British democracy it is entitled to break the law in such an operation. There is certainly no legal backing for this view and it is very doubtful if the home secretary gave his authority for the operation.

Once an intelligence agency believes it is above the law and can commit criminal acts without fear of prosecution it will inevitably encourage its members to engage in even more serious illegal acts. On 21 March 1984 78-year-old Miss Hilda Murrell was found murdered near her home in Shrewsbury in circumstances that had all the hallmarks of a botched MI5 operation using freelance burglars.[32] For many years Miss Murrell had been an active and articulate anti-nuclear supporter and was preparing a paper that she intended submitting as evidence to the Sizewell nuclear power-station inquiry. This alone would have placed Miss Murrell in MI5's subversive category and warranted her surveillance by Special Branch. Private security firms were also being employed to monitor the activities of protesters like Miss Murrell and these firms had unofficial links with MI5 and Special Branch.

Around midday on Wednesday 21 March Miss Murrell returned home unexpectedly and found an intruder or more likely intruders in her house. One theory is that at about 12.45 p.m. Miss Murrell was abducted while someone wearing her hat and a wig impersonated her in her own car. This was driven along a deliberately circuitous route during which several witnesses saw the car being driven erratically by a man apparently restraining someone in the passenger seat until it was abandoned in a ditch in Hunkington Lane 20 minutes later. A local farmer reported the car to the police at 5.20 p.m. that day and again two days later on Friday. During that period all the police did was to establish who the owner was and that Miss Murrell was not at home but they made no effort to find out if she was all right or how her car had crashed.

On Saturday morning, 24 March, a search of woods near the car revealed Miss Murrell's body but another farmer, Ian Scott, who had been in these woods on the Thursday, was quite certain that her body had not been there then. A search of Miss Murrell's house showed that the telephone had been professionally disconnected and that nothing was missing other than the balance of some money she had drawn from the bank on Wednesday. The officer in charge of the case was Detective Chief Superintendent David Cole, the same policeman involved in the case of Geoffrey Prime, the GCHQ spy, so he would certainly have been familiar with the work of MI5 and Special Branch. In April 1985, a year after the murder, a police inquiry conducted by the Assistant Chief Constable of Northumbria police, Peter Smith, concluded that British intelligence had not been involved in Miss Murrell's murder. How did he know this? Because Smith had asked the 'highest echelons' of the intelligence services and they had assured him they had not murdered Miss Murrell.[33] One is forced to conclude that Smith believes that had they done so they would have told him.

Despite the fact that over the years MI5 and Special Branch have maintained voluminous records on anyone they chose and could be remotely considered controversial or anti-government, this has neither helped to catch spies and traitors nor stopped the growth of terrorism. If MI5 had spent less time searching for subversives amongst those who use their democratic right to disagree with the government of the day it might have been more successful at protecting the nation's security which we have been assured at every spy trial has been irreparably damaged due to MI5's incompetence.[34]

While a security service is an essential part of a country's normal defences there is no reason why it should be politicised or secretive to the point of unaccountability in any worthwhile form. Simply passing more legislation will not change this. There has to be a genuine desire to make the security service more efficient. This can only be achieved by opening it to objective accountability. Politicians, being transient figures, lack the ability to challenge MI5's authority which they have allowed to grow unchecked until it is now more powerful than the democratically elected Parliament it is supposed to protect.

CHAPTER 8

TELLING THE TALE

Everyone enjoys a good spy story and though this is partly due to Ian Fleming's astoundingly successful, though very poorly written, stories about James Bond in the 1960s, in fact the popularity of fictional tales of espionage goes back into the last century.[1] The spy enjoys a peculiar brand of morality for although he is an enemy, rather like the Great Train Robbers, there is a sneaking regard for his exploits. And then there is the technical interest in the paraphernalia of his trade; the one-time pads, the silenced gun, and as a last resort the poison pill.

All spy stories need an easily identifiable and popular enemy.[2] Today it is the Libyans. At the turn of the century it was the Prussians. Tales were told of how they wanted to control Europe and had infiltrated Britain with hordes of their supporters who now lay waiting, Mauser rifle under the bed, for the signal that would send them into action. Looking back now we can laugh at these childish stories but they are not so different from the stories we hear today of Russian sabotage groups who have already recruited subversives in Britain and, when Moscow gives the signal, will emerge and destroy our airfields, dockyards and communication systems.

The real vogue for spy stories began during the 1930s and most were based on groups of well-educated upperclass rivals[3] who confronted one another in endless series of daring exploits in which the dull-witted police were only involved at the last moment, usually just in time to save the hero or his wife from a fate worse than death. Authors created chauvinistic characters like Bulldog Drummond and Richard Hannay who were for ever saving England and the rest of civilisation from the wiles of European maniacs with German-sounding names who wanted to dominate the world with the aid of poison gas sprinkled from airships which they had secretly manufactured in disused Cornish tin mines. Fortunately Drummond and Hannay were always con-

fronting decent sorts of enemies who knew their place and when it was time
to surrender.

It is perhaps convenient that the fictional exploits of the spies we see
continually in films or on television (including a reincarnation of Hannay)
convey the impression that they lead very exciting and glamorous lives,
surrounded by extremely clever people and beautiful women. A walk down
Westminster Bridge Road in London to the remarkably grubby office of MI6
would help dispel such myths.

It is often said that truth is stranger than fiction and nowhere is this more
apparent than in the world of intelligence. For every tediously invented story
in books or television, the real world of espionage can produce something
that is much more fascinating. It is this realisation that has brought about a
long drawn-out conflict of interests between the government and would-be
authors over the publication of true accounts of intelligence operations.

During the inter-war years there were few serious attempts to write about
the work of the intelligence services in World War I and these did not contain
any paticularly sensational material.[4] But it was after World War II that the
stories began to flow, or at least tried to. This was hardly surprising because
the war had seen a enormous number of brilliant intelligence operations.
Amongst these was the breaking of the German Enigma codes at Bletchley
Park and the Japanese naval codes in Singapore, the capturing and turning
round of all the German agents sent to Britain and using them to feed back
disinformation to the enemy, and the large number of deception schemes that
were used to fool the enemy, particularly before the D-Day landings.
However much post-war governments might try to prevent it, inevitably
some of these stories would eventually become known. Furthermore those
who had worked in wartime intelligence would also want to write their
autobiographies.

To cope with this obvious eventuality the most sensible course of action
would have been to set up some form of central vetting committee to whom
manuscripts could be submitted. They could then advise what sections, if
any, needed deleting or altering. Such an arrangement would have avoided
any conflict with the Official Secrets Act and yet permitted reasonably
complete and accurate accounts to be published. But this was not the case.
Instead, there was a running battle between would-be authors, publishers
and Whitehall. Generally speaking authors of this type of material fall into
three categories: those who have had first-hand experience, those who have
amassed information from their own researches and interviews, and those
who have been given stories to publish.

Despite all the restrictions some books did slip through the net. An early
example was the novel *Operation Heartbreak*, published by the British
ambassador to France, Duff Cooper, 1st Viscount Norwich. This tells the
story of Willie Maryngton who is an orphan and, following an unspectacular

army career, dies alone of pneumonia in his seedy London flat. British intelligence, operating from a headquarters disguised as a Soho brothel, acquire his body and having filled his pockets with false documents float Maryngton's corpse ashore off the coast of Spain hoping that the papers will be handed over to the Germans who will be fooled by them.

Duff Cooper's book was a great success but MI5 was furious because the basis of the story was true. Duff Cooper was threatened with prosecution under the Official Secrets Act if he returned to Britain but he countered by claiming that Churchill had personally given him details of the story on which his book was based. It is very doubtful that this was true. A much more likely source was his friend Ewen Montagu,[5] a wartime intelligence officer and post-war judge. However, MI5 did nothing further. Meantime the story had attracted the attention of a very experienced investigative journalist, the late Ian Colvin, who worked for the *Sunday Express* and suspected the novel was based on fact. Having been rebuffed by all official sources Colvin meticulously searched Spanish cemeteries until, in the Catholic section of the *Cementario de la Soledad* outside the little town of Huelva, he came across the grave of one William Martin.[6] Further local inquiries elicited that Martin had been a major in the Royal Marines whose body had been washed ashore on the coast nearby in April 1943, apparently after drowning following an air crash.

On his return to London Colvin sought permission to check through the personnel files of the Royal Marines to find out more about Major Martin. By early 1953 MI5 was thoroughly alarmed at what Colvin might write so it decided to spoil his scoop by publishing an official version of its own. For this they turned to Ewen Montagu who quickly cobbled together a suitably sanitised account. His story was serialised in the *Sunday Express* between 1 and 22 February 1953 and it was that newspaper's editor, Howard Keeble, who invented the classic title *The Man Who Never Was*. Despite being deliberately pre-empted by MI5, Colvin continued with his own book which was published later in 1953 under the title *The Unknown Courier*.

Montagu's book immediately became a best-seller. It fascinated readers all over the world as it was the first account of intelligence tricks that had been used in the war.[7] Two years later, in 1955, Montagu's book was made into a film of the same name by 20th Century Fox. Both the book and the film gave the impression that the deception plan, known officially as *Operation Mincemeat*, was Montagu's idea. This was not so. The idea had been that of Flight Lieutenant Charles Cholmondeley but because he was still working for MI5 his name could not be used and Montagu was able to downgrade his contribution to the plan.

Montagu not only received the kudos for the idea of *Operation Mincemeat* but also considerable financial reward. As a result, until his death in 1985 Montagu did everything possible to capitalise on the 'Major Martin' story and even claimed a bogus copyright in it alleging that there no other sources of information than himself. In fact Montagu's book is riddled with errors which he later claimed he introduced to protect the real identity of 'Major Martin', a ne'er-do-well living on his own in London who had committed suicide and for this reason his next-of-kin did not want his real name ever to be known.[8] All this is rubbish and the truth far simpler. Montagu never got the family's permission to use the body which is why he admits in the book he could not ask the next-of-kin for a photograph to use for his identity card. Cholmondley and Montagu simply hijacked a suitable body of someone who had died in the right sort of medical condition and the family were never told. This is why Montagu became so upset when anyone questioned him about the affair.

One possible candidate for the role of 'Major Martin' was a 45-year-old Welsh barman, Emlyn Howells, who died in Paddington General Hospital on 6 January 1943 from bronchial pneumonia after a long illness from tuberculosis.[9] But Howells's death certificate shows his date of death as 11 January so it is probably a forgery. The five factors that link Howells to 'Martin' are: he looks very similar to the photograph taken of 'Martin' in the Hackney mortuary,[10] he was Welsh, he died from pneumonia at the right time, both 'Martin' and Howells have a mark on the top of their right hand, and the little finger on the right hand of both men is bent under the palm. If Howells was used then certainly his next-of-kin were not consulted.[11]

The success of Montagu's book naturally irritated and encouraged others who had worked on similar operations and felt that they too had a tale of intrigue, daring and bravery to tell. Some of these were extremely interesting, others plainly ridiculous.

A story in the latter category appeared a year after Montagu's in 1954, called *I was Monty's Double*. Written by Edward Clifton James it told how in April 1944 (two months before the Normandy landings), when a lieutenant in the Royal Army Pay Corps, James was chosen to impersonate General Montgomery in what was officially known as *Operation Copperhead*. The idea had been proposed by Major-General H. R. Bull, of the G-3 Section at the Supreme Headquarters Allied Expeditionary Force (SHAEF), on 14 April 1944 in a letter to the commander-in-chief of the 21st Army Group.[12] The object was 'to lower German vigilance in north-west Europe prior to the invasion'. The plan was that 'General Montgomery' would meet with General Alexander and General Wilson in Algiers on or about 29 May 1944, and this would be carefully leaked to the media, hopefully persuading the Germans that if Montgomery was out of Britain the invasion could not be imminent.

In order to ensure that the Germans heard about 'Montgomery's' visit his personal aircraft would stop at Gibraltar en route for refuelling where he would be met by the governor and a guard of honour. News of this, it was confidently assumed, would be passed on by Spanish intelligence to the

Germans. Reports were also to be planted on the Germans by 'special intelligence' which meant the use of double agents controlled by the Twenty Committee. It was an elaborate plan first classified as Top Secret and then raised to BIGOT level. BIGOT was the highest security classification specifically used in connection with the forthcoming invasion and was a corruption of the expression TO GIB (to Gibraltar), that was part of the deception plan that the invasion would come from the Mediteranean.

Unfortunately, while James certainly looked like Montgomery and could imitate his movements and voice, he possessed two habits the general did not.[13] James smoked and drank heavily. On the flight out to Gibraltar James calmed his nerves with a hidden bottle of gin and the aircraft had to circle for an hour while he was sobered up sufficiently to play his part. Shortly after his arrival in Algiers, 'Montgomery' was seen staggering round the streets smoking a cigar. *Operation Copperhead* was quickly terminated and James flown home in disgrace. In fact, the entire operation was a waste of time. Post-war examination of German records showed that they had never noticed 'Montgomery' in either Gibraltar or Algiers, drunk or sober. Perhaps not surprisingly no attempt was made to stop James from publishing his book. However, such was the interest in this type of story that four years later, in 1958, an even more ridiculous film was made by Associated British Pathe of the same title, and this is still shown on television to this day, revered as one of Britain's great intelligence successes.

A much more important story involved the work of Special Operations Executives whose men and women, together with locally recruited agents, fought the Germans in occupied Europe with immense courage. Many died in appalling circumstances after torture and some of these stories had already begun to appear in the press. In 1953 a book written by Colonel H. J. Giskes, called *London Calling North Pole*, gave a rare German account[14] of how their intelligence had penetrated SOE's activities in Holland, turned them around and for over a year fooled SOE's headquarters in London who continued sending further arms supplies and agents, all of which were captured. Some fifty agents had gone to their deaths as the result of this intelligence coup.[15]

In 1961, after mounting pressure Edward Heath, then minister of state at the Foreign Office, asked M. R. D. Foot[16] to write the official history of SOE's French section[17] and in 1966 this was published as *SOE in France*. Although Foot was supposed to have had access to all SOE's archives (which were under the control of MI6), many were denied him with the result that the book was not complete. Added to this some of Foot's personal conclusions were bitterly resented in France, a feeling that still exists to this day. However, the fact that an organisation as secret as SOE could have its official history published made others ask why their agency could not as well.

One of these was Sir John Masterman who had been chairman of the Twenty Committee (sometimes called the Double Cross Committee from the use of the symbol XX), which controlled captured German agents, and imaginary ones as well, and fed back carefully prepared disinformation to the Germans throughout much of the war. Masterman had been asked to write a report on this work at the end of the war and prudently, but perhaps illegally, had kept a copy for himself. He now saw no reason why an accurate account of the work of the Twenty Committee should not be published, and thought it might help to salvage the reputation of MI5 following the series of post-war spy exposures in Britain. His suggestion met with no encouragement in Whitehall and it seemed that his account would never see the light of day.

Masterman sent the manuscript over to America where the Yale University Press agreed to publish it. Realising they could not prevent publication there in 1972 the British government belatedly agreed to allow the book to appear in Britain under the title *The Double Cross System*. Although it turned out to be a very interesting book there was certainly nothing in it that could possibly have affected national security so it is hard to see what all the fuss was about.

One particular story that many people wanted to tell was how the German Enigma codes had been broken. Britain, in conjunction with the Americans, had been very anxious that this story be kept secret because after the war they had persuaded many countries to adopt the Enigma cipher system and as a result were able to read their messages with ease. But the story was starting to come out on the continent where books and articles about Enigma had been written in both Poland and France. It was Group Captain Fred Winterbotham, who had worked with MI6, who eventually broke this particular log-jam and in 1974, after two years of Whitehall vetting, was allowed to publish *The Ultra Secret*.

As with Montagu, because Winterbotham was first in the field his book did extremely well, selling over four million copies, and it gave the first insight into the work of GCCS at Bletchley Park. Unfortunately, because Winterbotham was not allowed access to any archival material, his book was extremely inaccurate and gave rise to many misconceptions about Ultra that lingered on for years. At about the same time an American author, Anthony Cave Brown, had begun a definitive work on wartime intelligence and deception called *Bodyguard of Lies* which was eventually published in 1972. Cave Brown was greatly helped by the fact that the Americans had begun to declassify a large amount of material, enabling him to piece together much more information than was yet available in Britain. Although it had its faults and inaccuracies it was and remains a very good book. No attempt was made to stop this book being published in Britain.

The Ultra Secret sparked off an enormous amount of controversy because not only did it fail to explain how the Enigma keys had been broken, but also who had first broken them. The Poles felt their contribution had been deliberately ignored by Winterbotham but the truth was he knew nothing about it.[18] In 1982 an American, Gordon Welchman, published an account of his work at Bletchley Park called *The Hut Six Story*. This went far beyond anything available in Britain and was an excellent book, giving a highly technical account of how the Enigma keys had been penetrated.

Others who had worked with Welchman at Bletchley Park were very angry that their stories had been suppressed by GCHQ (GCCS's successor) while he was free to publish in America. One of these was the late Professor G. C. McVittie who had broken the Enigma weather keys but, although he had written a report about his work, he was not allowed to see it years later when he wanted to write about the subject.[19] In fact by the time Welchman's book reached Britain, Enigma had long been consigned to the museum and his technical details were of interest only to the *cognoscenti* of the cryptographic world, having no relevance to modern cipher machine technology. Under the circumstances it is difficult to understand why Sir Peter Marychurch, the head of GCHQ, wrote to Welchman[20] (who at the time was dying of cancer) claiming that his book would do great harm to national security, other than that it shows the permanent state of paranoia such people live in. Marychurch would have been better occupied looking after today's secrets at GCHQ which at the time he wrote to a dying man were leaking by the sackful to Russia and had been for the previous 14 years.[21]

This same paranoia expressed itself elsewhere when, encouraged by these stories of wartime intelligence operations, people began inquiring as to what was going on today in the same vein. On 21 May 1976 an article appeared in the magazine *Time Out* called 'The Eavesdroppers', written by Mark Hosenball and Duncan Cambell. Hosenball was an American journalist working in Britain, while Campbell was a British journalist who had a particular interest in military communications.

For its time 'The Eavesdroppers' was a revolutionary article because it described in hitherto unknown detail the workings of GCHQ, which in those days did not officially exist, and its American partner the NSA. The government was dismayed at the article but wisely chose to take no action because *Time Out* had a very small circulation and to prosecute would only have drawn attention to it. Unfortunately John Berry, who in 1970 had worked as a Sigint operator with the 9th Signals Regiment in Cyprus, saw the article and got in touch with *Time Out*. As a result on 18 February 1977 Crispin Aubrey, another journalist with the magazine, and Campbell went to see Berry at his flat and during a three-hour interview he told the two journalists about his work in Cyprus.[22] As they were leaving all three were arrested by waiting police and later charged under the Official Secrets Act.

Their trial opened at the Old Bailey on 5 September 1978 but had to be stopped because a chance remark on a television chat-show[23] revealed that the jury had been politically vetted by Special Branch which, at the time, was also secret.[24] The trial re-started on 3 October and one by one the charges against the three were dropped. It soon became obvious that Campbell had acquired all his extensive knowledge of Britain's civil and military communications systems simply by going round the country on his bicycle, or from freely available technical magazines. This had evidently never occurred to the police. In the end all three received minor, non-custodial sentences but in the process the government had drawn a lot of unwelcome attention to its Sigint operations and places like GCHQ, which until the trial few people had ever heard of. It was a classic example of overkill.

In 1978 Professor R. V. Jones, who had been a wartime scientific adviser to MI6, was allowed to write his account of technical intelligence during the war, and this was turned into a fascinating BBC television documentary series.[25] This described in detail such things as the method by which German bombers were able to fly to Britain, using a radio beam system for navigation, and drop their bombs automatically at a predetermined position, something Britain's Royal Air Force had never thought of. Jones was also able to refute the foolish rumour that Churchill had received advance warning through Ultra decrypts that the city of Coventry was to be attacked on the night of 14 November 1940.

By this time the literary intelligence battle had reached such proportions that the government agreed that a group of Cambridge historians should write a full history of British wartime intelligence.[26] The task was placed under the control of Professor F. H. Hinsley, who had worked at Bletchley Park. The first volume was published in 1979; the final one in 1988. Considering that Hinsley and his team were allowed access to many archives that have not been, and may never be, placed in the public domain it is remarkable that they managed to produce a series of books that was about as interesting as a railway timetable. The books were totally bland, devoid of personalities and comment and certainly, as far as the Polish contribution towards Enigma and the gift of two Purple decoding machines from America were concerned, inaccurate. Furthermore, Hinsley was not allowed to deal with British intelligence in the Far East against Japan, which would have shown the extent to which British codebreakers in Singapore were reading Japanese naval signals (as opposed to diplomatic) right up to Pearl Harbor and, therefore, the history is far from complete.

The trial of Aubrey, Berry and Campbell was to have been the subject of a BBC documentary[27] but when the trial collapsed so too did the plans for the programme. The idea was later revived by BBC's *Panorama* unit who in 1980 decided to make an investigative documentary into the work of MI5, MI6 and Special Branch, to be called *The Need To Know*.[28] The idea was most unpopular with the security services and Downing Street, who did everything possible to stop it, but the programme went ahead all the same.

In July 1980 I took part in the making of this programme and amongst the interviews I gave was one filmed outside the NSA eavesdropping station at Morwenstow, in Cornwall, where I explained how it scooped up all the communications passing through the British Telecom ground station at Goonhilly. During the filming the police arrived and ostentatiously noted down the registration numbers of our cars but made no attempt to stop us. About three months later, while the programme was still being edited, Vice Admiral Bobby Ray Inman USN, then Director of the NSA, personally telephoned the BBC to complain about my interview outside their Morwenstow station[29] and asked that it be removed from the final programme. Inman had evidently learned of my comments from the advance transcripts which the BBC had very cravenly supplied to Downing Street. By the time the two-part programme was shown in early 1981[30] that particular interview had been dropped and I was officially told that there had been a fault in the camera and the film had been unsuitable for transmission. This was quite untrue and a year later another producer found the film in perfect condition in the BBC's archives. Despite these problems the programme was very penetrating and amongst other things showed the extent of illegal telephone tapping by the security services in Britain, and how files kept on people contained totally false information which could materially affect their lives and careers.

By this time Mrs Thatcher's government had come to power and it was decided that no further official accounts of the intelligence services' work would be published. This included any record of Far East intelligence, an official history of MI5 by Anthony Simkins, and an account of British wartime deception plans by Professor Michael Howard. (In 1988 it was reported that, after all, these latter two histories would be published.) As a result, retired members of the intelligence services began to leak information to selected journalists and help others with their research.

One of the first to benefit was Rupert Allason now Conservative Member of Parliament for Torbay and the son of the Conservative MP for Hemel Hempstead from 1960 to 1975. The nearest Allason had ever come to the intelligence world was being a special constable with the London police, but writing under the name Nigel West he had helped research a book and BBC documentary in 1980 with Donald McCormick (who writes under the name of Richard Deacon), called *Spy*. Allason has always insisted[31] that his political connections had nothing to do with his subsequent literary career but the fact is that he suddenly emerged from literary obscurity with an incredible wealth of hitherto secret information about MI5 and MI6 that in the course of the next few years was to make him a well known author.

His books included *MI5: British Security Service Operations 1909–1945*, published in 1981; *A Matter of Trust: MI5 1945–1972*, published the next year; *The Branch*, a history of Special Branch, in 1983; *MI6: British Secret Intelligence Service Operations 1909–1945*, also in 1983, with the help of the former double-agent, Juan Pujol; *Garbo*, in 1985; and in 1986, *GCHQ: The Secret Wireless War 1900–86*. It was an impressive output but Allason would have been unable to write these books had he not received information from retired intelligence officers.

The books contained an enormous wealth of detail that could only have come from those with access to old records so it was obvious that someone, or a group of people, had decided that Allason was a sympathetic and convenient conduit through which to peddle their stories. Like Hinsley's, Allason's books were extremely dull and consisted of pages of names and dates cobbled together in a bland, impersonal style. And it was noticeable that when a particular source retired Allason's book could go no further. The best thing that can be said about them is that they are useful textbooks.

Most of Allason's books were published with no interference from the government despite the fact that they plainly contravened all the previous guidelines. *A Matter of Trust* ran into some problems and, after a lot of fruitless legal wrangling, Allason deleted a few names. A possible conclusion from all this is that the government was happy to see these tales told because they helped restore the image of MI5 and MI6 after all the previous disasters and it knew that Allason could do no research on his own that would turn up anything controversial.

In 1979 Andrew Boyle's *The Climate of Treason* skilfully unmasked the Russian spy Anthony Blunt and forced an embarrassed Mrs Thatcher to explain to a sceptical Parliament why Blunt had been granted immunity from prosecution in 1964 and allowed to continue in his prestigious position as Surveyor of the Queen's pictures. Many people wondered if this was not in some way connected with his post-war expedition, while still with MI5, to Marburg Castle in Germany where Blunt recovered for the royal family sensitive files[32] relating to the Duke of Windsor's wartime Nazi sympathies and currency-smuggling activities which have remained hidden in the royal archives ever since.

Then academics joined in the fray, notably Christopher Andrew and Anthony Glees, both of whom wrote very ponderous books about the intelligence services which were published without difficulty or literary impact. One thing all these books had in common was that their authors jealously guarded their own particular subject and much resented anyone else trying to intrude.

But without doubt the doyen of secondhand journalism in the field of intelligence must be 74-year-old Chapman Pincher who has been writing stories based on other peoples' information for 40 years. Known to his friends more accurately as Harry (Chapman was added to make his byline sound more impressive[33]), Pincher studied zoology and botany in his early life gaining an honours degree in 1935, and went on to serve with the 6th Armoured Division during the war.[34] In 1946 he joined the *Daily Express* as their science and defence writer. Pincher decided that the life of the common journalist was not for him and instead cultivated the right sort of contacts over expensive lunch tables in West End restaurants.

To begin with many of these contacts were wartime friends who gave

Pincher odd bits of gossip from which he could produce a reasonable story. On other occasions he was told of problems and fiascos in the armed services. After a while people realised that Pincher had little investigative ability of his own and seldom did any research, so he was an ideal person on whom to plant stories that would be published without difficulty in the *Daily Express* and *Sunday Express*, which in the 1960s were still important newspapers with large circulations.[35] Pincher was vain enough to believe he was being given all these stories because unlike other journalists he was a patriot and could be trusted to protect the national interest. Many of Pincher's articles carried the absurd headline 'the man who gives you tomorrow's news today'. As one commentator remarked: 'The columns of the *Daily Express* are a kind of official urinal where high officials of MI5 and MI6 stand side by side patiently leaking secrets to Mr Pincher who is too self-important and light-witted to realise how often he is being used.'[36]

Pincher also adopted hobbies like fishing and shooting which brought him into contact with the right sort of people. As a result his letters are littered with the names of senior members of government and the intelligence services, usually on a first name basis, thereby implying that he enjoys their confidence even in the most secret affairs.

The truth is that over the years Pincher was used to propogate inaccurate gossip provided by disaffected officials or to plant stories on behalf of government departments that would have been too ridiculous to print anywhere other than in the *Express* newspapers. An example of this occurred in 1957 after the disaster at Windscale. Downing Street wanted the public to believe that it would be told the truth about the accident. To make it sound more plausible Pincher was used to leak this and wrote one of his so-called exclusive articles in the *Daily Express* claiming that he alone knew that the prime minister would publish the report in full so that he could not be accused of using national security to hide damaging facts from the public.[37] Thirty years later the same newspaper carried front-page stories revealing how Macmillan had hushed up and rewritten the report to deliberately mislead the public.

Another example of Pincher's lack of journalistic ability is shown by his own account of how in 1959 he was told about the Ultra secret of breaking the Enigma codes.[38] It happened during one of his famous lunches, on this occasion with Air Vice-Marshal Kingston McCloughry. McCloughry told Pincher that Montgomery's success in North Africa had not been due to his tactical skill but because Montgomery had been able to read the messages passing between Berlin and his adversary Erwin Rommel.

How McCloughry got this information about Ultra is unclear. If he had been cleared to handle Ultra during the war it is most unlikely he would have mentioned its existence to a journalist. No one else ever did. The most likely explanation is that McCloughry picked up some information about Ultra after the war and decided to peddle it to Pincher in the hope of denigrating Montgomery's triumphs.

Pincher was intrigued by McCloughry's tale and sent a memorandum about it to Beaverbrook, the proprietor of the *Daily Express*. Beaverbrook, who had been in Churchill's War Cabinet, knew all about Ultra and guessed what McCloughry was trying to do. He therefore sent a message back to Pincher saying that as Montgomery was now an old man who had served his country well there seemed no point in bothering him about such a story. Pincher immediately agreed and it never occurred to him to follow up McCloughry's story himself. As a result he missed out on a genuine scoop instead of all the rubbish he usually wrote.

In 1979 Pincher retired and took up a country squire's lifestyle in Berkshire where he was able to enjoy his fishing and shooting and, when anyone gave him a story, continue writing about the intelligence world. Pincher's career came to an abrupt end when he foolishly allowed himself to be entrapped by Lord Rothschild in the Peter Wright affair.

The story of Peter Wright and his book *Spycatcher* remains a vital watershed because it brings together the two opposing forces of confidentiality and accountability. And although the matter has been thrashed out in the courts, no satisfactory solution to the problem has yet been found and, therefore, there is every likelihood that a similar situation will arise in the future.

Over the long months that the *Spycatcher* saga has been bandied about in both the press and courts some of the principal characters have changed their original attitudes, so to understand the story properly it is necessary to go back to the beginning. Only three people are involved: Peter Wright, Lord Victor Rothschild and Chapman Pincher.

Peter Wright was born on 9 August 1916. His father, Maurice, was an electronics engineer with Marconi. Peter has a sister Elizabeth and a younger brother Paul. After a traumatic childhood Peter and Paul followed their father into the world of electronics. Peter first worked for the Royal Navy's scientific warfare department during the war and later joined Marconi where his father still worked. Paul, who was a brilliant scientist, went to work for the Admiralty Research Laboratory. In 1957 Paul married my cousin Jean Reid Scott and I often had the pleasure of meeting Peter and his wife Lois when I visited Essex to go sailing with them all at the Heybridge Sailing Club on the Blackwater river.

Peter Wright was a very clever technician and in 1950 began work as an adviser to MI5 on bugging equipment, finally joining the security service in July 1955. By 1963 Wright wanted to become involved in catching spies and was promoted, ironically as it turned out by Roger (later Sir Roger) Hollis, and moved to D Branch. It is questionable whether this was a very good idea for, though a good technician, Wright was out of his depth as a spy hunter.

In December 1961 the Russian Anatoli Golitsin defected to the CIA and proceeded to make a series of startling allegations about Western intelligence, claiming that it had been completely fooled and penetrated at the highest level by the KGB. Wright was one of the minority in MI5 who chose to believe Golitsin's stories. The result was that every time an MI5 operation went wrong it was blamed on a Russian mole within the organisation. Past disasters, such as Kim Philby's defection to Moscow in January 1962, were minutely re-examined. MI5 assumed Philby had been tipped off by someone from inside its own organisation.

Every statement made by previous Russian defectors was meticulously re-translated and picked over word by word, and totally new meanings were extracted that no one seemed to have noticed previously. Eventually, the paranoia became so extreme that a special committee, called the Fluency Committee (codenamed K7), was set up, with Wright as a member which proceeded to investigate the loyalties of a number of senior members of MI5 including Hollis and Graham Mitchell.

One of the committee's primary sources of evidence was the *Venona* material.[39] This was a series of decrypts made by the FBI, beginning in 1944, of Russian messages sent from New York to Moscow encoded in the one-time-pad system. During World War II, US intelligence agents had recovered from a battlefield in Finland part of a Russian one-time code book which contained a list of words and phrases and their basic five-digit code group. But this alone did not enable them to strip away the five-digit additive taken from the one-time pad which together produced the final cipher text. In 1944 the Russians made the fatal error of sending out duplicate one-time pads to the Russian Trade Mission in New York and KGB agents. The FBI burgled the Mission's offices[40] and took copies of the plain texts of the messages they had intercepted. With these three components the FBI could then work out the additive tables on the other messages.

The *Venona* decrypts produced numerous codenames of Russian agents some of which had been identified, but others remained tantalisingly out of reach. Golitsin was allowed to look through these to see if he could identify any. One pair of codenames – David and Rosa – suggested a husband-and-wife team of agents. Golitsin identified them[41] as Lord Victor Rothschild and his wife Tess but there was no basis for this allegation. He had simply been inspired by the fact that David and Rosa are Jewish names.

The committee's two other primary sources were Konstantin Volkov and Igor Gouzenko. Volkov had been the Russian Consul in Istanbul and in August 1945 had walked into the British Consulate offering to supply information in return for political asylum and £27,500. Volkov claimed that he could provide the names of three Russian spies, two working in the Foreign Office (Burgess and McLean), and one who was head of counter-intelligence. Volkov's request was sent to MI6 in London where it was passed to Kim Philby to deal with. Philby warned the Russians and Volkov was taken back to Moscow and executed. All the Fluency Committee had to go on was Volkov's original statement in Russian about what he claimed he could reveal. Unfortunately, it was possible to translate this in different ways,[42] and some Russian experts took the view that Volkov was not referring to MI5, but to the counter-intelligence department in MI6 (Section V), which during the war had been headed by Kim Philby. Naturally the committee took the other view and argued that Volkov meant the head of MI5.

Igor Gouzenko was the cipher clerk at the Russian Embassy in Ottawa who had defected a month after Volkov, in September 1945. Amongst the information he gave was that there was 'a spy in five of MI'. The Fluency Committee assumed that Gouzenko meant MI5 but as Gouzenko did not know the difference between MI5 and MI6 he could equally have meant the fifth section in MI6. Further confusion surrounded the codename 'Elli' given by Gouzenko, since one spy with that codename had already been found. It turned out to be Kathleen Willsher who worked for the British High Commission in Ottawa and on 15 February 1946 was sentenced to three years' imprisonment for passing documents to the Russians. So were there two spies with the codename Elli? Or had Gouzenko made a mistake and lacked the courage to admit it, fearing it might downgrade his value as a defector? Or could Elli be an acronym for Guy Liddell who had worked in MI5 and was another suspect because of his friendship with Burgess, Philby and Blunt?[43] Over the years Gouzenko was to change his story several times and, as is always the case with defectors, it was soon impossible to separate fact from fantasy in what he said.

The more Wright and his Fluency Committee searched the more clues they seemed to find. Suspects were everywhere. Even Wright began to wonder if he was chasing shadows. The only thing lacking was proof. Of course, there was plenty of negative proof. If, for example, they discovered that Hollis had been in the habit of staying late in his office, they argued he was obviously copying secret documents for the Russians.

The whole affair reminded one of the 1939 British film *The Frozen Limits*. In this, a comedy team called the Crazy Gang arrive in the Yukon to join the gold rush 40 years too late. Nothing daunted, they create their own gold rush by burying a single nugget of gold in the plot of a prospector who, the next morning, excitedly descovers it. He brings it to the assay office where an 'expert', one of the Crazy Gang, appraises it and locks it away in a vast safe. What no one knows is that the back of the safe is false and when darkness falls the same nugget is taken out and reburied in another plot. The next morning a different prospector triumphantly brings 'his' nugget into the assay office. And so on. The problem arises when more than one prospector wants to look at his nugget at the same time.

The total amount of evidence the Fluency Committee managed to assemble was small and inconclusive. It could have fitted any number of people and, more important, was highly subjective in that it assumed the worst about all the suspects. Nevertheless, Wright and his colleagues claimed that they were 99 per cent certain that Hollis was a Russian spy and that this explained many of MI5's failures. On the other hand many others,[44] including Sir Dick White, a former head of MI5, and Sir Charles Spry, former head of the Australian security service ASIO, who knew Hollis well when he helped establish ASIO after the war, considered the allegations against Hollis pure fantasy[45] and pointed out that at no time had a single defector hinted that the Russians had a highly placed source like Hollis in MI5.

It doesn't seem to have occurred to the committee that there could be two quite different reasons for MI5's lack of success. First, MI5 was very inefficient and staffed with the wrong sort of people who spent far too much time squabbling amongst themselves. And second, MI5 wasted its resources worrying about alleged subversives, such as members of CND, instead of concentrating on the more dangerous enemies of the country.

In July 1974, the Fluency Committee asked the then prime minister, Harold Wilson, for an independent review of their evidence, and Wilson appointed Lord Trend, a former Cabinet secretary, to examine the committee's work. Eventually Trend reported that he could find no evidence against Hollis, Mitchell or anyone else. Perhaps Wilson wasn't very surprised because by then he suspected (rightly, as it turned out) that he too was under suspicion of being a Russian spy[46] and there appears to have been a group of disaffected MI5 officers who wanted to see him out of office. But Wilson had never had much faith in MI5 anyway.

Wright retired from MI5 early, in 1973, and continued as a part-time consultant until 31 January 1976 when he emigrated to Tasmania.[47] He remained obsessed that MI5 had been, and possibly still was, penetrated by the KGB, even though he had been unable to find any proof. It was an unsatisfactory and frustrating end to 21 years of work with MI5. To make matters worse there was a fuss over his pension due to the fact that in changing employment back in 1955 from the Admiralty to MI5, Wright had forfeited part of his pension rights which, he had always understood, MI5 would make up to him privately. They now refused to do this and Wright retired on only £2,000 a year.

At this point in the story it is necessary to introduce the second character – Lord Victor Rothschild. Born in 1910, Rothschild had pursued a career away from his family's banking empire and instead become a brilliant scientist. While at Cambridge in the 1930s he was by his own definition a socialist[48] (but never a Marxist), and as a member of the Apostles Club, whose members included many homosexuals and Communists, numbered Burgess and Blunt amongst his friends. Blunt was to remain one for 30 years.

During the war Rochschild had worked for MI5, and in 1943 was awarded the George Medal. Rothschild made no secret of the fact that he, like many of his generation and background, greatly admired the stand Russia was making against Fascism[49] and strongly argued that Britain should provide Russia with any information that might help it, including the Ultra codebreaking operations at Bletchley Park. Also during the war Rothschild and his first wife, Barbara Hutchinson, leased a property they owned at 5 Bentinck Street to two girls who, in turn, sub-let part of the house to Burgess and Blunt.[50] One of the girls was Tessa Mayor, an assistant to Rothschild at MI5, whom he later married in 1946 after his first marriage had collapsed.

Rothschild had left MI5 before Wright joined but they did meet occasionally as Rothschild retained some links with the security service. When Wright finally retired from MI5 he was due to receive a lump-sum payment of £5,000. He wanted the money in a hurry to help him start up his new stud farm in Tasmania and asked Rothschild if he could lend him £5,000 until the money arrived from MI5. This Rothschild did. Rothschild therefore knew two things about Wright. First, he was obsessed with the idea that MI5 was penetrated by the KGB; and second, he was short of money.

In 1979 came the dramatic unmasking of Blunt in Parliament; followed by Blunt's press conference at which he excused himself from answering questions about his activities on the grounds he might break the Official Secrets Act. Amongst the people this hypocrisy infuriated was Wright, who believed that Mrs Thatcher's statement to Parliament about Blunt on 15 November 1979 was either the product of a deliberate cover up or because she had been woefully misled. But the news about Blunt also shocked Rothschild. Rothschild had known about Blunt's confession to MI5 in 1964 and that he had been granted immunity from prosecution (Wright had been one of the interrogators involved), and he must have assumed the story would never be made public. Now the press was having a field day regurgitating all the past spy scandals. Rothschild's name cropped up because of his close friendship with Blunt and Burgess and it was no secret that in 1964 Rothschild had been questioned four or five times about his relationship with Blunt.

In August 1980 Wright received a letter from Rothschild asking for his help in preparing a list of Rothschild's achievements with MI5 which could be published to counter the current rumours that Rothschild had been a Russian spy.[51] Rothschild wrote, 'things are starting to get rough' but, in fact, there had only been one half-serious article about him by the waspish Auberon Waugh in the *Spectator* on 14 June 1980.[52] Rothschild's request to Wright was very strange. Wright had not been in MI5 with Rothschild so had no first-hand knowledge of his activities, let alone his achievements, and there were plenty of other retired MI5 officers who had worked with Rothschild whom he did not contact. And how were these achievements to be published? Like any retired intelligence officer, Rothschild was bound by the

Official Secrets Act and was thus prohibited from writing about his work with MI5. And even if such a list was published, surely it would only draw more attention to the rumours?

On 16 July 1980 Rothschild sent Wright an air ticket and £700[53] and asked him to come to England to discuss this 'list of achievements'. Again, this is very peculiar. The sum total of anything Wright could have said about Rothschild could have been written on one side of an airmail letter. So why go to the expense of bringing Wright all the way to London? Wright arrived in London with his wife on 22 August and brought with him a dossier he had prepared on the KGB penetration of MI5 which he wanted to present to the prime minister and hoped that Rothschild would help him. Rothschild agreed to do so and after a day in London took Wright to his house in Cambridge. Wright says that he promised Rothschild that he would not divulge what they discussed during these days.[54] Nevertheless, Wright later stated that he only agreed to meet Pincher and discuss the idea of a book because he was advised to do so by Rothschild.[55] He considered Rothschild to be an 'intimate confidante of successive heads of British intelligence' which meant that the plan had official backing because Rothschild assured him he would not get into trouble for working with Pincher.

At this point Pincher enters the story.[56] On the afternoon of 4 September Pincher received a telephone call from Rothschild who asked him to come to Cambridge and meet a friend of his. When he arrived Rothschild introduced him to Wright who, to conceal his identity, called himself Philip. Rothschild left the pair to talk together and by the time he returned Pincher had agreed to write a book based on Wright's dossier with them sharing the profits. Rothschild agreed to use his overseas banking facilities to get Wright's share of the money out to Tasmania. In October 1980 Pincher flew out to Tasmania and spent about ten days with Wright at his stud farm. During this visit Wright gave Pincher his draft manuscript, running to about 9,000 words in eight or nine chapters. Apparently Rothschild had removed one of the chapters but what it contained and why it was removed has never been explained.

Pincher was thrilled by what Wright told him and later described his visit as like being taken into an Aladdin's cave of secrets.[57] He also said that Wright had: 'a very good memory . . . allegations about Hollis had come from him. I was aware of [these] allegations but I would not have had enough information to publish without him [Wright].'[58]

Pincher flew back to Britain and settled down to write *Their Trade is Treachery*, which was published in March 1981 and also serialised by the *Daily Mail* who paid £35,000 for the rights.[59] There was no mention anywhere in the book of either Wright or Rothschild. According to Pincher, Wright received £31,827 in royalties[60] (all paid through Rothschild's Overbridge International in the Dutch Antilles),[61] although Wright subsequently disputed this amount.[62]

A copy of the manuscript was unofficially acquired by the government long before the book was published and MI5 soon deduced the identity of Pincher's source. They traced the counterfoil of the ticket on which Wright had travelled to London in 1980 and saw that it had been originally paid for by Rothschild and, with the help of ASIO, found out about Pincher's visit to Wright even though he had travelled under the name Dr Chapman. We can ignore all the subsequent tedious tales of an unknown arbiter and excessive secrecy having allowed *Their Trade is Treachery* to be published by mistake. The government could have stopped publication had it wanted to but did not bother because it thought the book very boring and full of arcane allegations without proof that would interest few people and soon be forgotten. They were right. Despite all the publicity it sold very badly.

The book's main problem was that its central thesis was fatally flawed. Pincher had written that:

> Trend concluded that there had been a strong *prima facie* case that MI5 had been deeply penetrated over many years by someone who was not Blunt and named Hollis as the likeliest suspect.

But in Parliament on 26 March 1981 the prime minister stated that:

> Lord Trend said neither of these things and nothing resembling them. He was satisfied that nothing had been covered up. He agreed that none of the leads identified Sir Roger Hollis as an agent for the Russian intelligence service, and that each of them could be explained by reference to Philby or Blunt. Lord Trend did not refer, as the book says he did, to the possibility that Hollis might have recruited unidentified Russian agents into MI5. Again he said no such thing.

Nevertheless, Pincher was very proud of the book and the intention was that Wright would sit in Tasmania and feed Pincher more material which he would turn into further books, pretending they were the product of his own researches, but Wright was concerned about having given information about MI5 to Pincher. On 16 September 1982 Pincher lunched with Sir Arthur Franks, director general of MI6. Some months later in January 1983 Pincher wrote to Wright warning him to have nothing to do with other writers such as Rupert Allason and two very experienced investigative journalists from *The Sunday Times*, Barrie Penrose and Simon Freeman, whom Pincher called 'arch shits'.[63]

He then described his lunch with Sir Arthur Franks and told Wright that Franks had assured him that the government had no intention of taking any action against him (Pincher), and that that included Wright. Pincher said that Franks had told him that the government had known all about *Their*

Trade is Treachery before it was published but preferred that he (Pincher) wrote the story rather than someone like Nigel West, Duncan Campbell or Barrie Penrose. If this weird conversation is true then either the head of MI6 had taken leave of his senses or Pincher was too vain to realise Franks was being sarcastic.

Shortly afterwards the relationship between Pincher and Wright ended and Wright decided to write his own version of events. The rest is history.

Throughout this curious Wright-Pincher saga the government faced a number of acutely embarrassing dilemmas. First, there was the question of why a senior retired MI5 officer like Rothschild, who was well aware of his responsibilities, brought Wright to London in the first place.

Pincher was later to claim,[64] apparently on Rothschild's behalf, that when Wright arrived at Rothschild's house in 1980 Rothschild discovered that Wright had already started work on a manuscript outlining his suspicions about Hollis. According to Pincher, Rothschild 'despaired of any action by MI5 to stop him' and decided that as the story was bound to come out through another author it was better that Wright give his story to Pincher who could be trusted to handle it properly. This explanation is typical Pincher bombast and lacks conviction. Instead of calling in a journalist, Rothschild's duty was to warn MI5 of what Wright was up to and leave it to them to try to stop him. Far from reminding Wright of his obligations, Rothschild effectively encouraged him to break the Official Secrets Act by giving information to Pincher and then personally involved himself in getting Wright's share of the money from the book out to Tasmania. One is tempted to ask why Rothschild appears to have wanted Wright's allegations against Hollis to be published as quickly as possible and, as it turned out, in a manner that would ensure the maximum publicity.

Yet in 1983, three years before Rothschild's involvement with Wright and Pincher became public knowledge, Rothschild was very contemptuous of people like Sarah Tisdall who leaked government secrets and told *The Times*:[65] 'As I am on the subject of leakers I believe they could be an excellent subject for the Think Tank ... and I have some ideas as to how to reduce leakages.' Attempts were made to have Rothschild prosecuted[66] and on 26 November 1986 Mr Campbell-Savours MP tabled a question asking the attorney general, Sir Michael Havers:

> ... if he will prosecute Lord Victor Rothschild under Section 7 of the Official Secrets Act 1920 for soliciting Mr Peter Wright by means of an offer of money to pass documents known or believed to contain official secrets relating to security services to Mr Chapman Pincher.

What made it particularly awkward for Mrs Thatcher was that Rothschild had been closely connected with the previous Conservative government, under the premiership of Edward Heath, as head of the Cabinet Office think-tank from 1970–74, where he had access to much secret material. To bring Rothschild to court under any section of the Official Secrets Act so soon after the Blunt revelation would inevitably dredge up yet again his long-standing friendships with people now known to have been Russian spies.

Although the government kept Rothschild out of court and denigrated Pincher's book to the point where everyone quickly lost interest in it, they unwittingly encouraged Wright to join forces with Paul Greengrass, a British television journalist, and publish *Spycatcher*. Had the government adopted the same course of action with this book it too would have been out of print very quickly and forgotten. But once entrapped in the whirlpool of litigation the government could not escape and was slowly drawn into the farcical situation whereby it became the book's best salesman.[67]

Pincher faced a similar dilemma. Soured at seeing sales of *Spycatcher* rocket past those of his own book into best-selling lists around the world, he joined in the general chorus of denigrating Wright's character and motives. No longer was Wright his great friend and keeper of that Aladdin's cave of glittering secrets he had so willingly exploited. Now Pincher suddenly decided[68] that Wright was an unreliable, untruthful, venal, revengeful traitor, only anxious to make money at the expense of betraying the innermost secrets of his country. But if this was true then plainly Wright was an unreliable source and since all of Pincher's allegations against Hollis were predicated on what Wright had told him they were no longer valid. In an effort to salvage something from his wrecked reputation Pincher hastily stitched together the book *A Web of Deception* in which he sought to explain away the inconsistencies of the Wright affair by claiming that he had known all about Hollis before he met Wright. But his account was unconvincing and, despite his publisher's efforts of dumping unordered copies on booksellers, the book flopped.

By now it was plain that Pincher was the victim of his own vanity. In his eagerness to capitalise on what seemed a very profitable scoop Pincher never stopped to ask himself why he had been chosen to handle the story nor why Rothschild was prepared to see the allegations about Hollis published even if it meant effectively encouraging another MI5 officer to break the Official Secrets Act.

Had he been a better journalist Pincher would have realised that he was being set up. For Rothschild, his use of Pincher to carry Wright's allegations resulted in unfavourable (and presumably unforeseen) publicity for him and in the end he was forced to write a bizarre letter to the *Daily Telegraph* pleading with the Director General of MI5 to: '. . . state publicly that he has unequivocal, repeat, unequivocal, evidence that I am not and never have been a Soviet agent.'[69]

The reponse to this extraordinary outburst was a deafening silence on the part of Mrs Thatcher who two days later issued the blandest of statements: 'I am advised that we have no evidence that he was ever a Soviet agent.'[70]

No mention was made of any unequivocal evidence so the whole episode only served to make Rothschild's position even more mysterious.

But the ultimate irony was reserved for the intelligence services themselves. Was there ever a mole? Or had all the hard work of the Fluency Committee been a waste of time resulting from some well-placed Russian disinformation designed to lower morale and cause confusion. Was this why the same information seemed to fit so many different people? After all, in 1987 Nigel West published his book *Molehunt* in which he took precisely the same evidence as had Pincher and proved that the mole with MI5 was not Hollis but Graham Mitchell. This caused Sir Dick White to comment wryly that when he died, doubtless the same evidence would be used to point the finger of suspicion at him.[71]

Was Wright deliberately fed the right sort of signals and then allowed to consume himself with his own obsessions? Or, worse still, had the entire Hollis affair been deliberately fabricated to create a diversion away from a far deeper and more important mole who remains undetected?

The *Spycatcher* case wound its way expensively and tediously through the Australian courts until in June 1988 the Supreme Court finally rejected the British government's case and Wright was free to call in at Heinemann's offices and collect his first royalty cheque, making him a millionaire. By now the book had sold some 1.8 million copies around the world in various editions. Paul Greengrass was less fortunate and as a British resident was warned by the government that any attempt by him to receive his share of the royalties would be countered by a seizure order in the British courts.

Rather more alarming for Downing Street was the news that Wright, perhaps inspired by the size of his royalty cheque, announced that he had ten other major intelligence stories to tell.[72] However, in the meantime, Wright's own credibility had suffered badly when on 13 October 1988, during an interview for the BBC *Panorama* programme,[73] he admitted to John Ware that his description in *Spycatcher*[74] of how a group of MI5 officers discussed with him ways of removing Prime Minister Harold Wilson from office was 'unreliable' and that instead of about 30 MI5 officers being involved there was only one.

The long-running legal battle over *Spycatcher* finally ended on 13 October 1988 when the British Law Lords unanimously dismissed the government's attempt to stop the media from reporting what Wright had said because it was already public knowledge everywhere else in the world. The judgement was long and complicated and raised a number of issues over how the media should report similar allegations about illegal yet confidential matters in the future. Lord Goff said, 'In a free society there is a continuing public interest that the workings of government should be open to scrutiny and criticism.'

But this apparent recognition of a public interest defence was reversed later in the judgement when it stated that where security matters are concerned secrecy must be absolute and the national interest is to be construed as the government of the day sees fit. Lord Griffiths chairman of the Security Commission, made the confused and naive comment, 'If we are to have an efficient security service we have to trust its members and if we are to have a free press we have to trust the editors.'

The judgement gave no guidance as to what a member of a secret organisation like MI5, MI6 or GCHQ should do if he or she genuinely believes there is some serious malpractice going on and has been unable to obtain any satisfaction from their immediate seniors or the Security Commission, as happened in the cases of Wright, Cathy Massiter and Jock Kane. Thus the Law Lords missed the opportunity to establish any sort of accountability for the intelligence services. Instead they fudged the issue and heaped a good many insults on Wright, accusing him of being a traitor, which was something the government had been unable to prove in a court of law.

In December 1987 (shortly before his death in May 1988), Kim Philby told Phillip Knightley that there had never been a Cambridge spy ring as so many people over the last 30 years had assumed.[75] Philby claimed that his recruitment, apparently through the Cambridge Marxist lecturer Maurice Dobb, was quite separate to the later recruitment of Burgess, Maclean and Blunt. According to Philby there was no Cambridge Comitern consisting of five people so the alleged 'fifth man' never existed. Philby's description of how he was recruited suggests that there was no central Cambridge spy recruiter, no highly organised preconceived plan, but that odd people were casually approached to see if they were interested in helping the fight against Fascism. If Philby was telling Knightley the truth (and there is no reason why he should), all this does is to throw more doubt on the concept of there having been a specific fifth man in the form of Hollis or Mitchell within MI5

But even before the *Spycatcher* affair could be settled the government got itself embroiled in two other rows over television programmes about the world of intelligence. The first of these was a Channel Four programme, made by 20/20 Vision, called *MI5's Official Secrets*, which was planned to be shown on 20 February 1985. The central figures of this film were Miss Cathy Massiter, a former librarian who had worked for MI5 for 13 years before resigning in 1983, and another unidentified woman clerk who had also recently left MI5.

The Independent Broadcasting Authority previewed the film and was advised by its lawyers not to let it be shown until the government had decided whether the two ex-MI5 employees were to be prosecuted. Unfortunately 20/20 Vision showed copies of the film to all and sundry, and even sold video cassettes of it together with copies of the transcript so the government, anxious not to have another fiasco on its hands like the abortive Ponting trial (see Chapter 9,) decided to do nothing. On 8 March 1985 Channel Four showed the complete film, and it was repeated again on 5 April 1988.

Miss Massiter turned out to be a very straightforward person who in simple and unemotive terms explained what she had been doing at MI5 and how she considered that many of her instructions from senior officials broke MI5's own guidelines, ultimately causing her to resign. She and her unidentified colleague (who, incidentally, Miss Massiter had not known while at MI5) revealed far more about the work of MI5 than those provided by Wright since his information was at least 20 years out of date and most of those he referred to were long dead. But the two women described events such as unwarranted telephone tapping that had happened only a year or so earlier. Together they gave a very disturbing account of how MI5 operates without control and accountability and made heavily politicised attacks against any person or organisation that criticised any aspect of the government's policies by claiming they were subversive.

In an effort to denigrate Miss Massiter's claims MI5 turned to its usual dirty trick of spreading smear stories about her. These were passed to Pincher-like journalists in pro-government newspapers who, under the pretence of wanting to protect national security, implied that Miss Massiter was unreliable and had been receiving psychiatric treatment and that she was a neurotic troublemaker anxious to draw attention to herself. But those who met Miss Massiter concluded she was a very honest, sane and well-balanced young woman who was telling the truth.[76]

The second fuss involved a set of six BBC television programmes, produced by Duncan Campbell, called *The Secret Society*, due to be shown in 1987. One of these was about a proposed geostationary satellite that GCHQ wanted to build called *Zircon*.[77] The government became terribly agitated about this and Special Branch officers raided the BBC studios in Scotland where the programme had been made, taking away van-loads of material while injunctions flew thick and fast in the courts. In fact, there was nothing particularly secret about *Zircon*. As its codename implies, it was part of the same generation of Sigint satellites as the NSA's *Rhyolite* and all the details of *Rhyolite* had long been known to the Russians anyway. There was little point in GCHQ copying NSA so late in the day other than that it wanted to impress the politicans with its hardware. After £70 million had been wasted on pointless development costs it was claimed that the *Zircon* project had been cancelled, although this may not be true.[78]

The *Zircon* film was finally shown by the BBC on 30 September 1988 and turned out to be remarkably dull, largely because Campbell missed the point as to why *Zircon* was ever started. The other films in the series were equally boring as Campbell tried to make controversial mountains out of unimportant molehills without offering any objective opinions to balance his arguments. Though Campbell is a brilliant investigative journalist he has yet to master the art of documentary television. The government could have saved itself a lot of trouble and expense had it let all six programmes go out without interference, when they would have attracted little public attention.

One strange book that appeared in 1987 while the *Spycatcher* saga was raging was an account of how MI6 bugged the Russian Trade Delegation's offices at Highgate in North London. Called *Break-In*, it was written by Bill Graham, a former member of the Royal Military Police who had served in Northern Ireland as personal bodyguard to Sir Brian Kimmons, the commander-in-chief. After leaving the army Graham had started up a double-glazing business.

Graham was first approached by Mike Carey of Special Branch who introduced him to MI6. They asked him to tender for replacing the windows in the Trade Delegation's offices. To ensure he got the contract MI6 subsidised his company so that his price was much cheaper than normal and, according to Graham, the Russians accepted his offer immediately. For the next two years Graham and his workmen were able to roam more or less as they pleased, watching what went on inside the office complex, planting electronic bugs in the window sashes, and even stealing documents for MI6 to photograph. Apparently it was a great success.

Despite the fact that Graham had obviously signed the Official Secrets Act while in the army and had voluntarily agreed to work for MI6 from whom he received money, the government made no effort to stop him from publishing his book which in terms of national security revealed far more about the current work of the security services than had *Spycatcher*. Furthermore, if the MI6 operation against the Russians had been so successful, why blow it publicly when the same trick might be used against some other foreign diplomatic mission?

One reason could be that the operation was not the success that Graham believed. It seems odd that the Russians, who are always short of foreign currency, were so anxious to sign a contract (and after only 45 minutes' deliberation) with a British company to fit new windows at their Trade Delegation when it would have been cheaper to bring the windows in from Russia and fit them with their own labour. Siberian winters must have taught the Russians more about double-glazing than anyone in Britain. And it is remarkable that security within the Trade Delegation was so lax that Graham could carry out much work for MI6. Perhaps the Russians were not quite as stupid as it seems. The KGB watches events in Northern Ireland very carefully and at least one Russian Sigint trawler is permanently stationed off the coast monitoring military and civil traffic. As Graham was the C-in-C's bodyguard he could well have been photographed at some time and the Russians therefore may have guessed that Graham was now working for British security, snapped up his cheap offer and then fed back disinformation through him. Nevertheless, whether the operation was a success or not, writing about it in such detail constituted a breach of the government's oft-repeated policy.

Also in 1987 the BBC decided to emulate the 1981 *Panorama* programme on the security services with a new investigative documentary called *State of Secrecy*. On this occasion the producers either lost their way or were pressured into avoiding any controversial subjects so when the programme appeared on 14 September it was boring to the point of inducing sleep. Not surprisingly the government made no attempt to stop it from being shown.

Later that same year BBC Radio 4 planned to broadcast a three-part series called *My Country Right or Wrong*, which was to be an innocuous discussion about various aspects of the security services but was not intended to reveal anything secret or controversial. A number of retired intelligence officers from MI5, MI6, GCHQ and the CIA, together with former home secretaries and even Lord Hailsham, recorded interviews and before any of this material was used the producer contacted the D-notice Committee. However before the first programme could be broadcast the government rushed off to court to obtain an injunction banning it even though it already knew what it contained.

The effect of this, of course, was to concentrate the media's attention on the programme and soon its contents were being merrily leaked in every paper and debated in Parliament. It was then revealed that Sir Anthony Duff, the former head of MI5, had circulated a memorandum throughout MI5 stating that there was nothing to worry about in the programme. So all the government achieved was to give greater prominence to a programme which had it gone out in its original mid-morning slot would have been heard by very few people. Eventually in July 1988 the government relented and the broadcasts went ahead.

To compound the government's misery Allason appeared on the literary scene for the first time since becoming a Conservative politician with a new book called *The Friends*, about the post-war history of MI6. As usual Allason had simply used information given him, either in the form of interviews or documents by retired members of MI6, with the result that the book was extremely dull mainly consisting of various covert operations most of which had already appeared in *Spycatcher*. Allason's book was submitted to the D-Notice Committee which asked that a number of names be deleted from the manuscript.[79] But Allason evidently baulked at all these deletions and the book was published containing at least 13 names of MI6 officers that the government had wanted removed.

On the face of it the book would appear to breach the guidelines laid down by the government over the *Spycatcher* affair. Yet when questioned about it in Parliament the attorney general, Sir Patrick Mayhew, replied:

> The government deplores the publication of books of this nature especially when advice from the D-notice Committee has to any extent

been disregarded. As regards legal action this is not a case of an author who is or who has been a crown servant ... the government concluded that an application for an injunction ... would be unlikely to succeed.[80]

It is a curious bit of legal hairsplitting. Plainly, Allason could not have written the book without the help of MI6 officers, past or present (whose identities must be known to the government), since he knows nothing about intelligence affairs and admits there are no MI6 archives in the public domain. It is ridiculous to pursue Wright through the courts in order to stop him giving away so-called secrets that are at least 20 years old when Allason can be given exactly the same sort of material to publish with impunity. Whether Allason will write any more books like this will depend upon the willingness of other intelligence officers to feed him further information and documents from official files and on whether he wants promotion within the Conservative Party. It is hard to see how Allason could enjoy ministerial rank and still apparently be embarrassing the government with his books. The only consolation for the government was that *The Friends* was so dull that very few copies were sold. Indeed, it must have been a relief when a threatened libel action caused some bookshops to take it off their shelves altogether.[81]

In the autumn of 1988, while the dust from the *Spycatcher* ruling was settling, fresh controversy broke out around a new book about the traitor Anthony Blunt. Called *The Mask of Treachery*,[82] it was written by John Costello, a British author living in America who had over a four-year period uncovered a hitherto unknown mass of MI5 papers in American archives. These showed that British intelligence had concealed from the Americans its knowledge of Blunt's treachery. The book also revealed that he had joined MI5 on the recommendation of Victor Rothschild and confirmed Blunt's role, while still with MI5, in recovering sensitive royal documents from Germany in 1945 which had ensured his subsequent royal patronage and employment even after he had confessed in 1964 to his work for the Russians.

An advance proof of the book was sent to the British publishers, William Collins, in July 1988 and, as happened to one of Chapman Pincher's books, it found its way without either the author's or the American publisher's knowledge into the hands of Admiral William Higgins, secretary of the D-notice Committee. Eventually Collins admitted it had given Higgins a proof which he had circulated to MI5, MI6 and GCHQ. In mid-September Higgins wrote saying he would like the names of John Hilton (an MI6 undercover agent in Cyprus 20 years ago), Alastair Macdonald (a wartime intelligence officer) and Geoffrey Sudbury (a GCHQ codebreaker already identified in *Spycatcher*) deleted. In the end the unnecessary fuss surrounding this trivial matter ensured that the three names enjoyed far wider circulation than had Higgins said nothing, although the publicity did the book's sales no harm.

Meantime a long line of other retired intelligence officers are alleged to be planning books.[83] The include John Day, a senior MI5 officer who had worked with Wright on the Fluency Committee; Nicholas Elliott of MI6 who had been responsible for the Crabb fiasco; and Desmond Bristow, also of MI6, who accused two former colleagues of being Russian spies. It was also alleged that Sir Dick White who had been head of both MI5 and MI6 had agreed to let Andrew Boyle (who exposed Blunt) ghost his autobiography. Dick White subsequently issued a statement denying this, claiming Boyle was writing the book without his authority.[84] Anthony Cavendish is to write a biography of Sir Maurice Oldfield, former head of MI6, and others anxious to break into print include Fred Winterbotham (of Ultra fame), David Smiley, an ex-SOE and MI6 officer, and the Russian spy George Blake.

It is hard to see what some of these people can have to say that would be of interest after so many years but others' stories ought to be very interesting if they are willing to tell the whole truth. But as we have seen with *Spycatcher*, not only is the truth elusive but it is frequently obscured by subjective memories and opinions.

Over the 40 years during which all these cases of alleged breaches of national security have occurred, the only people who have benefited have been the armies of lawyers who have enriched themselves at the taxpayer's expense. The *Spycatcher* case alone is estimated to have cost over £3 million. But *Spycatcher* was never a matter of national security, simply one of the government's embarrassment at having MI5's illegal practices publicly exposed. Nor is national security in any way impaired because the public knows that a corpse dressed as a major in the Royal Marines was floated ashore on the coast of Spain in 1943, or that there is a place called GCHQ at Cheltenham, or even that the head of MI5 was an alleged Russian spy.

Governments pay far too much attention to the ludicrous world of secrecy that is, in the main, designed only to protect its own privileged inefficiency. Other countries, notably Australia and America, have managed to find a sensible balance between accountability and responsibility.[85] Had Wright been a retired employee of the CIA, his book *Spycatcher* would have been published, with a few deletions and without any fuss. Whatever legislation the government finally introduces public interest in the intelligence world will continue. The sooner it accepts this and establishes a method by which such books can be written without a lot of fuss, the better it will be for the government and the nation's secrets.

CHAPTER 9

DEFENCE OF THE REALM

National security is a convenient phrase. It rolls off the tongue easily and commands respect. Yet it means quite different things to different people. Essentially national security is related to secrecy and, conversely, secrecy is related to national security. So the two are inextricably connected.

All countries have secrets. Some believe they have more than others. Exactly what ought to be secret is seldom debated. Like weeds, secrecy grows continuously and drastic action is required if it is to be held in check, let alone pushed back. Most countries have some type of law that makes it an offence to pass on details of their secrets to someone else. In Britain we have the much-debated Official Secrets Act (OSA) first introduced in 1911 during the great German spy scare which was a complete invention.[1]

The OSA is divided into two parts. Section 1 concerns spying and sabotage and carries a maximum penalty of 14 years' imprisonment. There is no doubt that this part of the act is perfectly sensible. But Section 2 concerns the communicating of official information[2] without authority, or receiving such information believing it to have been passed on in breach of the Act. It is this part of the OSA that has fallen into disrepute through misuse.

At the outset it is perhaps worth mentioning that everyone in Britain is bound by the OSA.[3] People often talk about 'signing the OSA' as if this alone made them answerable. But the purpose of signing the official form is simply to remind someone of their responsibilities.

In America there is the National Defense Act of 1911[4] and the Espionage Act of 1917, introduced when America entered World War I.[5] Additionally many government departments, such as the CIA and NSA, require their employees to sign additional documents reminding them of the secret nature of their work, particularly connected with various forms of Sigint and code breaking.[6]

But the problem is that everyone has their own idea of what ought to be secret in the interests of national security. Politicians tend to adopt an ambivalent and hypocritical attitude. When in opposition many advocate a reduction in secrecy and criticise the government of the day for not providing a greater degree of accountability, calling for the introduction of some form of freedom of information legislation like that which exists in America and elsewhere. But as soon as these same politicians come to power and start running the country a remarkable change comes over them.

New ministers quickly succumb to the fascination of secrecy because secrecy is power and power is the all-important talisman of politics. Permanent civil servants are also quick to remind their temporary masters of the advantages of secrecy: how disasters can be hidden, bad news massaged to make it look better, and good news leaked to those who will give it the right publicity.

National security and secrecy are not party-political matters. They are used by whatever party is in power. Take as an example the dilemma facing Harold Wilson during his first term as Labour prime minister between 1964 and 1969.[7] At the time Britain's independent nuclear deterrent, of Polaris missiles in our own nuclear submarines, was growing old and would either have to be replaced or the whole concept of an independent nuclear deterrent scrapped.

Labour had come to power on an election promise not to extend the nuclear deterrent beyond Polaris. At the time America was developing two new missile systems, Antelope, basically a Polaris improvement, and Poseidon, a totally new missile. Wilson was offered Poseidon by President Lyndon Johnson but refused it because it would have taken his government beyond its political promise. Wilson expected to get Antelope which he hoped to be able to persuade his party to accept on the grounds that it was merely maintaining Polaris. But the Americans suddenly cancelled Antelope.

Wilson then decided to authorise British scientists to begin their own programme to improve Polaris. On the grounds of national security, but in reality to conserve Labour Party unity, the work was to be done in total secrecy and Parliament was not told. The project was codenamed *Chevaline*.

In 1970 Wilson lost the general election and Edward Heath became prime minister. When Wilson returned to Downing Street in 1973, still on a manifesto that promised no extension of the nuclear deterrent beyond Polaris, he discovered that *Chevaline* was still ticking over, but no real progress had been made in its development. In October 1974 Wilson went to the country again and was returned with a larger majority. Now he felt safe to press ahead with *Chevaline*. Only one problem remained and that was his Cabinet, which contained several stalwart unilateral disarmers including Michael Foot and Barbara Castle.

Once again secrecy and national security won the day. Without realising what they were agreeing to the Cabinet accepted that Polaris should be improved at a cost of £24 million. They were not told that they had agreed to fit Polaris with a completely new and far more advanced weapons system using multi-warheads which would include numerous decoys intended to baffle the Russian anti-missile defence system. Within two years the cost of *Chevaline* had risen to £584 million, but neither the Cabinet nor Parliament were told. In April 1976 Wilson resigned and James Callaghan took over as prime minister. Still no one was told about the project yet within two years the cost had risen to £1 billion and *Chevaline* was still five years off entering service.

In 1979 the Conservatives swept into power. For them there was no political problem about replacing Polaris. In January 1980 Defence Secretary Francis Pym told Parliament of the government's intention to order Trident, which immediately provoked the inevitable opposition from the Labour benches. Pym then revealed that the two previous Labour governments had spent £1 billion on *Chevaline*. Not surprisingly, Labour supporters through-out the country were furious while the leadership found its defence policy in tatters from which it has never recovered. *Chevaline* continues to haunt the Labour Party to this day.

What is particularly interesting about the *Chevaline* affair is how national security was invoked to keep it secret. Yet the whole purpose of a deterrent is to show your enemies not only that it exists but is a viable threat. Under the circumstances it would have been perfectly logical and sensible to make a public anouncement about replacing Polaris with *Chevaline* even if the cost overruns were concealed.

Plainly the government had used national security and secrecy as an excuse because it knew it was going against the policies of its own party and did not want the embarrassment of debating this either in Parliament or at the Labour Party's annual conference. Yet this was the very same party which when in opposition had been so keen to see more openness of government and less secrecy. The civil servants must have found all this most amusing.

Back in 1939 Churchill remarked, 'The Official Secrets Act was devised to protect the national defences and ought not to be used to shield ministers who have strong personal interests in concealing the truth about matters from the country.'[8]

Fine words indeed. But in post-war years Churchill was not above concealing embarrassing truths from the people. His own illnesses, even when they rendered him incapable of carrying out the daily responsibilities of prime minister, were hidden from public view by misleading and untruthful statements peddled to sycophantic lobby correspondents and editors.

The leaking of political secrets by the government in power is another example of how the mythology of national security can be invoked as and when it is convenient. There is a charming anecdote told about Clement

Attlee when he became prime minister at the end of World War II.[9] His staff suggested that a news agency teleprinter be installed in Downing Street. Attlee, who came from a generation that did not understand such things, was not impressed until, that is, his staff pointed out that the same machine would relay the latest cricket scores. An avid cricketer, Attlee agreed. Some days after the machine had been installed Attlee stopped to read what it was printing. Horrified, he rushed into the Cabinet Secretary's office to complain that the cricket machine was printing out the details of that morning's Cabinet meeting. Attlee was evidently unaware that it was the custom to brief selected journalists with summaries of Cabinet business.

Today Downing Street leaks like a rusty bucket when convenient and is quite prepared to blackmail the media into getting stories published as it wants. In early January 1983 Mrs Thatcher flew to the Falkland Islands but because her visit had to be made in secret the usual lemming-like press contingent could not be given advance warning. By chance the BBC's Nicholas Witchell and a camera team happened to be out there and so were the only television crew on hand to record the prime minister's regal progress around the islands.

Mrs Thatcher's press officer, Bernard Ingham (who in theory is supposed to be an impartial civil servant), wanted full coverage of the visit as part of the build-up to the forthcoming general election. He therefore told the assistant director general of the BBC, Alan Protheroe, that unless the BBC agreed to share its exclusive material with Independent Television News and Independent Radio News the RAF would be told not to fly out the BBC's tapes.[10]

Normally no one would have known of Ingham's behaviour and had anyone alleged that he had blackmailed the BBC the claim would have been instantly denied as rubbish and political spite against Mrs Thatcher's visit. Unfortunately Ingham's radio-telephone conversation between the Falklands and London was monitored by a radio ham. He gave a copy to Channel Four television who broadcast it in their programme *The Friday Alternative*.

After some blustering Protheroe cravenly acquiesced and shared the BBC's material with ITN so that for five days Mrs Thatcher enjoyed peak-time coverage on all four channels. If the BBC had had any courage it would have not only rejected Ingham's threats but issued a public statement as to why its film was being held up in the Falklands. It is, incidentally, open to question whether the Downing Street press secretary has the authority to forbid the RAF to carry a legitimate piece of film cargo for the BBC.

Having got Protheroe's agreement Ingham then telephoned his office in Downing Street boasting that he had won. That conversation was also monitored. Naturally Ingham was furious at having his telephone call tapped and claimed it was illegal. That sounded a shade ironic coming from a civil servant who knows perfectly well that every telephone call entering and leaving Britain is illegally intercepted by GCHQ.

A more serious example of how confidential material can be leaked to the media to suit government ministers occurred in January 1986 during the long drawn out saga of the Westland affair. Westland, Britain's only manufacturer of helicopters, was in financial difficulties and since the government was not prepared to help it were advised to look for a partner. This resulted in a division of opinion within the Cabinet. The Secretary of State for Defence, Michael Heseltine, wanted Westland to merge with a European consortium. But the Secretary of State for Trade and Industry, Leon Brittan, preferred Westland to join forces with the giant American helicopter company Sikorski. Inevitably there was a great deal of lobbying behind the scenes with each side peddling the enormous benefits of its particular recommendation.

In the course of this power struggle on 3 January 1986 Heseltine wrote to Lloyds Bank, who were Westland's financial advisers, pointing out in some detail why the European deal was better. When the prime minister heard about this she referred the letter to the Solicitor General Sir Patrick Mayhew. Mayhew was unhappy about some of the things Heseltine had written because he felt that they might affect a proper unbiased commercial judgement of the rival bids. On 6 January Mayhew wrote to Heseltine asking him to clarify a number of points, which he did. The entire exchange was in total confidence as befits correspondence with the country's most senior law officer. But almost immediately a copy of Mayhew's letter to Heseltine was somehow shown to Brittan who discussed it with Sir Peter Carey, a director of Morgan Grenfell, the bankers who were advising Sikorski.

What happened next was quite incredible. Brittan told his department's chief information officer, Miss Colette Bowe, to leak selective extracts from Mayhew's letter to the public. Later that same day Miss Bowe telephoned the political correspondent at the Press Association and read out to him parts of Mayhew's letter, in particular the phrase that Heseltine's letter had contained material inaccuracies. Not surprisingly the press had a field day with this revelation coming from the very heart of government.

Mayhew was furious and wrote to Heseltine but by the time the letter arrived things had changed again, because on the previous day Heseltine had resigned from the government by storming out of a Cabinet meeting. In Parliament all sorts of accusations were bandied about and Brittan invoked some dubious legalistic hairsplitting to deny having received a letter from the head of British Aerospace, and then had to return to Parliament later in the evening to apologise for misleading the House. Eventually he had to resign.

As usual an inquiry was set up which ponderously sifted through what evidence could be found. Everyone including the prime minister and her Cabinet secretary (the luckless Sir Robert Armstrong) had ingenious and feeble explanations as to what had happened and what they had known about the affair. No one seemed anxious to investigate whether Brittan, even though a Cabinet minister, had the right to leak documents belonging to the solicitor-general to the press. In fact, he had not. Anyone else would have certainly been prosecuted with all manner of claims about endangering national security. The whole affair was a sordid example of how the world of secrecy is used to the advantage of the government in power. It leaks when convenient and then prosecutes others for doing the same.

Brittan leaked state secrets to the press in order to thwart his rival Heseltine. He was an experienced politician, a privy councillor, an eminent lawyer and a QC, so could hardly be unaware of the law. He was not prosecuted.

Sarah Tisdall was aged 23, a junior civil servant working in the Foreign Office. She too leaked state secrets to the press to thwart Heseltine. On 21 October 1983 she obtained access to two documents prepared by Heseltine about the manner in which Cruise missiles were to arrive at Greenham Common airbase in November. Anticipating demonstrations from the anti-nuclear protestors camped at the base Heseltine's memoranda explained that the missiles would be flown in overnight from America so as to arrive early in the morning. He also dealt in some detail with the number of police and troops that would be on hand including references to armed American air-force police who in a last resort would be authorised to open fire on any protesters who invaded the airbase and got close to the missiles themselves.

Exactly why Miss Tisdall thought these documents were worth leaking to the press is hard to understand. Despite their ridiculously high-security classification, 'Secret – UK Eyes A', they contained nothing new or surprising. Nevertheless Miss Tisdall felt that Heseltine was misleading the country and Parliament and decided to pass a copy of the two documents on to the press. She was not as well organised at leaking material as Brittan and all she did was to run off photocopies using the machine in her own office and hand them in anonymously at the offices of the *Guardian* newspaper that afternoon. During the next few days the paper published some stories based on Miss Tisdall's documents which, apart from causing questions to be asked in Parliament, also alerted the government to the fact that there had been a serious leak of information.[11]

Had the *Guardian* copied the information off the documents left by Miss Tisdall and then destroyed them that would have been an end to the matter. Foolishly the paper retained Miss Tisdall's copies and when they were subsequently forced to hand them back[12] investigators quickly traced the machine on which they had been made from the drum identification marks. Miss Tisdall was interviewed by police on 6 January 1984, later confessed, and pleaded guilty at her trial on 23 March 1984 which, unfortunately for her, was before Mr Justice Cantley (who presided at the trial of Jeremy Thorpe). She was sentenced to six months' imprisonment.

The sentence was quite out of proportion to the offence and simply reflected the government's embarrassment over the premature announcement which caused them to delay the arrival date of the Cruise missiles by a fortnight. Miss Tisdall's career with the civil service was obviously in ruins and she would now have a criminal record for the rest of her life which would inevitably restrict her chances of getting another decent job. For a young woman of 23 that alone was a severe punishment. At worst a suspended sentence would have been more than adequate.

So Miss Tisdall lost her job and went to prison. Brittan was rewarded by Mrs Thatcher with a £95,000 a year sinecure with the Common Market and a knighthood.[13]

The severity of Miss Tisdall's sentence did not deter another civil servant, 39-year-old Clive Ponting, who worked in the Ministry of Defence, from also leaking papers. While Miss Tisdall was still in prison on 16 July 1984 Ponting sent some papers to Tam Dalyell MP concerning the background to the sinking of the Argentine cruiser, *Belgrano*, during the Falklands War in 1982. Ponting also was not very clever about concealing the source of the documents and it was not long before they were traced back to him. On 28 January 1985 Ponting stood trial at the Old Bailey charged under the Official Secrets Act.

The judge, Mr Justice McCowan, in a very strong summing-up, lectured (some might say hectored) the jury, encouraging them to ignore Ponting's claims and any other arguments about the rights and wrongs of the Official Secrets Act. Plainly this upset the jury and after a three-hour retirement they unanimously acquitted Ponting much to the chagrin of the government. Most people accepted that Ponting, like Miss Tisdall, had done wrong and should have been dismissed from his job. But taking into account the way politicians behave over secrets when it suits them, prosecuting people under the OSA and sending them to prison was not the correct answer.

Brittan leaked purely out of spite. But Tisdall and Ponting leaked because they felt the public and Parliament were being deliberately misled. So too did Peter Wright and Cathy Massiter. And Jock Kane tried to. This highlights the problem of trying to reconcile confidentiality to one's employer, the nation's security, and accountability over illegal activities.

There is nothing odd in expecting an employee to respect his employer's secrets. This applies just as much in private industry as it does in a government department. But what happens if an employee discovers that his employer is doing something illegal? For example, labelling toxic waste as harmless in order to dump it cheaply? Or putting pressure on employees to ignore safety regulations in order to increase output? Few employees will want to risk their jobs by making a direct protest to their employer but they might be willing to pass on incriminating documents to a newspaper in the hope that the subsequent investigation will publicise the illegality and put an end to it. Most of us would applaud such action.

Ponting believed that his department's minister was not telling Parliament the truth.[14] He evidently felt there was no point in approaching one of his senior colleagues about this. Should Ponting have gone public or was the matter not important enough to breach his employer's confidentiality? Should Parliament and the public always be told the truth and is it the duty of the civil service to see that this is done? The government claims that it has a right to expect its employees like Ponting to respect its secrecy, but equally it can be argued that if the government had not tried to mislead Parliament over the *Belgrano* affair, which was unconnected with national security, Ponting would have had nothing to leak.

Cathy Massiter was a junior employee of MI5 who came to the conclusion that MI5 was breaching its guidelines by tapping telephones and keeping dossiers on people and organisations that were neither subversive nor a threat to the state but merely disagreed with government policies. She believed there was no point in making a complaint about this to her seniors since they were responsible for this highly politicised attitude. So she resigned and then went public. In her television interview[15] she gave specific details of how MI5 was breaking its guidelines but the government did nothing about these allegations except attempt to smear Miss Massiter's character.

Jock Kane was neither a whistleblower nor troublemaker.[16] He was a dedicated employee at GCHQ who over 25 years worked his way up through the organisation with an impeccably loyal record. He became genuinely worried about the level of fraud and lack of security within the organisation and approached senior management about it giving details of specific incidents. But he was laughed at for taking matters too seriously and no action was taken.

Peter Wright served his country loyally for over 25 years and genuinely believed MI5 was penetrated by the KGB and that Mrs Thatcher, Parliament and the country were being deliberately misled by security advisers who would not face up to the facts. He tried sending reports directly to the prime minister but these were intercepted by civil servants. He gave his facts to Chapman Pincher (see Chapter 7) but still nothing happened, as the Bettaney case showed. When he published his own account in *Spycatcher* the government spent millions trying to stop him. It is not hard to see why. His story showed that MI5 consistently breaks the law and the Maxwell Fyfe guidelines, something that governments have always denied.

This mania for secrecy based on the excuse of protecting national security has steadily grown until today it has become a form of paranoia that intrudes into every aspect of British life, often to the detriment of the very people it is supposed to be protecting. Time and again, when something embarrassing happens the immediate bureaucratic instinct is to hide it away from public view on the spurious grounds that it would not be in the public interest to reveal it. To civil servants, everything they do is secret and should be kept from public view for ever. If civil servants had their way the Public Record

Office would be closed down and no government documents would ever be released for inspection. Even the thought of having their mismanagement exposed after 30 years upsets bureaucrats.

In October 1957 a fire in one of the Windscale nuclear reactors in Cumbria released a cloud of radioactive gas over the surrounding countryside. Today the reactor still remains sealed like a tomb as it was in 1957. Naturally there was an inquiry headed by Sir William Penney, chief of the Atomic Weapons Research Establishment, to find out what had happened, how it had occurred and what dangers the public had been exposed to. Penney's report concluded that the accident had happened, as had a previous unreported accident in 1952, because of bad judgement by the staff and faulty instruments. The Ministry of Defence had no objection to Penney's report being published as there were no security considerations involved.

But the prime minister, Harold Macmillan, believed he knew what was good for ordinary members of the public and in his lordly detached manner decided not to be honest with them. His excuse was that if Penney's report was published in full it would make America less willing to cooperate with Britain in developing nuclear weapons, shake public confidence in future nuclear power-stations, and most important of all embarrass Britain's Atomic Energy Authority. Macmillan decided that it would not be in the public interest for the truth to be told and ordered that only a watered-down version of the report should be published. For 30 years the facts lay hidden. It is now believed that up to 33 deaths resulted from this accident.

We now have many more nuclear power-stations in Britain. If the same sort of accident occurred again now and an employee believed the truth was being concealed, would he be justified in telling the media or should he stay silent so as not to embarrass the government? We are quick to criticise the Russians for being secretive but they were more open about the Chernobyl reactor disaster in 1987 than Macmillan was about Windscale in 1957.

Many claims of official secrecy are simply made to hide inefficiency. In the late 1960s Peter Laurie, a journalist with the *Sunday Times* became interested in Britain's civil-defence plans for protecting the public against nuclear attack. The government was not anxious to help so Laurie started going round the country on his own and gradually put together details which he published in an intriguing book called *Beneath the City Streets*.

Laurie discovered that although the government had spent a lot of money building elaborate secret underground funk-holes for civil servants and ministers the general public would be left to fend for itself. Laurie's book was not at all popular with the government, although ironically the Home Office found it ideal as a training manual because, like the BBC film *The War Game*,[17] which the government managed to suppress, it came very near the truth. So here was an example where the claim of national security was being used, and still is to this day, to conceal the embarrassing fact that in a war the public is unprotected while the government has plans to look after itself.

Apart from fudging the truth, threatening to prosecute under the Official Secrets Act and going to the courts for injunctions, the government has another useful weapon at its disposal to prevent the truth from being told. This is the D-notice system operated by the Defence, Press and Broadcasting Committee. Introduced in 1912, its duties were taken over by formal censorship during World War I. During the inter-wars years the committee did not meet and from 1939 to 1945 formal wartime censorship was again in force. It was during the post-war Attlee government that the D-notice system began to operate again, mainly because of the development of the atomic bomb which at the time we fondly assumed the Russians knew nothing about.

The D-notice system is a quaint British compromise that no other country would tolerate. The committee has no legal powers to stop publication but can only request that a particular subject not be reported in the national interest. There are some nine permanent D-notices in force covering matters like defence plans, radar stations, wartime contingency arrangements including civil defence, and of course details about MI5 and MI6. Other D-notices are issued on a temporary basis for specific items. There are about a thousand people on the D-notice list, mainly editors of newspapers, television and radio news, and defence journals.

Over the years the D-notice system has been mainly used by governments to prevent embarrassing stories from being reported rather than those that might genuinely affect national security. D-notices are also used to frighten off timid editors from a story long enough so that the government can leak its own version.[18] The D-notice system has now fallen into disrepute but since the government can so easily blackmail organisations like the BBC or bribe tame journalists with hints of scoops it really no longer matters.

The result of this hypocritical ambivalence has been to encourage the investigative journalist, not to be confused with Pincher-style journalism where planted stories are published as real news. In the dog-eat-dog world of mass circulation, one newspaper's scoop is derided by another as a breach of national security. The journalistic world is full fictitious claims of loyalty which in reality conceal disappointment at having missed a good story. When Pincher was peddling Wright's story (pretending it was the product of his own investigations), the *Daily Mail* was only too happy to serialise it. But when the *Sunday Times* bought the serial rights of *Spycatcher* Wright became a venal traitor. The *Daily Express* criticised Duncan Campbell[19] for exposing the profligacy of the useless *Zircon* satellite project at GCHQ, conveniently forgetting that Pincher embarrassed a government in the *Daily Express* in 1967 by revealing that GCHQ read all Britain's cable traffic.[20] The *Daily Telegraph* rubbished Wright's book[21] and roundly condemned him for revealing the nation's secrets[22] yet were willing to publish precise details as to how Britain's nuclear submarines avoid Russian detection when leaving their base in Scotland.[23]

Revision of the OSA has been talked about for 60 years but each government in turn has baulked at doing anything because they have found the Act's bewildering complexity and ambivalence useful to concealing their own mismanagement. The first serious attempt at reform came in 1969 when the Labour government published a White Paper, *Information and the Public Interest*. This was a very muddled document but before it could even be debated the Labour government was defeated in the 1970 election.

Edward Heath became prime minister promising to review the OSA and a committee was set up under Lord Franks. The civil service was very hostile to the idea of any changes and Sir Burke Trend, then Cabinet secretary, plaintively argued, 'Once you embark on the striptease of government, where do you stop?'[24] In September 1972 Franks produced a draft Official Information Bill which though long on words was short on any great changes and while Heath's government was still considering his ideas it was defeated in the February 1974 election following the miners' strike.

The Labour Party returned to office, once again promising to replace the OSA with a new Act which would place the responsibility on individual government departments to justify withholding information from the public. But despite these fine words nothing happened for five years until the Liberal politician, Clement Freud, introduced his private Official Information Bill in March 1979. But although the Labour government indicated it would not oppose his ideas, before the Bill could make progress through Parliament the government was defeated in the June 1979 election.

From the start Mrs Thatcher made it clear that she was against any reform of Section 2 of the OSA, just as she also refused to permit any further official histories of World War II intelligence operations to be written. One of her arguments was that if there was more freedom of information ministers' accountability to Parliament would be reduced and the importance of Parliament diminished. This was nonsense. The Thatcher administration consistently misled Parliament and concealed information from it whenever it was faced with an embarrassing fiasco as happened, for example, with the Prime affair.

During the years that Britain was fumbling with the idea of reforming the OSA, America, Australia and Canada all introduced Freedom of Information Acts. In general these allow citizens to obtain details of information held by the government on a wide range of subjects, the single most important being files kept on themselves which they have the right to challenge and amend if the details are inaccurate. In each country a request can be denied if the release of the information is considered to be against the national interest[25] and there are various forms of appeal against such a refusal.

In Australia and Canada the operation of this legislation has worked very smoothly with few people making use of it and even fewer finding anything incorrect in files kept about them. Agencies like ASIO, Australia's MI5, have welcomed the legislation, claiming that it helps them keep more accurate records while at the same time removing the mythology that they have a lot to hide. In America the Freedom of Information Act has certainly revealed a number of unsavoury details about the past work of the FBI, CIA and the NSA, even though the bulk of their files are still protected from inspection. There is of course always the danger that if an agency like the CIA knows that there is a chance that its files may be made public in the future, it will conceal its dishonest and illegal activities within even more secret and unaccountable cabals, as happened in the Iran/Contra affair. But accepting that no legislation will ever overcome deliberate dishonesty, these forms of Freedom of Information Acts have worked well in all three countries without affecting their genuine national security. Under the circumstances there is no reason why a similar Act would not work equally well in Britain but the present government has no intention of permitting any such thing.

It was therefore a shock to Mrs Thatcher when one of her own back-benchers, Richard Shepherd, proposed his own bill – the Protection of Official Information Bill – to replace the outworn OSA. The Bill carefully avoided altering Section 1 of the OSA which deals with espionage but with regard to Section 2 proposed some revolutionary changes.

One of these was contained in the proposed new Section 7:

> It shall be a defence for a person charged with an offence under this Act
> to prove that the disclosure or retention of the information or article
> was in the public interest insofar as he had reasonable cause to believe
> that it indicated the existence of crime, fraud, abuse of authority,
> neglect in the performance of official duty or other misconduct.

But this clause was qualified by Section 8 that stated that such a defence would fail unless the person charged: 'had taken reasonable steps to comply with any established procedures for drawing such misconduct to the attention of the appropriate authorities without effect.'

This would apply for instance in the case of Jock Kane who went through all the correct complaint procedures yet was still unable to find anyone willing to take action. The proposed Section 7 also opened up a very dangerous area for the government because if an employee of MI5 or MI6 like Massiter gave details of how MI5 had tapped telephones without a warrant or burgled someone's house she would be entitled to make the information public.

Section 6 was even more controversial because Shepherd proposed that it would be a defence under the act if it could be proved that the disputed information had been publicly available either in Britain or abroad. The obvious and valid objection to this is that stories could be leaked overseas first and then reprinted in this country. On the other hand it would stop a ludicrous situation arising, as happened with *Spycatcher*, whereby everyone else in the world, including Russia, can read the 'secret' information, but not those in Britain.

But perhaps the worst part of the new Bill as far as the government was concerned was the idea that in order to claim that a particular piece of information was secret a minister would have to give a certificate stating that its unauthorised disclosure would endanger national security. Shepherd then proposed that a defendent would have the right to challenge such a certificate by referring it to a Judicial Committee of the Privy Council (actually the Law Lords so there was little danger of any sudden surge of liberalism) who would have the right to cancel the certificate. So for the first time there would, in theory at least, be an independent outside body that would have the right to decide what was secret or not.

Other unpopular proposals included a definition of protected information held by Crown and government contractors outlawing unauthorised disclosure where serious injury would be caused to the national interest or the safety of a British citizen; government departments required to make an annual report on measures taken to increase access to official information, and to compel the civil service minister to make regulations governing the classification of documents. Apart from Shepherd's Bill highlighting government inaction, the whole tenor of his proposals sent cold shivers down the spine of every civil servant. What he was proposing was that they would have to prove something was secret rather than rely on the time-honoured custom that everything, even the number of cups of tea they drank daily, was part of national security.

As Bernard Levin put it, 'the government decided the Bill must be defeated because ministers and civil servants must retain the unfettered right to deceive, to cover up misconduct, and cheat the public in the darkness they wrap round themselves in the name of the law.'[26]

Shepherd received many hints that if he withdrew his Bill the government would put forward its own proposals. But Shepherd and his supporters, including such right-wing stalwarts as Sir Nicholas Bonsor, Sir Ian Gilmour and Teddy Taylor, persisted. Eventually on 15 January 1988 the government issued a three-line whip ordering its party to vote against Shepherd's bill. Despite a surprisingly large backbench revolt the government won the day but lost the moral argument.

In one of his most pathetic performances Douglas Hurd, the home secretary, performed an even more puppet-like dance than usual, appealing for an 'orderly path' to revised legislation to replace Section 2 of the OSA. 'It is simply not sensible to scratch and scramble at this,' he whined, 'it is not sensible for us to take at a gallop the necessary detailed work in order to get round a tactical difficulty.' As his government had been in power since 1979 it is hard to see that much galloping had been done about this matter in the previous eight years.

When the proposed Official Secrets Bill, which would replace Section 2 of the present Official Secrets Act, finally came before Parliament in December 1988 it was marginally more liberal than the original proposals first published in July. Hurd made much of the fact that numerous trivial subjects previously covered by the old Act, such as the menu in the Home Office canteen, would no longer be protected by criminal law. To cover these minor issues there will be changes in the civil service rules that will enforce greater loyalty and discipline.

But although the new Bill appears more liberal in fact it removes the 'public interest' defence from anyone who is handling, or has handled, secret information and discovers some illegality. Any member of the intelligence services who discovers instances of illegal telephone tapping, burglary, mail interception, bugging or other dirty tricks would be breaking the law if they revealed to anyone that the agency was breaking the law. This means that a future Cathy Massiter or Jock Kane would be unable to claim that it was in the public interest to reveal such malpractices.

But it is not only serving or retired intelligence officers who are gagged. Two obscure clauses in the Bill which Hurd naturally did not mention concern 'notified persons' and 'classes or descriptions of information deemed likely to cause damage (to national security)'.[27] A 'notified person' can be anyone. All that is required is the serving of a ministerial notice on any member of the public stating that 'in the interests of national security they be subject to the provisions of the Act' which compels them to remain silent on a state subject for life.

This would mean that if a journalist or author found out something about the security service or any other government department that showed it was engaged in some illegal activity that he could be made a 'notified person' in order to stop him from writing about it. Authors like Rupert Allason (Nigel West), who have used information supplied by former intelligence officers, could also be prevented from publishing any of this in a book.

Addressing Parliament on 21 December 1988 Hurd said:

We are asking Parliament to say that it is not in the public interest to knowingly damage the work of the security and intelligence services, knowingly to prejudice the capabilities of the armed forces, knowingly to jeopardise the country's interests abroad, knowingly to put our citizens' lives at risk, knowingly to add to the crime rate, or knowingly to disclose details relating to special investigations under the authorised warrants.

These fine words neatly gloss over the fact that both this new Act and the Security Service Act to control MI5 have been the result, not of government altruism in a search for greater accountability, but of a number of embarrassing revelations which have shown that illegalities have been taking place with the tacit approval of ministers who have been too lazy or incompetent to ensure that the law is obeyed.

If any damage has been done to MI5 over the years it is entirely of its own making. Not only has it failed to fulfil its primary duty of catching spies and traitors but it has broken its own rules with impunity while searching for non-existent subversives.

Typical examples of embarrassing revelations within the armed services which could now be suppressed include the failure of the Nimrod early-warning radar system that was scrapped at a cost of £850 million in favour of the American system, and the radar for the Tornado fighters defending Britain's airspace which does not work so that aircraft have had to be kept out of service until it does. Under this new Act such costly fiascoes could not be reported by the media thus allowing inefficient suppliers and civil servants to escape public criticism while the armed services would have to use sub-standard equipment. Thus it is not investigative journalists and authors who are prejudicing the capabilities of the armed services but the government itself.

As former Conservative prime minister Edward Heath pointed out, the new Act would prevent the exposure of any ministerial scandal like the Iran/Contra dealings in America which exposed the hypocrisy and incompetence of the president much to the dismay of Mrs Thatcher who was opposed to any such investigation.[28] In truth this new Act has nothing to do with more openness about government affairs but, like the new Act covering the work of MI5 and the whole history of official secrets legislation, is a cosmetic exercise designed to make it more difficult to expose scandals and corruption.

The reason for disallowing a 'public interest' defence is to prevent the repetition of a case like Clive Ponting's. After such a case, and after the *Spycatcher* fiasco the government is well aware the public does not trust it to tell the truth. If therefore journalists who revealed embarrassing illegalities went for trial before a jury – no matter how carefully selected by Special Branch – there would be few convictions. Instead the government is retreating behind this blanket ban on reporting fondly believing that if embarrassing details are kept out of the public eye by legislation, the public will believe that everything is all right. Effectively the government is saying that it cannot trust the public. The public is saying it does not trust the government. Or to misquote the old saying, 'National security is the last refuge of a scoundrel'.

Despite this new legislation could the situation ever arise when an employee in some government department – no matter how secret – would be justified in whistle-blowing?

In an article in *The Times* on 15 October 1988 Lord Armstrong, he of *Spycatcher* fame, wrote: 'I too could envisage a public interest defence of a breach of confidentiality – but only after every possible course of action short of such a breach had been tried and exhausted.'

Intrigued by this definition I asked Lord Armstrong if he could explain his 'public interest' defence in the context of a real example.[29] In his charming reply Lord Armstrong wrote: 'I cannot cite a 'real example' of this because I never experienced one during my time as Secretary of the Cabinet.'[30]

I then reminded Lord Armstrong of the cases of Cathy Massiter and Jock Kane, pointing out that the latter had used every avenue of complaint, including a former prime minister, without success.

Lord Armstrong replied:

I am afraid I could not trust my memory sufficiently to comment on particular cases in detail ... so I am afraid that I am precluded from entering into a debate about whether Mr Kane's and Miss Massiter's cases were 'real examples' ... Nowadays [they] would have access to the staff counsellor and would have been able to take their allegations and complaints to him if they had felt that they were not being taken sufficiently seriously by their superiors.[31]

Allowing for some economy of memory this is an interesting reply. It suggests that a future Cathy Massiter who discovers that colleagues are breaking the Security Service Act would be able to go to this counsellor only after she had complained to her superiors, even though they had presumably approved the illegal operation in the first place. By any standard that seems a very naive conception of employee relationship.

This new Act will do nothing to solve the problem of those who have served in various official capacities and wish to publish their memoirs. There are plenty of people who were involved in intelligence during the last war whose knowledge is over 45 years old and of no current relevance. It would be far more sensible to adopt a procedure similar to the American vetting committee.[32] Further, this new Act will mean an investigative journalist who discovered that the government had concealed the story of a Chernobyl-type disaster would be in breach of the law if he revealed the facts even if by so doing he saved lives.[33] Obviously Hurd wants to blunt the role of the media as the public watchdog. The Act will produce a situation where Ingham in Downing Street could leak any tale he wanted to enhance Mrs Thatcher's status yet a journalist would be in breach of the law if he reported how this had been done.

To some extent the media has only itself to blame for the cavalier fashion in which Hurd feels he can treat them. Most editors and journalists, especially in television, are so lazy and ill-informed that all too often they readily acquiesce to official tricks and report stories verbatim from press releases without bothering to check the facts because this is such an easy way of filling space to suit a deadline. For them Hurd's new secrets Act would make things very easy. There would be no investigative journalism and scoops would be handed out to sycophantic lobby correspondents and others willing to toady to government press officers. If a government has such a compliant and feeble media it can hardly be blamed for taking advantage of it.

The irony is that the country will not be better protected by hiding away incompetence and disasters like the cases of Blake and Prime behind a wall of secrecy. It may make the intelligence services feel better and enable civil servants to secure their place in the honours' list but it will also make them lazier at tracking down the real enemies in our midst. Openness and frankness frightens the intelligence world because it knows how fraudulent are its claims about its work, which would not stand up to a moment's scrutiny by any competent outside observer. If we could strip away this bureaucratic fraud we could then see what secrets we need to protect and the country would be a safer place. Truth never did a country any harm.

Intelligence is like pornography. It is secret and forbidden. Sealed from inspection it looks exciting and important. But behind the plastic wrapper it is really very boring. The more you know about it the less interesting it becomes and the more obviously a confidence trick.

Just as a pornographic bookshop keeps its wares hidden, so an intelligence agency creates mystique and mythology behind drawn curtains because without it ordinary people would start to ask questions about necessity and cost-effectiveness.

At the beginning of this book I likened intelligence to advertising. One of the joys of advertising is that if sales go up you claim it was because of the advertisements but if they do not go up or go down you argue it was because there was not enough advertising. We shall never know if the IRA really intended to attack the wedding of Prince Andrew and Miss Sarah Ferguson. The fact that the IRA said they had no such plans is proof to MI5 that they did.

The wonderful world of intelligence needs no proof. If you cannot find the right facts you hold up those you have in front of the mirror and it produces the image you need. If challenged you say it is so secret that it cannot be discussed. The intelligence fraternity is never wrong.

What does the future hold? Despite all the legislation governments introduce to hide their intelligence failures the public is tiring of being treated like fools. After the revelations of the Iran/Contra affair, which is more dangerous – secret White House cabals illegally shipping arms to Iran with the help of Marine Corps' colonels and presidents who fall asleep, or the KGB? After *Spycatcher* why should we believe that Douglas Hurd is interested in openness? Is it better to have Israeli-backed terrorist teams in this country than the IRA? Does it really help the security of Britain to allow

MI5 and CIA teams to attempt the kidnapping of foreign diplomats on London's streets? What is the difference between the CIA letting off car bombs in the Lebanon, killing innocent people, and religious fanatics doing the same.

Suppose Gorbachev is successful and steers Russia on to a less abrasive political course with the West and, also coping with his own domestic problems, has less time to bother about invading Europe. Could Gorbachev ever be strong enough to wind down the KGB and GRU? Or are they, like the agencies in the West, also beyond his control? And if he did so would the CIA, NSA, MI6 and MI5 go to their masters and say there was less demand for their services. It has never happened yet. Like drunken sailors, the KGB needs the CIA who in turn needs the GRU who needs MI6 and it needs the NSA who needs MI5. If one collapsed the rest would fall like dominoes because they would be deprived of the 'enemies' who prop them up. So the game has to continue.

CHAPTER 10

WHERE NOW THE ENEMY?

When peace breaks out it is hard to believe that soldiers will ever be needed again. It happened in 1815, in 1918, and again in 1945. At the end of World War II, Western Europe demobilised rapidly and turned its efforts towards reconstruction and recovery, aided by the far-sighted Marshall Plan. Not so the Soviet Union, at first. Wherever possible they encouraged communism and civil war, took control of Czechoslovakia by force and subterfuge, blockaded Berlin to test the nerve of the West, and finally erected the wall that physically divided East from West and stood thereafter as the evidence of communism's bankrupt philosophy.

Throughout the next 45 years Western intelligence had it all their own way. It was easy for them to construct sinister scenarios because everyone wanted to believe the worst about Russia's intentions, given its boorish behaviour in Berlin, endless espionage against the West, and the build-up of all sorts of weaponry far in excess of anything needed to defend the Soviet Union.

The defence of the West through NATO absorbed a vast amount of money and resources. In 1988, the defence budgets of the NATO countries totalled $404 billion. A quarter of America's entire military budget of $295 billion was spent on the NATO alliance. Although it is harder to quantify the split in intelligence budgets, it would seem that as much as 75 per cent of all Western intelligence expenditure was directed against the Soviet Union and Eastern Europe. Huge networks of eavesdropping stations have been built, and a galaxy of satellites launched, so that armies of experts might provide an ever-increasing tide of electronic dross. No matter that intelligence failed to work on every major occasion during these four decades. The creation of an ever bigger bogeyman sustained a huge and very profitable industry, representing an important slice of the economy of the West.

At a certain point in the evolution of that process, exactly the same things could have been said about Russia and her former allies. That the Soviet Union ever really intended to invade the West – the magical Fulda Gap scenario – is extremely doubtful. But the same paranoia that gripped the West was equally useful in promoting military and intelligence budgets in the East, especially as their citizens were not permitted the luxury of debate or dissent. Surplus manpower was absorbed into conscripted armies, uneconomic factories went on producing armaments, and civilian production dwindled. Armies of KGB and GRU agents spied and listened both at home and abroad, culling an unending stream of apparently priceless information with which to impress their superiors, though in fact, most of it could be found in technical journals.

And now, quite suddenly, it has all vanished. The wall has come down. The sentry boxes are empty and the minefields cleared. Even Margaret Thatcher, the most ardent supporter of the cold war, had to admit – albeit reluctantly – that the Soviet threat, or what President Reagan called the 'evil empire', has now been forced to retreat so far in political and psychological terms that it is no longer capable of launching a surprise attack upon the West.

Its forward bases in Eastern Europe have gone, so too have its communications and pre-positioned supplies, while the Soviet army has been significantly weakened by ethnic strife, insubordination, and forced demobilisation into an uncaring and unprepared civilian environment, and severe budgetary cuts. It would now take the Russians at least six months to mount an attack on the West and, since they would have to fight their way across unfriendly countries, their flexibility of movement no longer exists.

But even more important than the military retreat is the complete change in East-West relations that have for so long been dominated by America and the Soviet Union, with Britain attempting to play the role of the honest broker. The Soviets, until yesterday a great world power, are now racked with internal divisions that have produced bloody confrontations, and are tottering on the brink of economic collapse. By contrast the united East and West Germany – so long divided and bitter enemies – look set to form once again the most powerful nation in Europe. America's position in Europe is already diminished and, if the American army is ejected from Germany, it is unlikely that it will find a new place to stay in Europe, and once the army goes home, that will be the end of NATO. Britain's position is even less secure because there is now no need for her as an intermediary. Moreover, her independent nuclear deterrent, bought so expensively from America, is increasingly irrelevant as time passes.

For all intelligence agencies – East and West – this is terrible news. It is as bad as President Richard Nixon opening up relations with China and wiping out the CIA's China desk at a stroke. Now the entire CIA Soviet desk is under scrutiny and threat. Gorbachev is counting on disarmament to produce a peace dividend that will help set the Soviet Union on a new course towards economic prosperity. In America a similar battle is brewing in Congress and the media about future military spending. Already embarrassed by the abandonment of his 'No New Taxes' election pledge, President Bush is struggling with massive budget cuts that will affect all defence spending – and inevitably turn the spotlight onto the intelligence agencies, among which the CIA will reflect the brightest image.

The Gulf War has given Bush some breathing space but, in the long term, Congress will start slashing budgets, first with the armed forces, and then in the peripheral intelligence areas – such as CIA support for anti-communist forces in Afghanistan that now cost $400 million a year, help for the Unita forces in Angola, around $50 million, and aid to Cambodian rebels running at $10 million. Small though such cutbacks may seem when set against the CIA's total budget of around $2.5 billion, they will whet the appetite of Congress to look even closer at other activities, and turn their attention to the National Security Agency (NSA), and the National Reconnaissance Office (NRO).

Roger Morris, a former National Security Council member under Presidents Nixon and Johnson, recently described the CIA as:

An obese tunnel-vision relic, slouching towards Capitol Hill for still more, and with still more ominous briefings on a world already past.

The same argument is being heard in Britain, where a substantial peace dividend is badly needed to cut back Britain's £21.2 billion annual defence budget and divert these funds to vote-winning civilian projects such as education and hospitals. Already plans are being made to reduce the number of troops, tanks, aircraft, and ships. Now unwelcome attention is being turned to the intelligence services with their secret and unaccountable budgets.

Suggestions already publicly made include the merging of MI5 and MI6; the abolition of MI5 altogether and transferring their duties to the smaller and more efficient police Special Branch; a cutback in GCHQ's size and budget now that there are far fewer potential enemies on whom to eavesdrop, and an end to continuing the £500 million *Zircon* satellite programme for eavesdropping on Russia.

In the face of such criticism, it is hardly surprising that the intelligence agencies are mounting a counter-attack, and there are certainly arguments they can adduce in their favour. For a start, although the Russian threat is smaller and farther away, it has not disappeared. Nor can there be any certainty that Gorbachev and his policy of *perestroika* will survive. In March 1990 a secret NATO meeting was addressed by three experts on Russian

Affairs: Peter Frank, professor of Soviet studies at Essex University in Britain, Christopher Donnelly, a NATO specialist, and Philip Peterson, a similar expert from the Pentagon. They outlined three sombre scenarios. First, that Russia would decline into civil war similar to that which followed the 1917 revolution. Second, a slow collapse of central government as the Communist party disintegrated. And third, the least likely, that Gorbachev's reforms would succeed.

There are signs that the first two scenarios have already begun to unfold. As with so many colonial empires (for example, those of Britain, Belgium, and Portugal in Africa), once the central authority weakens, internecine fighting begins between ethnic groups and already a bewildered KGB and Soviet army have had to deal with civil disturbances on a scale unheard of since 1917, resulting in many deaths and hideous atrocities. The collapse of the old-style, rigidly controlled central government has also begun, with key figures like Boris Yeltsin openly challenging the Communist party's control, winning wide support and becoming president of the Russian Federation. All this comes at a time when there is little evidence that Gorbachev's reforms are working, and many ordinary people are saying publicly that they were better off under the old regime when at least there was some food in the shops. Food lines in Moscow, even for the most basic items, are now worse than at any time since the Second World War.

Gorbachev's ability to alter the Soviet economy is like that of the captain of a fully laden supertanker ploughing its way through the sea. He has put the helm hard over to change course and rung the engine room for full speed, but it takes a long time before the bow starts changing direction. And however appealing the fruits of Western-style capitalism may seem to younger Russians who want to see more CD players, jeans, and video recorders in the shops, it certainly does not appeal to the managers of Soviet factories who have long enjoyed a lethargic lifestyle cushioned from the harsh world of competition. For them there is nothing to be gained by helping Gorbachev.

A far more worrying aspect of Gorbachev's predicament is what to do with the thousands of conscripts now returning form their old Warsaw Pact bases in Eastern Europe. Not for them a heroes' welcome. Quite the reverse. They are being brought home almost as if they were in disgrace. After enjoying the better living standards in Eastern Europe, these unwanted soldiers and their families – including officers as senior as colonels – suddenly find themselves being treated like refugees and forced to live in old factories and empty office blocks because no proper housing is available.

The Red Army has always enjoyed a special place in the history and minds of the Russian people who remember that fifty years ago it saved them from the Nazis. For the past forty years the same army has kept them safe from an attack by Western imperialists. As a result the military has always had unrestricted access to the nation's finances. The generals will not take kindly to seeing service personnel treated thus, and demobilised in haste into an already declining civilian economy without chance of decent housing and employment. The army's concern is shared by the thousands of bureaucrats and high-ranking party officials who now seem likely to lose their once secure jobs under Gorbachev's new policies.

The paradox facing the West is that if we want Gorbachev to succeed, and thus continue the easing of East-West tension, we must be willing to give Russia massive financial aid (on a scale similar to the $70 billion West Germany is providing to finance the reconstruction of East Germany's economy over the period 1990–94), – something that Western governments have so far refused to sanction. If Gorbachev falls, and is replaced by a hardline government backed by the military, it would certainly please Western hawks and the intelligence fraternity, because not only could they claim 'I told you so', but it would again present the West with a bogeyman that automatically justified a return to the cold-war budgets for espionage activities.

If, however, Gorbachev remains in power, so that guarantees against any renewal of the cold war remain in place, where else can the intelligence agencies look for work to justify their profligacy? The Iraq crisis and subsequent war could not have come at a better time. If the West's agencies are criticized for not having warned their leaders of Hussein's invasion more precisely, they have two stock replies. First, they gave the right warnings but the politicians chose not to listen. Second, the warning would have come sooner, and in more detail, had their budgets for new technology and manpower been larger. So this is a time for expansion, not cutbacks. Neither of these arguments is likely to impress the more experienced members of Congress, especially as the American ambassador in Baghdad, April Glaspie, had a personal call from Saddam Hussein who assured her that Iraq's differences with Kuwait were just an Arab family quarrel and, on that assurance, she felt able to leave the embassy for a vacation back in the United States. Politicians may begin to wonder how it is that every time some significant military event takes place the expensive American intelligence infrastructure is wrongfooted.

Another argument is that in times of uncertainty there is a greater need for intelligence, because with chemical and nuclear weapons proliferating amongst smaller and often unstable nations, the threat against the West is actually greater than when dealing only with a single enemy like Russia. Modern technology makes it quite possible that small weapons of terrifying destructive power can be smuggled into the West with reasonable ease. Unfortunately, the planning of such operations is unlikely to be detected by electronic intelligence, but would require deep Humint penetration, which, in countries like Libya and Iraq, is almost impossible for the West to achieve.

Terrorism has never proved easy to monitor by conventional intelligence because it is usually a fragmented and amateurish affair. This has been demonstrated in Northern Ireland where, despite a vast array of sophisticated technology ranging from widespread telephone tapping, long-range microphones, and huge computer data banks keeping watch on the movements of everyone remotely connected with para-military activities, the IRA still manages to attack more or less any target it chooses. While it is true that security forces in Northern Ireland are able to target the movements of all known suspects, the IRA overcomes this simply by using new recruits with no previous terrorist connections to carry out the attacks while the godfathers stay quietly in the shadows providing advice and equipment.

The terrorist situation in Northern Ireland has now become one of attrition and stalemate in which neither side can win. But the IRA cannot lose. If they choose to bury their Semtex explosive and *Kalashnikovs* and do nothing, eventually the security forces will be reduced and, as soon as that happens, there is nothing to stop the IRA from starting the campaign all over again.

Another area where intelligence agencies claim their expertise remains essential is fighting the international drugs war. In theory some of the technology for detecting military operations could be used for monitoring the activities of South American drug barons in their remote hideaways, eavesdropping on their international communications, and even spotting their illegal shipments. In practice, however, organisations like Britain's Customs & Excise, and America's Drug Enforcement Agency (DEA), do not like sharing their drug-smuggling secrets with agencies such as the CIA and MI6, because from past experience they know that such agencies are often involved in such illegal activites in order to further their own operations.

An embarrassing – and very typical – example of this is the case of the former president of Panama, General Manuel Noriega, who was deposed and eventually captured by the Americans after their invasion in late 1989. Noriega is now in custody in Florida awaiting trial on drug trafficking charges, including the allegation that he accepted a $4.6 million (£2.8 million) bribe from the Colombian Medellin drug cartel to protect drug shipments passing through Panama. However, for over 10 years the CIA paid Noriega $200,000 (£125,000) a year for intelligence gathering in Latin America – especially against Cuba – and he remained on the CIA's payroll even though they knew from the DEA that Noriega was helping the Medellin drug cartel to smuggle cocaine into America.

Noriega was also alleged to have made a deal with the former White House aide, Oliver North, to train Contra terrorists in Panama, and to have provided Russian weapons that could be planted in El Salvador and then 'captured' to falsely link the Sandinista government with the Russians. All this is very typical of CIA morality, and consequently telling them to combat the drug trade is unlikely to prove very useful.

Again, it has been suggested that American agencies could deploy their expertise in the field of economic intelligence. This would include monitoring the revival of economic progress in Eastern Europe, and in other parts of the world, to ensure that American companies stayed ahead, and also covering industrial espionage on the part of Japanese and European firms. Apart from the fact that the CIA and the NSA have been illegally monitoring economic communications around the world for the past 25 years or more, these agencies are not in a position to assist their respective countries in that way since they would be openly violating the law instead of doing it clandestinely.

The legacy of the Noriega and Iran-Contra affairs – and many other similarly dubious operations – have left the CIA in a very vulnerable situation, since even the Senate Intelligence Committee believes that they are not being told the whole truth. At the beginning of 1990, Congress exercised its ultimate power of censure over the CIA by voting to appoint an independent inspector-general to oversee its activities. Both Bush and William Webster, the current director of the CIA, bitterly resented this step, claiming that it would prevent the CIA from operating efficiently. But both Congress and the State Department insist that in the future the CIA should not be allowed to tamper with America's foreign policy as it has done so disastrously in the post-war era.

For the moment the American intelligence agencies seem to have escaped any immediate budgetary cuts, since it is reported that the Bush administration has set the classified intelligence budget for 1991, which covers the activities of the CIA, NSA, NRO, and the Pentagon's Defence Intelligence Agency (DIA) , at a record $30 billion, more than half of which is to be spent for intelligence gathering in the Soviet Union and Eastern Europe. Already this has generated considerable criticism that the budget is a leftover from the cold war and ignores new realities. Proof that this expenditure is justified can come only when the agencies mentioned above have delivered the goods. They have for so long a time relied almost entirely on advanced technology and computer-generated intelligence to count submarines, aircraft, and tanks, that it remains to be seen if they are capable of interpreting something far more important, the political motivation of the new leaders of Eastern Europe, with any greater success.

In Britain it is reported that although the budgets for GCHQ and MI5 would be held at their present levels, Mrs Thatcher had agreed to an increase in the budget for MI6 to cover the cost of a new directorate to handle counter-terrorism by Arab and IRA groups – which sounds suspiciously like an encroachment on MI5's responsibilities that may lead to duplication of effort and bureaucratic jealousies. Like the Americans, the British government is acutely interested in monitoring Gorbachev's chances of survival, and a special 'Gorbachev Committee' has been set up, co-ordinated by Sir Patrick Wright, permanent under-secretary at the Foreign Office, Sir Christopher Curwen, in charge of co-ordinating intelligence at the Cabinet Office, and Sir

Colin McColl, head of MI6. If past experience is anything to go by, this type of prestigious committee will be the last to learn of Gorbachev's overthrow.

If the political changes have caused headaches for Western intelligence agencies, the fallout for the KGB has been even more painful. For a start they are having to come to terms with a radically new regime that is not only talking about democracy but is actually encouraging it to happen on the streets of Moscow and elsewhere. KGB officers, who only a year or so ago would have been clubbing demonstrators over the head and dispatching them to psychiatric hospitals or *gulags*, are now obliged to stand around and hear radicals, including senior politicians like Yeltsin, publicly denounce the whole fabric of the communist system. Even worse, Oleg Kalugin, the retired head of KGB operations in Leningrad, (and before that station chief in Washington), has given a long interview in *Komsomolskaya Pravda* revealing all manner of unsavoury secrets about how the KGB operated in Russia. Far more embarrassing are his claims that while in Washington he had close contact with the CIA and State Department and regularly exchanged information with them. Although stripped of his rank and decorations, and with his pension at risk, Kalugin is now besieged by Western publishers who want him to write his memoirs – which might well become a KGB *Spycatcher*.

To counter this unexpected aspect of *glasnost* the KGB have embarked on a massive public relations programme both at home and abroad. The KGB are shown to be loyal and heroic servants of the state, not only protecting the borders of the Soviet Union from drug smugglers and illegal immigrants, (which will surprise those who are trying to get out of the country as fast as possible), but also combating black market activities, corruption, and even aircraft hijackings. Gruesome revelations that 3.5 million Soviet citizens have been executed by the Russian government since the revolution, and details about other mass murders and deportations, are skilfully brushed aside and blamed on past enemies of the state who just happened to be head of the KGB at the time. Amazingly, the KGB have promised full investigations into the murder of the Tsar and his family, the fate of Raoul Wallenberg, the Katyn massacre, and the cover-up after the Chernobyl nuclear disaster.

On the question of spying abroad the KGB have decided to bring their heroes out of the closet and make a series of six documentary films praising their achievements. This decision was influenced by MI6, who allowed the Soviet defector, Oleg Gordievsky, to appear on British television, write a series of articles, and co-author a book for which the American publishers paid $200,000, the French publishers £32,000, and the German publishers £55,000. As the book portrays Gordievsky as a great hero, and the KGB consider him a traitor, they responded by holding an unprecedented press conference in London on 22 March 1990, and issuing a long statement which denounced the affair as:

... part of a plot to disrupt growing relations between London and Moscow. In whose interest is it to remind us about Gordievsky, and who sanctioned the staging of this undignified campaign, carried out in the worst traditions of the 'cold war'? There are some in Britain who don't favour the present developments in Soviet-British relations and are trying to cast a shadow over a constructive dialogue. Gordievsky is presented today as a kind of expert, who knows the answers to all the questions concerning ... the Soviet Union. But to what extent can one trust assessments coming from a traitor, smuggled out of the USSR illegally five years ago, when the policy of *glasnost* and *perestroika* was just beginning to take shape? Not to mention the fact that the status of Gordievsky at that period hardly gave him any access to really important political information. Gordievsky claims to be a sort of 'saviour of mankind from nuclear disaster' This is simply a laughable claim.

The bitter tone of this remarkable statement was largely due to the fact that Gordievsky had, surprisingly, been permitted to disclose that he had been smuggled out of Russia hidden in a false compartment of a vehicle belonging to the British embassy, which was accorded diplomatic immunity from search at the Finnish border. Aside from being a clear breach of diplomatic protocol, it was an act of foolish vainglory to boast about it publicly.

The first KGB film was about Kim Philby and was made by *Gostelradio*, the state broadcasting system, which sold the British rights to a small independent company in London, Walberry Productions. They added some local British interviews together with a suitably Russian sounding commentary, and the film was shown on Channel 4 in Britain in May 1990. It turned out to be a disaster because the British company failed to carry out the necessary research, with the result that Britain's Secret Intelligence Service, or MI6, was called MI5, and Philby was credited with being in MI6 in May 1941 when, in fact, he was working for Special Operations Executive. Other claims made in the film about Philby's achievements also lacked credibility.

Mortified by the Western reaction, the KGB decided to make a second film about George Blake, (see Chapter 2), who had the advantage over Philby of still being alive. To give the production a more professional gloss, the Russian press agency, *Novsti*, approached British television with offers of co-production. One independent company turned down the proposal because they were unable to secure full editorial control, but the BBC decided to go ahead and are said to have spent around £200,000 on making the 75-minute film. Blake's own book about his career as a spy, which he had written several years ago had difficulty finding a publisher, wad due to be published in late 1990.

Bearing in mind that for many years Blake was a professional double agent, indeed a triple agent, of great skill, and is now working under orders from the KGB, it is unlikely that anything he says will be of any value or should be taken seriously. Nevertheless, it is an embarrassment British intelligence could do without, and it also raises the question of whether the government, after having pursued Peter Wright and *Spycatcher* so expensively through the courts, should allow royalties to be paid to a convicted traitor who should still be in prison.

Perhaps it would have been wiser for MI6 not to have allowed Gordievsky to go public for, if this type of frankness is to continue, it will probably prove more embarrassing for the British than the KGB, especially if they decided to release details and archive documents relating to the Soviets' recruiting of spies in Britain at Cambridge and elsewhere in the 1930s, and the true extent of Prime's activities. (See Chapter 4.)

But the changes that may affect the size and direction of British, American, and Soviet agencies is nothing compared to the upheaval caused in other East European countries as the tide of democracy batters down the gates of the various secret headquarters. Two of the most interesting organisations are the secret police, or *Stasi*, and the *Hauptverwaltung Aufklarung*, or *HVA*, (Chief Administration, Intelligence), in East Germany. From 1956 to 1987, the HVA was run by one of the most talented spymasters, Lieutenant General Markus Wolf, who concentrated his activities mainly against West Germany where he established his prize agent, Gunter Guillaume, in the heart of the West German government as Chancellor Willy Brandt's aide.

Markus was equally successful in running a spy ring in Britain of which only a small part was exposed when Reinhard and Sonja Schulze (not their real names), were caught in July 1986 operating a clearing house for information at Hounslow, near Heathrow airport, in west London, and were sentenced to 10 years' imprisonment. Although much equipment was found in their house for preparing coded messages for transmission, the police were unable to discover a transmitter, which suggests that it was operated elsewhere by other members of the ring who remained undetected. The Schulzes were released from prison in June 1990 and, before long, will doubtless be writing a book or appearing on television.

A spokesman for the West German justice ministry in Bonn has said:

> Any East German who has served a sentence for spying or any other crime is entitled to live freely in West Germany because we do not recognise East and West Germans as being people having different nationalities.

This raises the question of the extent to which the East German Interior Ministry will share its intelligence files with the West Germans and, through them, with the CIA, MI6, and Mossad. Recalling the ease with which

Gehlen, Hitler's intelligence chief, changed sides after the war (see Chapter 2), it would not be surprising if the same thing happened again. Although there have been pictures on Western television of the *Stasi* offices in East Berlin being ransacked by angry crowds, it is remarkable that not a single dossier or document taken from their vast files has been reproduced in the media, which suggests that some other agency may have got there first. If East Germany does share all its intelligence archives with the West it would seriously undermine the KGB, since the two have worked very closely together throughout the cold war.

Another country that has begun to open its intelligence files to the West is Czechoslovakia. President Vaclav Havel has already admitted that his country supplied Libya with 1,000 tons of Semtex explosive, (although the head of the Semtex company later denied this was correct), but it remains to be seen whether Havel will go further and unravel details of some of the covert operations of the Czech intelligence service, the *STB*, against the West. In 1988, a Czech spy using the false name of Erwin von Haarlem was arrested in his apartment at Friern Barnet, in north London, but although a mass of espionage equipment was seized together with a powerful shortwave radio, MI5 were unable to find a transmitter nor establish what information von Haarlem had been passing on to Prague. Another case that Havel could explain is the defection of Major Josef Frolik in 1969 (see Chapter 2), who made so many allegations against members of the Wilson government.

Although the future of the intelligence agencies in the East European countries may look uncertain at the moment, one should never forget that the profession is a great survivor and, like the chameleon, able to adapt to new surroundings very quickly. In the excitement of new-found democracy, security services, counter-intelligence, secret police, and spies may all seem redundant. But, as we have seen in Romania, democracy is fragile and things can change very quickly.

Decades of communist mismangement will take many years to put right. Rising inflation, foreign debts, and trade deficits in free international markets will not only inhibit growth but also create massive unemployment as the old subsidised industries disappear. None of the Eastern European countries have the machinery to deal with unemployment because it has never happened before, and, inevitably, there will be much hardship and discontent amongst those who find their heady aspirations come to nothing. East Germany will survive because it will be supported by its wealthy brother in the West, but the poorer countries like Poland, Hungary, Romania, and even Czechoslovakia will face many disappointments and, like the Soviet Union, see a reduction in their living standards.

The charismatic leaders who have taken over the running of these new democracies with such enthusiasm and naivete, will find themselves faced with a fragmented and angry population. If shortages persist there will be demonstrations which can quickly get out of hand. Rival political parties will be formed and election results challenged.

History shows that in such circumstances the first thing that happens is that liberal leaders who championed democratic rights either get overthrown or, to protect their office, become paranoid about opposition on the part of internal and external ememies, real or imaginary. Predictably, they look for help to control their opponents and – it will also come as no surprise – the same secret police and intelligence experts that existed under the old regimes will quietly creep out of the woodwork, complete with files containing the names of the new subversives, and equipment to keep them under surveillance. In a remarkably short space of time, using a new and more friendly name that conceals their true role, these agencies will begin their operations again for their new masters with exactly the same zeal and technology. At first their operations will seem quite simple and mundane, since they will merely be feeding their new masters what they want to hear. But gradually the well-oiled wheels will turn and their activities become less accountable until, without anyone realising it, they have reestablished their secret empires again.

Although the scenarios will be far less sinister in the West, the political paranoia will be much the same, and past experience shows that if the intelligence fraternity maintains a low profile and bides its time, before long some incident will occur that will restore its fortunes once more.

The intelligence game has survived, and will continue to do so, because it is all things to all people. No leader willingly admits that he needs an intelligence service. Indeed many governments go through elaborate charades to pretend that no such organisations exist. But equally, no government, East or West, really wants to eradicate completely the web of deceit and lies in which the intelligence fraternity operates, because there is always the likelihood that one day it may need it to conceal some dubious political policy. All the intelligence world has to do is to wait and be available to serve any master that pays its price.

NOTES

INTRODUCTION *(Pages 1–12)*

[1] This was the Chiefs of Staff report COS(40)592 of 31 July 1940, (now CAB 66/10, Public Record Office, Kew). *The Sinking of the Automedon, The Capture of the Nankin*, James Rusbridger, (Encounter, May 1985), *The Pacific War*, John Costello, (Collins, 1981) page 614, and Intercept SRNA 0020, RG 457, (National Archives, Washington DC).

[2] The 7,528-ton Blue Funnel Line steamer *Automedon* that sailed from Liverpool in late September.

[3] On 11 November 1940 off the Nicobar Islands in the Indian Ocean. The master of the *Automedon*, Captain McEwen, two officers, and a steward, were killed by the *Atlantis'* attack. (Modern Records Centre, Blue Funnel Line Archives, Liverpool), and *The War at Sea – 1939–45*, Stephen Roskill, (HMSO, Volume I), page 282.

[4] The 7,862-ton *Atlantis*, or *Schiff*-16, known to the Royal Navy as Raider C. The *Atlantis* sailed from Kiel on 11 March 1940 and by the time it was sunk 622 days later by HMS *Devonshire* on 22 November 1941 had sunk or captured 22 allied merchant ships totalling 145,697 tons. *German Raiders of World War II*, August Muggenthaler, (Robert Hale, 1978), page 16.

[5] Captain Bernard Rogge whose first officer was Lieutenant Ulrich Mohr.

[6] The Chiefs of Staff report and all the other secret mail from the *Automedon's* strongroom which included new code books for the Royal Navy and the entire post for MI6 in the Far East reached Tokyo on 5 December 1940. Hitler saw a summary of the report in Berlin on 7 December and the Japanese had copies by 12 December. *The Price of Admiralty*, Dr J. W. M. Chapman, Sussex University, (Saltire Press, 1984), Volume III, and German naval attaché telegrams

209/40–212/40 gKdos, OKM Signal Log. (Military Reference Section, National Archives, Washington DC).

[7] Nor was the governor of Singapore, Sir Shenton Thomas, told and even the C-in-C Air Chief Marshal Sir Robert Brooke-Popham, for whom the report had been intended, was not told. Private correspondence August 1984 with Colonel Brian Montgomery, author of *Shenton of Singapore*, (Secker & Warburg, 1984), and Hugh Humphrey CMG OBE who was Sir Shenton's private secretary in 1940, also Historical Section, Cabinet Office, London, letter to author 23 August 1984, and letter from Squadron Leader G. H. Wiles, Air Ministry 15 July 1948 to Brooke-Popham explaining that his copy of the report was lost when the *Automedon* was sunk by a submarine. Forty years later the British Foreign Office refused to admit the Cabinet papers had been captured, suggesting that they had been passed to the Russians by Donald McLean, the long-exposed Russian spy, and thence to the Germans who in 1940 were their allies. In fact the Foreign Office knew perfectly well that the papers had been captured in 1940.

[8] The Japanese 25th Army forces under the command of General Tomoyuki Yamashita, totalled 15,000 with a few light tanks. Total allied forces, British, Australian, Indian, and local, totalled 130,000, all of whom surrendered on 15 February 1942.

[9] Operation *Market Garden*, launched on 17 September 1944 with the intention of securing the main bridges across the rivers Maas, Waal, and Lower Rhine.

[10] The Contra rebels, officially backed by the American government, were called freedom fighters because they were attempting to overthrow a pro-Communist government.

[11] Based on a report in *The Washington Post*, May 1986, see Cryptolog Magazine, June 1986.

[12] Allen Dulles in evidence to Congressional Committee on the National Security Act, 27 June 1947.

[13] In September 1984 President Reagan wanted the American people and the Western world to believe that the Russians were supplying MiG-21 fighters to Nicaragua, in order to justify his support for the Contra terrorists of freedom fighters. The CIA conveniently produced some fuzzy photographs of the Russian freighter *Bakuriani* which had twelve large crates on its deck which the CIA claimed contained MiG-21 aircraft. The *Bakuriani* eventually reached the Nicaraguan port of Corinto on 6 November 1984 surrounded by US Navy ships and aircraft amidst much publicity created by leaks from the CIA to the Western media. When the *Bakuriani* was unloaded the crates were found to contain four small patrol boats and two light helicopters. *Deep Black*, William E. Burrows, (Transworld, 1988), pages 292–295.

[14] One such magazine was *Encounter*, which in the 1950s and early 1960s received some funding from the CIA. Journalists who are willing to print these pro-intelligence stories are naturally afforded all manner of facilities and overseas visits that are denied to their more skeptical colleagues.

15 *Maggie is IRA's Missile Target, Sunday Express,* 19 June 1988. 'An IRA murder squad equipped with a deadly Stinger missile is planning an atrocity as seven world leaders gather in Toronto today. This urgent warning comes from the American CIA.' Canadian intelligence authorities later denied knowledge of any such threat. Ironically these emotive headlines are the best recruiting campaign the IRA could have, since they bestow upon them an expertise far in excess of their real capabilities.

16 Report by the Chemical Defence Research Establishment, Porton Down, quoted by Mr Leo Abse MP. (*The Times,* London, 13 May 1986).

17 Typical examples of this type of article are *D-Day in the 1980s,* John Keegan. *The Sunday Times,* London, 10 June 1984; *All Quiet on the Central Front,* Ian Mather, *The Observer,* 14 December 1986; *The Tank Trap NATO must now avoid,* John Keegan, *The Daily Telegraph,* 22 September 1987.

18 Exactly what the Russians would do, having conquered Western Europe and presumably Britain, is never made clear. As their leaders are so incompetent that they cannot run or feed their own country properly and spend their time coping with one economic disaster after another, it is hard to see what value a devastated nuclear wasteland would be to them – especially if in the process they had lost 100 million Russians as the result of NATO's retaliatory nuclear strikes. The Russian government seems more likely to have its hands full in the future with internal problems as various ethnic communities demand more autonomy. Perhaps there are some Russians who genuinely want to go to war, but in the light of the 12 million casualties they suffered in World War II they must be a fast-disappearing minority.

19 *Red Army's secret invasion,* John Beattie, SUNDAY EXPRESS, 4 January 1987.

20 The official excuse is that it would not be in the national interest for the British people to know what the Russians have been privy to for years. The real reason is that the ineptness of our security services is too embarrassing to reveal in public.

21 Gordievsky was supposed to have been able to advise both President Reagan and Mrs Thatcher on how to deal with Gorbachev. It certainly did not do Reagan much good in Reykyavic when he met the Russian leader who completely outwitted him. In 1990 Britain's MI6 decided to allow Gordievsky to go public (under their close control), and give a series of interviews in the media about his alleged achievements, and also co-author a book with Dr Christopher Andrew. The Russians were furious at seeing a traitor portrayed in this way, and besides issuing a press statement deriding Gordievsky's claims, embarked on a series of television films showing their spies Kim Philby and George Blake also as heroes.

22 *Soviet Military Power – The Annotated and Corrected Version,* Tom Gervasi, (Random House, 1987).

23 In 1955 the American air attaché in Moscow, Colonel Charles Taylor, was at a Russian air force display and witnessed a flypast of M-4 Bison four-engined bombers. To his amazement Taylor counted twice the number of M-4s as he had

seen the previous year. On the basis of his report the US Senate began investigations in April 1956, and with the help of US Air Force experts concluded that Russia would have 800 M-4s operational by 1964. In fact Taylor had been hoaxed and 18 M-4s had flown past him three times. By 1961 the Russians only had 190 M-4s. The missile gap of the late 1950s was similar, and experts concluded that Russia would have 1,000 intercontinental ballistic missiles by 1961. In fact, by 1961 Russia had twelve. *The Soviet Estimate*, John Prados, (Dial Press, New York, 1982), page 43.

24 Britain's civil defence organisation has an annual budget of around £70 million and is an amateurish mixture of long wordy documents and a handful of dedicated emergency planning officers. In reality most of the plans are connected not with an external attack but in controlling civil disorders. There are elaborate underground bunkers for selected civil servants in London and dotted around the country, and a main government emergency headquarters at Westwells Road, in Corsham, Wiltshire. None of these would survive a nuclear attack, but they would allow the government to continue operating if civil disorders had reached the point that mobs were roaming the streets of Whitehall. *Beneath the City Streets*, Peter Laurie, (Granada, 1983), and *War Plan UK*, Duncan Campbell, (Burnett, 1982).

25 The exact number of people killed is unknown, but estimates range from 100,000 to 300,000. About 700,000 were left homeless, and the cost of rebuilding the devastated cities has been estimated at £1.5 billion. *The Independent*, London, 20 December 1988.

26 Tass newsagency, 14 December 1988. Mr Gorbachev, who had been in New York where he announced a 10 per cent reduction in Russia's conventional forces, flew back home to take charge of the disaster. He soon found that the lack of organisation and resources made his presence of little value. Gorbachev used the opportunity to tell his colleagues the folly of wasting huge resources on the armed forces when the country is so ill-prepared for natural disasters.

27 *The Second Oldest Profession*, Phillip Knightley, (Deutsch, 1986), pages 13 et seq.

28 *Soviet special forces dig in*, Blake Baker, *The Daily Telegraph*, 23 January 1986, quoting from *Jane's Defence Weekly*, and also *Russian agents were involved at Greenham*, Charles Lawrence, *The Daily Telegraph*, 22 January 1986.

29 Rust was released in August 1988.

30 Gorbachev used the incident to get rid of a lot of old diehards in the armed services who were opposed to his reforms, so he may be one of the first political leaders to realise that what he is told by his experts is largely inaccurate.

31 *Inside Intelligence*, Anthony Cavendish, (privately published, 1987), preface by George Kennedy Young, deputy head MI6, and see 'Peterborough', *The Daily Telegraph*, 29 December 1987, *Frankly Speaking*.

32 *The Second World War*, Winston Churchill, (Cassell, 1950), Volume 3, page 319, and *Ultra Goes to War*, Ronald Lewin, (McGraw Hill, 1978), Chapter 7. Ultra was the expression used for decrypts of German signals encoded on the *Enigma*

cryptograph which were decoded by GCCS at Bletchley Park some forty miles north of London. Major Desmond Morton had first met Churchill on the western front in France during World War I. From 1929 through 1939 Morton had been head of the Industrial Intelligence Centre (IIC), the cover name of a government agency responsible for discovering the true nature of Germany's economy and war plans. Although the IIC was notoriously inaccurate, Morton illegally gave Churchill secret information so that he could harrass the pacifist governments in Britain during the 1930s about their lack of preparedness for war.

[33] When George Brown was Foreign Secretary in the mid-1960s he decided to visit the headquarters of MI6 at Century House, Westminster Bridge Road, in southeast London, on the grounds that if he was to be in charge of MI6 he wanted to know how they worked. His officials were horrified at the idea, since no previous Foreign Secretary had ever made such a visit, and naively argued that if he was recognised it would reveal the connection between the Foreign Office and MI6 which, in fact, was widely known. *Inside Story*, Chapman Pincher, (Sidgwick & Jackson, 1978), pages 24–25. Another reason why ministers are discouraged from knowing too much about the intelligence agencies is that much of their work is illegal, and therefore the less the minister knows the fewer lies he has to tell in Parliament.

[34] Before the Falklands War the Americans were deeply concerned about the proposed rundown of Britain's naval forces, and in 1981, when Mrs Thatcher visited President Reagan in Washington, he offered Britain two US Navy aircraft carriers, the 45,000-ton USS *Oriskany* and USS *Hancock*. The offer was rejected by Britain because of the cost of re-establishing a new fixed-wing Fleet Air Arm which had disappeared following the scrapping of HMS *Ark Royal* in 1978. At the time of the Falklands War Britain was planning to sell one of its two carriers to Australia, which would have further reduced its operational capabilities outside the NATO north Atlantic area, but as a result of the war not only was this sale cancelled but a third carrier was built. So at the end of the war the Royal Navy's rundown had been reversed and Britain was committed to the huge expense of constructing the £600 million airfield and military base at Mount Pleasant in the Falklands. *The Daily Telegraph*, 12 March 1984.

[35] Such as the Thorn-EMI *Cymbeline* system. Iraqi officers were still being trained by Thorn-EMI in its use after the Kuwait invasion.

[36] In April 1990, British customs officials stopped the exports of several large sections of pipe to Iraq because they believed they were parts of a 'super gun'. It eventually transpired that the Conservative politician, Sir Hal Miller, had in 1988 several times warned the government that Iraq was trying to have a 'super gun' made under cover of pretending the parts were for their oil industry. Britain had sold Iraq $8.8 billion worth of arms between 1984 and 1988, and it became apparent that the government had known about this order but did not want to upset such a profitable customer. The 'super gun' was to a design of Dr Gerald Bull who had done similar work for the American government under the *Harp* programme in the 1960s. But the idea and technology were much older and first developed by two Americans – Lynn and Haskell – in 1880. Because of technical

problems nothing came of the idea until it was revived by Hitler in 1943, who planned a battery of 50 such guns inside a hill near Calais, in France, with which to bombard London, but before the guns could be installed the site was destroyed by allied bombers. The 'super gun' suffers from two basic problems: first, the barrel explodes after firing a few rounds, and second, once fired its fixed position is easy to locate and destroy. It is a bizarre idea that only appeals to dictators.

[37] Bazoft, who was a young and somewhat naive journalist, had gone to Iraq in 1989 on behalf of *The Observer* newspaper to investigate an alleged explosion at a military installation. He asked Mrs Parrish to drive him out to the site in her car, which carried markings of the hospital where she worked. Both were arrested and in March 1990 Bazoft was hanged.

[38] Mrs Parrish's sudden and unexpected release occurred in July 1990, allegedly as the result of a letter sent to Iraq's president by President Kaunda of Zambia. Exactly why Hussein should have responded in this fashion to Kaunda is unclear. A more likely explanation is that Mr Tiny Rowland, who owns *The Observer* newspaper, was closely involved in Mrs Parrish's release, perhaps through his international company Lonrho which has very large business interests in Zambia.

[39] The Australian Security Intelligence Organisation, ASIO, their equivalent of MI5, has come under continuous attack from left-wing governments and organisations in recent years, even to the point of having its offices raided on 16 March 1973 by the Australian Attorney General Keith Murphy, who was looking for his own ASIO file as he was suspected of being a KGB agent. At the moment ASIO hardly dares to keep track of anyone for fear of upsetting politicians, and it cannot veto a person's appointment to a sensitive defence area, with the result that Australia's government is heavily penetrated by the KGB. Plainly this is just as absurd as the unnecessary secrecy in Britian.

CHAPTER I *(Pages 13–39)*

[1] Cathy Massiter answered an advertisement through her university appointments board for a job with the Ministry of Defence 'processing information' but only after she had been accepted did she find she was actually working for MI5. (*20/20 Vision* television documentary, Channel Four, 20 February 1985.)

[2] So many books and articles have been written in recent years about MI5 and MI6 that there is little that is secret left to tell. For a quick reference guide Richard Norton-Taylor's article in the *Guardian*, 6 April 1988 'Picking the lock of Britain's security', is both concise and accurate. Nigel West's books are excellent text books but make dull reading.

[3] There has always been some controversy as to whether every German spy was caught. But in the absence of any German account of their spying activities the

British version is the only guide. In 1982 Leonard Mosley wrote *The Druid* (Methuen), claiming that an agent was parachuted into Wales on 10 May 1941 and spied for the Germans undetected throughout the war. Unfortunately Mr Mosley was unable to supply the author with any evidence which he regarded as satisfactory proof of this extraordinary claim.

[4] For a complete account see J. C. Masterman, *The Double Cross System in the War of 1939–45* (Yale University Press, 1972).

[5] The British government's attempt in Australia during 1987 to stop the publication of Peter Wright's *Spycatcher* which ended in failure and a legal bill of £3 million.

[6] *Spycatcher* (Viking, New York, 1987) page 38.

[7] *On the Record*, Duncan Campbell & Steven Connor (Michael Joseph, 1986).

[8] Eight CTL 8050 with 75 terminals. *On the Record*, page 64.

[9] *20/20 Vision*, 20 February 1985.

[10] *Spycatcher*, page 360.

[11] Department of Health & Social Security advertisement, *The Times*, London, 15 May 1983.

[12] *The Times* Diary, London, 12 October 1983.

[13] The government has approved the establishment of a Government Data Network combining the computers of the DHSS, Inland Revenue, Customs & Excise and possibly the police and MI5. *Daily Telegraph*, London, 6 February and 20 May 1988.

[14] Claridges Hotel in Mayfair is one of these. *Spycatcher*, page 72.

[15] During the conference in 1979 to determine the future of Rhodesia not only was Lancaster House fully bugged but so too were all the hotel rooms used by the various delegations.

[16] A1A (Technical Operations).

[17] When a minister, or even the prime minister, assures Parliament that everything in MI5 is all right what he really means is that this is what he has been told by the head of MI5, which is about as much use as sending a rabbit to fetch a lettuce.

[18] Whenever questions about alleged illegal activities of MI5 have been raised in Parliament ministers have always used the excuse of 'national security' to avoid giving a reply.

[19] 'The Spies Who Stay Out In the Cold', James Rusbridger, *Western Morning News*, 28 November 1988.

[20] *Most Secret War*, R. V. Jones (Hodder & Stoughton, 1979); and *The Griffin*, Arnold Kramish (Macmillan, 1987).

[21] *The Secret Servant*, Anthony Cave Brown (Michael Joseph, 1988).

[22] *SOE*, M. R. D. Foot (BBC Publications, 1984).

[23] 'Between Bluff, Deceit, and Treachery', James Rusbridger (*Encounter*, May 1986), and *All The King's Men*, Robert Marshall (Collins, 1988).

[24] *Inside Intelligence*, Anthony Cavendish, preface by George Kennedy Young.

[25] *Spycatcher*, pages 160–1. The first plan apparently approved by the prime minister Sir Anthony Eden was to kill Nasser using nerve gas while a second plan called for his murder using renegade Egyptian army officers. Mainly due to inefficiency, neither plan was put into effect but they indicate the sick and paranoid condition of Britain's prime minister and his secret service.

[26] *Spycatcher*, page 73. The submarines were the Royal Navy's *X-craft* used during World War II to try to sink the German battleship *Tirpitz*.

[27] On 14 April 1988 the government announced that GCHQ had been ordered to make financial cuts of 1.8 per cent in all departments. The management anounced the closure of interception stations at Hawklaw in Scotland, Culmhead near Taunton, and Cheadle in Staffordshire. But these closures owe more to new technology rather than any financial saving. (*Observer*, London, 15 April 1988.)

[28] *Denniston Papers*, 2 December 1944, a report on the history and work of GCCS (Churchill College, Cambridge); *GCHQ*, Nigel West (Weidenfeld & Nicolson, 1986); and interviews with Captain T. E. Nave OBE RN (Ret'd), Melbourne, Australia, January/April/May 1988.

[29] Senate Committee on Interstate Commerce, *Cable Landing Licenses*. 66th Congress, 3rd Session, 1921, Page 193. (Library of Congress, Washington DC.)

[30] *The Ultra Secret*, F. W. Winterbotham (Weidenfeld & Nicolson, 1974).

[31] *Enigma*, Wladyslaw Kozaczuk (Arms & Armour Press, 1984), and *Intercept*, Jozef Garlinski (Dent, 1979).

[32] In the absence of any official history the best sources are *GCHQ*, Nigel West (Weidenfeld & Nicolson, 1986), and *The Ties That Bind*, Jeffrey Richelson and Desmond Ball (Allen & Unwin, 1985), pages 20–2.

[33] GCHQ still retains the use of part of Bletchley Park for training purposes. (Private information GCHQ)

[34] The revelation that Neil Kinnock had telephoned Malcolm Turnbull on nine occasions emerged during a House of Commons debate on 27 November 1986. (*Hansard*, cols 426–7). The Labour Party had hoped to embarrass the government over their handling of the *Spycatcher* affair in Australia and it is fairly obvious that GCHQ and the NSA, via MI6, briefed the government about the number and content of Kinnock's calls. Although this information certainly helped Mrs Thatcher at the time politically it was very foolish to have publicly revealed the extent to which the government taps telephones in this way.

[35] Neither the CIA nor NSA are allowed to tap American telephone calls but there is nothing to stop GCHQ doing this for them and giving them the transcripts just as the NSA taps calls in Britain for GCHQ. This arrangement allows both governments to claim that their own agencies do not tap domestic and international calls.

[36] Built in great secrecy at a cost of $25 million, *Project Lightning* began in June 1957 and the Harvest computer first started work in February 1962 with the ability to read 1.3 million characters per second. In 1976 Harvest was superseded by the Cray-1 computer which cost $15 million and was able to read 320 million words per second or roughly 2,500 average-size hardback books. By the mid-1980s the NSA was working on even faster computers. With this sort of computer power it is very simple to monitor hundreds of thousands of circuits around the world. *The Puzzle Palace*, Pages 100–2.

[37] The most common is transmitting a message both in a high-grade cipher and then inadvertently in a low-grade variety.

[38] *The Ties That Bind*, pages 177–81.

[39] *The Last Hero: Wild Bill Donovan*, Anthony Cave Brown (Times Books, New York, 1982); *The Ties that Bind*, Jeffrey Richelson & Desmond Ball; and *The Shadow Warriors*, Bradley Smith (Deutsch, 1983).

[40] Peter Wright deals at some length in *Spycatcher* with the suspicions of the Americans, especially against the Wilson government in 1964, and recounts (page 364) how James Angleton of the CIA told MI5 that Wilson was a Russian agent. The Czechoslovakian defector, Josef Frolik, named a series of Labour MPs and trade-union officials who had been recruited by the KGB. Certainly Wilson did have some odd friends with close East European connections but most people now believe that any plot against Wilson was a mixture of the CIA's and Peter Wright's own paranoia. *The Wilson Plot*, David Leigh (Heinemann, 1988).

[41] *The Second Oldest Profession*, Phillip Knightley (Deutsch, 1986) pages 250–3.

[42] Fletcher Knebel & Charles Bailey (Weidenfeld & Nicolson, 1962).

[43] *The Ties that Bind*, page 99 *et seq*, and *The Codebreakers*, David Kahn (Macmillan, 1967).

[44] 12 August 1988 by Duncan Campbell.

[45] First Session, Volume 5, *NSA & 4th Amendment Rights*, October 29 and November 6, 1975. Intelligence activities, Senate Resolution #21. US Senate, 94th Congress (Government printing office, Washington DC) and *The Puzzle Palace*, James Bamford (Sidgwick & Jackson, 1983) pages 253–4.

[46] *The Ties that Bind*, page 193.

[47] The best known of these was the Battle of the Bulge the German counter-offensive in the Ardennes in December 1944.

[48] *The US Intelligence Community*, Jeffrey Richelson (William Morrow, New York, 1987), and *Deep Black*, William Burrows (Transworld, 1986).

[49] *The Ties that Bind*, pages 177–9.

[50] All evidence suggests that the Russians knew how to produce an atom bomb around the same time as British, German, French and American scientists were working on the same basic idea. This is what happens with most inventions which are seldom the work of one country. Certainly spies like Fuchs, May, Pontecorvo and Maclean helped Russia to take short cuts but it would have got there in the end. 'Entering the Nuclear Arms Race', David Holloway (*Social Studies of Science*, 1981).

[51] *The Man from Moscow*, Greville Wynne (London, 1967).

[52] Andrei Niklaievich Tupolev born 1888 and the Father of Russian Aviation designed his first aircraft in 1923 and in 1934 built the then world's largest landplane, the ANT-20 *Maxim Gorki*. After the war Tupolev designed Russia's first jet passenger aircraft the Tu-104 and then went onto the design of the Russian version of Concorde, the Tu-144. Tupolev died in 1972.

[53] 'Secrets safe with Russians', *Daily Telegraph*, 10 June 1986.

[54] See Chapter 3.

[55] Arafat's speech was a lengthy and flowery affair largely because he found it necessary to repeat everything. At the end of it both the Americans and inevitably the Israelis rejected his call for peace. There then followed intensive lobbying between Arafat and the Americans and the former made another speech this time including the necessary formula rejecting terrorism. To the horror of the Israelis

the Americans then began direct talks with the PLO. The most likely outcome of this affair is that Mossad will attempt to sabotage the peace process by staging terrorist incidents in Europe leaving behind enough evidence to suggest they are the work of the PLO or other Arab organisations.

[56] Nevertheless Israel is still paying Pollard $5,000 a month while he is in prison, *Newsweek*, 10 April, 1989.

[57] 'Israeli intelligence cell pulled out of Britain', *Sunday Telegraph*, 24 July 1988. 'Israel halts secrets trade with MI6 after expulsion', *Sunday Telegraph*, 21 August 1988; 'The presence of a new Mossad operation in London is being tolerated as a goodwill gesture.'

[58] See Chapter 6.

CHAPTER 2 *(Pages 38–61)*

[1] British Lion/London Films, 1949, written by Graham Greene, directed by Carol Reed.

[2] *A Matter of Trust*, pages 57–8.

[3] *The Second Oldest Profession*, page 249; *The Dictionary of Espionage*, page 104; *George Blake: Double Agent*, E. H. Cookridge (Hodder & Stoughton, 1970) pages 120–3.

[4] *George Blake: Double Agent*, page 139.

[5] *Spycatcher*, page 156.

[6] *A Matter of Trust*, page 58.

[7] *George Blake: Superspy*, Montgomery Hyde (Constable, 1987).

[8] *George Blake: Superspy*, page 39.

[9] *George Blake: Double Agent*, page 128 *et seq*.

[10] See chapter 6.

[11] *Spycatcher*, page 128; *A Matter of Trust*, page 66.

[12] *A Matter of Trust*, page 70.
[13] Private information to the author.

[14] *Inside Story*, page 94.

[15] Ibid, page 94.

[16] Ibid, page 94.

[17] *Spycatcher*, page 47.

[18] *Report of the Inquiry into Prison Escapes and Security*, (HMSO, Cmnd 3175, 1966) page 7 *et seq.*

[19] *George Blake: Double Agent*, page 186.

[20] Pincher claims that Mountbatten assured him that Blake's escape had only been made possible by appalling laxity in the prison. *Traitors*, Chapman Pincher (Sidgwick & Jackson, 1987) page 205. It is hard to believe that Mountbatten would have genuinely believed this so he was presumably using Pincher as a means of passing on false information. The Home Office file containing the details of Blake's escape is embargoed for 75 years which is a privilege normally only given to very sensitive intelligence material which suggests the published report does not contain the whole story. (Home Office to author May 1989.)

[21] In September 1988 Blake, now 65, gave an interview to the Russian weekly magazine *Socialist Industry*. In this he stated that he 'effectively began working for' the Soviet Union in 1953' and had been converted to Communism while studying Russian at Cambridge for MI6. About his escape from prison Blake said, 'Even today nothing can be said about who helped me escape' adding that there were other people in addition to Sean Bourke. Blake claimed to be very happy in Russia and his Dutch mother has visited him there several times. Blake confirmed that he had given the Russians details of the Berlin tunnel before it was even built and that while in West Berlin with MI6 he was head of Britain's agent network in East Germany and Czechoslovakia. Since this interview would have been made with the approval of the KGB its credibility must be treated with considerable reserve.

[22] *The Springing of George Blake*, Sean Bourke (Cassell, 1970). Interestingly, when Bourke was interviewed by E. H. Cookridge for his book in 1970 Bourke made no mention of two-way radios or car jacks.

[23] The author bought some of these two-way radios in the 1960s and used them (illegally) at equestrian events in the south-west. Even in open country they were very inefficient with a range of less than a mile and consumed batteries extremely quickly. Such radios should not be confused with today's portable cellular telephones.

[24] Prison officers at Exeter prison use powerful two-way radios of the latest design to keep in touch with the central prison control when in the exercise yard immediately outside the main building. Yet these need an external aerial system to enable their signals to be received (private information to author).

[25] Letter to author from Mr Keith Bannister, HM Prison Service HQ, 11 April 1988.

[26] Official Report, page 12.

[27] Held by Kevin O'Connor, of RTE, Irish Television, in Dublin.

[28] Official Report, page 23.

[29] *Sunday Times*, 27 March 1988.

[30] *The Spy Who Got Away*, David Wise (Collins, 1988). Wise alleges that there is a remarkable degree of cooperation between the CIA and KGB even to the point of the CIA agreeing to allow the KGB to have some of their agents on the Russian staff inside the American Embassy in Moscow.

[31] *Gouzenko: The Untold Story*, John Sawatsky (Macmillan Canada, 1984).

[32] Top Secret cipher telegram #241 from Australian Mission at the United Nations personal to Australian Prime Minister, 14 April 1954. (Australian Archives ACT CRS A/6213 RCE/L/1). At the time the telegram was sent the Petrovs had just defected and the Australian government was cautiously finding its way as to how to deal with them. The telegram ended 'Gouzenko is somewhat of [a] prima donna and Petrov may be a horse of another colour but it would be well to proceed cautiously with Greeks bringing gifts'.

[33] *Molehunt*, pages 79–80.

[34] Ibid, page 82.

[35] *The Petrov Affair*, Robert Manne (Pergamon Press, Sydney, 1987).

[36] Private information to author from ASIO sources (Interview, Melbourne, May 1988). The pages in the Australian Archives file relating to this are still classified.

[37] Australian Archives ACT CRS A/6283/XR1.

[38] *Philby: KGB Masterspy*, Phillip Knightley (Deutsch, 1988). Philby, who died on 11 May 1988, had been married four times, first to Litzi Friedman, an Austrian; next to Aileen Furse in 1946; and then Eleanor Brewer. For some while his fourth wife Rufa who he married in 1970 was mistakenly referred to as Nina. This came about because a photograph taken by Tom Philby of his father and Rufa together with George Blake and his wife Ida at their dacha, and originally published in the *Daily Mail*, was incorrectly captioned.

[39] *Traitors*, page 199.

[40] In October 1988 the *Sunday Telegraph* ran a series of articles about Gordievsky in

which it was claimed he was a man of great moral courage despite the fact he had betrayed his country's secrets. It is a curious paradox that Peter Wright, who tried to alert his country to what he believed, rightly or wrongly, was a disastrous security situation within MI5, was branded a traitor. Perhaps it is true that no man is a prophet in his own land.

41 *Spycatcher*, page 305.

42 *The Wilson Plot*, David Leigh (Heinemann, 1988).

43 The 222 exchange prefix belongs to a special government telephone exchange, built in 1938 in the basement of the War Office in Whitehall, that in the old days when British telephone dials used a combination of letters and numbers, was called FEDeral. Its purpose is to provide the prime minister, ministers and senior civil servants with a secure secret communications system. In 1963 it was moved to beneath the Department of the Environment's offices in Marsham Street, near Horseferry Road, and linked to the larger government exchange there called Horseferry Tandem, or YTAN (Y being a British Telecom prefix meaning secret). This is the central exchange in the Government Telecommunications Network, a private telephone system linking government offices around the country with its own private circuits intended to be free from industrial disputes. Outsiders wanting access to the 222 exchange need to dial 222 8080 first and then ask with the necessary authority for the number they want. As MI5's offices are in Curzon Street their normal exchange prefix should be either 499 or 629. MI5's bogus travel agency, Casuro Holidays, used the number 222 7443.

44 Howard was allowed to join the CIA in January 1981 despite having a history of drug abuse which came to light during his security vetting procedure. While working at the CIA it also became evident he was an alcoholic yet a year later in January 1982 he was selected to work in the CIA's most secret department at the American Embassy in Moscow. For the next 18 months Howard underwent intensive training and was indoctrinated into all the CIA's secrets about its Russian operations. However in May 1983 Howard failed a polygraph, or lie detector, test and on 2 May was dismissed from the CIA. Greatly embittered by his treatment Howard contacted the KGB while in Vienna in September 1984 and started selling them secrets. Yurchenko only knew Howard by his codename 'Robert' but on 6 August 1985, five days after his defection, the CIA identified Howard to the FBI who then placed him under surveillance. On 19 September Howard was questioned by the FBI but denied being a spy. Two days later, 21 September 1985, Howard eluded the FBI watchers and made good his escape eventually surfacing in Moscow. Howard had $150,000 in a Swiss bank account which he took with him to Moscow while the FBI later found $10,000 worth of silver and gold coins buried in the New Mexico desert all of which was presumably the rewards of his spying. The CIA later claimed he had completely wrecked their Moscow operation. *The Spy Who Got Away*, David Wise (Random House, 1988).

45 Pelton joined the National Security Agency in 1965 and resigned in 1979. He had

previously served in the US Air Force where he had a poor disciplinary record. While with the NSA he had become bankrupt but apparently no one at the agency knew this. Pelton telephoned the Russian Embassy in Washington at 2.30 p.m. on the 15 January 1980 seeking an appointment but although the call was monitored by the FBI it had no idea who he was until Yurchenko told them the caller worked at the NSA. Pelton made two trips to Vienna to meet with the KGB at much the same time that Geoffrey Prime was visiting them there. Although he had worked in a relatively unimportant capacity Pelton had access to the *Ivy Bells* project. This was a hazardous operation begun in 1977 when the US Navy placed eavesdropping induction pods over Russian undersea telephone cables in the Sea of Okhotsk near the naval bases on the Kamchatka Peninsula and monitored the signals. The pods containing the tape recorders had to be recovered by underwater specialists every six weeks using a robot submarine. Pelton told the Russians about *Ivy Bells* in 1981 and they immediately hauled up the NSA's pods. Pelton also gave the Russians details of the NSA's 60-page reference file, called the Signals Parameters File, on its knowledge and penetration of Russian communications. In all Pelton was paid $35,000. He was arrested on 24 November 1985 and sentenced to life imprisonment in December 1986. *Deep Black*, William Burrows (Transworld, 1988) page 139; *The Spy Who Got Away*, page 246; and *Veil*, Bob Woodward (Simon & Schuster, 1987) pages 448–9.

46 After Yurchenko returned to Moscow the KGB claimed the CIA had offered him $1 million tax-free and a lifetime annual salary of $62,500 a year with built-in cost of living adjustments. *The Spy Who Got Away*, page 181.

47 It is difficult to decide whose behaviour was the most bizarre – Angleton's or Golitsin's. Towards the end of his career Angleton became completely out of touch with reality and lived in a convoluted world of his own making beset with his twisted theories that the West was riddled with KGB moles and false defectors. He was eventually sacked from the CIA by the director William Colby in 1974. Angleton died on 11 May 1987.

CHAPTER 3 *(Pages 62–84)*

1 The priest in question was St Thomas Becket (1118–70) who became chancellor to Henry II in 1154 and archbishop of Canterbury in 1162. After quarrelling with the king he refused to swear allegiance to the Constitutions of Clarendon and was exiled to France from 1164 to 1170. Attempts to resolve the dispute failed and at Henry II's instigation Becket was murdered in Canterbury Cathedral on 29 December 1170. Henry II later claimed he had not intended his remarks to be taken as wanting to have Becket killed.

[2] Technical information kindly supplied by Jane's Publishing Company Ltd, London.

[3] *Spycatcher*, page 73.

[4] 'Russian tantrums', *Sunday Times*, London, 7 September 1986.

[5] *Spycatcher*, page 72.

[6] *A Matter of Trust*, Nigel West, (Weidenfeld & Nicolson, 1982) page 59.

[7] One version of events claims that Crabb abandoned the attempt until the next day, but the most reliable account confirms that he went on with his mission that same day. (Correspondence with Chapman Pincher, 1986–87.)

[8] *Inside Story*, Chapman Pincher (Sidgwick & Jackson, 1978) page 180.

[9] *West Sussex Gazette*, Chichester, 10 June 1957 and until the inquest has very comprehensive coverage of the affair.

[10] *The Truth Twisters*, Richard Deacon (Macdonald, 1987) page 86.

[11] Letter from Mrs Pat Rose to Martin Flannery MP, 11 December 1960, kindly made available to the author by Richard Deacon. Mrs Rose died in 1987 and Mr Douglas Rose in a letter dated 19 May 1987 refused to give the author any further help or information.

[12] Kindly made available to the author by Richard Deacon.

[13] *Frogman Extraordinary*, (1960); *Commander Crabb is Alive*, (1968); and *The Fake Defector*, all by Bernard Hutton.

[14] *Rainbow Warrior*, *Sunday Times* Insight Team (Hutchinson, 1986); and *Sink the Rainbow*, John Dyson and Joseph Fitchett (Gollancz, 1986).

[15] *The Times*, 15 December 1987.

[16] Information kindly supplied by Greenpeace 1988.

[17] *The Times*, 5 August 1988.

[18] Prieur gave birth to a son on 21 December 1988.

[19] 'Warrior bomber's top posting', *Daily Telegraph*, 29 March 1988.

[20] *Veil*, Bob Woodward (Simon & Schuster, 1987).

[21] *Sunday Times*, 9 November 1986.

[22] TOW is a two-stage solid fuel-propelled rocket using a command guidewire control system with a range of 3,280 yards launched from a light vehicle, ground tripod, or aircraft.

[23] The proposal was made via David Kimche of the Israeli foreign ministry.

[24] Another intermediary was Cyrus Hashemi who died in mysterious circumstances in London in July 1986.

[25] *Veil*, page 416.

[26] The main justification for the attack was that the Libyans were responsible for the bomb attack on a West Berlin nightclub on 5 April 1986 in which one American soldier and a Turkish woman were killed and 230 people injured. In fact it later transpired that the attack had been the work of Syrian intelligence.

[27] *Sunday Times*, 9 November 1986.

[28] Waite returned to the Lebanon in 1987 in an attempt to free more hostages and on 20 January 1987 was himself kidnapped.

[29] It was also very embarrassing for the federal law-enforcement agencies who in September 1986 had arrested two West Germans in San Diego for allegedly trying to export goods from America to Iran. *Broker of Death*, Hermann Moll with Michael Leapman (Macmillan, 1988).

[30] *Sunday Telegraph*, 27 March 1988.

[31] *Sunday Times*, 27 March 1988.

CHAPTER 4 *(Pages 85–110)*

[1] *Time of Trial*, Rhona Prime (Hodder & Stoughton, 1987); BBC Television, *Everyman*, 15 November 1987; *The Puzzle Palace*, James Bamford (Sidgwick & Jackson, 1983); and *The Report of the Security Commission* (HMSO, Cmnd 8876 May 1983).

[2] Report of official inquiry, page 6 *et seq*.

[3] Private information from FBI and GCHQ.

[4] Private information GCHQ.

[5] *A Matter of Trust*, Nigel West (Weidenfeld & Nicolson, 1982) pages 126–127. For some years the author's brother, then in the Royal Navy, was engaged in the positive vetting of *Polaris* submarine crews and it was always a very difficult task to find completely suitable referees.

[6] Employees of GCHQ are forbidden to visit a number of countries, especially those in Eastern Europe, and were supposed to tell their superior officer of any foreign travel. It is strange that Prime's journeys were never noticed by Special Branch at the airports (private information GCHQ).

[7] *Political Intelligence Digest*, Australia, Volume 2, Nbr.4, 1987 and *The Falcon and the Snowman*, Robert Lindsey (Simon & Schuster, 1979).

[8] Private information GCHQ.

[9] *Political Intelligence Digest*, page 6.

[10] Private information GCHQ.

[11] 'Soviet mole sought after GCHQ leaks', and 'Cheltenham worker sends submarine secrets to Moscow', both by Norman Kirkham, *Sunday Telegraph*, 20 September and 22 November, 1987. Both articles stated that the Americans had learned that secrets from within GCHQ were still reaching the Russians.

[12] Privately to the author, pointing out that giving lectures would be a very unimportant part of Prime's duties and certainly not one that would justify his resignation.

[13] Private information GCHQ.

[14] On 10 July 1986 two East Germans, Reinhard and Sonja Schulze (not their real names which are unknown), were sentenced to ten years imprisonment for spying. Their task was to act as postmen, to pass on messages from other spies in Britain. If Prime had access to a transmitter this is the sort of cut-out arrangement he would have used so that the arrest of one party does not lead to any other part of the network.

[15] *Bodyguard of Lies*, Anthony Cave Brown (W. H. Allen, 1976) page 19.

[16] Mr Paul Greengrass, Granada Television. The telephone conversation was at 12.30p.m. to Sir James Waddell's office on (01) 275 3236 at the Police Complaints Board.

[17] *GCHQ: The Negative Asset: The Failure and the Cover-up.*

[18] On 12 May 1983 Mrs Thatcher told Parliament:'The [Security] Commission conclude that the polygraph is the only measure of which it could be said with any confidence that it would have protected GCHQ from Prime's treachery, because it would either have deterred him from applying to join or could have exposed him in the course of examination.'

The trade unions at GCHQ had bitterly opposed the use of the polygraph and on 25 January 1984 were banned from GCHQ ostensibly because they had taken part in industrial action in 1981.

On 8 December 1988 Mrs Thatcher told Parliament that after more than five years' study the government had decided to abandon plans to introduce the polygraph at GCHQ and similar agencies. Dr Archibald Levey of the Medical Research Council had submitted a 200-page report which concluded that: 'the polygraph is probably incapable of achieving a high level of accuracy and reliability when used for screening purposes [and] individuals trained in the use of counter-measures would have a good chance of escaping detection.'

It seems probable that the whole matter of the polygraph was raised so as to antagonise the trade unions and thus provide an excuse for banning them from GCHQ. Failure to introduce the polygraph will not impress the Americans which suggests that GCHQ know the NSA will not share their most sensitive material with them.

[19] In 1980, the NSA did warn GCHQ that it believed there was a top-level leak of information to the Russians but as it could provide no definite information, and MI6 had picked up nothing similar, it was discounted by GCHQ. This may have been an attempt by the KGB to expose Prime.

[20] *Report of the Security Commission October 1986* (HMSO, Cmnd 9923) page 7 *et seq.*

[21] Amongst the various claims was that defence counsel for the eight accused had held a secret meeting at which it was agreed they would all use their right of challenge so as to get rid of all pro-government members of the jury. In fact no such meeting was held and the allegation is quite untrue but unfortunately has found a place in mythology (*Sunday Times* letters, 12 June 1988). It was also argued that the eight servicemen should have been tried by court martial, rather than a criminal court with a jury, so that they would have automatically been found guilty. This does not say much for the quality of justice meted out by military courts martial.

[22] It is a well-worn theme by several right-wing commentators that by challenging a juror, counsel can somehow anticipate the personal beliefs of their replacement simply by their clothes or hairstyle.

[23] The inquiry was conducted by David Calcutt QC (HMSO, Cmnd 9781), who may be a brilliant legal expert but plainly has no first-hand experience of life in the services and has never experienced the bullying tactics that NCOs indulge in nor the pressures induced by long periods of solitary confinement. The entire report reads as if it were a philosophical discussion between academics and has no relevance to the affair at all.

[24] *Stand By Your Man*, producer Angela Kaye.

[25] Rhona Prime's explanation was far from convincing. One could have understood her telling the police about her husband's assaults on small girls because she was the devoted mother of three children. But Prime's spying at GCHQ was in the past, a technical matter of no interest to Rhona, and no individual had been harmed by the information he gave to the Russians. If Rhona had thrown her husband's spy kit away and said nothing, no one at GCHQ would have been any the wiser. The information about *Rhyolite* had already been given to the Russians by Boyce and Lee. Plainly the Russians would never have approached Prime again. Why she chose to tell the police and thus ensure her husband spends the next 20 years in prison is a mystery, unless Rhona enjoys a convoluted form of religious martyrdom.

[26] Private information BBC.

[27] Considering the importance of GCHQ and its close links with the NSA, it would indeed be remarkable if Prime was the Russians' only spy.

[28] They continued long after Prime's arrest was public knowledge (*The Puzzle Palace*, British edition preface page 49). This was one of the facts of the case carefully omitted from the official report.

[29] *Molehunt*, Nigel West (Weidenfeld & Nicolson, 1987), Chapter 9.

[30] *Security Commission Report* (Cmnd 9514, HMSO, 1985).

[31] *I Pledge Allegiance*, Howard Blum (Weidenfeld & Nicolson, 1988) pages 97 *et seq*.

[32] This was a rotor cipher machine descended from the German Enigma of World War II.

[33] Some less sensitive material was allowed past unaltered to provide bait for the rest.

[34] By comparison in July 1974 the CIA and US Navy spent over $500 million raising the wreck of an old Russian *Golf* class submarine from the bed of the Pacific Ocean in order to get a few obsolescent secrets. *A Matter of Risk*, Roy Varner & Wayne Collier (Random House, 1978). Prime cost the Russians about £20,000 which shows that money alone is not the key to good espionage. Bribing a junior clerk who operates a photocopier is less risky and far more cost-effective than trying to blackmail a leading scientist.

[35] 'Trident subs face Soviet threat due to US spy family', John Keegan, *Daily Telegraph*, 30 December 1987. Quoting the editor of the 1988 edition of *British Warships and Auxiliaries*, Keegan alleges that Walker handed over the secrets of the silent-running pump-jet propulsion system which is to be fitted to the Royal Navy's *Vanguard*-class submarines. No member of the Walker spy ring could have

known anything about this development work so if there has been a leak, and there is no evidence there has been, it is more likely to have occurred in Britain. But Keegan is one of those right-wing journalists that is always peddling the theory of Russia's invincibility.

[36] 'NATO's New Spy Scandal', (*Newsweek*, 5 September 1988).

CHAPTER 5 *(Pages 111–132)*

[1] During the Korean War film coverage was mainly in the hands of newsreel cameramen whose output took a week or more to reach audiences back home. Vietnam was the first war covered by television although, lacking satellite links, film had to be flown to the west coast of America before being fed into the networks. For a long time only journalists sympathetic to Washington's policies were given access to front-line areas but in the end it was television pictures of American troops destroying villages that changed public opinion throughout America. As the Falklands War of 1982 showed, engaging in wars that do not enjoy complete domestic support will be far more difficult in the future.

[2] The expression 'wind of change' was first used by British Prime Minister Harold Macmillan in a speech during his visit to South Africa in 1958 which marked the government's support of independence for African states.

[3] *The Friends*, Nigel West (Weidenfeld & Nicolson, 1988) page 99.

[4] A treaty between Turkey, Iraq, Iran, Pakistan, and Britain, signed in 1955 its goals being military, economic, and social cooperation. When Iraq withdrew from it in 1959 its headquarters were moved from Baghdad to Ankara and it was renamed the Central Treaty Organisation.

[5] It was not until November 1956 that Britain and France were able to launch the invasion by which time world opinion had hardened against them and even as troops were landing Britain accepted an UN truce and within 24 hours the Anglo-French force was evacuated.

[6] See Chapter 1, note 25.

[7] *Spycatcher*, pages 83–4. Wright states that GCHQ's H Division could calculate the new rotor settings on the Egyptian Hagelin cryptographs simply by listening to the cipher clerk re-setting them but this is impossible. In fact one operator read out the new daily setting and the other operator then set the rotors accordingly (private information GCHQ).

[8] Ibid, page 85.

[9] Eden had just been involved in a major row with MI6 over the Crabb affair earlier in the year (see Chapter 3) and neither MI6 nor GCHQ (the latter in those days being an unknown organisation) would have told Eden the extent of their cooperation with the NSA while Eden would not have had the expertise to ask.

[10] During the Six Day War, 5–11 June 1967, Egypt lost over 300 aircraft, mainly MiG-17s and MiG-21s, in the first day, and by the end of the fighting had also lost seven fully equipped divisions, 800 tanks, 450 guns and 10,000 vehicles, while 10,000 soldiers were killed and over 20,000 wounded. A great deal of this equipment was captured intact by Israel who passed on samples of Russia's latest hardware to the West.

[11] *The Times*, 28 October 1988.

[12] *KGB/CIA*, Celina Bledowska and Jonathan Bloch (Bison Books, 1987) pages 82–6.

[13] *KGB*, John Barron (Hodder & Stoughton, 1974) pages 252–4.

[14] 'Southern Africa in Soviet foreign policy', Kurt M. Campbell, Adelphi Papers 227 (International Institute for Strategic Studies, 1987) pages 19–21.

[15] Ibid, page 14.

[16] Ibid, page 9, *KGB/CIA*, pages 91–8.

[17] Adelphi Papers 227, pages 32–4.

[18] *The Dictionary of Espionage*, page 107, *Spyclopaedia*, page 298.

[19] The promise to buy this sugar was a great embarrassment since Russia and its partners are large sugar producers and exporters and had no use for the Cuban sugar. Early in 1961 I was asked by the Russians to see if I could secretly arrange to divert this sugar elsewhere, have it refined, and sold for hard currency without the Cubans finding out. With the aid of some expertly forged documents supplied by the KGB I did this and it became known as The Cuban Sugar Laundry. Ironically some two years later the CIA approached me to see if I could deliberately push prices down on the London sugar market in order to reduce Cuba's earnings. At the time prices were high following cyclone damage to the Caribbean sugar harvest. The CIA spent around $1 million on this harebrained project and although sugar prices did fall this was entirely due to the natural balance of supply and demand reasserting itself. Oddly enough, at the same time, a member of Cubazucar's staff in London asked me if it was possible to push prices up but as Cuba did not have sufficient foreign currency to sustain such an operation nothing happened and the person handling the idea defected anyway.

CHAPTER 6 *(Pages 133–157)*

[1] 'Between Bluff, Deceit and Treachery', James Rusbridger, (*Encounter*, May 1986); 'All The King's Men', (BBC Television, *Timewatch*, May 1986); *All The King's Men*, Robert Marshall (Collins, 1988); *Déricourt: The Chequered Spy*, Jean Overton Fuller (Michael Russell, 1989); *SOE in France*, M. R. D. Foot (HMSO, 1966). Claims and opinions about the true role of Henri Déricourt vary enormously. The author and Robert Marshall remain convinced he was working for MI6 which explains why he escaped any punishment for his betrayals. M. R. D. Foot believes he was merely a rogue who took care of himself without regard for others. Miss Overton Fuller, who met him after the war, believes he was a clever SOE agent who did a deal with the Germans that saved many lives. Colonel Buckmaster (head of F Section) claims he ran Déricourt as a double agent with the help of Sir Dick White of MI5. Sir Dick White denies this. The only person who knows the truth is Déricourt himself who, it has been alleged, is alive and living in Barcelona.

[2] *Sunday Telegraph*, 24 July 1988.

[3] *Sunday Telegraph*, 21 August 1988.

[4] Leaving behind his wife and two children.

[5] Cuban authorities identified Palsencia as having been born in Cifuentes, Villa Clara, and the holder of identity card #650/1300/3052, but whether she was also a member of Cuban intelligence is unclear.

[6] Cuban newspaper *Granma*, 25 September 1988.

[7] Evidently the CIA planned to kidnap Perez by force and then announce his 'defection' through carefully placed leaks in the media which would also claim that Perez had denounced other Cuban agents. It would then be impossible for Perez to return to Cuba and establish his innocence so he would be forced to accept CIA money and thus become a real defector.

[8] The British and Cuban versions of the shooting incident are contradictory. The British version was that the injured man, later said to be a member of MI5, 'had been interviewed by the Anti-Terrorist Squad who are satisfied he was not posing a threat to anyone.' The Cuban version was that Perez fired only at Lombard from very close range hitting him in the chest. He fell to the ground seriously wounded while the CIA and MI5 team ran off.

[9] 'Failure of Castro's trap led to shooting', *Sunday Telegraph*, 18 September 1988.

[10] 'Obey our laws or go home', *Mail on Sunday*, 18 September 1988.

[11] *The Independent*, 1 October 1988.

12 'CIA chief warns media over intelligence stories', *Guardian*, 8 May 1986.

13 *Observer*, London, 27 April 1986.

14 *The Times*, London, 12 January 1988.

15 On 17 April 1986 Hindawi gave a suitcase to his pregnant Irish girlfriend, 32-year-old Ann Murphy, after booking her on to El Al flight 016 from London to Tel Aviv. When El Al security staff checked Miss Murphy's suitcase it was found to contain a bomb and Hindawi was later arrested in West Kensington. At Hindawi's trial in October 1986 the court was told that the bomb had been supplied by Syrian intelligence and following his conviction the British government broke off diplomatic relations with Syria. In his defence Hindawi claimed he thought the suitcase contained drugs and that the bomb had been planted on him by Mossad agents posing as El Al security staff who switched suitcases. The court disbelieved this explanation although in the light of the Sowan affair it is exactly the sort of dirty trick Mossad engages in and would also explain why Hindawi was apparently willing to murder his girlfriend. It was also very strange that the Syrian ambassador and his staff should have allegedly been so closely involved in such an operation.

16 *Guardian*, London, 23 December 1988.

17 Stormont Castle press office.

18 Sometimes the official line is reversed and claims of enormous capabilities are leaked to compliant sections of the press. On 2 October 1988 the pro-government *Sunday Express* reported that the IRA possessed four tons of Semtex, several SAM-7 surface-to-air missiles, numerous armour-piercing heavy machine guns and at least 2,000 Kalashnikov automatic rifles. The strength of the IRA had dramatically increased to 650 men and women 200 of whom were in Ireland. Reports such as this must provide wonderful recruiting material for the IRA.

19 Politicians often make the point that the IRA have not achieved anything in Northern Ireland. But terrorism, urban guerrilla warfare, or freedom fighting, depending upon which title you choose to use, is not necessarily about achievement but rather destabilising the authority in power by creating mayhem and murder. This is precisely what President Reagan's Contra rebels, or terrorists, are trying to do in Nicaragua. On this basis the IRA have been extremely successful and are no nearer defeat than they were 20 years ago.

20 Notwithstanding the deaths of many servicemen Northern Ireland has proved an extremely valuable training ground not only for military operations in a horribly realistic scenario but also for a variety of intelligence operations which can be carried out without any of the normal judicial controls that exist on the mainland. ('The Need to Know', BBC Television, *Panorama*, February/March, 1981.)

21 Stormont Castle press office, November 1988.

22 '£1.5m guard for Maggie', *Mail on Sunday*, 11 September 1988. Both Mrs Thatcher and the chief constable of Sussex, Roger Birch, were keen to declaim that 'terrorism will not win' but by the time the conference began Brighton was more heavily defended against the IRA than it had been against Hitler's armies in 1940.

23 On 27 September 1988 Israel's defence minister Yitzhak Rabin stated that the Israeli army was deliberately shooting at and wounding Palestinian demonstrators to try to crush the nine-month uprising in the occupied Arab territories (*Daily Telegraph*, 28 September 1988). The next day a Foreign Office minister, William Waldegrave, told Israel's ambassador in London that the British government was distressed that there should be a deliberate policy of inflicting injury and said it was difficult to see how such action would bring peace.

24 Article 15 of the European Human Rights Convention gives member countries the right to ignore, or derogate, rulings 'in time of war or other public emergency threatening the life of the nation'. The dilemma facing the government is that if it derogates it shows that the IRA is threatening the whole of the United Kingdom, which is exactly the sort of publicity the IRA would like to enjoy. If it derogates only for Northern Ireland then it is giving that part of the United Kingdom an unwanted special status. Under British law a defendant has the right to know what is alleged against him if he is to be detained but the RUC fears that if it had to tell a suspect this then he could warn accomplices for whom the police were still searching.

25 'Nameless accusers', *The Independent*, 15 December 1988.

26 For the full text see *The Times*, London, 14 December 1988.

27 *The Times*, London, 15 December 1988.

28 'The Jury on Trial', a three-part series in *The Times*, London, October 1988, contained many of the well-worn arguments including the opening statement 'there are now grave doubts that justice is being done'. In a summary of the views expressed, Steward Tendler wrote on 31 October, 'jurors were entirely dominated by emotional, social or political responses'. It is of course precisely this argument that has led to claims that Irish people appearing before British courts find juries prejudiced against them from the start because of the automatic link made between Ireland and terrorism.

29 'Witnesses afraid to testify', *The Independent*, 23 December 1988.

30 Hendrik Botha, Stephanus de Jager, William Metelerkamp and Jacobus le Grange were arrested in March 1984 with five Britons who were tried at Birmingham Crown Court in July 1985 four being sentenced to between three and 15 months' imprisonment and the fifth fined £2,500.

[31] *Daily Mirror*, 22 December 1988. When asked about this case the Home Office said 'These things take time'.

[32] Written Parliamentary answer by Roger Freeman MP, junior defence minister, 23 March 1988.

[33] In an article in the *Sunday Telegraph* on 28 February 1988 Bruce Anderson commented, 'If Pte Thain had been ... luckier in his lawyers – he might well have been acquitted.' As a result the lawyers involved issued a writ for libel against the newspaper.

[34] *The Independent, The Times,* 27 September 1988.

[35] The SAS greatly enjoys its Rambo-like reputation but because so many of its operations are carried out by its members wearing plain clothes, in total secrecy and with a marked reluctance to account for their actions afterwards, it is inevitable that the spectre is raised that the SAS is a form of unofficial assassination squad called in to do the politicians' dirty work in situations like Northern Ireland. In Gibraltar the SAS apparently accepted MI5's briefing about the three suspects without any further checking and evidently did not consider that a Renault 5 car containing 220lbs of explosives and shrapnel would have shown some obvious signs of such a weight. The SAS must have known that MI5 had previously been involved in at least one of the shooting incidents in Northern Ireland involving unarmed civilians investigated by John Stalker. The lesson the SAS should learn from Gibraltar is that it ought to be more careful in acting on informaton of this kind from MI5 without first checking, otherwise it may find itself drawn into similar dubious situations in the future and end up a politicised killing machine.

[36] One quaint suggestion made after the Gibraltar inquest was that the SAS should be placed under the control of the Home Office. Since the Home Office cannot control MI5's activities it is hardly likely Whitehall bureaucrats would have any more success with soldiers. The idea came from John Keegan of the *Daily Telegraph* (1 October 1988).

[37] On 3 October 1988 BBC *Panorama* planned to show a documentary film about the role of the SAS in Northern Ireland presented by Tom Mangold and produced by Eamonn Matthews. In the film Enoch Powell, the former MP for South Down, said:

Gibraltar was a catastrophe. There was at no time a car bomb in Gibraltar but nevertheless three human beings have been shot to death by soldiers without being in possession of arms or a method of detonating a car bomb had there been one ... responsibility must be taken at a visual level to Parliament and to the public ... [the SAS] are being used in place of a civil power and essentially as a killing machine ... it may be that ministers of the crown may wish to indicate that they are witholding information. That is perfectly conceivable but still does not detract from their duty or responsibility.

Lord Prior said that 'there was little day-to-day political control of the SAS' when he was secretary of state for Northern Ireland. Two days before the film was due to be shown John Birt, the BBC's deputy director-general, postponed the transmission on the grounds that the film raised questions about the conduct of the SAS in Northern Ireland but offered no solutions (*Daily Telegraph*, 3 & 4 October 1988). The film was also shown in advance to the D-notice Committee who asked that a section of the SAS training film be deleted because it showed soldiers using a door to break into a room holding hostages. The film was finally shown on 17 October 1988 and Powell's comments about the SAS being used as a 'killing machine' had been removed. In the end the film concentrated on the procedures used at inquests in Northern Ireland and was remarkably uninteresting and the connection with the SAS of peripheral value. The delay in screening happened to coincide with the Conservative Party conference at Brighton.

38 *Guardian*, 19 September 1988.

39 *Stalker*, John Stalker (Harrap, 1988).

40 It is a remarkable coincidence that Mr Stalker's personal friendships which he made no secret about never became an issue affecting his police career until he was on the point of making specific allegations against a number of senior RUC officers in May 1986.

41 Max Hastings, editor, *Daily Telegraph*, 8 February 1988, reviewing John Stalker's book said: 'A fair cop in the wrong place: the real blunderers are those that sent him [Stalker] to the province four years ago. Responsibility must presumably extend to the British Cabinet. To satisfy public unease, they foolishly initiated an inquiry which they then could not bring themselves to see concluded.'

42 'Stalker escapes prosecution over RUC memoirs', *Daily Telegraph*, 12 February 1988.

43 'Murder case hits SA police morale', *Guardian*, 4 April 1988.

44 *Sunday Times*, 13 March 1988. At first the intelligence services seemed anxious to detail the extent of their surveillance of the quartet in Spain prior to the shootings but as the inquest drew near stories were put about downgrading this and the cooperation received from the Spanish police who seemed to conveniently lose the suspects at every important moment.

45 There were plenty of other static military targets in Gibraltar the IRA could have attacked causing heavy casualties that would have required far less planning than the guard parade on Tuesdays, so the fact that MI5 could be so certain as to the target's identity plainly shows the extent of their monitoring operations in Spain.

46 The clerk at the rental office of Marbesol remembers serving Farrell who paid the £90 deposit in sterling.

[47] One report claims the Semtex was brought ashore at the port of Puerto Banus but Spanish police denied this. Another possibility is that MI5 supplied the Semtex to the gang using a double agent in a sting operation. In November 1988 a number of senior Spanish police officers were charged with supplying guns and explosives to the Basque terrorist movement ETA. One of the accused, Chief Superintendent Francisco Alvarez, testified that such sting operations had been approved in advance by their superiors in order to get information about ETA's future plans. However the idea of setting up the IRA trio with the help of the Spanish police is a typical intelligence operation often used by American law-enforcement agencies to catch drug smugglers (*Guardian*, 13 November 1988).

[48] On 28 April 1988 Thames Television transmitted a documentary called *Death on the Rock* produced by Chris Oxley and presented by Julian Manyon. The programme went ahead despite strong protests from the government to the Independent Broadcasting Authority that it was pre-judging the outcome of the Gibraltar inquest. During the second half of the programme Julian Manyon said:

> We have obtained a dramatic account of [the shootings] from another witness who was in a car only a few yards back. Also wishing to protect his identity he has given a detailed statement to a lawyer representing *This Week*: 'The man on the ground was lying on his back, the man standing over this man had his foot on the man's chest. I could see that he also had a gun in his hand. I then saw the gunman point his gun deliberately at the man that was lying on the floor and fire two or three times in him at point blank range. I was horrified by what I saw.'

Although not mentioned in the programme this unsigned and unsworn statement had been made to a Gibraltar lawyer, Peter Finch, acting on behalf of Thames Television by Kenneth Asquez, a 20-year-old clerk working for the Algemene Bank. It was Asquez's second statement. His first, in his own handwriting, had been made to Major Robert Randall around about 19 March or some 13 days after the shooting. In this Asquez also said that he had seen the man doing the shooting pull on a black beret, show an ID (identity) card and shout, 'Stop, it's OK, it's the police.' This part of his statement was omitted from the television programme *Death on the Rock*.

Another person who took part in the documentary was Mrs Carmen Proetta who said she saw two of the terrorists put their hands up as if they wanted to surrender and were then shot with their hands still up. As soon as the programme had been transmitted several pro-government newspapers received supposedly anonymous telephone calls implying that Mrs Proetta had a criminal record, was involved in vice and drug activities and hated the British so much that she had fabricated her story. The *Sun* newspaper called Mrs Proetta 'the Tart of Gib' while other newspapers carried similiar but less salacious stories about her morals and character. On 16 December 1988 the *Sun* paid Mrs Proetta libel damages of around £75,000 and the editor and journalists involved apologised for the distress they had caused her, admitted the allegations were untrue, and that Mrs Proetta was a 'wholly independent person who had given an honest account of what she remembers seeing'. Mrs Proetta believed the smear story had emanated from the Gibraltar police and at least one senior officer in the force who had originally been anxious for the *Sun* to print the story refused to give evidence on behalf of the newspaper at the libel hearing.

[49] *Daily Telegraph*, 24 May 1988; *Sunday Telegraph*, 10 June 1988.

[50] 'Gibraltar', Ian Jack, *Granta* magazine, Autumn 1988.

[51] On 23 September 1988 Kenneth Asquez appeared as a witness at the inquest and during a bizarre cross-examination retracted his original statement claiming he had only made it to stop Major Randall from pestering him. The coroner asked, 'Was this statement true or parts of it true and parts of it not true?'

Asquez replied, 'At the moment I'm a bit confused because my mind is not so clear.'

Later the coroner asked, 'The trouble is, Mr Asquez, that this question of the beret, the ID card, and the words to the effect 'Stop, it's OK, it's the police', have only come out for the first time in this court subsequent to the time you made the statement. Can you try and explain a little further?'

Asquez replied, 'No, as I said before I'm a bit confused. My thoughts are vague from that time.'

Asquez claimed that he had made up the part about the soldier pulling on the beret, the ID card, and the shouted warning, after reading about it in the newspapers but Mr Hucker, counsel for the SAS, pointed out that these details had never been mentioned in any newspaper. To this Asquez lamely replied that he must have heard it on the streets. Nor could Asquez explain why he voluntarily went to see the lawyer, Peter Finch, who was acting for Thames Television and repeated the same statement again when he could have easily told Finch his original statement was untrue. Asquez later admitted in evidence that he had problems at the bank because his daily cash statement did not balance, which had happened before. On 26 September 1988 Major Randall, then on holiday in America, sent a sworn affidavit to the inquest stating that at no time had he pestered Asquez into giving the first statement nor had he offered him any inducement to do so. Mr Asquez's two companions, Mr and Mrs Polson, who were with him in the car at the time he claimed to have seen the shooting, were not called to give evidence at the inquest. Mr Polson's father was a member of the Gibraltar police and evidently did not wish his family to become involved. (Official transcript D/14S2301A/1 pages 1–69, and affidavit sworn before Mrs Carol Wellner, Notary Public, Mecklenburg, North Carolina, USA.)

[52] On 22–4 September while the inquest was taking place Mrs Thatcher made an official visit to Spain and had a long private discussion about Gibraltar with the Spanish premier. From that moment onwards the Spanish decided not to give evidence at the inquest.

[53] There was a great deal of hypocritical criticism in some newspapers about Asquez's unsworn and unsigned statement having been used by Thames Television in *Death*

on the Rock. In fact everything suggests Asquez was telling the truth in his first statement because it contained details not known anywhere else at the time. He then voluntarily repeated the same details again to TTV's lawyer so it is hard to see how a signature would have made any difference. As to why Asquez suddenly became so confused, one can speculate that in a small community like Gibraltar it might not have been popular to give the only evidence that could have resulted in soldiers beng convicted of killing IRA terrorists.

[54] *Daily Telegraph*, 1 October 1988.

[55] *Veil*, Bob Woodward (Simon & Schuster, 1987) page 396–7.

[56] 'MI6 linked to Contra sabotage', David Leigh and Paul Lashmar (*Observer*, 31 July 1988).

[57] *The Prime Minister Was A Spy*, Anthony Grey (Weidenfeld & Nicolson, 1983). On 5 October 1988 the *Observer* paid Titcombe damages and costs in settlement of his libel action against them for having accused him of a 'hoax' over the Holt affair. (*The Times*, 6 October 1988.) Titcombe dropped a similar action against the *Sunday Telegraph*.

[58] While visiting Cheviot Beach in February 1988 I was told by Australian Army officials who still controlled the area and local coastguards that there had been over 70 drownings off this stretch of the coast in recent years and few bodies had been recovered as sharks frequented the area. Furthermore Holt had nearly drowned when he went swimming in rough seas a few weeks earlier. Royal Australian Navy sources confirmed to me that the waters off Cheviot Beach were extremely hazardous and shallow with many rocky outcrops and it would be impossible for a submarine to venture anywhere near the shore.

[59] 'The mercurial career of Ronald Mervyn Titcombe', *Melbourne Age*, 19 November 1983.

[60] Philip Chambers told Ronald Titcombe that he was a former Regular Army Intelligence Corps analyst trained at GCHQ Cheltenham. (Chambers report, page 1.)

[61] 'I am now satisfied that I have identified a number of code systems in the text of the diaries.' (Chambers report, page 2.)

[62] Harold Holt letters, pages 63 and 104, London 1953.

[63] Chambers report, page 6.

[64] Chambers report, page 25.

[65] Supplied by Ronald Titcombe on 15 January 1985 for my analysis. On 2 February

1985 I wrote Titcombe advising that I could find no evidence to support the claim of the hidden code thesis.

[66] *Vassall: The Autobiography of a Spy*, John Vassall (Sidgwick & Jackson, 1975).

[67] *A Matter of Trust*, page 79.

[68] *Spycatcher*, page 165.

[69] Private information to author.

[70] 'An odd collection of Spies', Andrew Lownie, *The Times*, 30 March 1988.

[71] *Spyclopaedia*, Richard Deacon (Macdonald), 1988 page 234.

[72] Interview with his brother Lt Col G. B. Courtney MBE MC, Toorak, Australia, May 1988.

[73] 'Briton given spy grilling in Bulgaria', *Sunday Telegraph*, June 1962.

CHAPTER 7 *(Pages 158–173)*

[1] *State of Secrecy*, BBC Television, 14 September 1987.

[2] *Guardian*, 23 January 1988.

[3] Evidence to the House of Commons Treasury and Civil Service Select Committee, 12 February 1986.

[4] *The Branch*, Nigel West (Secker & Warburg, 1983) is a straightforward account of their activities in the Metropolitan Police area but does not deal with their role elsewhere in the country. Writing to the author, 25 March 1983, West said, 'I share your misgivings about some of the County Forces. I think they watch too much television! Fortunately the Special Branch in London are thoroughly professional and do not appear to get up to such tricks.'

[5] In January 1982 shortly before he resigned as chief constable of the Devon and Cornwall police John Alderson claimed he had destroyed many Special Branch files because they contained details of people who were not subversive in any way but merely held legitimate views against foxhunting, apartheid, nuclear power-stations and so forth. (*Cornish Guardian*, 14 January 1982.) It was a nice piece of publicity for someone about to stand as a Liberal Party candidate but had no real meaning

since Special Branch keeps all its files on a computer in London over which no chief constable has any control.

6 Home Secretary Douglas Hurd opening Second Reading, Security Service Bill, 15 December 1988.

7 Mr Hurd described the new Bill as being necessary for the 'survival or the well-being of the nation as a whole' but failed to explain why this could not have been achieved equally successfully if MI5 adhered to the terms of the 1952 directive.

8 The annual Security Commission report about telephone tapping has never mentioned that any requests have been refused so one must assume all are issued.

9 A similar situation arises when police ask a magistrate to sign a search warrant. Few if any ever bother to check to see if the facts are true and if they made a habit of doing so the police would soon find a more compliant colleague.

10 Under the new Bill MI5 will not be allowed to burgle or bug the private property belonging to Members of Parliament. The question of MPs' immunity from such operations is a complex one. The 1957 Birkett Report stated that MPs were in exactly the same position as any private citizen in regard to the interception of their communications unless they were in connection with Parliamentary proceedings when they would be fully privileged. In 1966, when Harold Wilson was Labour prime minister and had been warned by MI5 that several of his colleagues were suspected Communist sympathisers, he gave orders that there should be no tapping of MPs' telephones. The question of bugging their homes was not mentioned. Mrs Thatcher reaffirmed this policy on 6 February 1980 and again on 10 December 1986. MI5 regarded this directive as nonsense and either used freelances or handed the task over to the CIA and the NSA operating in Britain, which is how Neil Kinnock's telephone calls to Malcolm Turnbull came to be tapped during the *Spycatcher* saga in 1986 (see Chapter 1).

11 House of Commons Home Affairs Committee inquiry, May 1984.

12 'The Need To Know', BBC *Panorama*, 23 February 1981. After leaving the British police force Salisbury became police commissioner for South Australia and in 1978 was dismissed for repeatedly misleading the State government over what Special Branch was doing. In 1977, on the instructions of South Australian Premier Donald Dunstan, Judge White carried out an inspection of the South Australian Special Branch records and found them to be 'scandalously inaccurate, irrelevant to security purposes, and outrageously unfair to hundreds, perhaps thousands, of loyal and worthy citizens.' Judge White found that Special Branch had kept files on members of the local and national Labour Party, half the judges of the Supreme Court, trade-union officials, homosexuals, members of conservation groups, members of peace and anti-nuclear movements, and thousands of others who had taken part in political activity. The judge commented that the files had been opened 'on the unreasoned assumption that any person who thought or acted less

conservatively than suited the security services was considered potential dangers to the security of the state.' Most of the files were destroyed. Since the entire Australian security service was originally established with the help of MI5 and based on its system it would be reasonable to assume that the South Australian files mirror those held in Britain. *Who's Watching You?*, Crispin Aubrey (Penguin, 1981) pages 54–55.

[13] 'The Need To Know', BBC *Panorama*, 23 February 1981.

[14] House of Commons, 3 December 1986.

[15] *The Times* and *Daily Express*, 21 September, *Daily Telegraph*, 22 September and *Daily Telegraph*, 17 November, 1983.

[16] When a complaint is made against the police it is at least investigated by other policemen who know the system and how evidence can be concealed or altered. Even so some investigations make little progress because of the unwritten rule that no police officer will expose another's malpractices. MI5 is a very large and complex organisation and only someone who had actually worked in it would have the slightest idea of where to look for evidence of illegal operations. The belief that some worthy outside body could discover such things is farcical.

[17] *Who's Watching You?*, page 27.

[18] Correspondence with Mrs J. A. Davies, 18 January–30 July, 1982.

[19] 'Terrorists Target the Networks', James Rusbridger, *Sunday Times*, 29 May 1988.

[20] Cmnd 351 (HMSO, March 1988).

[21] This is a deliberately misleading statement because it only refers to the warrants in force on that one day and does not give the cumulative total of warrants issued during the year; furthermore warrants issued by the Foreign Secretary (responsible for MI6 and GCHQ) and the Northern Ireland secretary are not included. A single warrant can cover the tapping of an individual's telephone or of an entire organisation like CND or the National Union of Mineworkers involving several hundred telephones. As the commissioner always chooses 31 December as the day for calculating warrants in force one can assume that British Telecom ensure he is given the lowest figure possible which Lloyd has no way of checking anyway. One estimate puts the total number of telephone taps in the course of a year at over 30,000, three-quarters of which are on behalf of MI5, MI6 and Special Branch, for security purposes and not connected with criminal activities. Private information from British Telecom and the *Observer*, 30 October 1988.

[22] The Security Commission never investigated any of her claims despite the fact that if she was right MI5 had breached the rules. This hardly suggests the Commission is endowed with much investigative zeal.

23 'The Need To Know', BBC Television, *Panorama*, 23 February 1981.

24 Page 72.

25 *Operation Julie*, Dick Lee and Colin Pratt (W H Allen, 1978) page 161.

26 All tapping operations are conducted from British Telecom's headquarters. The special British Telecom staff who handle telephone tapping work in Section AES/9, the cost of this department being around £10 million a year.

27 *20/20 Vision*, 20 February 1985.

28 *ibid*.

29 House of Commons, 15 January 1988.

30 *New Society*, 31 May 1984.

31 *Spycatcher*, pages 54–6.

32 The author is grateful to Commander Robert Green RN (Ret'd) for personal details concerning his aunt and her murder, to Graham Smith for permission to quote from his carefully researched book *Death of a Rose Grower* (Woolf, 1985), and also 'Who Killed Miss Murrell?', *Daily Mail*, 14 March 1985.

33 *Daily Telegraph*, 27 June 1985.

34 This is what the judges have been saying for the past 40 years every time they sentence a spy or traitor that has been found in our midst – not by MI5 – but either because of their own stupidity, like Prime, or because a defector has told MI5 about them. If what judges say is true then by now there can hardly be a secret left in Britain not known to the Russians. It is hard to see what difference all this has made to Britain's security or position in the world today.

CHAPTER 8 *(Pages 174–200)*

1 One of the earliest was William Le Queux, born in 1864, who as a writer and journalist pestered the Foreign Office and War Office before World War I with endless tales of imaginary German spies until he was actually believed. *The Second Oldest Profession*, Phillip Knightley (Deutsch, 1986) pages 13 *et seq*.

2 Not only authors need a popular enemy but so too do the intelligence agencies

which is why no matter what happens on the political front stories are always being fed to compliant sections of the media about terrible enemies lurking round every corner.

3 As well as the snobbery there was also a strong anti-semitic streak running through all Buchan's books.

4 In 1932 Sir Compton Mackenzie published the second volume of his trilogy *Greek Memories* concerning his work for MI6 in Greece during World War I. At a bizarre trial Mackenzie was prosecuted under the Official Secrets Act and fined £100 with £100 costs. An original copy of his book remains in the British Library but can only be seen with the permission of MI5 who over the last 55 years have never given their approval to anyone. This example alone gives an idea of the paranoia that grips the intelligence services.

5 Montagu and Duff Cooper were at Trinity College, Cambridge together.

6 No. 46, Row 14.

7 The idea of planting false documents on the enemy was not new. Apart from the Wooden Horse of Troy it had been used with great success during World War I on 17 October 1917 during the fighting between Britain and Turkey in the Middle East. An intelligence officer, Colonel Richard Meinertzhagen, arranged that a bag containing supposedly secret papers about British plans was 'lost' so that it would be found by a Turkish patrol. *Bodyguard of Lies*, Anthony Cave Brown (W H Allen, 1976) pages 278–82. The story is also told in the 1987 film *The Australian Light Horse*.

8 Colonel John Bevan, a member of the deception organisation the London Controlling Section, was told by Montagu that 'Martin' was a Welsh gardener who had committed suicide by drinking weedkiller. (Interviewed by the late Randolph Churchill, 9 May 1967, information kindly supplied by Martin Gilbert.) Montagu confirmed after recording a BBC television interview that Martin was Welsh but not that he necessarily died in Wales. (Information kindly supplied by Roy Davies, BBC *Timewatch*.)

9 The author is greatly indebted to Mr Colin Gibbon of Pontypridd for his help in researching these details.

10 WO 106/5921, Public Record Office, Kew.

11 According to his next-of-kin, Howells entered hospital immediately after Christmas 1942 in the terminal stages of illness. They confirm that he died on 6 January and the headstone on his grave in Wales bears this date. The death certificate shows he died on 11 January and that he underwent a post-mortem which under the circumstances would have been unnecessary. Hospital records contain no mention of Howells having undergone a post-mortem and Dr A. L.

Jacobs who is shown as having carried this out cannot now recall any details. If Howells's body underwent a post-mortem it could not have been used for the deception plan so perhaps this detail was added to the death certificate as a red herring. A further complication is that Howells is officially buried in South Wales so does he have two graves? (Author's correspondence with Howells's relatives, North West Thames Regional Health Authority, Dr A. L. Jacobs, and Kenyons Limited, 1987–88.)

[12] SHAEF/18229/Ops, File 381, RG 331, Military Reference Section, National Archives, Washington DC.

[13] *Bodyguard of Lies*, pages 608–9.

[14] There are virtually no other German accounts of intelligence operations including codebreaking against the allies.

[15] 'The Great Game of the Secret Agents', Professor Louis de Jong (*Encounter*, January 1980) and *Errors of Judgement*, Nicholas Kelso (Robert Hale, 1988).

[16] 'As for the identity of our author . . . in order to prevent his being distracted from getting on with the job, we decided not to reveal his name to anyone.' Letter from Edward Heath to Dame Irene Ward, 9 May 1961.

[17] 'A pilot project on the history of SOE was being prepared but without any guarantee as to its publication. Publication would depend entirely on seeing what the finished product looked like.' Letter from Edward Heath to Dame Irene Ward, 23 February 1961.

[18] In 1988 Professor Hinsley's final volume of the official history of World War II intelligence contained an appendix in which he belatedly set the Polish and French contribution in its proper perspective.

[19] Correspondence with the late Professor G. C. McVittie from 1983 to 1987.

[20] 'It is a bitter blow to us . . . when valued ex-colleagues decide to let us down,' 12 July 1985.

[21] While Marychurch was worrying about the 40-year-old secrets of Enigma one of his senior ex-employees, Geoffrey Prime, had been spying inside GCHQ for 14 years.

[22] *Who's Watching You?*, Crispin Aubrey (Penguin, 1981) pages 20–2.

[23] *Saturday Night People*, Russell Harty, 17 September 1968, London Weekend Television.

[24] On 11 October 1978, mid-way through the trial, the attorney general, Sam Silkin, admitted he had only learned about jury vetting in 1974.

25 *The Secret War*, BBC Television, 1977, producer Brian Johnson, six 30-minute episodes.

26 *British Intelligence in the Second World War* (HMSO, 1981–88).

27 *The Technology of Espionage*, James Rusbridger, for David Wilson, BBC's Science Correspondent.

28 Producer John Penycate, presenter Tom Mangold.

29 Letter to author from Tom Mangold, 28 June 1983.

30 Part 1 screened on 23 February; Part 2 on March 2, BBC–1.

31 Letter to author, 18 August 1983.

32 But not all of them. Other equally embarrassing files include those held by the FBI in Washington concerning the Duke of Windsor's currency-smuggling activities while governor of the Bahamas during the war, his involvement in the unsolved murder of Sir Harry Oakes, and J. Edgar Hoover's recommendation that the Duke and Duchess of Windsor be interned as traitors.

33 'Spy-watching Trade Booms', Michael Davie, *Observer*, 10 May 1987.

34 Biographical details courtesy of Sidgwick & Jackson.

35 When Beaverbrook died in 1964 the *Daily Express* still sold around 4.2 million copies a day. Between 1970 and the mid-1980s the newspaper had seven editors, its cover price rose in 11 jumps by 1,440 per cent, changed to tabloid size, and had three different owners with a fourth in 1986. By then daily circulation was around 2 million copies and by mid-1988 this had slumped to 1.68 million. Over the same period circulation of the *Sunday Express* declined from over 4.4 million to 2.14 million.

36 *New Statesman*, E. P. Thomson, June 1978.

37 'Windscale: The Whole Truth. The prime minister has decided to publish the report on the atomic accident at Windscale IN FULL'. *Daily Express*, 1957. 'Supermac's Big Cover-up after Windscale Blaze', *Daily Express*, 1988.

38 *Inside Story*, pages 220–221.

39 Known as *Bride* to British intelligence, the material concerned Russian signals traffic that had been intercepted at the end of the war, mainly at an American Sigint station at Shoal Bay, near Darwin, in Australia, but also between the Russian Trade Delegation in New York and Moscow. *The FBI–KGB War*, Robert Lamphere (Random House, 1986) pages 78–86; *Spycatcher*, pages 179–185; *A*

Matter of Trust, page 28, and author's correspondence with Robert Lamphere 1986–1988.

[40] *Newsweek*, 19 May 1980, page 32.

[41] *Spycatcher*, page 317.

[42] This was explained in detail during *The Trial of Sir Roger Hollis*, London Weekend Television, 3 April 1988, a dramatised courtroom 'trial' that ended with a verdict of not guilty.

[43] This thesis is dealt with in detail in *Mask of Treachery*, pages 602–7.

[44] Author's correspondence with Sir Dick White 1985–1988, and various conversations with Sir Charles Spry, Toorak, Victoria, Australia, January/February 1988.

[45] One of the allegations made against Hollis was that in 1954 he warned the Russians that Vladimir Petrov, a Russian diplomat in Australia, was planning to defect. But Sir Charles Spry has shown that this is completely untrue. *The Petrov Affair*, Robert Manne (Pergamon Press, 1987) pages 227–8.

[46] In 1964 James Angleton, then head of the CIA, had claimed that Wilson was a Russian agent (*Spycatcher*, page 364). There has also been considerable controversy about the true reason why Wilson suddenly resigned as prime minister in 1976. There seems little doubt that MI5 suspected Wilson and some of his friends of being Russian agents, but whether MI5, in part or whole, ever tried to destabilise the entire Wilson government is another matter. *The Wilson Plot*, David Leigh (Heinemann, 1988).

[47] Author's conversation with Peter Wright in Australia January/February 1988.

[48] *A Spy's Revenge*, Richard Hall (Penguin, 1987) page 42.

[49] 'Rothschild – as wrong as Wright?', *Private Eye*, December 1987. In 1951 Rothschild was a member of the Labour Party, contributed money to the *Tribune* magazine, and a close friend of prominent left-wingers like Leslie and Beattie Plummer.

[50] *A Web of Deception*, Chapman Pincher (Sidgwick & Jackson, 1987) page 8.

[51] *A Spy's Revenge*, page 45; *Web of Deception*, page 10.

[52] It was titled 'Lord Rothschild is Innocent' and dealt with his links with Burgess and Blunt. On 2 November 1979 the *Evening Standard* carried an article about Blunt's exposure adding that 'Rothschild himself is known amongst the *cognoscenti* as the First Man'.

53 *A Web of Deception*, page 10.

54 To the author, Australia, January/February 1988.

55 To the author, Australia, January/February 1988, and *A Spy's Revenge*, page 50.

56 *A Web of Deception*, pages 1–14.

57 *Molehunt*, Nigel West (Weidenfeld & Nicolson, 1987) page 138.

58 *Daily Telegraph*, Stephen Bates, 25 November 1986.

59 *A Web of Deception*, page 66.

60 *A Web of Deception*, page 66.

61 'A Wilderness of Mirrors', John Ware, BBC *Panorama* (*Listener*, 6 August 1987).

62 Letter from David Hooper (Peter Wright's London solicitor) to the *Guardian*, 16 January 1988.

63 *A Spy's Revenge*, page 49.

64 Chapman Pincher, *Daily Express*, 14 December 1986.

65 *Listener*, 6 August 1987.

66 *Daily Telegraph*, 26 November 1986.

67 It was September 1985 when the government first obtained temporary injunctions against Wright and his Australian publishers. In July 1986 the attorney general won a High Court ban preventing the *Guardian* and the *Observer* from reporting any of Wright's information. During November–December 1986 the government's case was heard in the New South Wales Supreme Court and on 12 March 1987 the court ruled against the British government. On 12 July 1987 the *Sunday Times* published extracts from *Spycatcher* and the attorney general commenced contempt proceedings. On 24 September 1987 the Australian appeal court gave the go-ahead for publication. On 23 November 1987 the government sought a permanent ban on the media reporting Wright's allegations and on 21 December the High Court rejected this. On 10 February 1988 the Appeal Court also rejected the call for a permanent ban. On 2 June the Australian High Court rejected the government's appeal. On 14 June the government appealed to the House of Lords.

68 'How the author of *Spycatcher* kept altering his story', Chapman Pincher, letter to the *Guardian*, 14 January 1988.

69 4 December 1986.

[70] House of Commons, 6 December 1986.

[71] Letter to author, 26 February 1988.

[72] 'Wright hints at ten new major secrets', Christopher Morris (*The Times*, 15 June 1988).

[73] Producer Elizabeth Clough.

[74] Page 369.

[75] *Sunday Times*, 27 March 1988 and *Philby: KGB Master Spy*, Phillip Knightley (Deutsch, 1988).

[76] Including John Cartwright MP (Social Democratic), Steven Norris (Conservative), and Alf Dubs (Labour), who listened to her various claims and concluded she was a very sane and serious person. *Official Secrets*, page 180.

[77] Following the Prime affair (see Chapter 4) a team of NSA experts came to GCHQ Cheltenham to review the agreement by which NSA shared with GCHQ most of their technology and information. Despite desperate attempts to play down the importance of the Prime case (hence the useless official report), the NSA was far from convinced that it was safe to share such secrets with GCHQ in the future because it believed further spies existed within GCHQ. In September 1983 Michael Heseltine approved *Project Zircon* so that GCHQ would have its own satellite system. However, if the Russians knew about *Rhyolite* they could hardly mistake *Zircon* when it was launched. (Private information GCHQ.)

[78] *Daily Telegraph*, 7 August 1987. It was later revealed that one of the BBC governors, Dame Daphne Park, who wanted to suppress the series *The Secret Society* had been a senior MI6 officer. *The Friends*, Nigel West (Weidenfeld & Nicolson, 1988); and 'MI6 Career of BBC Governor Revealed', David Leigh (*Observer*, 26 June 1988). It is quite possible that production of *Zircon* continues secretly since the Marconi factory that was specially built for the project at Portsmouth where it was being made still seems remarkably active.

[79] '13 ex-MI6 men named in book', Michael Evans (*The Times*, 16 June 1988), and 'Tory's spy book escapes MI5 ban', David Leigh, (*Observer*, 19 June 1988).

[80] 'Author MP in spy book row' (*Western Morning News*, 23 June 1988).

[81] Greville Wynne who had worked for MI6 and been imprisoned by the Russians for his part in the Penkovsky affair took exception to some of the remarks West made in the book. Conflicting reports then followed as to whether the book had been withdrawn or not, but W. H. Smith commented that it did not matter much as it had only sold a total of 60 copies in its 435 shops. 'Peterborough' (*Daily Telegraph*, 21 July 1988).

82 William Morrow, New York, 1988.

83 'Former MI5 men queue up to publish memoirs', *The Times*, 12 October 1988.

84 *The Times*, 13 October 1988.

85 It has often been suggested that there should be a committee of Privy Councillors who would oversee security matters. But past experience, such as the inquiry into the Falklands War in 1982, shows only too clearly that the idea that because someone is a Privy Councillor he is an expert on intelligence and can therefore ask the right questions and understand the answers is totally false.

CHAPTER 9 *(Pages 201–218)*

1 The OSA began life in 1888 as the Breach of Official Trust Bill and was formerly introduced on to the statute book in 1889. But the Act we all know today dates from 17 July 1911.

2 There is no definition as to what official information means. In theory it can mean any piece of information that a civil servant wants to keep secret, and frequently it does.

3 Someone like Rupert Allason, who writes books under the name Nigel West, signed the OSA whilst a special constable yet is not prosecuted for publishing details of the intelligence services.

4 Introduced on 3 March 1911.

5 In addition there is the Communications Act passed in 1950 at the start of the Korean War.

6 The CIA requires employees engaged in particularly sensitive work to sign #2441 Special Project Secrecy Agreement, while the NSA is protected by Section 6 of Public Law 86–36 passed by Congress in 1959 which effectively gives it the right to deny its own existence and exempts the NSA from the Freedom of Information Act. *The Puzzle Palace*, James Bamford (Sidgwick & Jackson, 1983) pages 88–9. Anyone trying to write about their work with such agencies without permission has their book royalties seized by the government. But since America has a perfectly sensible system for approving manuscripts, this seldom happens.

7 *Sunday Times*, 7 April 1985.

[8] *Official Secrets*, David Hooper (Secker & Warburg, 1987) page 8. During the 1930s Admiral Sir Hugh 'Quex' Sinclair, head of MI6, withheld secrets from Britain's Labour Prime Minister Ramsey MacDonald because he did not like his policies yet leaked the same secrets to Churchill, then in the political wilderness. This is an early example of the politicisation of the intelligence services and one wonders if the same thing would happen today if the Conservative government was defeated by Labour who then embarked on an anti-nuclear defence policy against the advice of the chiefs of the defence staff.

[9] *The Abuse of Power*, James Margach (W. H. Allen, 1976).

[10] *Daily Telegraph*, 24 January 1983.

[11] *Guardian*, 22 October, 1 November, and 18 December, 1983.

[12] The newspaper was obliged to hand them back under a court order on 16 December 1983.

[13] In August 1988.

[14] The whole affair concerned the circumstances under which the Argentine cruiser *Belgrano* was sunk on 2 May 1982. Some people, notably Tam Dayell MP, claimed Mrs Thatcher had ordered the attack even though the vessel posed no threat in order to prevent any peaceful settlement of the Argentinian invasion of the Falklands so that the re-taking of the islands could go ahead with all the glory the eventual victory bestowed upon her. The government refused to give exact details of the information it had known about the *Belgrano*'s movements, even to a Commons select committee, claiming it was a secret.

[15] *20/20 Vision*, 8 March 1985.

[16] See Chapter 4.

[17] Produced by Peter Watkins in 1965. The government of the day asked the BBC not to show the film on television because it claimed it might cause mass suicides. The BBC agreed to this censorship. What the government really feared was that it might cause people to ask what civil defence precautions existed. The film had a limited cinema release, causing no suicides, and was finally shown on television in 1985. It remains a powerful film because of the simplicity of the story and the gritty documentary style of black and white photography no longer seen in today's sanitised television dramas.

[18] In 1957 the *Daily Sketch* was threatened with prosecution by the D-notice Committee if it published a photograph of an early version of the vertical take-off aircraft. Two weeks later the Minister of Aviation, Duncan Sandys, made a speech about the aircraft at the Farnborough Air Show and released pictures of it to the press (*Official Secrets*, page 11).

[19] 'With friends like Duncan Campbell, who needs the Russians?', Peter Hitchens, *Daily Express*, 26 January 1987. 'Harry Pincher himself told me that he takes seriously the affidavit from Sir Peter Marychurch [head of GCHQ] which says the *Zircon* leak is a genuine breach of security' (letter from Peter Hitchens to author 27 January 1987). What Marychurch forgot to tell Pincher, and Pincher did not bother to find out before selling the tale to the *Daily Express*, was that *Zircon* only became necessary when, following the Prime scandal in 1982, the NSA decided GCHQ's security was so bad it would not share further secrets with it. This was why Mrs Thatcher would not publish the Waddell Report about Jock Kane's allegations, because had she done so it would have exposed the misleading statement she made to Parliament in 1980 that Kane's allegations were unfounded and that everything was all right at GCHQ.

[20] 'Cable Vetting Sensation', *Daily Express*, 21 February 1967. Pincher had been given the story by Robert Lawson who had worked for two cable companies in London. Pincher assumed this vetting procedure was a recent affair and completely missed the nub of the story that it had been going on since 1919. The story had first been offered to the *Daily Mail* who were persuaded by the D-notice secretary, Colonel Sammy Lohan, not to print it. The government claimed that by publishing the story it warned our enemies not to use the cable systems.

[21] John Keegan, Defence Correspondent, 15 July 1987.

[22] 'A Wretched Affair', main leader, 14 August 1987; 'Mr Wright is a sorry figure and a wholly unreliable witness, driven to betray his employers, and his country, by a mixture of bile and cupidity. His book . . . is of negligible worth.'

[23] 'The strange case of the invisible submarine', Adela Gooch, *Daily Telegraph*, 14 December 1987.

[24] *Official Secrets*, page 229.

[25] In many instances the government in question is willing to release the information but is asked not to do so by Britain. On several recent occasions the author had files declassified to him in Australia without difficulty only to find them reclassified again later at the request of GCHQ. In every case the information was 45 years old and could have no bearing on any country's national security. This gives a good idea of the paranoia prevailing in Whitehall and places like GCHQ.

[26] *The Times*, 11 January 1988.

[27] 'Secret police to gag public', David Leigh *Observer*, 11 December 1988.

[28] It was particularly galling for Mrs Thatcher who had strongly criticised other Western governments for doing secret deals with countries like Iran to find that her great friend and ally had been doing exactly the same. The extent to which the British government knew about American arms' shipments to Iran has naturally

never been revealed but since several of the shady middlemen involved operated out of London it would be strange if even MI5 did not know what was going on. As with the case of the bombing of the *Rainbow Warrior* in New Zealand by France, when the full extent of America's duplicity became known a strange silence descended on Downing Street and Whitehall and no criticism was made of the affair. Of course the British government has never criticised the Americans for their armed intervention in Nicaragua which is terrorism under another name precisely the same as the IRA activities in Northern Ireland. But all governments possess this chameleon-like ability to switch morality on and off to suit. An interesting British view of the Iran/Contra arms scandal can be found in *Broker of Death*, Hermann Moll with Michael Leapman (Macmillan, 1988).

[29] 15 October 1988.

[30] 11 November 1988.

[31] 1 December 1988.

[32] With such a system, the *Spycatcher* fiasco could have been avoided. Malcolm Turnbull, Wright's lawyer, offered to submit the manuscript to the government and remove any offending passages. The government refused patronisingly saying they would see how good Turnbull was in court. Indeed they did to the tune of £3 million of wasted taxpayers' money. *The Spycatcher Trial*, Malcolm Turnbull (Heinemann, 1988).

[33] As occurred at Windscale 35 years ago and the details concealed by the then prime minister.

BIBLIOGRAPHY

Agee, Philip, *Inside the Company: the CIA Diary*. Penguin, 1975.

Andrew, Christopher, *Secret Service*. Heinemann, 1985.

Aubrey, Crispin, *Who's Watching You?* Penguin, 1981.

Bamford, James, *The Puzzle Palace*. Sidgwick & Jackson, 1983.

Barron, John, *KGB*. Hodder & Stoughton, 1974.

Bledowska, Celina and Bloch, Jonathan, *KGB-CIA*. Bison Books, 1987.

Blum, Howard, *I Pledge Allegiance*. Weidenfeld & Nicolson, 1988.

Bourke, Sean, *The Springing of George Blake*. Cassell, 1970.

Boyle, Andrew, *The Climate of Treason*. Hutchinson, 1979.

Burrows, William, *Deep Black*. Transworld/Bantam, 1988.

Calvocoressi, Peter, *Top Secret Ultra*. Cassell, 1980.

Campbell, Duncan, *War Plan UK*. Burnett, 1982.

Campbell, Duncan and Connor, Steven, *On the Record*. Michael Joseph, 1986.

Campbell, Keith, *ANC: A Soviet task force?* Institute for the Study of Terrorism, 1986.

Campbell, Kurt M., *Southern Africa in Soviet foreign policy*. International Institute for Strategic Studies, 1987.

Castle, Barbara, *The Castle Diaries 1964–70*. Weidenfeld & Nicolson, 1984.

Cave Brown, Anthony, *Bodyguard of Lies*. W. H. Allen, 1976.

   The Last Hero: Wild Bill Donovan. Times Books, New York, 1982.

   The Secret Servant. Michael Joseph, 1988.

Cecil, Robert, *A Divided Life*. The Bodley Head, 1988.

Chapman, Dr John, *The Price of Admiralty*. Saltire Press, 1984.

Churchill, Rt Hon Winston S., *The Second World War*, 6 Volumes. Cassell, 1948–54.

Cockburn, Andrew, *The Threat: Inside the Soviet Military Machine*. Hutchinson, 1983.

Colvin, Ian, *The Unknown Courier*. Kimber, 1953.

Cookridge, E. H., *George Blake: Double Agent*. Hodder Paperbacks, 1970.

Cooper, Duff, *Operation Heartbreak*. Rupert Hart Davies, 1950.

Costello, John, *The Pacific War*. Collins, 1981.

   The Mask of Treachery. William Morrow, 1988.

Cox, Barry, *Civil Liberties in Britain*. Penguin, 1975.

Cruickshank, Dr Charles, *Deception in World War II*. Oxford University Press, 1979.

Deacon, Richard, *The Israeli Secret Service*. Hamish Hamilton, 1977.

    The Truth Twisters. Macdonald, 1987.

    Spyclopaedia. Macdonald, 1988.

Deavours, C. A. and Kruh, Louis, *Machine Cryptography & Modern Cryptanalysis*. Artech Press, USA, 1985.

Dobson, Christopher and Payne, Ronald, *The Dictionary of Espionage*. Harrap, 1984.

Dyson, John and Fitchett, Joseph, *Sink the Rainbow*. Gollancz, 1986.

Foot, M. R. D., *SOE in France*. HMSO, 1966.

    SOE. BBC Publications, 1984.

Fullick, Roy and Powell, Geoffrey, *Suez: The Double War*. Hamish Hamilton, 1979.

Garlinski, Jozef, *Intercept*. Dent, 1979.

Gervasi, Tom, *Soviet Military Power: The Annotated and Corrected Version of the Pentagon's Guide*. Sidgwick & Jackson, 1988.

Gilbert, Martin, *Finest Hour*. Heinemann, 1987.

    Road to Victory. Heinemann, 1986.

Giskes, H. J., *London Calling North Pole*. Kimber, 1953.

Glees, Anthony, *The Secrets of the Service*. Cape, 1987.

Golitsin, Anatoly, *New Lies for Old*. The Bodley Head, 1984.

Graham, Bill, *Break-In*. The Bodley Head, 1987.

Grey, Anthony, *The Prime Minister Was a Spy*. Weidenfeld & Nicolson, 1983.

HMSO, *Report of the Inquiry into Prison Escapes and Security*. Earl Mountbatten of Burma, 1966.

    Report of the Security Commission. May 1983.

    Report by David Calcutt QC – Service police in Cyprus. May 1986.

    Report of the Security Commission. October 1986.

    Interceptions of Communications Act: Report for 1987. March 1988.

Hall, Richard, *A Spy's Revenge*. Viking Penguin, 1987.

Handel, Michael (ed), *Strategic and Operational Deception in the Second World War*. Frank Cass, 1987.

Higham, Charles, *Wallis – Secret lives of the Duchess of Windsor*. Sidgwick & Jackson, 1988.

Hinsley, Professor F. H., *British Intelligence in the Second World War*. HMSO, 1981–1988.

Hodges, Andrew, *Alan Turing: The Enigma*. Burnett, 1983.

Hollingsworth, Mark & Norton Taylor, Richard, *Blacklist*. Hogarth Press, 1988.

Hooper, David, *Official Secrets*. Secker & Warburg, 1987.

Johnson, Brian, *The Secret War*. BBC Publications, 1978.

Jones, Professor R. V., *Most Secret War*. Hodder & Stoughton, 1979.

Kahn, David, *The Codebreakers*. Macmillan, New York, 1967.

Kennedy, William V., *The Intelligence War*. Salamander, 1983.

Knebel, Fletcher and Bailey, Charles, *Seven days in May*. Weidenfeld & Nicolson, 1962.

Knightley, Phillip, *The Second Oldest Profession*. Deutsch, 1986.

    Philby: KGB Masterspy. Deutsch, 1988.

Knightley, Phillip and Kennedy, Caroline, *An Affair of State*. Cape, 1987.

Kozaczuk, Wladyslaw, *Enigma*. Arms & Armour Press, 1984.

Kramish, Arnold, *The Griffin*. Macmillan, 1987.

Lamphere, Robert and Shachtman, Tom, *The FBI-KGB War*. Random House, 1986.

Laurie, Peter, *Beneath The City Streets*. Allen Lane, 1970.

Lee, Dick and Pratt, Colin, *Operation Julie*. W. H. Allen, 1978.

Leigh, David, *The Frontiers of Secrecy*. Junction Books, 1980.

The Wilson Plot. Heinemann, 1989.

Levchenko, Stanislav, *On the Wrong Side*. Pergamon-Brassey, New York, 1988.

Lindsey, Robert, *The Falcon and the Snowman*. Simon & Schuster, 1979.

McLachlan, Donald, *Room 39: Naval Intelligence in Action 1939-45*, Weidenfeld & Nicolson, 1968.

Manne, Robert, *The Petrov Affair*. Pergamon, 1987.

Margach, James, *The Abuse of Power*. W. H. Allen, 1976.

Marshall, Robert, *All The King's Men*. Collins, 1988.

Masterman, J. C., *The Double-Cross System in the War of 1939-45*. Yale University Press, 1972.

Moll, Hermann, with Leapman, Michael, *Broker of Death*. Macmillan, 1988.

Montagu, Ewen, *The Man Who Never Was*. Evans, 1953.

Montgomery Hyde, H., *George Blake: Superspy*. Constable, 1987.

Moss, Norman, *Klaus Fuchs*. Grafton, 1987.

Overton Fuller, Miss Jean, *Dericourt: The Chequered Spy*. Michael Russell, 1989.

Penrose, Barrie and Freeman, Simon, *Conspiracy of Silence*. Grafton, 1986.

Pincher, Chapman, *Inside Story*. Sidgwick & Jackson, 1978.

Their Trade is Treachery. Sidgwick & Jackson, 1981.

Too Secret Too Long. Sidgwick & Jackson, 1984.

Traitors. Sidgwick & Jackson, 1987.

A Web of Deception. Sidgwick & Jackson, 1987.

Prime, Rhona, *Time of Trial*. Hodder & Stoughton, 1984.

Richelson, Jeffrey and Ball, Desmond, *The Ties that Bind*. Allen & Unwin, 1985.

Rusbridger, James, 'The Sinking of the Automedon, the Capture of the Nankin'. *Encounter*, May 1985.

'Between Bluff, Deceit, and Treachery'. *Encounter*, 1986.

Sakharov, Vladimir with Tosi, Umberto, *High Treason*. Robert Hale, 1981.

Sawatsky, John, *Gouzenko: The Untold Story*. Macmillan, Canada, 1984.

Shuckburgh, Evelyn, *Descent to Suez: Diaries 1951-1956*. Weidenfeld & Nicolson, 1986.

Smith, Graham, *Death of a Rose Grower*. Woolf, 1985.

Stalker, John, *Stalker*. Harrap, 1988.

Straight, Michael, *After Long Silence*. Collins, 1983.

Sunday Times Insight, *Rainbow Warrior*. Hutchinson, 1986.

Sweetman, Bill, *Stealth Aircraft*. Motorbooks International, 1986.

Trethowan, Ian, *Split Screen*, Hamish Hamilton, 1984.

Tuck, Jay, *High-Tech Espionage*. Sidgwick & Jackson, 1986.

Turner, Admiral Stansfield, *Secrecy and Democracy: The CIA in Transition*. Sidgwick & Jackson, 1986.

Varner, Roy and Collier, Wayne, *A Matter of Risk*. Hodder & Stoughton, 1979.

Vassall, John, *Vassall: The Autobiography of a Spy*. Sidgwick & Jackson, 1975.

Welchman, Gordon, *The Hut Six Story*. Allen Lane, 1982.

West, Nigel, *MI5: British Security Service Operations 1909–1945*. The Bodley Head, 1981.

A Matter of Trust: MI5 1945–1972. Weidenfeld & Nicolson, 1982.

MI6: British Secret Intelligence Service Operations 1909–1945. Weidenfeld & Nicolson, 1983.

The Branch: A History of the Metropolitan Police Special Branch, 1883–1983. Secker & Warburg, 1983.

GCHQ: The Secret Wireless War 1900–86. Weidenfeld & Nicolson, 1986.

Molehunt. Weidenfeld & Nicolson, 1988.

The Friends. Weidenfeld & Nicolson, 1988.

Winterbotham, F. W., *The Ultra Secret*. Weidenfeld & Nicolson, 1974.

Wise, David, *The Spy Who Got Away*. Collins, 1988.

Woodward, Bob, *Veil: The Secret Wars of the CIA*. Simon & Schuster, 1987.

Wright, Peter, *Spycatcher*. Viking, 1987.

Wynne, Greville, *The Man From Moscow*. London, 1967.

Young, G. K., *Subversion*. Ossian Publishers, 1984.

Yost, Graham, *Spy-Tech*. Harrap, 1985.

INDEX